Reading/Thinking/Writing

A Holistic Language and Literacy Program for the K–8 Classroom

Iris McClellan Tiedt
Northern Kentucky University

and National Writing Project Teacher-Consultants:
Ruth Gibbs, San Diego, California
Martha Howard, Cupertino, California
Marylue Timpson, Los Altos, California
Mary Young Williams, Milpitas, California

Allyn and Bacon
Boston   London   Sydney   Toronto

Copyright © 1989 by Allyn and Bacon
A Division of Simon & Schuster
160 Gould Street
Needham Heights, Massachusetts 02194

Library of Congress Cataloging-in-Publication Data

Tiedt, Iris M.
    Reading/thinking/writing : a holistic language and literacy program for the K–8
classroom / Iris McClellan Tiedt, and National Writing Project teacher-consultants,
Ruth Gibbs . . . [et al.].
    p.   cm.
    Bibliography: p.
    Includes index.
    ISBN 0–205–11856–9
    1. Language arts (Elementary)—United States. 2. Reading (Elementary)—
United States. 3. Thought and thinking—Study and teaching (Elementary)—
United States. 4. English language—United States—Composition and exercises.
I. Gibbs, Ruth. II. National Writing Project (U.S.) III. Title.
LB1576.T558 1989   88–23484
372.6—dc19   CIP

Printed in the United States of America
10 9 8 7 6 5 4 3 2   92 91 90

Contents

Preface   ix

1   Reading/Thinking/Writing: An Adventure in Learning   1

Reading/Thinking/Writing: Making Connections   2
    Recommended Resources   5
Designing a Reading/Thinking/Writing Program   6
    An Integrated Model   6
    Building a Language and Thinking Foundation   8
    Discovering Basic Reading and Writing Concepts   9
    Gaining Power Through Reading/Thinking/Writing   10
    Strengthening Reading/Writing Connections   11
    Learning Advanced Thinking Skills   12
    Reading/Thinking/Writing Across the Curriculum   13
    Reading and Responding to Literature   14
    Developing a Student-Centered Curriculum   15
    Basic Assumptions Underlying the Program   15
    Summary   16
Recommended Instructional Strategies   16
    Reading Aloud to Students   17
    Literature as a Text   18
    Presenting a Well-Designed Lesson   20
    Your Professional Library   22
Summary   23
Challenge   24

2   Building a Language and Thinking Foundation   26

Implementing the Program   26
Thinking Awareness for Students   27
       A Useful Strategy: Visualization   28
       A Useful Strategy: Classification   32
Listening for Comprehension   38
       A Useful Strategy: Story Theater   38
       A Useful Strategy: Music and Rhythm   41
Speaking to Communicate Thinking   47
       A Useful Strategy: Puppetry   47
       A Useful Strategy: Preparing and Presenting Speeches   51

3   Discovering Basic Reading and Writing Concepts   56

Implementing the Program   57
Early Experiences with Written Language   58
       A Useful Strategy: Choral Reading   59
       More Lessons to Introduce Written Language   63
Discovering Sound-Symbol Relationships: Phonics   68
       More Lessons to Discover Sound-Symbol Relationships   81
Extending Reading/Thinking/Writing Abilities   82
       A Useful Strategy: Language Experience   82
       A Useful Strategy: Comparing   88
Developing a Thematic Module: Self-Esteem   95

4   Gaining Power Through Reading/Thinking/Writing   101

Implementing the Program   102
Developing Reading/Thinking/Writing Fluency   103
       A Useful Strategy: Time on Task with Reading and
          Thinking   103
       More Lessons to Promote Fluency   109
Thinking About What We Read   113
       A Useful Strategy: Transaction Logs   114
       More Lessons to Promote Thinking About What We
          Read   119
Sharing Reading Orally and in Writing   126
       A Useful Strategy: Readers' Theater   129

More Lessons to Promote the Sharing of Reading and
        Writing   136
Focusing on a Theme: Love   141

5   Strengthening Reading/Writing Connections   148

Implementing the Program   148
Writing Begins with Thinking and Leads to Reading   149
        A Useful Strategy: Clustering   150
        A Useful Strategy: Venn Diagram   156
Learning to Write by Reading   163
        A Useful Strategy: Patterning   163
        A Useful Strategy: Literature Models for Good Writing   168
Writing to Be Read   172
        A Useful Strategy: Editing Skills   172
        More Lessons to Promote Writing to Be Read   181

6   Learning Advanced Thinking Skills   193

Implementing the Program   194
Gathering Data at the Knowledge Level   195
        A Useful Strategy: Mapping   195
        More Ideas to Promote Skill in Data Gathering   202
Working with Data in Varied Ways   208
        A Useful Strategy: Planning Questions   209
        More Lessons to Promote Working with Data   214
Integrative Thinking   221
        A Useful Strategy: Journals   221
        More Lessons to Promote Integrative Thinking   228
Focus on a Theme: Understanding Our Diversity   233

7   Reading/Thinking/Writing Across the Curriculum   238

Implementing the Program   239
Reading/Thinking/Writing in Social Studies   239
        A Useful Strategy: The I-Search Paper   240
Reading/Thinking/Writing in Science   248
        A Useful Strategy: The Learning Log   248
Reading/Thinking/Writing in Math   252
        A Useful Strategy: Identifying Key Words in a Problem   253

Reading/Thinking/Writing in Art   258
    A Useful Strategy: Publishing Books   258
Reading/Thinking/Writing in Music   263
    A Useful Strategy: Songs and Mood   263

8 Reading and Responding to Literature   269

Implementing the Program   270
Learning to Read/Think/Write with Literature   272
    A Useful Strategy: La Dictée   272
    More Lessons to Teach Reading/Thinking/Writing with
      Literature   278
Exploring Literature Concepts and Forms   285
    A Useful Strategy: Working with Point of View   286
    More Lessons to Teach Literature Concepts   290
Experiencing Drama: Process and Product   296
    A Useful Strategy: Creative Dramatics   297
    More Lessons to Promote the Use of Drama   303
Developing a Thematic Module: Freedom   309

9 Developing a Student-Centered Curriculum   316

Implementing the Program   317
Carrying Out the Reading/Thinking/Writing Literacy Program   318
    Characteristics of a Strong Reading/Thinking/Writing
      Program   319
    Objectives for Student Learning   320
    Skills of a Good Teacher   321
    Communicating with Parents   322
Involving Students in Learning   323
    Working in Small Groups   323
    Holistic Scoring of Student Writing   330
    Evaluating Progress   337
    Publishing Student Work   342

10 Resources for Students and Teachers   345

Especially for the Primary Grades   345
    Caldecott Award Books   345
    Read Books Aloud to Stimulate Thinking   351
    Wordless Books   354

Reading in the Middle Grades   356
      Children's Classics   357
Especially for Upper Elementary and Junior High   359
      Newbery Award Books   359
      Literature with High Appeal for Young Adult Readers   366
Language Books for K–8 Students   374
Books for the Teacher: Reading/Thinking/Writing   381
      Teaching Reading   381
      Thinking: Information and Stimulus   382
      Books about Writing and Teaching Students to Write   383

Index   385

Preface

Every teacher needs to believe in a philosophy that fits experience—a sense of direction. And every teacher searches for a program that exemplifies this intuitive knowledge—a program designed for teachers who recognize children's natural propensity for learning.

The integrated language and literacy program described in *Reading/Thinking/Writing* meets that need. This program begins with the learner's language, first acquired naturally during preschool years, but continuing to grow as the student matures. The program facilitates students' beginning work with written language—reading and writing supported by oral-aural abilities and the students' prior knowledge. Literature supports the entire program, extending knowledge and opening doors. Children learn to read by reading, to think by thinking, and to write by writing, but the three processes are integrated within meaningful studies that allow for individual progress and interest.

The teaching ideas in this book are enjoyable; they have been selected to motivate students to read, to think, and to write with pleasure. At the same time, each teaching strategy is also based on a sound theoretical base that is outlined in the first chapter. Drawing from the fields of linguistics, psycholinguistics, and English education, we clearly understand how children begin to read most naturally, supported by a strong thinking and language base. This book shows you how to help students gain reading power and to respond to literature first orally and then through writing, as suggested in the many lessons presented.

Written by experienced, practicing teachers, each teaching strategy is described in clear language, step-by-step, so that you can put the ideas to work in your classroom immediately. The whole strategy is described from start to finish. You are told how to introduce the lesson, carry it out, follow up the lesson, and evaluate the results. The lessons follow a process that is easy to put into practice in your classroom, and the strategies will make your teaching more effective.

The holistic model on which this program is based provides the organization for the book. The program begins with each student as he or she comes to work in a classroom with a teacher. The child progresses from the benchmark established at that time, continuing to achieve—to read, think, and write—according to each one's individual potential. The program is designed for children. It is also designed for you.

The Authors

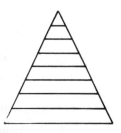

1

Reading/Thinking/Writing: An Adventure in Learning

Learning to read opens doors to an exciting world for any child—a world of shared adventure, fantasy, and humor; a world of information and amazing facts; and a world of thought and beauty. As teachers, we know the keys that will open these doors.

We know, for example, that reading cannot be taught in isolation. What the child brings to the reading task, the child's prior knowledge, is an important prerequisite for successful reading. Therefore, we emphasize the necessity of a strong thinking-language-experiential base for beginning reading experiences.

We also recognize the connections between reading and writing. As students read, they think about what they read and respond to the author's ideas orally and in writing. They learn to see literature as an example of writing, and they observe how skilled authors use words and how they express their ideas. Through reading, students develop a sense of form, voice, and style; they learn to create "reading" by writing.

Clearly, a reading program must encompass thinking, listening, speaking, reading, and writing as related language skills. We have written this book to aid you in developing an integrated language and literacy program that is enjoyable, efficient, and effective. The reading/thinking/writing program presented crosses K–8 grades so that sample lessons presented in each chapter can be adapted for various developmental levels. These teacher-tested strategies suggest ways of beginning your own holistic language and literacy program by selecting ideas from each chapter.

In this introductory chapter, we give you an overview of the program presented in *Reading/Thinking/Writing*. This chapter is important because it explains the theoretical base from which we authors are operating. In this chapter you can expect to learn:

- A rationale for integrating reading, thinking, and writing
- The assumptions underlying our holistic literacy program
- A model for integrating language and literacy instruction
- Teaching strategies that you can begin using immediately
- Recommended resources for your continued growth

Reading/Thinking/Writing: Making Connections

The newborn child begins to think and to learn language at birth. Without formal instruction, children eagerly attempt speech, beginning with experimental babbling and gradually producing recognizable words. Other humans around him provide positive encouragement: "Hear that? Johnny said, 'Mama.' "

We talk and children listen. We provide language information on which the baby's mind can work. Soon, the child moves beyond single-word utterances, producing two-unit messages, such as, "Go car" or "All gone Daddy." The child has abstracted sentence structure from the language heard, applying this knowledge to create a child grammar that will slowly evolve into the sense of grammar that we adults share.

Studies show that children do not learn language simply through imitation, however, for they can generate sentences they have never heard before. Clearly, they have learned the underlying grammatical structure identified by Noam Chomsky and other researchers of English grammar.[1] We can observe the learning process children go through in their speech, much to our amusement and enlightenment; for example:

Timmy: "I holded the rabbits."

Mother: "Did you say you *held* the rabbits?"

Timmy: "No, I holded the rabbits."

Timmy does not need or want help in conducting his language experiments. He is operating with a hypothesis about forming past tense in English verbs that he will self-correct as he gathers new data about irregular verbs from the language around him. Timmy is an independent thinker, happily working to solve this complex language puzzle.

Long before entering school, children become aware of meanings in the world around them. They read the meaning of a green light at the street corner; they understand the meaning of a cat's contented purr. Soon, they begin to observe the strange markings of written language—the street signs their parents seem to understand, cautioning to "Drive carefully," or the ice cream store's enticing "31 flavors." They enter school eager to learn to read.

Viewing reading as "gaining meaning from written language," we share books—predictable, funny, beautiful—with children, leading them to understand and respond to what the author has written. We celebrate authors and view them as friends. We also encourage children to begin putting their own ideas into writing, using invented spelling, rereading and revising the familiar language, as they produce books. We celebrate every child author, too, and display their books on the bookshelf beside the works of Dr. Seuss, Marcia Brown, Ezra Jack Keats, and Byrd Baylor. Thus, children become confident readers and writers, each working at his or her level of competence, and each eager to learn new information and new abilities.

Being aware that the reader brings much to the reading act, we see reading as a transaction between the reader, with his or her prior knowledge, and the writer, as they work together to construct "meaning." Language experiences, vocabulary development, and motivating activities move the young reader toward achieving the goal of comprehension. The child learns to think about what he or she reads and to respond through speaking and writing. Learning is taking place.

As studies of children's acquisition of spoken language demonstrate, children are able to abstract the complex rules of English grammar from speech they hear. No one tells children the rules for constructing a sentence, yet they learn to speak readily in order to function in the world. In the same way, they can learn to read, for children are literally programmed to learn how to read. Our job, then, is to supply written language from which young readers can abstract the system.[2] We also supply the pencils and paper for writing so children can create "reading." And, of course, our adult role includes providing enthusiastic, positive support.

Current understandings of the reading process come to us from studies in psycholinguistics, cognitive psychology, and language studies (child acquisition of language, English grammar, and phonology). Observation of children reading enables researchers to determine how the reading process works. We are learning how the good reader reads. We are also learning that reading is a language process that includes thinking before, during, and after the reading experience. Frank Smith, a foremost researcher of the reading process, notes in *Reading without Nonsense:* "The teacher's role is to motivate, encourage and help children to learn to read. To do this teachers must make reading meaningful, which means seeing how it looks from the child's point of view."[3]

Children who read fluently with a high degree of comprehension have a number of skills in common. For one thing, they use oral language easily. Based on experiences and concept development, their vocabulary is larger than that of less able readers, which enables them to understand what they read. They come to the reading task with a well-fed brain, usually the result of an enriched home environment where parents listen, talk, and read to children. They have already begun to "read the world" around them and are thus well-prepared to read books. These children are actively thinking as they read, and they are eager to respond to literature they have shared.[4]

Good readers learn to read by reading. After discovering the basic relationships between sound and print, they quickly learn to discriminate among words, using whatever clues are available to them—letters, spelling patterns, the meaning context, and illustrations. They grab just enough to make sense of what they are reading, and on they go. If the passage is suddenly no longer meaningful, they quickly check back to discover their error. Through reading, they learn new vocabulary, new grammatical structures, and stylistic devices used by skillful writers; they also learn more of the generalizations about words and spelling patterns that we call *phonics*.[5]

Reading is not taught in isolation, however; it is supported by thinking, listening, speaking, and writing abilities. In turn, learning to read supports the development of the other language abilities. Integrated lessons that reflect these understandings will best meet student needs. An integrated language program can be depicted thus:[6]

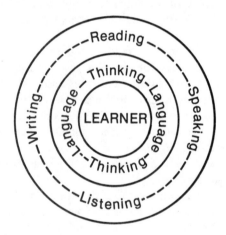

Current research tells us that reading and writing are complementary processes. Therefore, we will plan instruction that reflects research findings as recommended by James Moffett and Betty Jane Wagner:

> The best way for the receiver to learn to comprehend is to compose. Communication is a game like any other in some respects. To play well you have to play all roles in it. You cannot be a good fielder in baseball if you are not also a base runner, because to know which teammate to throw the ball to you must know what the runner is most likely to do. This is why a good theory of language arts should make clear that composition and comprehension are equal and reciprocal.

Chess players role-play each other in order to read each other's mind, and that is what readers and writers have to do. A learner needs to practice all roles and relations of the communication structure. This amounts to being sender, receiver, and sometimes even subject in all kinds of discourse.[7]

Our aim in this book is to share teaching ideas that engage students in relating thinking, reading, and writing processes in meaningful lessons and learning experiences that are based on whole language. Our intent is also to suggest ways of involving students in learning that is enjoyable and motivating for them and, therefore, more stimulating for you.

RECOMMENDED RESOURCES

If you want to know more about research findings related to reading, thinking, and writing, you may want to investigate the works of writers from whom we have gathered our information. The following reports of research can be found in most university libraries, or you may wish to order them directly from the publisher (see the Directory of Addresses at the end of Chapter 10).

Britton, James. *Language and Learning*. Penguin, 1970. A report of how children learn language and how language becomes an essential aspect of learning.

Goodman, Kenneth. *What's Whole in Whole Language?* Heineman, 1986. A parent/teacher guide to children's language and literacy learning.

Goodman, Kenneth and Yetta. "Reading and Writing Relationships: Pragmatic Functions." In *Composing and Comprehending*, ed. Julie Jenson. National Council of Teachers of English, 1984. See also "Learning to Read Is Natural." In *Theory and Practice of Early Reading*, ed. L. Resnick and P. Weaver. Erlbaum, 1979.

Graves, Donald. *Writing: Teachers & Children at Work*. Heineman, 1983. A report of his observations of children's writing and how teachers work to encourage writing development. See also *Write from the Start*, co-authored with Virginia Stuart. Dutton, 1985.

Moffett, James. *Teaching the Universe of Discourse*. Houghton Mifflin, 1968. A seminal work that has influenced current thinking in the language arts. His *Active Voice* (Boynton/Cook, 1981) makes connections between thinking and language arts across the curriculum. See also *A Student-centered Language Arts and Reading Curriculum, K-13: A Handbook for Teachers*. Houghton Mifflin, 1983. (Latest edition is co-authored by Betty Jane Wagner.)

Rosenblatt, Louise. *Literature as Exploration*. Noble, 1976. See also *The Reader, the Text, the Poem*. University of Illinois, 1978. Deals with transactions between reader and author.

Smith, Frank. *Reading without Nonsense*. Teachers College Press, 1978. Presents a sound analysis of the reading/language processes that we need to recognize and suggestions for applying these cognitive understandings; based on his earlier work, *Understanding Reading* (Holt, 1973). See also *Comprehension and Learning*, (Holt, 1975) and *Writing and the Writer* (Holt, 1982).

Tiedt, Iris M. *The Language Arts Handbook*. Prentice-Hall, 1983. Provides an up-to-date overview of integrated language arts instruction, including chapters on thinking, language growth, and reading instruction. Former editor of *Language Arts*, her work includes *Teaching Writing in K–8 Classrooms* (Prentice-Hall, 1983), co-authored with a team of elementary teachers who attended the California Writing Project Summer Institute, and *Teaching Thinking across the Grades* (Allyn and Bacon, 1989).

As you peruse copies of the current issues of educational journals, we recommend that you become acquainted with work by the following scholars who are also influencing thinking related to language and literary instruction:

James Squire	David Pearson
Jeanne Chall	Anne Haas Dyson
Arthur Applebee	Richard Andersen
Robert Calfee	Dolores Durkin
Stephen Tchudi	Judith Langer
Michael Halliday	Courtney Cazden
Carol Chomsky	Don Holdaway
Jean Piaget	Jerome Bruner
Charles Cooper	Marie Clay
Charlotte Huck	Walter Loban
George Miller	Robert Tierney
Jeannette Veatch	Lev Vygotsky

An excellent summary of ideas related to literacy instruction is provided by articles in *Composing and Comprehending*, edited by Julie Jensen (National Council of Teachers of English, 1984). A second collection of informative articles is *Convergences: Transactions in Reading and Writing*, edited by Bruce T. Petersen (National Council of Teachers of English, 1986).

Designing a Reading/Thinking/Writing Program

If we accept the findings of current research relating reading, thinking, and writing, then we should design a reading program that carries out the ideas we have just summarized. That, of course, is what we hope to do in this book.

AN INTEGRATED MODEL

The ideas we present are organized around a holistic model that clarifies the interrelationships among the language arts thus:

This program describes what the learner is doing, beginning with a firm foundation of thinking and oral language, which has its roots in the early years of the young learner's life. As children gain facility with oral English, they move naturally into working with written language, discovering encoding-decoding information and developing reading fluency. Gradually, they connect reading with composition, using higher order thinking skills. Literature, then, becomes the students' text as they listen to and read books for pleasure and information, entering into transactions with each author, and then responding to the experience with original thinking expressed orally and in writing. Evaluation, both formative and summative, is on-going throughout the program, but it is not the learner's primary concern.

Thus, this book is organized along the lines of this model. Following the introductory chapter that you are now reading, chapters focus on each developmental level of the integrated reading/thinking/writing processes. We provide suggestions for classroom activities that cover the information described below. You can use these activities immediately.

CHAPTER 2
BUILDING A LANGUAGE AND THINKING FOUNDATION

Children learn language orally at an early age. At this stage, a child can learn any language in the surrounding environment—German, Sioux, Tagalog, English. In this book, we are talking primarily about children who speak English, although the ideas presented are applicable to instruction in any language.

"As children learn their language, they learn to think," writes James Squire, former President of the National Council of Teachers of English. Although we recognize that language is not necessary for all forms of thought, "for most children language is the major vehicle through which thinking occurs, and it is through language that children learn to label ideas, to classify, to relate the new to the known, to construct ideas or compose, to reconstruct or comprehend."[8]

After hearing and speaking their native language for five years, children usually enter school able to converse readily. They have a functional vocabulary and often understand such concepts as colors and numbers. The range of abilities in any kindergarten or first grade is broad, however, and we need to plan learning activities appropriately. Children who have heard book language since the age of two readily move into beginning reading and writing activities, but slower learners or children who are learning English as a second language need more time with thinking and oral language to form this foundation for reading and writing. This oral language foundation will continue to support experiments with written language.

What the child has learned through listening and speaking provides the foundation for reading and writing—what is often referred to as *readiness*. As Squire points out, "A critical factor in shaping the quality of both composing and comprehending is the prior knowledge the pupil brings to reading and writing."[9] Knowing the structure of English sentences, for example, enables beginning readers to predict the meaning of an unknown word in the context of a sentence. For example:

At the zoo Joe saw a big, gray *elephant*.

Preceded by the determiner *a* and two adjectives, the word has to be a noun. The experience of going to the zoo or reading books about elephants also assists the reader in narrowing the possibilities for identifying this unfamiliar word. The prior knowledge that is stored in the student's brain thus enables him or her to predict meaning with reasonable certainty and to move on with the story.

Our first consideration, therefore, in this program is to strengthen children's use of oral language and their general fund of information—their experiential backgrounds. This knowledge prepares them to read and write successfully. Prereading and prewriting activities will continue to develop the child's "ear for language" and to assure that students develop a positive attitude toward reading and writing.

In this chapter, we describe such activities as:

- Visualization
- Developing comprehension through listening
- Storytelling and puppetry
- Talking in small groups

Oral-aural activities blend naturally into the first stages of learning to recognize symbols and to relate them to spoken sounds, as presented in the following chapter.

CHAPTER 3
DISCOVERING BASIC READING AND WRITING CONCEPTS

In order to learn to read and to write, students must first become aware of written language. Usually, this awareness happens naturally through observation of the environment—learning about functional signs, noticing parents reading the newspaper, and being read to. Before coming to school, many children recognize letter symbols that we use to represent the sounds we speak. We build our reading/thinking/writing program, then, on what children bring to school—their prior knowledge.

The most natural way to begin work with written language is to encourage children to write, using whatever knowledge of written language they have, expressing their own ideas. Children use invented spelling as they write in journals and create original books. These eager learners acquire literacy as they did oral language—reaching out for what they need, asking questions, observing, and discovering. A rich language environment provides the information they need for learning.

Gradually, students *discover* information about the sound-symbol relationships, what we commonly call *phonics*. For instance, they learn that the letter symbol *b* is used to begin spelling such words as *bird, boy,* and *beautiful*. Through writing and reading, they discover more complex sound and symbol relationships. For example, they learn that the *ch* spelling can represent a number of sounds: /s/, /c/, or /k/. Because multiple spellings (graphemes) are used for many of the forty phonemes (sounds) used in speaking English, the full range of the sound-symbol relationships will be explored over a number of years. Children will continue to reinforce their knowledge of the phoneme-grapheme relationships through extensive reading/thinking/writing experiences—gathering data, analyzing, synthesizing, and applying.

In this chapter, we present such ideas as:

- Beginning journals
- Webbing and mapping
- Writing books
- Simple bookbinding
- Tape-assisted reading

CHAPTER 4
GAINING POWER THROUGH READING/
THINKING/WRITING

Our overall goal is to produce self-motivated students who read and write easily. Students will learn to read by reading, and they will learn to write by writing. Of course, they need help as they engage in these processes, and that is your function as planner, facilitator, and co-worker.

As children engage in purposeful reading and writing tasks, we circulate throughout the room to serve as a resource to assist learners in what they are trying to do. Students also learn to use each other as resources. We try to help students solve their own problems as much as possible, by asking a question or pointing out an illustration that provides a clue to unlocking the meaning of a word. Talking about a story you have read aloud and webbing key words on the board assists students as they write their reactions to the behavior of a main character. This individualized approach to instruction permits children to progress at their own pace and level of ability, and it answers the questions individual learners have immediately so they are able to continue with the task at hand.

We select learning activities that engage students in "really" reading and in "really" writing whole language. We avoid wasting student time with fill-in-the blank activities or trying to read lists of unrelated words. As much as possible, new skills develop in the context of reading or writing whole language, discovered by the learner. Therefore, we favor such practices as free reading and writing, teaching around a theme of general interest, and introducing students to tools or strategies they can use when they seem appropriate. Time-on-task studies remind us of what most of us already know: Learners need to read and write frequently, and they must also see a purpose in the tasks they undertake—enjoyment, information, communication, and learning.

As students read and write, we reinforce their awareness of the inter-relationships between the reading and writing processes. We also guide them to recognize the thinking-language processes that underlie both composition and comprehension.

In this chapter, we present such ideas as:

- Creating a classroom library
- Developing a unit of study

- More bookbinding ideas
- Stimulating ideas for writing

CHAPTER 5
STRENGTHENING READING/WRITING CONNECTIONS

Throughout the elementary and middle school years, we help students observe the relationships between reading and writing, as two sides of the same coin. We help students become aware of the ways that reading and writing are connected. For example:

Both involve thinking-language processes.

Both utilize the phoneme-grapheme or phonology system of the English language.

Both require a transaction between reader and writer.

Both support the learnings that make up comprehension and composition.

Helping students become aware (metacognition) of the complementary nature of these processes is efficient in terms of learning and teaching time. The students are learning both encoding and decoding skills as they write a sentence that they have spoken or contribute to a class story the teacher is printing on the board. They are learning both reading and spelling skills as they construct a list of rhyming words or observe words that begin with the same combination of letters. We can eliminate divisions between reading, language arts, spelling, and handwriting instruction to take full advantage of whatever language experiences offer student learners.

As students hear you read "book language," they enjoy a good story, but they are also learning how to construct sentences. They are expanding their knowledge of vocabulary, concepts about the world, and how we string words together to make varied sentences. They are developing an "ear for language" that will enable them to edit their writing as they test their sentences by reading them aloud. This basic knowledge of grammar is learned before children enter school, but it continues to grow through reading and writing experiences in the classroom.

As students engage in reading and writing activities, they also become aware that what they are reading is "writing." The author who produced a book went through the process of writing a first draft, reading and revising until a final copy of the manuscript was prepared for the publisher. Seeing the author as a writer experiencing the same problems they do may enhance student interest in observing how the author wrote, the stylistic devices used, varied idioms, and figurative language. They will find that they can follow an author's sentence structures as they write in the manner of Maurice Sendak or Madeline

L'Engle. Reading "writing" is a new way of perceiving the reading act as students learn to read like writers!

In this chapter, we stress such activities as:

- Celebrating authors
- Imitating the writing of an author
- Keeping reading logs
- Writing for varied audiences

CHAPTER 6
LEARNING ADVANCED THINKING SKILLS

Remembering that reading is equated with "making or composing meaning," we emphasize the teaching of comprehension skills at all levels of learning. We also place a higher value on the ideas expressed by the student writer than on the correct use of such conventions as spelling and the placement of quotation marks.

We help children "read between the lines" for hidden meanings as we read, for example, *Charlotte's Web*. They infer the character traits of Templeton, the rat, by observing E. B. White's description of his behavior. As young authors, they learn, conversely, to hide some of the messages they want to convey by writing sentences that "show, not tell" what they want the reader to understand. Learning to use such thinking skills helps students grow toward more mature responses to the literature they read and toward expressing more sophisticated ideas in their writing.

Both comprehension and composition are predicated on the assumption that two persons are involved. Therefore, students need to develop a sense of audience as they write. As they read, assuming the role of responder, they must work with the author to understand the message being communicated; they compose meaning as they engage in the reading process. They also need to recognize the influence that what they bring to this transaction has on the success of communication.[10] Lack of knowledge about a subject, for example, may make it impossible to understand the author's work, no matter how well it is written. We think of the reader-writer transaction like this:

The Author/Reader Transaction

Author-writer's Contribution	Reader-responder's Contribution
Think; talk; read	Think; intend to read
Select theme, message, plot	Understand literal-factual meaning; vocabulary
Organize presentation; compose meaning	Compose meaning; comprehend

Author-writer's Contribution	Reader-responder's Contribution
Address audience	Interpret meaning—inferences, perceive relationships
Write with style—imagery, idiom, rhetoric	React personally
Communicate with clarity	Respond—summarize, generalize, evaluate
COMPOSITION	COMPREHENSION

We can show students how to deal with meaning at different levels of sophistication by planning activities that engage them in consciously moving from facts presented to generating ideas themselves. We can guide students to respond to a story at different levels as they write questions based, for example, on "Little Red Riding Hood":

Fact: Why was little Red Riding Hood called by that name?

Inference: Is this a true story?

Judgment: Which character would you like to play?

Creativity: How would Little Red Riding Hood tell this story to her mother?

Talking and writing in this manner reinforces thinking skills that can be used as students read independently.

In this chapter, we emphasize:

- Thinking awareness
- Using various levels of thinking
- Integrating instruction
- Figurative language

CHAPTER 7
READING/THINKING/WRITING ACROSS THE CURRICULUM

Reading and writing are basic learning processes across the curriculum, and thinking underlies every learning activity we can devise. As teachers, we need to ensure that students are reading and writing in all subject areas for purposes that they understand. We need to help them determine varied purposes that are clearly their own so that students are not always reading and writing because you made an assignment. Furthermore, purposes for reading and writing should include enjoyment as well as information.

In any curriculum area students should perceive reading as a way of discovering what they want to know. As we guide them in planning an I-Search paper, for example, we will begin by visiting the library to determine what resources are available (see pages 241–245). We will also help them learn skills of evaluating what they read and considering the validity of what authors present. On the other hand, students should begin to view composition as a means of expressing their own thoughts. We can give them opportunities to clarify what they believe and to substantiate their positions through rational thinking that provides evidence to support their arguments. Reading, writing, and thinking are integral components of learning in any classroom. We need to take full advantage of strategies that will enhance student growth in using these processes as they learn the content of a subject that we teach.

In this chapter, we focus on:

- Teaching around themes that cross disciplines
- Using writing to clarify thinking
- Using reading to discover information
- Helping students use thinking skills as they engage with content-specific ideas

CHAPTER 8
READING AND RESPONDING TO LITERATURE

Once students are "hooked on books," they will read widely along lines of their own interest. They will enjoy sharing books with their classmates—a surefire way to stimulate reading, writing, and thinking. They will investigate different forms of literature, perhaps drama motivated by seeing a play or producing one in school. Writing original poetry often leads students to reading the poetry of others with genuine appreciation. We can encourage them to respond openly to literature, making personal judgments about what they like or do not like, selecting the books they want to read. They are applying the higher order thinking skills that we want them to know.

Throughout this growth as responsible readers, students reinforce the perception of what they read as "writing." They observe the writing of the authors they read, and perceive these writers as real people. More and more, their own writing is a response to literature, and their writing is influenced by literature models. Instruction directs these observations and encourages students to observe and discuss writing styles. The teacher also provides information about the authors as real people who engage in writing much as the students do. By consciously reading like a writer, the student is learning how to write.

In this chapter, we stress:

- The wide reading of varied authors
- Exploring our literary heritage
- Reading different genres
- Writing varied forms of literature
- Learning to write by reading

CHAPTER 9
DEVELOPING A STUDENT-CENTERED CURRICULUM

Our goal is to create a strong reading/thinking/writing program that meets student needs. We begin, therefore, with a statement of the characteristics of a program that emphasizes student discovery and individualization of instruction. Objectives the the program are spelled out in terms of student learning, and teacher behaviors are recommended that support student involvement in assessing their own progress. We also suggest ways of communicating to parents.

We involve students in assessing their own learning and we use evaluation as a positive means for helping students consider what they are learning—the learning process itself. We encourage students to evaluate their progress continuously as they maintain a reading log and collect writing in individual portfolios. They learn to work in small groups and to apply holistic methods of responding to the writing of their peers. Publication of student work provides purpose for student editing of their writing as they prepare to make their work public.

The information in this chapter is divided into two parts:

- Designing the curriculum
- Involving students in learning

BASIC ASSUMPTIONS UNDERLYING THE PROGRAM

This holistic model depicts a reading/thinking/writing program based on the following assumptions:

1. A strong thinking-language base is necessary for success in reading and writing. Thinking and language permeate all learning.
2. Reading and writing cannot be taught in isolation. Integrating the language arts reinforces learning efficiently and effectively.

3. Children need to learn basic phonics information, but they can best learn and then reinforce this learning through reading and writing whole language. Decoding and encoding should always be presented as complementary processes applied during reading and writing activities. (Note, too, that both decoding and encoding require the application of thinking skills.)

4. Students learn to read, write, and think by engaging frequently in composing and comprehending activities that emphasize quality of the learning experience as well as quantity or frequency.

5. Literature must be an integral part of instruction across the curriculum at all levels. It should be presented as something to be read and also as an example of good writing by a real person who is sharing his or her thinking.

6. Both reading and writing entail a transaction between author and audience as they work together to construct meaning. The work of both reader and writer are influenced by prior knowledge—what each brings to the task of making meaning.

7. Reading, writing, and thinking abilities grow uniquely for each individual. Instructional strategies (for example, the discovery method) should allow for individual progress—interest, pacing, self-esteem, and accomplishment. Evaluation must also be geared to individual growth with appropriate expectations established for each learner.

SUMMARY

The holistic language and literacy program described in this section is based on individual student growth. Designed for all learners at all levels, it begins anew each time a student and teacher come together. Learning begins, quite literally, with what the learner brings to the encounter, and growth continues from this benchmark. Progress recorded in a writing portfolio and recordings of reading performance demonstrate clearly to student, teacher, and parent the learning that is taking place.

Recommended Instructional Strategies

Throughout this book of ideas, we stress learning activities that emphasize reading, thinking, and writing as languaging processes—integral components of the language arts program. We present activities that incorporate oral language to support growth in working with the written language, and we try to make students aware that thinking is part of everything we do. We stress the importance of showing students how all of the language skills connect and how their own thinking processes work. Talking with students might result in a class poster—a motto—like this:

THINK ABOUT IT!

The more you read, the better you read.

The more you write, the better you write.

The more you read, the better you write.

The more you write, the better you read.

And all the time, you are thinking!

In this section, we describe several teaching strategies that integrate language arts instruction. Each strategy engages students in "really" reading and "really" writing rather than focusing on isolated drill typified by most workbook pages or duplicated sheets. These strategies pay off in terms of student involvement and, therefore, achievement, and lead to positive attitudes toward reading and writing as having purpose in an adult life.

READING ALOUD TO STUDENTS

An effective method of engaging students in reading is your reading aloud to them. A strategy readily available to any teacher, reading aloud is not just a special treat used to give students a break or a last resort of a tired teacher to calm a group of unruly students. Reading aloud is an excellent technique for teaching students how to read. Listening to the oral presentation of a book also teaches students how to write!

As you read, for example, *Tom Sawyer*, to a class, the students are learning:

1. What fluent reading sounds like—the cadence of English sentences, the varied intonation appropriate for questions or a sense of excitement, and the way to pronounce words.

2. A positive attitude toward reading and toward being in school—teacher and students are sharing an enjoyable experience. Laughing together about Tom and Huck's escapades makes for cohesive group dynamics.

3. English grammar—what book language sounds like, how English sentences are structured, and sentence variety.

4. Writing style—interesting ways of using language, figurative language, and imagery.

5. Characteristics of one form of writing (narrative)—plot development, characterization, setting, mood, theme, and dialogue.

6. Comprehension abilities—same ones used in reading independently are introduced through listening—vocabulary, inference, generalization, and evaluation.

7. Perception of the author as a writer—information about the man, Samuel Clemens, who wrote this book, the difficulties of his life, his familiarity with the setting, and issues presented.

In order to take full advantage of reading aloud as a teaching strategy, of course, you guide students to recognize what they are hearing and what they are learning. Plan follow-up oral or written activities based on student understanding of the work you are sharing. Every literature selection—short story, novel, article, or essay—will suggest a number of ideas to develop. Some choose others for fuller development. Examples of lessons that begin with oral reading are presented throughout this text.

Good stories to read aloud include:

Primary Grades
Where the Wild Things Are, Maurice Sendak (Harper)
Crow Boy, Taro Yashima (Viking)
Swimmy, Leo Lionni (Pantheon)
The Relatives Came, Cynthia Rylant (Bradbury)

Middle Grades
Mary Poppins, Pamela Travers (Harcourt)
The Lion, the Witch, and the Wardrobe, C. S. Lewis (Macmillan)
The Genie of Sutton Place, George Selden (Farrar)
Island of the Blue Dolphins, Scott O'Dell (Houghton)

Upper Grades
It's Like This, Cat, Emily Neville (Harper)
Dragonwings, Lawrence Yep (Harper)
Watership Down, Richard Adams (Collings)
The Twelve and the Genii, Pauline Clarke (Faber)
Sarah, Plain and Tall, Patricia MacLachlan (Harper)

LITERATURE AS A TEXT

The very moment the raccoon opened his eyes he knew it was the day to decide. The pines of his forest gloomed dark against the almost brilliant oaks and maples hung with leaves of rose and pale yellow and green turning scarlet. His nose lifted to taste the air, and found it already cinnamoned with autumn, already pungent with damp earth smells like the undersides of mushrooms. Even the tips of his delicate racoon paws were no longer quite warm.

An exciting way to teach students to write is to guide them to observe the writing they read! Although it was certainly not her primary intention, Julia Cunningham provides a ready-made lesson in using descriptive detail and colorful language in the first paragraph of a charming book, *Macaroon* (Pantheon).

Throughout the chapters that follow, we share ideas that demonstrate how you can teach students to write by using literature in enjoyable and effective ways. You can use literature models to show students how to write more effective sentences and also longer forms—paragraphs, fables, and short stories. You can use literature to teach grammatical structures. You can even use literature as a text to teach the mechanics of writing!

As an example, you might read the touching book *Nonna* by Jennifer Bartoli (Harvey) in which a child tells of the death of his grandmother. After responding to the book informally and identifying with the feelings expressed, you might suggest borrowing one of the author's sentences as a way of experimenting with writing.

For beginning writers, print the sentence on the board, thus:

Amy came out of the kitchen carrying a big plate of cookies.

Read the sentence aloud, pointing to the words that you read. Then have students read the sentence aloud. Ask them to see if they can copy Jennifer Bartoli's sentence. Dictating the sentence as it is written may be helpful, too. These techniques also work well for ESL and bilingual students. After students have copied the sentence, read it aloud again together. (Many children will, of course, have memorized the sentence, so they will memorize-read, which is a supportive learning process.)

Next, rewrite the sentence on the board, showing only the structure with blanks where words are omitted, thus:

_____ came out of the _____ carrying a
_____   _____ of _____.

Have students suggest various ways of completing this sentence framework borrowed from Bartoli:

Joe came out of the garage carrying a big box of tools.
Mildred came out of the bedroom carrying a little bag of toys.

Then ask students to write sentences of their own following the framework. Have students read their completed sentences aloud in small groups so all have an audience. Children can choose their best sentences to display on the bulletin board where others can read them.

The purpose of this experiment with language is to extend students' awareness of sentence structure. It demonstrates to them explicitly what they are already doing intuitively—borrowing structures from the language they hear or read.

Leave *Nonna* on the reading table where students can find it. They will be especially interested in discovering the sentence used in the writing experiment.

PRESENTING A WELL-DESIGNED LESSON

An important ressponsibility for the teacher is planning the curriculum and how it will be carried out over a period of time. As we plan and develop learning experiences with students, we consider all that we know about good teaching.

Effective teachers have learned that a warm-up period or preparation time, a *stimulus*, is essential if students are to perform an activity well. Before students write or read, we plan prewriting or prereading activities that stimulate students' thinking. We talk about the topic, write words on the board that may be used, even begin composing collectively, as we did in the lesson above. We literally prepare students to succeed.

The learning *activity* must have purpose that is clear to the student. The warm-up period engages students in thinking—greases the skids, so to speak. As students work at a given task, the teacher and aides act as resource people, facilitating the child's performance, but being careful to allow time for thinking and working out problems independently. Positive reinforcement encourages students to tackle the work of learning. Praise and self-satisfaction are the rewards of their efforts.

Equally important is the *follow-up*, or what happens after students complete the learning activity. Students might act out a story they have read; they could meet to read their fables in a read-around group; or they might work at the Publishing Center to make a booklet of their original poems. The follow-up reinforces learning, establishes purpose for the activity, and motivates subsequent learning. It also assists the instructor in evaluating the success of the lesson.

Evaluation is written into every lesson, for it is important to know our objectives and to know if they have been met. You can evaluate the success of a lesson by simply observing student performance. Evaluation may also take the form of retelling, acting out, making a timeline, or producing a well-structured written fairytale. If grades are to be placed on student work, students should know the criteria you are applying. (See Chapter 9.)

A well-designed lesson, then, contains four components: the *stimulus* or warm-up, the learning *activity*, the *follow-up*, and the *evaluation*. We form an acronym to remind you of these components as you plan, using the SAFE Model:

S   timulus

A   ctivity

F   ollow-up

E   valuation

Following is a lesson that demonstrates how the model works in the classroom.

SAFE Lesson: Example

TITLE: ROCK WRITING

DIFFICULTY LEVEL: GRADES 2–8 (Orally with teacher in K–1)

OBJECTIVES:

Students will:

1. Collect data using their senses
2. Record notes about a natural object, a rock
3. Arrange ideas noted in poetry form

DESCRIPTION:

As part of a science study of local landforms, students select a rock that they observe carefully, using all five senses. They then write words and phrases based on their observations. After reading and thinking about their notes, they write an ode to their individual rock, beginning, "Oh, rock. . . ."

PROCEDURES:

Have students gather rocks as part of a field trip. You may prefer to bring in enough rocks so that each student will have one to observe.

Stimulus:

Each student has a rock on his or her desk. Discuss what the students can observe about a rock based on each of the senses. Have a student recorder write key words on the board, such as:

Sight—size, shape, color

Hearing—rattle, scraping

Taste—mineral content, dirt

Touch—shape, roughness, smoothness, unevenness, bumps

Smell—sweet fragrance, earthiness

Have students fold a sheet of composition paper in thirds, labeling one section for each sense, and the sixth one entitled Other Ideas. Ask students to observe their rocks and to jot down notes about what they observe.

Activity:

After students have had time to observe and write notes, tell them that they can use their observations to write an ode to their rocks. Tell them that an ode is a song that begins, "Oh, _____" and that it usually praises a person. They can begin their poem with "Oh, rock . . ." and speak to their rock as a person, using personification.

Follow-up:

After students have written for a while, have them read their poems to a partner. Partners can assist each other in adding ideas or revising the poem, as needed. Their poems might be something like this:

Ode to a Rock

Oh, wonderful little gray rock,
Bumpety, lumpety, and tough.
You have tumbled down from the high mountain.
You have survived the trampling of many rough feet,
The crush of an automobile's wheels.
I will give you an easier life now
Perched on my bedroom windowsill.

Evaluation:

Circulate around the room to observe student participation as they observe, write, and share. Have students determine the criteria for an especially good poem after they have shared, answering the question: What made some poems stand out as especially effective? Students can revise their poems based on the criteria established. Have students display the rock writing with the rocks laid on a table or shelf.

The SAFE Model, demonstrated in lessons in every chapter of this book, assures you that your lessons will be theoretically sound, including a warm-up or prewriting activity and a follow-up or postwriting activity as well as evaluation. This lesson plan also integrates all of the language skills, including thinking, into a meaningful holistic learning experience that students enjoy.

YOUR PROFESSIONAL LIBRARY

If you want to know more about the teaching of an integrated reading/thinking/writing program, you will continue to read books and journals that present research, theory, and current practice. We recommend the books listed earlier in this chapter on page 5. We also recommend two journals that will keep you up-to-date in the years ahead. You can read these journals in a college library or obtain an individual subscription by joining the organizations that publish them. Write for information about the following:

Language Arts. National Council of Teachers of English. 1111 Kenyon Road, Urbana IL 61801.

Reading Teacher. International Reading Association. Box 8139, Newark DE 19711.

In addition, you will begin collecting books to help you expand the ideas we share with you. We recommend one or two books of poetry, as well as collections of fairytales, myths, and literature that you enjoy yourself and would like to share with students. You might begin with these:

Arbuthnot, May H., and Root, Shelton. *Time for Poetry*. Scott Foresman. A favorite collection of poetry for all occasions and seasons.

Arbuthnot, May H., et al. *Books for Children*. Scott, Foresman. An overview of children's literature; up-dated regularly.

Carpenter, Humphrey. *Secret Gardens: The Golden Age of Children's Literature*. Houghton Mifflin.

Mother Goose. Varied editions.

Silverstein, Shel. *Where the Sidewalk Ends*. Harper. Funny poetry that students of all ages love.

We also recommend that you begin collecting copies of your favorite books written for children—books too good to miss, books you would like to share with children in school or out. For example:

Carroll, Lewis. *Alice in Wonderland*. Varied editions.

Grahame, Kenneth. *Wind in the Willows*. Varied editions.

McCloskey, Robert. *Make Way for Ducklings*. Viking.

Milne, A. A. *Winnie the Pooh*. Dutton.

White, E. B. *Charlotte's Web*. Harper.

The choices are up to you! The important thing is to get to know good books for children that will help you teach reading, writing, and thinking. Go to the library and read.

Summary

This integrated language and literacy program provides for each individual's level of ability, for the children operate with the prior knowledge of language with which they enter the classroom. Establishing that individual performance level as the benchmark from which the child begins, we plan language experiences from which all children can learn—the intervention strategies in our on-going classroom research. Continuously we question, searching for the most effective strategies for encouraging each child to move onward.

At any period of time, we can observe an individual child's performance compared to that initial benchmark and note the amount of growth and the effect of the classroom learning experiences. Student, teacher, and parent work together to support growth.

The teacher of a holistic language and literacy program is a facilitator of learning, planning activities that will engage students in exciting content and resulting in language use. Developing a rich language environment, both oral and written, to provide information about content and language itself, the teacher guides students to extend themselves to their fullest potential. The students read, think, and write in response to new experiences, and the reward is their own achievement.

"Idealized," you say? "Impossible!"

"No, *wonderful*," we answer. "And, it is happening in classrooms across the country today."

Challenge

The ideas suggested here will help you begin developing a holistic language and literacy program right now!

1. Schedule an afternoon at your local public library. Find out what they have to offer—books, records, films—resources you can use for planning or presenting activities in your classroom. Browse through the fiction and nonfiction sections. Locate the collections of Folktales (398) and collections of poetry (811). Ask the librarian to help you locate what you are interested in.

   Inquire where they keep the *Children's Catalog*, an index of literature written for children. Published by the Wilson Publishing Company, this index, updated quarterly, includes annotations and categorizes literature by subjects. It is a very useful reference when you want books about certain themes.

2. Begin a file of "Books for Children." Refer to the lists in Chapter 10 to suggest titles that might interest you. As you read or browse through books, complete a 4" x 6" card like this:

Simon, Seymour.	NF Sci
How to Talk with Your Computer.	K-4
Crowell, 1984.	29 pp.

Very clear directions for beginning programming—BASIC, LOGO

Illustrated.

Even older kids could use independently.

As you begin your file, setting up a form like this will make it easy to jot down all the information you might later need. Include any information that would be useful to you.

3. Plan two lessons following the SAFE Model described on page 21. Think through each lesson before you begin writing the plan. What objectives will you meet? What will the children learn? You might develop one lesson around the sharing of a book that you read aloud to a class. Planning these lessons will give you the feel of the total learning experience as you go through it on paper. Then try at least one of the lessons with a group of students. Summarize how this lesson model worked for you.

Endnotes

1. Aaron Bar-Adon and Werner F. Leopold, eds. *Child Language: A Book of Readings*. Prentice-Hall, 1971. Anne Haas Dyson. "Reading, Writing, and Language: Young Children Solving the Written Language Puzzle." In *Composing and Comprehending*, ed. Julie Jensen. National Conference on Research in English, 1984, pp. 127–142.

2. Frank Smith, ed. *Pscholinguistics and Reading*. Holt, 1973, p. 180.

3. Ibid., p. 195.

4. Iris M. Tiedt. *The Language Arts Handbook*. Prentice-Hall, 1983.

5. Kenneth Goodman. *What's Whole about Whole Language?* Heineman, 1986. Also, "Basal Readers: A Call for Action." *Language Arts*, 63, 4 (April 1986): 358–363.

6. Tiedt. *Language Arts Handbook*, p. 6.

7. James Moffett and Betty Jane Wagner. *Student-Centered Language Arts and Reading, K–13: A Handbook for Teachers*. Houghton Mifflin, 1983, pp. 10–11.

8. James R. Squire. "Composing and Comprehending: Two Sides of the Same Basic Process." In *Composing and Comprehending*, p. 23.

9. Ibid., p. 24.

10. Louise Rosenblatt. *Literature as Exploration*, 3rd ed. Noble, 1973.

2

Building a Language and Thinking Foundation

"As children and young people learn their language, they learn to think." Thus, James Squire, former president of the National Council of Teachers of English, begins his list of "The Ten Great Ideas in the Teaching of English During the Past Half Century."

As they learn to speak, young children learn to relate ideas, experiences, concepts, and words. Noting similarities and differences, they begin to classify animals, colors, people, and language. They are learning to think with language. This language and thinking development provides a firm foundation for learning to read and to write.

Oral language and thinking continue to support comprehension and composition at all levels. In this chapter, we will explore ideas for developing thinking, listening, and speaking abilities.

Thinking Awareness for Students

Listening for Comprehension

Speaking to Communicate Thinking

Implementing the Program

Research related to thinking and language development can be summarized as follows:

1. Thinking and language acquisition, which develop together, provide the foundation for all learning. These skills continue to grow throughout the learning experiences in which children engage.

2. The prior knowledge acquired by a child determines success in reading and writing tasks at all stages of development.

3. Children need to be aware of thinking processes and the potential power of their brains (metacognition).

4. Children learn most readily through listening. Listening comprehension is closely related to reading comprehension. Both involve higher level thinking skills.

5. Speaking is a productive skill that reveals thinking. As such, it is akin to composition.

6. No language skill is taught in isolation. As children listen and speak, they are thinking and they are preparing to read and write. Listening and speaking continue to be integral aspects of the reading and writing processes at all levels.

Selected Resources

You may wish to explore the following resources from which we drew the ideas summarized above.

Baghan, Marcia. *Our Daughter Learns to Read and Write*. IRA, 1984.

Britton, James. *Language and Learning*. University of Miami Press, 1970.

Goodman, Kenneth. *What's Whole in Whole Language?* Heineman, 1986.

Jaggar, Angela, and Smith-Burke, M. Trika, eds. *Observing the Language Learner*. NCTE and IRA, 1985.

Standiford, Sally. "Metacomprehension." ERIC Clearinghouse on Reading and Communication Skills, 1985.

Tiedt, Iris. "English in the Elementary School: What, How, and Why We Teach." In *Education in the 80's: English*, ed. R. Baird Shuman. National Education Association, 1981.

Thinking Awareness for Students

Thinking and language grow together as the young child first abstracts the complex English grammar system and then begins putting words together to communicate. Although thinking can take different forms, for the most part human thinking involves language. Thus, thinking deserves a foremost consideration in a language and literacy program.

Because thinking processes are largely invisible, we tend to take them for granted. Therefore, a first task is to help students become aware of the thinking processes they are engaging in (metacognition) as they act out a situation, respond to a story, or write even a simple sentence. We can talk about thinking and how we make decisions. We can visualize scenes depicted by an author who shares a story. We can ask questions about historical events and people who live in different parts of our country. Students of all ages need to think about thinking.

The lessons in this section of the chapter begin with leading students to visualize. This aspect of thinking is important for students of all ages. Adapt the lessons presented to fit the grade level you teach by selecting appropriate literature or topics for discussion.

A USEFUL STRATEGY: VISUALIZATION

Visualization is a method of producing mental images. It helps students translate words they hear or read into detailed colored pictures in their minds. It enables students to understand new concepts and understand their relationships to concepts previously introduced. The ability to visualize is necessary for comprehension of what is read, and visualizing helps writers express ideas more clearly.

SAFE Lesson No. 1

TITLE: INTRODUCING VISUALIZATION
DIFFICULTY LEVEL: GRADES K–12
OBJECTIVES:

Students will:

1. Experiment with a visualization method
2. Improve recall and comprehension skills

DESCRIPTION:

The students will listen to a paragraph and recall as many details as they can. The second time you read the paragraph, students will draw pictures about the story as it is being read.

PROCEDURES:
Stimulus:

Introduce the method of visualization to your students. They will need to have pencils and paper. You will need two or three paragraphs to read.

Tell the students that you are looking for ways to help them learn more easily.

Ask them to experiment with a method called *visualization,* which some people find very helpful.

Activity:

Ask the students to listen as you read a descriptive paragraph. When you have finished, ask them to tell you what they remember about the paragraph. List their oral responses on the board.

Read another paragraph. Ask the students to draw pictures relating to the ideas presented in the paragraph while it is being read. When you have finished, ask them what they remember about this paragraph.

Was it easier for them to remember when they drew pictures as the story was read? Discuss the value of this process as a study aid.

Follow-Up:

When reading aloud, occasionally ask that students draw pictures to help with recall and comprehension. For example, when reading a fairytale such as "Cinderella," have a group of four children draw the sequence of events.

Evaluation:

Students will determine whether or not this method has value for them. Two or three times a week, after a reading assignment has been completed, ask the students to report on their experiences using this method.

Record any improvement in the students' ability to recall and comprehend a story when this method is used.

SAFE Lesson No. 2

TITLE: WHICH WAY DID THEY GO?

DIFFICULTY LEVEL: GRADES 3–10

OBJECTIVES:

Students will:

1. Learn or review the directions north, south, east, and west as shown on a map

2. Use these directions to follow and visualize the action in a story (older students)

DESCRIPTION:

Students will listen to a story and sketch the route of the action. This activity should help them visualize the action in the story.

PROCEDURES:

Stimulus:

Visualization skill is very important to understand the action in adventure and mystery stories.

Review with your students the directions north, south, east, and west as they appear on a map. For very young students, this may be the whole content of the lesson. With older students, *discuss* treasure maps and road maps.

Discuss with them the value of being able to read a map and follow the action in a story.

Activity:

Give students a set of oral directions and check their comprehension. Ask the students to write *N* at the top of their papers, *S* at the bottom, *E* on the right, and *W* on the left.

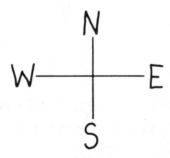

Ask them to draw a circle in the middle of their papers. Then ask them to draw a tree near south, a lake near east, a mountain near north, and an ocean along the west side.

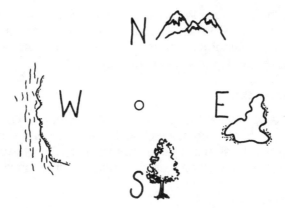

Be sure that the students understand that a map is a small representation of a larger area. Tell them to listen as you tell a story and to sketch the route of the action in the story. Tell a story similar to the following:

John and Mary set out from the circle to go fishing in the ocean. They walked south for a while, and they met a fisherman walking from the west. He was going fishing at a lake and he invited them to go along. They walked with him to the lake. They didn't catch anything so they decided to go and eat their lunch under a big tree down south.

After lunch they walked to the ocean. It was too late to fish because the sun was going down. Soon, the moon came up over the mountain to the northeast. They decided to sleep on the beach and walk home in the morning.

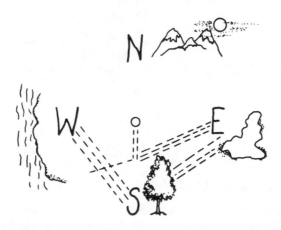

Ask the group the following questions: What direction would you go to go swimming? What direction would you go to climb a mountain? If you were under the tree in the south, what direction would you have to go to get home to the circle?

Follow-Up:

Make up stories that are increasingly difficult. Put the students into groups to make up stories, too. Have the students sketch the route as you or your students tell or read stories. Make it difficult. Later, ask them to wait until the story is ended and then draw the map.

Evaluation:

Check the students' sketches of the route to see if they have visualized the action.

Display the student-made maps. Give each student one blue ribbon. Have them walk around and place a ribbon on their favorite map.

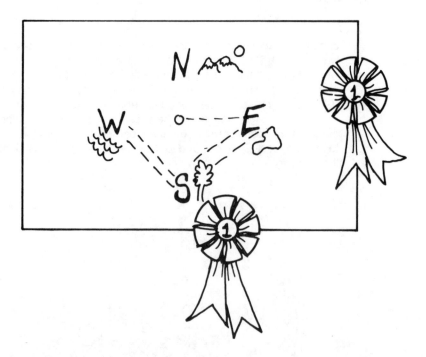

A USEFUL STRATEGY: CLASSIFICATION

The ability to classify helps students draw conclusions. Very young students should use concrete objects in their first experiences with classification. Older students can handle abstract representations. This process requires students to observe closely to see likenesses and differences, to group objects or ideas, and to label the groups. These skills are important to reading, writing, and thinking.

SAFE Lesson No. 3

TITLE: CLASSIFYING LEAVES
DIFFICULTY LEVEL: GRADES K–5
OBJECTIVES:

Students will:

1. Learn to observe likenesses and differences
2. Practice grouping objects and labeling the groups

DESCRIPTION:

Students will group leaves according to colors, sizes, and other characteristics. They will label the groups.

PROCEDURE:

Stimulus:

The beginning of the school year is a good time to use leaves for any activity. They are large enough and hardy enough for even young students to handle.

Display the leaves and have each student select one. Tell them to look closely at their leaf and be prepared to tell one thing about it.

Activity:

Call on students to tell one thing about their leaf. List the words they use on the board. For example, if one child states, "My leaf is red," list *red*.

When all the observations are listed, ask each student to use masking tape to fasten his or her leaf near the words that describe it. Help the students list the specific attributes in the statements about the leaves. Discuss color, size, shape, and other characteristics. Regroup the leaves if indicated.

We have three smooth leaves. One smooth leaf is red.

Write a sentence about the results. For example: "We have ten green leaves, five pointed leaves, two red and yellow leaves, and ten round leaves."

Follow-Up:

Ask students to bring in leaves to add to the chart. Tell them that some leaves can be properly placed under more than one heading.

Help students make generalizations about the groups, such as, "Pointed leaves are usually yellow." Have students summarize what they learned in this lesson.

Evaluation:

Note the students' ability to label groups and to place leaves in proper groups. Observe their accuracy as they tell why they placed a leaf under a specific category.

SAFE Lesson No. 4

TITLE: CLASSIFY GAMES
DIFFICULTY LEVEL: GRADES K–5
OBJECTIVES:

Students will:

1. Practice classification methods using games
2. Think about different categories

DESCRIPTION:

Students will classify games.

PROCEDURES:

Stimulus:

Most students enjoy games. Games can be classified in many ways, depending on the age and experience of the student.

Discuss favorite games. Ask the students to name their favorites as you list them on the board.

Activity:

Ask the students to look at the list and decide which games should be placed together and why. For example, they may decide to use Games with Professional Teams and Games Played on a Table.

Games with Professional Teams	Games Played on a table
1. Basketball	1. Checkers
2. Football	2. Chess
3. Hockey	3. Monopoly
4. Tennis	4. Hearts
5. Bowling	5. Parcheesi

As a group is labeled, list it on chart paper or the board. Have the children write the names of the games that belong in that group underneath it. Create new labels when needed.

Ask the students to make statements about games using the information on the board. For example: Games played with a ball are not usually quiet games. Table games often have game boards.

For more capable groups, ask them to compare the games in one group to games in another, such as: Card games can be played in small spaces, but ball games need lots of room.

Follow-Up:

Use TV shows, movies, popular songs, or school lunches and follow the same procedure.

Evaluation:

Note the ability of the students to put objects into groups and name the groups.

Have groups exchange their lists and judge whether the games were classified accurately.

Still More Ideas to Try

These activities will provide practice in classification and visualization. They will help students learn to make discoveries and judgments for themselves, and understand the implications of this information.

- Story Rating: At the end of a unit in any curriculum area, classify the stories or lessons.
- Book Rating: Put up a chart with such headings as "Don't Miss This One," "Don't Waste Your Time," "Funny Story," and other headings suggested by the students. When they have read a book, help them list the title under the proper heading.
- Picture Perfect: Bring a picture of a friend, pet, toy, car, or bike to school. Don't show it to anyone. Describe this person or object to the class and have the students draw pictures of the way they visualize it. Put the original picture on the board and the class pictures around it for comparison.

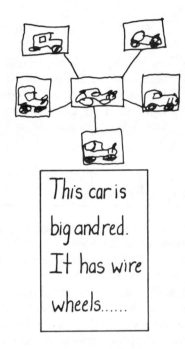

- **What Color Do You See?**   When reading to the students, stop occasionally and ask what colors they saw in their mind when you read about articles that were not completely described.

- **Do You Know the Way?**   Make a map of the way you come to school.

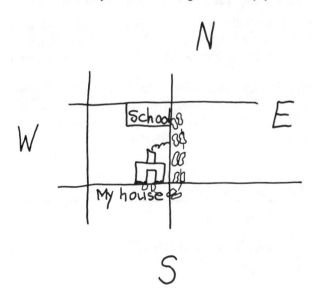

Each map should include directions (north, south, east, and west) and a sketch of the school.

- What Did We Learn Today?   At the end of the class, have students make summary statements about something they learned. Statements made by one person will trigger the thoughts of others. You might add something you consider important, if no one mentions it. Thus, students will be ready with an answer when their parents ask, "What did you learn today?"

Listening for Comprehension

Listening is the primary way of learning language, and it should continue to support learning throughout the school years. We need to plan lessons that teach listening skills, for listening comprehension is akin to reading comprehension. Through well-planned listening lessons we lay the foundation for thinking expressed orally and in writing. Thus, listening, an essential part of every learning experience, should be presented with clear objectives in mind.

The lessons in this section illustrate the kinds of classroom activities that involve listening and, of course, speaking, for the two oral skills cannot be separated. We begin with story theater, a dramatization strategy for all ages that involves students in listening, talking, and thinking.

A USEFUL STRATEGY: STORY THEATER

Story theater is an activity in which you read a story aloud while the students dramatize it. There are no special parts, and all the students are involved. The students do not speak, but they may make motions or noises to make the action clear.

When students dramatize a story, they develop greater comprehension of the words and phrases they hear. Begin with a good story and help your students build bridges to new understandings of language.

SAFE Lesson No. 5

TITLE: SHOW US

DIFFICULTY LEVEL: GRADES K–4

OBJECTIVES:

Students will demonstrate understanding of the words.

DESCRIPTION:

Students will dramatize the events of a story to demonstrate comprehension of events.

PROCEDURES:

Stimulus:

Choose a story that has a great deal of action. Tell the students that one group will read and the other group will act out the story.

Tell the students that we can let others know what is going on and how we feel without saying a word.

As a warm-up activity for pantomime, ask the class to show you fear, annoyance, surprise, amusement, impatience, and happiness without saying a word.

Activity:

Give the students who will be readers copies of Maurice Sendak's *Where the Wild Things Are*. Have the group practice reading the story in unison. Assign parts. While one group reads, the other students will act out the story. They cannot use any words.

For variety, let *all* students play *all* parts. Say, "All play the part of Max/Wild Thing/Tree/Mother/Boat/Vines/King of Wild Things/ at the same time."

Follow-Up:

Use other stories to repeat the process:

The Elephant's Child by Rudyard Kipling

Chicken Little by Steven Kellog (Reteller)

The Funny Little Woman by Arlene Mosel, illustrated by Blair Lent

Ol' Paul, The Mighty Logger by Glen Rounds

John Henry, An American Legend by Ezra Jack Keats

Evaluation:

You will have an opportunity to check the comprehension of students as they dramatize the story. Try to discover what causes some students to have difficulty with comprehension. It may be that they do not understand the words or are unable to visualize the scene. A discussion following student disagreement as to what the action should be can lead to greater comprehension.

SAFE Lesson No. 6

TITLE: WHAT HAPPENED NEXT?
DIFFICULTY LEVEL: GRADES K–8
OBJECTIVES:

Students will learn to use evidence in the story to predict the outcome

DESCRIPTION:

You will tell or read a story, stop at an appropriate place, and ask the students to dramatize what happens next. Older students will be asked to cite evidence from the story that helped them with their prediction.

PROCEDURES:

Stimulus:

Ask the students to recall the story "The Three Little Pigs." Retell the story together. What would the wolf do if he could catch the three little pigs? How do the students know? Ask them to cite evidence from the story.

character	What he/she will do next	How do you know?
Wolf	hurt pigs	he said he would blow house down.
Pigs	stand up to wolf	they said "Not by the hair of my chinny chin chin"

Activity:

Tell the students that this activity is called "What Happened Next?" (Activities are more interesting when they have names.) In this activity you read a story while the students listen closely. Stop suddenly and ask the students to dramatize what happens next.

Tell the class that they will work together on the first one to see if they understand.

> You are very hungry. You find a bag of cookies. Show me what you do next.

For young students use a very simple story.

> A little boy named Joe loved to scare people. He would walk up quietly behind his father and say, "Boo." He would laugh when his father jumped. He would walk up quietly behind his mother and say, "Boo." He would laugh when she jumped. He would walk up quietly behind his sister and say, "Boo." He would laugh when she jumped. One day his mother had a friend come over for lunch. They were standing in the hall talking . . . .

Stop here and ask the students what they think happened next. Ask them to give evidence from the story to support their answers.

For older students, read or tell a story suitable for the ages and interests of the students. Stop at an appropriate place and ask the students to act out what they think happens next. If students disagree, have them give evidence from what they have heard and present their end to the scene.

Follow-Up:

Change the nature of the characters (pretty is ugly; good is now bad) in the story and have the scenes dramatized. Discuss the reasons for the changes in the outcome of the story.

Evaluation:

Evaluate the ability of the students to cite evidence from a story and predict how the story will end by watching them.

Give each student a card labeled "Next?" As a student tells a story, have classmates hold up a card when the storyteller gets to a "What Happens Next?" scene.

A USEFUL STRATEGY: MUSIC AND RHYTHM

Lowell Mason (1792–1872) from Boston, Massachusetts, was responsible for the inclusion of music in the public school curriculum. He believed that children should commence learning to sing as soon as they are able to read, and should continue to sing as long as they continue in school.

Music and rhythm help students to relax and can motivate even reluctant learners. Think of the commercials we can remember from radio and TV. Even kindergarten students can sing the commercials. Young students first learn the alphabet as a song, and many nursery rhymes are learned as songs. When you add music and rhythm to any lesson, you are integrating learning from both sides of the brain. The result is that learning is accelerated and the information is more likely to be retained.

SAFE Lesson No. 7

TITLE: SING ME A SKILL

DIFFICULTY LEVEL: GRADES 1–6

OBJECTIVES:

Students will:

1. Teach a rule to the class using music and rhythm
2. Decide whether or not this mode of learning is easier and more motivational than other methods
3. Discover that teaching a skill helps to learn it more thoroughly

DESCRIPTION:

Students will use music and rhythm to teach skills to the class.

PROCEDURES:

Stimulus:

Ask the group how they first learned to recite the alphabet and nursery rhymes and to count. (They probably sang them first.)

Tell them that some people think music helps students to learn more quickly and to retain knowledge longer. You want to test the theory with their help.

Activity:

Decide which writing skills you want your class to learn and list them on the board.

Divide the class into groups so that there is a group for each rule. Demonstrate how easy it is to write words to an old song to teach a rule. For example, to teach a rule about capital letters, set the rule to the tune of "My Bonnie Lies Over the Ocean."

Oh, when you are writing a sentence   remember as you work along, if

it doesn't start with a capital   the teacher will say it is wrong.
(end with a period)

Have the students sing along. Ask each group to write words to a familiar song that will teach the writing skill they have been assigned. Tell them they will be asked to sing the song for the class. Have them make a great presentation out of it and teach the class to sing it. Tell them to prepare a test for their skill which they give to the class and correct. Have each group select a date to present their song, teach it, and test it.

Follow-Up:

Make copies of the original songs and give them to the students to bind together so each student will have a "Writing Skill Songbook." Have them write songs to teach other skills.

Evaluation:

Ask the group to evaluate this method of teaching. Write yes or no to these questions or give oral answers:

1. Were the students enthusiastic?
2. Did the groups enjoy teaching?
3. Did the class learn the skill?
4. Which techniques were most effective?
5. Would you like to try this again?

Give your own test on the skills to see if this method of teaching is effective.

SAFE Lesson No. 8

TITLE: THE SNOWY DAY

DIFFICULTY LEVEL: GRADES K–2 (ADAPT FOR UPPER GRADES)

OBJECTIVES:

Students will:

1. Demonstrate good listening skills
2. Retell a story in sequence
3. Write a sentence about a book
4. Be aware of the pleasure of reading a good book

DESCRIPTION:

Children will listen to a good winter story, talk about it, outline the sequence of events, and compose a statement about the book. They will make snowflakes to display with their writing.

PROCEDURES:

Obtain as many copies of *The Snowy Day* by Ezra Jack Keats as you can from your school library or the public library.

Stimulus:

Talk about the coldness outdoors, the coming of winter, snow, and snowflakes. Read *The Snowy Day* aloud to the class.

Have students retell the events of the story in sequence. Print on the board as the sentences are composed. Read this summary aloud, encouraging students to read with you.

Activity:

Ask the students, "Did you like this story?" Print these words on the board: I liked this story because _____. Next, ask, "Why did you like this story?" Print answers on the board, leaving out sentence markers.

it was funny

I like Peter

the pictures are pretty

Read the beginning sentence aloud several times using different endings that are on the board. Have children copy the sentence using the ending they choose.

Follow-Up:

Prepare a bulletin board entitled "Winter Fun." Let students display their writing as completed. Then have students cut out snowflakes to scatter across the board.

Evaluation:

Observe student participation. Circulate around the room to see that students are writing and to assist in the selection of an ending for the sentence. Praise their display when completed.

Note:

1. To make snowflakes: Fold paper in fourths, then thirds, then cut small shapes on the folds.
2. Have students read each others' writing.
3. Talk about the fun of sharing a good book (metacognition).
4. Use film of book from Weston Woods.
5. Good display for Open House.

SAFE Lesson No. 9

TITLE: ECHO READING WITH RHYTHM
DIFFICULTY LEVEL: GRADES 1–3
OBJECTIVES:

Students will:

1. Gain confidence in their ability to read aloud before a group
2. Read more fluently

DESCRIPTION:

Many teachers use echo reading (reading a line from the reading book, followed by the group reading the same line in the same way) to help students become better oral readers. This activity uses a group of students in place of the teacher and adds rhythmic activity.

PROCEDURES:

Stimulus:

Ask how many students have seen cheerleaders at a football game. Discuss the activities of the cheerleaders. Did they clap, stomp, and snap their fingers? What did the rooting section do?

Pretend that you are a cheerleader. Read a line in a book and have the students echo it. Use rhythm and clapping.

Activity:

Divide the class into two groups. One will start as cheerleaders and the others as rooters.

Ask the cheerleader group to choose a word, line, or paragraph from a story that you assign. The cheerleaders will decide how that part of the story should be read and read it for the group. They can add any rhythmic activity to the reading.

The group echoes the cheerleaders.

Follow-Up:

Have the cheerleaders read a whole paragraph and see if the other group can echo it. Allow individual students to be cheerleaders.

Evaluation:

Notice students who continue to read very slowly or word by word and give them extra echo reading practice with you.

Still More Ideas to Try

Retelling messages, stories, jokes, or movie or TV plots involves many skills. It is necessary to comprehend what was heard or read and be able to recall and repeat or summarize. Retelling is very difficult for some students. They may need to be given very simple assignments until they develop confidence in their ability to retell.

- Cut-Up Stories: Cut up a story and give a numbered part to each student in the group. Have each part read or retold in order. When the story is finished, the students will tell or write it in their own words.

- Half-Minute Memories: One student talks about any topic for thirty seconds. Another student repeats as much as he or she can remember.

- Did You Hear That?   When students ask questions, ask other students to repeat or use their own words to ask the same question.

- Echoes: When giving an assignment to the class, ask a student to repeat the assignment.

- Make Us Laugh: Each day assign a student to prepare a good joke or funny story to tell to the class the next day.

- Telephone Talents: Simulate a telephone call. Give the students a message of three or four items. Allow them to make notes. Ask them to write down at least three important parts of the message.

- Daily Diary: At the end of a school day or class period, ask a student to summarize the activities of the day or period. Have the class evaluate the summary.

- TV Plots: Ask the students to tell and then write in twenty-five words or less the plot of their favorite TV show.

Speaking to Communicate Thinking

Speaking is a basic method of communicating our thinking. We ask and answer questions. We tell stories to our friends. We provide information. Although we talk more than we read or write, we do not allocate much classroom time to teaching students to speak more effectively.

Talk in the classroom is an integral aspect of learning. It provides the foundation for writing, and it is an important way of responding to reading. Students will benefit from talking through the learning processes they are experiencing, the thinking they engage in, and the problems they are having. Talking permits students to learn from each other.

In this section, we begin with a focus on puppetry, which is an exciting way of promoting speaking in the classroom. The emphasis here is on making simple puppets that can be used for classroom learning experiences immediately.

A USEFUL STRATEGY: PUPPETRY

Puppets and puppet shows have been enjoyed for thousands of years. The enchantment is still evident today. Students who find it difficult to speak before a group can gain confidence as they first hide themselves and speak as a puppet character. Students learn about cause and effect, sequencing, predicting, and drawing conclusions as they combine their ideas and write a play for their puppets.

Puppet shows can be used in conjunction with all curriculum areas. At the end of a unit, puppet shows written and produced by the students demonstrate to the teacher what the students have learned about the subject. They can be used to teach skills in a manner that motivates students to learn. Simple puppets can be made quickly and easily to teach and reinforce a skill, or beautiful, more elaborate puppets can be made as part of an art and language project.

Following is a simple puppet pattern:

1. Cut a strip of tagboard or construction paper 12" x 3".
2. Fold it in the middle.
3. Fold each half in half away from the center.
4. Cut a piece of red construction paper 3" x 6" and fold it in the middle.
5. Glue it to the center of the strip (the parts shaded in the diagram). This is the mouth of the puppet.
6. Color or paste eyes, hair, nose, and ears on the head.
7. Staple arms and legs on the body.

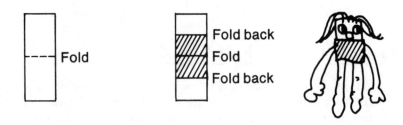

SAFE Lesson No. 10

TITLE: PUPPETS AS TEACHERS
DIFFICULTY LEVEL: GRADES 3–8
OBJECTIVES:

Students will:

1. Evaluate skills they have learned
2. Use puppets to teach skills they think are important

DESCRIPTION:

Students will decide which skills they think should be taught to younger students. Each one will have an opportunity to use puppets to teach one of these skills.

PROCEDURES:

Stimulus:

Ask students if they have ever had older students help them with learning. Bring out in the discussion the advantages and any disadvantages that they remember. Ask them what they have learned that they think is important for younger students to learn. List these topics on the board.

1. How to draw animal pictures

2. How to draw a map

3. How to skim a selection for answers to questions

4. How to write an outline

5. How to make a new friend

Activities:

Have each student choose a skill from the list on the board and write a few sentences telling why that skill is important. Form groups of students according to the skill chosen. They will meet together to prepare a puppet show that will teach this skill. Each group will present their show to the class.

Follow-Up:

After each presentation, have the group decide whether or not the skill was really taught and how the presentation might be improved. (Be sure the suggestions are presented in a positive manner.) A teacher in a lower grade will welcome your class members as they come in to teach skills that they think the younger students should learn.

Evaluation:

You and the students can evaluate the performances and decide whether or not the skills were taught.

Ask younger children to rate the performances. Make this simple by having them judge it as "yes" or "no" when you ask them, "Did you like this?"

SAFE Lesson No. 11

TITLE: MAKE IT LIVE WITH PUPPETS

DIFFICULTY LEVEL: GRADES 3–10

OBJECTIVES:

Students will:

1. Evaluate lessons at the end of a unit
2. Demonstrate and extend their learning of the unit through puppet show presentations

DESCRIPTION:

Students will choose a favorite lesson at the end of a unit of study. Students are often good judges of the quality of their lessons. They will work in groups to prepare and present puppet shows to share these lessons.

PROCEDURES:

Stimulus:

At the end of a unit in reading, social studies, literature, science, music, or sports, discuss the lessons in the unit with the students.

Ask the students to list their favorite lessons such as:

Events

Poems

People

(or whatever has been the subject of the lessons).

Activity:

Have the students select from the list one in which they have the most interest. Ask them to prepare a short dramatization for puppets using this lesson. Students who have similar interests may work together. Puppets can be made at home. Families usually get involved when such an assignment is given and this adds interest and motivation to the lesson. Parents who have an interest in puppets are often willing to help.

Follow-Up:

After these plays have been presented to your class, present them to primary classes.

Stories and events concerning the subject that were not part of the unit may be researched and presented to the class in puppet shows to extend the learning of all the students.

Evaluation:

You and students can evaluate the performances and the knowledge of the subjects presented. Base the grade on: Was it interesting? What was the quality of the puppets? Was the skill taught?

A USEFUL STRATEGY: PREPARING AND PRESENTING SPEECHES

Other than answering questions and reading reports and stories, most students have few opportunities to speak before a group. That may account for the fact that the greatest fear many adults have today is that they will be called on to speak. If we can provide opportunities and motivation for students to speak, give them feedback about their speeches, and show them how they can improve, we will help them develop confidence in this skill.

Preparing and presenting a speech requires the speaker to choose a topic, organize ideas, present them in a manner that is interesting to others, speak loudly enough to be heard and in a dignified manner, and know when to stop.

SAFE Lesson No. 12

TITLE: SPEAKER OF THE WEEK

DIFFICULTY LEVEL: GRADES 2–8

OBJECTIVES:

Students will:

1. Present their ideas in speeches before the group
2. Develop more skill in their abilities to speak before a group
3. Learn to give and accept critical evaluation of speeches

DESCRIPTION:

Students will prepare and present speeches to the group. The group will evaluate the presentation and choose a "Speaker of the Week."

PROCEDURES:

Stimulus:

Tell the class about an interesting event in your life, such as an embarrassing moment or a funny experience. Ask students to share similar experiences with the group. Tell them that once a week you will schedule time for students to share thoughts and ideas with the class. Tell them that this will not be a "Show and Tell" or sharing time. They are now ready to learn more about speaking before a group.

Ask the students to help you list on the board the qualities of a good speaker. Keep the list on a chart or ditto and add to it as the students think of additional qualities.

A Good Speaker...

• speaks loudly enough to be heard

• doesn't move around too much while speaking

• makes eye contact with the audience

• has an interesting speech

Activity:

Make a list of dates for the speeches and ask students to sign up for a turn. The speeches are usually quite short (two to three minutes) when this activity starts in order that a number of students can be scheduled to speak each time. After a speech, go down the list on your chart; for example, could you hear? Was the talk interesting? and so on. Ask for other comments, but be sure the comments are designed to help. An award or certificate for the Speaker of the Week may be presented to the speaker chosen by student vote.

Follow-Up:

Invite other classes to hear outstanding speeches.

Evaluation:

Videotape students at the beginning of this activity and later in the year. This shows the student how he or she is seen by the other students and indicates problems and progress. If a video recorder is not available, a tape recorder will provide partial feedback. Student evaluation of other students will need direction from you so that it doesn't become a popularity contest. Show students how to evaluate their peers. Accept positive, constructive feedback only.

SAFE Lesson No. 13

TITLE: SHARING FAVORITE POEMS
DIFFICULTY LEVEL: GRADES K–12
OBJECTIVES:

Students will:

1. Hear and enjoy poetry
2. Develop skill in reading poetry aloud

DESCRIPTION:

If students are introduced to poetry and find it enjoyable when they are young, they are likely to enjoy it as older students and adults. When students prepare a poem to present to the group, they are learning rhythm, new words, and how poets use words in many unusual ways to express their feelings.

PROCEDURES:

Stimulus:

Share a favorite poem with the group and tell them why you enjoy it. Ask the students to name some of their favorite poems.

"My Shadow" Robert Louis Stevenson

"Arithmetic" Carl Sandburg

"The Moon's the North Wind's Cooky" Vachel Lindsay

"The Animal Store" Rachel Field

Activity:

Ask the students to prepare to read a poem to the group. Ask them not to share the entire poem if it is very long. With the group, list suggestions for sharing a poem, such as, "Be sure you have practiced so you will not stumble over words" or "Keep the rhythm while you read." Make out a schedule and let students schedule themselves. After each presentation, check the list of suggestions to see if they were followed. Ask the students to make comments about the poems and the presentations.

Follow-Up:

Make copies of the poems presented and put them into a class book, entitled "Our Favorite Poems." Invite other classes to come and hear poetry and share some of their favorite poems.

Evaluation:

You and students will evaluate the presentations and the growing appreciation of the students for poetry. Ask these questions and have them write "yes" or "no":

1. Did you learn some new poems that you enjoy reciting or reading?
2. Do you share your poems with your friends and family?
3. Can you recite or read a favorite poem to a friend or a family member?
4. Are you, or would you like to be, a poet?

Discuss their answers.

Still More Ideas to Try

There are many firmly held and sometimes conflicting viewpoints as to how children should be taught to read and to write, but there is common agreement among theorists and practitioners that an oral language foundation is crucial to the process. These activities involve oral language practice.

- Lip Synch Poetry: Play a record or a tape of a poem being read. Have students lip synch while the record or tape plays (good for fluency, rhythm, and slow or beginning readers).

- Extemporaneous Speaking: Name a topic and call on students to speak without preparation.

- Get a Word In: Write some words on large cards. When a speaker begins to speak, hold up a card. Tell the speaker that he or she must work the word into the speech in the next few sentences.
- Puppet Professor: Let a puppet teach a new skill to your group.
- Proliferating Puppet Plays: Put up a schedule for weekly puppet shows. Students prepare shows at home or during free time. They fill in a date when they are ready to perform.
- Parents Prefer Puppets: Have parents with skill in puppetry come and teach the class to make puppets.
- Cloze Commercials: Have students watch a commerical and write down the important words. Read it to the class, omitting the name of the product. See if the students can tell you the name of the product.

Exploring Further

Almy, Millie, et al. *Young Children's Thinking: Studies of Some Aspects of Piaget's Theory*. Teacher's College Press, 1966.

Bloom, Benjamin. *All Our Children Learning: A Primer for Parents, Teachers, and Other Educators*. McGraw, 1981.

Canfield, Jack, and Wells, Harold. *100 Ways to Enhance Self-concept in the Classroom*. Prentice-Hall, 1976.

Kroll, Barry, and Vann, Roberta. *Exploring Speaking-Writing Relationships: Connections and Contrasts*. NCTE, 1981.

Pinnell, Gay Su, ed. *Discovering Language with Children*. NCTE, 1980.

Tiedt, Iris M. *Exploring Books with Children*. Houghton, 1979.

Trelease, Jim. *The Read-Aloud Handbook*. Penguin, 1982.

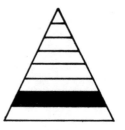

3

Discovering Basic Reading and Writing Concepts

As children begin to explore their world, they usually show a natural curiosity about written language. Observed in their surroundings, the strange markings clearly carry meaning, so it is not surprising that many young children begin to scribble-write with pencils and crayons in combination with their drawing. Furthermore, they are pleased to read what they have written, improvising happily about the meaning they intend to communicate. Naturally, they can read their messages because they "wrote" them. Thus, they begin to write and to read, as naturally as they learned to speak.

Beginning reading and writing should be supported by familiar oral language with storytelling preceding the writing and reading of stories. Children quickly learn that they can write what they can say, using invented spelling, at first, to ease them through the maze of English spelling. Gradually, the more specific relationships between spoken sounds and the letter symbols we use to represent these sounds is discovered as children observe written language in books and the language their teacher writes as they develop ideas in the classroom together. Confidently, children begin to build the foundation for independent decoding (reading) and encoding (writing or spelling) as connected language skills. The phonics skills or sound-symbol relationships that they learn operate on a two-way-street, applied in the complementary functions of reading and writing.

Once this information has been discovered, students will continue to learn more and to reinforce this knowledge as they apply it during the reading and writing process. As much as possible, we try to encourage the learning of these skills in the context of whole language. Reading a good story, for example, motivates a reader to use whatever skills he or she knows to construct meaning. In the same way, the desire to communicate meaning in writing to other students stimulates children to work hard on revising their writing, to learn more and more complex spelling information, and to work on forming letters more clearly. Children who acquire literacy skills in this way develop a strong sense of self and never become dependent on the teacher to tell them what to think or how to learn.

In this chapter, we present ideas for ensuring that children begin to read and write successfully. The ideas are grouped under the following headings:

Early Experiences with Written Language

Discovering Sound-Symbol Relationships: Phonics

Extending Reading/Thinking/Writing Abilities

Developing a Thematic Module: Self-Esteem

Implementing the Program

We follow each individual child's lead in moving ahead toward literacy. These first experiences strengthen what each has learned by acquiring oral language—an amazing demonstration of thinking abilities. Our job is to support the child's acquisition of literacy in a similar manner based on the findings of research and what we know from experience.

1. A child's ability to use oral language determines success in beginning to read and write.

   Children are learning to think as they begin processing real language. Application of these thought processes is crucial to both composing and comprehending written language. In the classroom we should continue to include oral language experiences as a foundation for reading and writing instruction at all levels of instruction.

2. Interaction with other language users is essential for continued language growth. Children need to work together as they communicate orally and in writing.

   Watching television extensively is not sufficient to promote language growth. In the classroom we need to schedule retelling, acting out, and communicating in varied ways to other students to ensure that learning is taking place. Your reading books aloud followed by talking about events, characters, and ideas is a recommended practice for helping students to think, learn new concepts, and write "thinking." Sharing what they write and read aids learning as students progress throughout the grades.

3. Children need to develop a sense of story and knowledge of other forms of writing as a direct aid to composing and comprehending.

   Telling stories, acting out event sequences, and listening to literature read by you are excellent ways to introduce various forms of literature in the early years. Knowledge of these forms will continue to grow at all levels as students read independently. Thus, they can make choices as they select an appropriate form for presenting their thinking in writing.

4. Written language is a puzzle that students are motivated to solve. It is a code that we use for both writing (encoding) and reading (decoding).

   Children's earliest independent writing often provides the avenue to interest in forming letters, reading the meaning a child has put on paper, and gradual learning of conventional spellings. Encoding (writing what the child thinks or says) and decoding (reading or giving meaning to written symbols) begin naturally with child-initiated writing and reading. Children learn best by working with the whole language—a complete message. They will abstract the many connections between reading, writing, and oral language as they work with written language. Our job is to help children do what they are trying to do to become literate, just as we supported their earlier attempts to speak.

Selected Resources

You may be interested in reading more about the ideas we have summarized above.

Applebee, Arthur. *The Child's Concept of Story*. University of Chicago, 1978.

Dyson, Anne Haas. "Reading, Writing, and Language: Young Children Solving The Written Language Puzzle." In *Composing and Comprehending*, ed. Julie Jensen. NCRE, 1984.

Goodman, Kenneth. *What's Whole About Whole Language?* Heineman, 1986.

Holdaway, Donald. *The Foundations of Literacy*. Ashton Scholastic, 1979.

Loban, Walter. *Language Development: Kindergarten Through Grade Twelve*. NCTC, 1976.

Miller, George. *Spontaneous Apprentices: Children and Language*. Seabury, 1977.

Tierney, Robert, and Pearson, P. David. "Toward a Composing Model of Reading." In *Composing and Comprehending*, ed. Julie Jensen. NCRE, 1984, pp. 33–45.

Squire, James. "Composing and Comprehending: Two Sides of the Same Coin." In *Composing and Comprehending*, ed. Julie Jensen. NCRE, 1984, pp. 23–31.

Early Experiences with Written Language

Students need to hear language, any language, to understand the meaning communicated and to be able to talk before they begin to read or write. First-grade students often come to school with an oral vocabulary of 2,500 to 5,000 words and an understanding of more than 20,000 words.

The student who does not have this language base for learning—this prior knowledge—is probably not ready to read or write. For this reason, with each new group of students at any level, we first assess their facility with the spoken language. The student's experience may be with any language, for the learning processes are the same, but in this book we assume that we are working with English-speaking students.

Our first reading and writing activities, then, may be purely oral, designed to develop concepts through experience, to stimulate vocabulary growth, and to promote self-esteem. Oral language continues to support reading and writing activities throughout the elementary and secondary grades. We stress the fact that young people are learning to read and to write as they listen and speak.

We begin our Reading/Thinking/Writing Program with whole language methods that engage children individually in writing their own stories, using whatever knowledge they have of written language. Relying on familiar rhymes or information known to most of the children, we create reading material together. Beginning experiences with reading and writing should show children that they can read and write from the very first day of class, as in the lessons that follow.

A USEFUL STRATEGY: CHORAL READING

Choral reading allows students to try new words and sounds with the support of the group. Individual voices, hidden among the other voices, gain confidence as students memorize-read nursery rhymes, jump-rope chants, songs, and poems. This first exposure to reading is pleasant, designed to provide a good feeling about reading and a positive attitude toward school.

SAFE Lesson No. 1

TITLE: GET GOING WITH MOTHER GOOSE

DIFFICULTY LEVEL: GRADES K–2 (upper grades to strengthen reading abilities or to introduce this literature)

OBJECTIVES:

Students will:

1. Hear, repeat, and enjoy many nursery rhymes
2. Read a nursery rhyme together from a chart
3. Illustrate the rhyme to make it easier to memorize-read independently

DESCRIPTION:

Students begin to read familiar rhymes written on large experience charts.

PROCEDURES:

Write a nursery rhyme on a large chart, such as:

Jack and Jill went up the hill

To fetch a pail of water.

Jack fell down and broke his crown

And Jill came tumbling after.

Add simple illustrations that students can use as clues to help them read the words.

Stimulus:

Before showing children the chart, share a number of rhymes orally. Ask if anyone can say such verses as:

Little Miss Muffet

Hey, Diddle Diddle

Humpty Dumpty

Have the children join the lead speaker in saying each verse. Children may clap to the rhythm or act out the meaning.

Activity:

Ask children if they know the verse "Jack and Jill," the rhyme you have printed on your chart. Recite the poem aloud, letting them join in. Then place the chart before the group. Read the verse aloud as you point to the printed words.

Have children draw pictures to illustrate the words of the rhyme. Paste them near the words on the chart.

Follow-Up:

Give each student copies of this rhyme, one line on a sheet. They can illustrate each page. Have students read the pages aloud as they illustrate them. Staple the pages together to form a book.

Bring in collections of rhymes from the school or public library, for example:

Book of Nursery and Mother Goose Rhymes by Marguerite de Angeli

Favorite Nursery Rhymes, by Randolph Caldecott

Mother Goose Rhymes, by Arthur Rackham

Read rhymes the children may know and show them the illustrations. Leave the poetry collections on the reading table where the children can look at them later.

Evaluation:

Ask students to take their poetry books home to read to someone at home. The next day talk about their successful experiences in reading. If any had difficulty, see that they have a chance to read to a partner at school.

SAFE Lesson No. 2

TITLE: JUMP ROPE AND READ

DIFFICULTY LEVEL: GRADES K–4

OBJECTIVES:

Children will:

1. Chant jump-rope verses
2. Read familiar verses printed on a chart

DESCRIPTION:

Children review jump-rope rhymes that they know and learn new ones that they can use on the playground. They use this familiar material as beginning reading texts.

PROCEDURES:

Prepare a chart of the familiar rhyme, "One, Two, Buckle My Shoe."

> One, two, buckle my shoe;
> Three, four, shut the door;
> Five, six, pick up sticks;
> Seven, eight, lay them straight;
> Nine, ten, a big, fat hen!

Stimulus:

Before using the chart, ask students to share jump-rope rhymes they know. If the weather is pleasant, you may want to go outdoors to try the rhymes. You can teach children new rhymes. For example, try these humorous ones:

> Salomi was a dancer.
> She danced before the King.
> And every time she danced,
> She wiggled everything!
> "Stop!" said the King.
> "You can't do that in here!"
> Salomi said, "Baloney,"
> And she kicked the chandelier.

> My father is a butcher.
> My mother cuts the meat.
> And I'm the little weeniewurst
> That runs around the street.

Activity:

Show the chart of the rhyme "One, Two, Buckle My Shoe." Have students put numerals by number words.

Illustrate other words so that students will know what they are. Even if you are not a great artist, the students will enjoy the lesson and remember the words because of the association.

One, two, buckle my shoe.

Three, four, shut the door.

Have the group chant the rhyme while some students jump in rhythm.

Follow-Up:

Chart other rhymes and follow the same procedure. Give students dittos of the rhymes to illustrate and read at home. Make a big class book of your charts. Ask children to bring in rhymes from their parents and relatives. Chart them and add them to your class book. As a group, write your own class rhyme. Have individuals write and share rhymes.

Evaluation:

Discuss with students why it is easier to read material that has rhythm in it. Note students who have difficulty reading in rhymes and give them more practice time in jumping and reading.

Observe students' interest in the collections of rhymes you placed on the reading table.

Note:

Repeat this lesson with different rhymes at regular intervals to reinforce children's knowledge of their literary heritage as well as to support beginning reading experiences.

MORE LESSONS TO INTRODUCE WRITTEN LANGUAGE

In addition to such strategies as choral reading, we can use other activities that reinforce the relationship between spoken language and written language.

We can also provide lessons designed to support children's beginning efforts at writing as well as reading. Both reading and writing should be taught as "two sides of the same coin," so the same lesson may teach both encoding and decoding and the thinking skills that underlie comprehension and composition. The following lessons are examples of what you can do.

SAFE Lesson No. 3

TITLE: BE A SECRETARY

DIFFICULTY LEVEL: GRADES K–2

OBJECTIVES:

Children will:

1. Improve their listening skills
2. Reinforce their knowledge of sound-symbol relationships

PROCEDURES:

Stimulus:

Read Bernard Waber's book, *Ira Sleeps Over* (Houghton Mifflin), aloud to the students. Make the most of the words spoken by Ira's older sister who taunts him about his attachment to his teddy bear, "Tah Tah." Encourage the students to join in on the lines repeated by Ira's parents.

Talk about the story, answering the questions:

Who? (the characters)

When? Where? (the setting)

What? Why? (the plot)

How? (the conclusion)

Through such discussion, students are developing a sense of story. This knowledge is crucial for reading comprehension and composition of narrative forms.

Activity:

Give students lined paper on which to write several sentences taken from Waber's story. You may choose lines that are repetitive, like these:

"Take him," said my mother.
"Take him," said my father.

According to the students' abilities, dictate the sentences one by one. Have students listen first, then write. After students write the first sentence independently, have several children write the sentence on the board. Talk about spelling and punctuation as students correct their own sentences. Dictate the second sentence, observing that many of the words are the same as those in the first one.

Follow-Up:

Have students act out the story as you read it aloud again. All students can perform at once as they remember the sequence of the story and the dialogue together.

Students can take their dictation home to share with their family. Encourage them to tell their family the story of Ira. The next day ask students if they can write the same sentences again with less help.

You may wish to have a Teddy Bear Day when children bring in their bears or other stuffed toys. Special recognition may be given to the oldest bear, smallest bear, bear with the funniest name, and any other special category. Children may write stories about their bears to be placed in bear-shaped books like this:

Evaluation:

Observe student participation. Walk around the room as students write the first dictation. Collect the second set of papers to examine (not grade or correct) as a guide for further instruction. Plan small group instruction for those who have similar problems.

Have students evaluate their own writing, working in pairs as they each assess their own progress.

Place student writing in individual portfolios to begin an accumulation of individual work showing each student's development. (This provides an excellent sampling to share with parents during conferences.)

SAFE Lesson No. 4

TITLE: FLOOR WRITING
DIFFICULTY LEVEL: GRADES K–2
OBJECTIVES:

Children will:

1. Write messages independently
2. Share their writing with others
3. Develop their self-esteem and positive feelings toward school

DESCRIPTION:

Children "write" on large pieces of butcher paper on the floor where they are not confined by space. Each child performs according to his or her individual level of ability and interest.

PROCEDURES:

Stimulus:

Prepare large pieces of butcher paper (one per child) and gather boxes of crayons. Say to the children: "Today we are going to write a letter about going to school. What can we write about?" Encourage students to list things they have done during the first days of school—taking a listening walk, reading *A Tree Is Nice* together, going to the cafeteria, singing "I've Been Working On the Railroad," and so on.

Ask the children to whom they can give their letter. Elicit a variety of responses—Mommy, Daddy, Grandmother, Mrs. Jordan, my sister, Milly, and so on.

Activity:

Have each student take a piece of paper and a box of crayons and find a place to work on the floor. As the students begin "writing" their letters, walk around the room to observe and encourage them. The messages will be a combination of pictures, letters, and words—whatever children produce is accepted.

Ask for volunteers to share their letters. Have two students hold a big letter so all can see while the author "reads" what he or she has produced. Because they wrote it, they will be able to read the message, embellishing it as they go along.

Follow-Up:

Show students how to roll their letters and give each one a rubber band with which to hold it securely. They will take the letters home to read to a person they choose.

Evaluation:

Unobtrusively take notes as you move around the room. Note students who have any problems and those who perform particularly well. This early holistic evaluation of student writing will guide your planning for further teaching.

Prepare duplicated copies of your class list for this purpose. Keep them on a clipboard. Use at least one daily on which you make such observations.

Notes:
1. Use this same type of lesson with older students in mapping a story or events in history.
2. Encourage students to share with their families.

Still More Activities to Try

Young students increase their vocabulary and learn to classify and compare as they create word books. Students whose native language is not English may write the words in both languages. Word books can be made for any subject of interest to the student. Any activity that gives the student practice in using words and sounds and promotes enjoyment of language helps the student become a better reader.

- **Alphabet Books:** Alphabet books can be made for any subject. Holidays are especially good topics.
- **Friendly Books:** Books that describe friends are popular with young students.

- Beautiful Word Books: Students choose words they think are beautiful. They write one word on each page, illustrate it, and tell why they think it is beautiful.

- A Book About Me: Students draw pictures of their families, their houses, their friends, their favorite foods, and any other items they want to draw or write about.
- Favorite TV Show Books: Students draw pictures and tell why they enjoy their favorite television show.
- Animal Books: Students can decide which animals belong in circus animal books, wild animal books, or pet books, and make pictures of them.
- Funny Word Books: Students can choose words that they think are funny and illustrate them.
- Words I Can Read: Students cut words from papers and magazines that they can read, and paste them in the book.

Discovering Sound-Symbol Relationships: Phonics

Students are encouraged to write and draw as their first efforts in communicating through writing. Naturally, they can read the messages they write, even though they are not completely or correctly spelled. Gradually, however, instruction leads them toward a greater command of the written language and the ability to write so that someone else can also read what they have written.

Handwriting (printing) focuses on forming letters and learning to identify sounds associated with the various letters. Spelling and reading abilities progress together as children learn to associate the sounds they hear in words (phonemes) with specific letters or combinations of letters (graphemes).

SAFE Lesson No. 5

TITLE: WRITING SYMBOLS FOR SOUNDS
DIFFICULTY LEVEL: GRADES K–3
OBJECTIVES:

Students will:

1. Use manuscript printing in writing
2. Reinforce knowledge of sounds and symbols

DESCRIPTION:

Through an integrated approach, students will learn to write the manuscript alphabet as they also learn to read and spell many words. They are beginning to associate sounds with symbols that we use to represent the sounds in writing.

PROCEDURES:

Stimulus:

Students are excited about learning to read and write. As they learn to identify letters, they can also learn to form them. We usually present the letters in groups according to the difficulty of forming the letters, such as:

Straight lines	i, l, t
Circles	o, a, b, d, p c, e g, q
Curves	n, m, h, u f, j, r, s
Slanted lines	v, w, y k x, z

Students can act out the shapes of the letters or form them in clay as they are introduced. As handwriting lessons are presented, we try to use the letters in words and sentences. The word *lit,* for example, incorporates the first straight-line letters. We can write the word and talk about its meanings in oral sentences, such as:

> A bird lit on the tree.
> Mother lit the candle.

We introduce most of the commonly used letters fairly quickly so that students can draw upon the full set of tools to read and write meaningful ideas. Then, they can practice them as they write for real purposes, referring to the alphabet chart as needed.

Activity:

Begin a class "Big Dictionary," which includes one large page for each letter of the alphabet. To avoid confusion, begin with pages for the regular consonants. On the page for *b*, students will paste pictures cut from magazines or ones they have drawn, such as boy, bug, bird, and baby.

Have students say the words aloud to test the beginning sounds. This will be fairly easy for regular consonants:

> /b/, /d/, /h/, /l/, /m/, /n/, /p/, /t/, /v/

Later, you can add other pages as students become aware that letters are associated with more than one sound. The following is an example:

> /f/ spellings: f, ph
> /s/ spellings: s, c, ss, and others

Then, we have letters that represent more than one sound, such as:

> letter *c* used in *cake* or *cent* to represent /k/ and /s/

As students prepare the pages, they can print words beneath each picture. They may also write short sentences, including the appropriate words.

Follow-up:

Continue to develop the class dictionary as students learn more about the phoneme-grapheme relationships. The followiwng chart will guide you in introducing this information.

CONSONANTS

PHONEMES	GRAPHEMES					
	Difficulty Level			Examples		
	1	2	3	Initial	Medial	Final
/b/	b			bill	tuber	cab
		bb			rubber	ebb
/d/	d			dill	coding	hard
		ed				pulled
		dd			sudden	Fudd
		ld				could
/f/	f			fill	fifer	loaf
		ph		phone	telephone	
		gh			roughing	cough
		ff			ruffle	off
			v			Chekhov
			pf (Ger.)	pfennig		
/g/	g			gill	tiger	bug
		gu		guest		
		gh		ghost		
		gg			logging	
			gue			catalogue
/h/	h			hill	unhappy	
		wh		who		
			j	José		
/j/	j			jam		
		g		giant	imagine	wage
		dg			judger	judge
			di		soldier	
			du		graduate	
			de		grandeur	

Source: Iris M. Tiedt, *The Language Arts Handbook,* © 1983, pp. 208–212. Reprinted by permission of Prentice Hall, Inc., Englewood Cliffs, New Jersey.

CONSONANTS

PHONEMES	GRAPHEMES					
	Difficulty Level			Examples		
	1	2	3	Initial	Medial	Final
/k/	k			kill	raking	look
		ke				lake
		c		cat	act	
		qu (1)*		quit	equinox	
		qu (2)*			liquor	
		ck			lacking	pick
		cc			accost	
		x			fix	
			cu		biscuit	
			cch		bacchanal	
			ch	chorus		
			kh	khaki		
			cqu		acquit	
			que (1)		barbeque	
			que (2)			plaque
/l/	l			like	failing	fatal
		ll (1)**	ll (2)**	llama	calling	doll
/m/	m			mill	timer	ham
		me				come
		mm			simmer	
		mb			climbing	lamb
			mn			hymn
/n/	n			no	lining	fun
		ne				line
		kn		knot		
		gn		gnat		feign
		nn			runner	

*In the initial position the grapheme qu(1) spells the blended phonemes /kw/; in other positions qu(2) is usually an alternate spelling for /k/.

**The grapheme ll (2) is very rare in the initial position. For that reason it is considered a difficult spelling while the ll (1) grapheme is rather common.

CONSONANTS

PHONEMES	GRAPHEMES					
	Difficulty Level			Examples		
	1	2	3	Initial	Medial	Final
			pn	pneumonia		
/p/	p			pill	caper	top
		pp			copper	Lapp
/r/	r			rose	caring	fair
		rr			carry	Carr
		wr		write		
			rh	rhyme		
/s/	s			so		thus
		c		cell	receive	
		sc		scent		
		ss			classes	toss
		x				fox
			ps	pseudo		
/t/	t			to	later	hit
		tt			hotter	mutt
		bt			debtor	debt
		ed				licked
			pt	ptomaine		receipt
			dt			veldt
			th	Thomas		
/v/	v			very	cover	
		f				of
		ve				weave
			ph		Stephen	
			vv		flivver	
/w/	w			will	slower	how
		one		one		
		wh		while	awhile	
			qu (kw)		quit	

CONSONANTS

PHONEMES	Difficulty Level			Examples		
	1	**2**	**3**	**Initial**	**Medial**	**Final**
			ui		suite	
			oui	ouija		
/y/	y			yes	lawyer	
			j		hallelujah	
			io		onion	
			ll		bouillon	
/z/	z			zoo	dozing	whiz
		s (e)			miser	lose, is
		zz			dazzle	buzz
		ss			Missouri	
			sc		discern	
			x	xylophone		
			cz	czar		
/č/	ch			child		much
		tch			matches	hutch
			c	cello		
			cz	Czech		
			eou		righteous	
			t		nature	
/š/	sh			shoe	worship	rush
		s		sugar		
		ch		champagne		
			sch	schist		
			ce		ocean	
			si		mansion	
			ss		mission	
			sci		luscious	
			ti		patient	

CONSONANTS

PHONEMES	GRAPHEMES					
	Difficulty Level			Examples		
	1	2	3	Initial	Medial	Final
			xi		anxious	
			chs		fuchsia	
/ž/		g		gendarme (Fr)	adagio	garage
		s (i)			pleasure, Asia	
		z (i)			brazier	
			j	jejeune		
/θ/	th			thimble	ether	loathe
/ð/	th			the	either	breath
/ŋ/	ng				ringer	wing
	nk				think	
			ngue			tongue

DIPHTHONGS

PHONEMES	GRAPHEMES
/iy/ (long e)	see, sea, me, deceive, believe, carbine, ski, gladly, Aesop, people, quay, key, suite, equator, Phoenix
/ey/ (long a)	bay, rain, gate, they, gauge, break, neigh, rein, straight, care
/ay/ (long i)	kite, right, I, by, cries, find, buy, height, eye, stein, aisle, dye, aye, lyre, iodine
/ow/ (long o)	lone, road, foe, slow, dough, beau, sew, yeoman, whoa, odor, oh, solo, soul, brooch
/yuw/ (long u)	use, few, view, beautiful, queue
/oy/	toy, moist
/aw/	now, out, bough
/uw/	too, blew, tune, suit, lose, flu, do, canoe, through, tomb, blue, group, prove, maneuver

SIMPLE VOWELS

PHONEMES	GRAPHEMES	
/i/	give, pit, myth, quilt, busy, women, England, sieve, been	
/e/	red, said, breath, friend, any, leopard (leisure), says, aesthetics, their, foetid	
/æ/	had, have, laugh, plaid	**Unaccented Syllables**
/ə/	nut, flood, rough, son, of, dove, was, does	cattle ahead fountain parliament
/a/	ah, halt, hot, mirage, cart, heart, fault, sergeant	moment happily burgeon porpoise
/u/	good, full, put, wolf, could	
/ɔ/	caught, jaw, talk, fought, daughter, watch, broad, toss, otter, Utah	
/ʌ/	her, sir, fur, work, satyr, journey, heard, grammar	

Encourage students to read the pages that are developed as the book grows. Place it on the floor or on a large table where students can turn the pages readily.

Evaluation:

Observe student participation. Praise students for their contributions. Guide students to be sure pronunciation and spelling of words is accurate. You may want an aide to assist you.

SAFE Lesson No. 6

TITLE: SING A SONG OF LETTERS

DIFFICULTY LEVEL: GRADES 1–4

OBJECTIVES:

Children will:

1. Begin to learn the order of letters in the alphabet
2. Learn a song about the alphabet
3. Share this information with their parents
4. Create a class dictionary

DESCRIPTION:

Students will become aware of the order of the alphabet. They will begin to memorize the letters in order and learn how to use a dictionary.

PROCEDURES:

Be aware that knowledge of alphabetical order is not a reading skill. This skill is useful only when putting words in order or when locating words in an alphabetical list such as a dictionary or index. We will not be concerned about mastery of this skill at beginning levels.

Stimulus:

As we work with beginning readers, ESL students, or older students who need extra help, our first effort is to make students aware of how spoken and written language are related. We need to identify specific sounds (phonemes) and to recognize the written symbols, letters, that we use to represent these sounds (graphemes). These understandings are the basic tools for reading and writing.

Display a large chart of the printed alphabet in the room to which you can refer as you introduce the letters to students. Small copies of the alphabet chart can be taped to each student's desk. This is very helpful to the student who has difficulty copying from a chart at some distance.

Give each student a printed nameplate to place on his or her desk that all can see, such as:

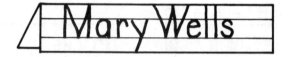

Say the alphabet letters in order together. Have children get a sense of alphabetical order by using this information in various ways. Have children display their nameplates on their desks. Using only first names, ask students to get in line alphabetically with your assistance. Call out: "Anyone whose name begins with *A* or *B* may get in line. *C* or *D. E* or *F. . . .*" Help students recognize their letters and encourage them to help each other.

Display words around the room that students will gradually get to know, for example: *door, window, fish, plant, chalkboard.* Ask students to find the word that goes first according to the alphabet.

Activity:

Teach children the "Alphabet Song," which they will enjoy singing.

Sing the song aloud or play it on the piano or xylophone. Point to the letters on the alphabet chart as you sing each one slowly. Have the students sing with you as you repeat the song and point out the letters as before.

This song becomes part of the class repertoire of songs.

Follow-Up:

You may reproduce this song on a transparency to show students the music as well as the lyrics. Thus, they will be reinforcing knowledge of music as well as the alphabet.

Give children large letter cards. As you point to the letter on the chart, the class says the name of the letter, and the child who has that letter comes to the front of the room to stand in line.

Continue to reinforce knowledge of these letter symbols so that students recognize them easily. As much as possible, present the symbols in the context of written words and relate the written symbols to sounds they represent (e.g., *b* stands for the sound we hear at the beginning of *bird*).

Send a list of suggested activities home to parents so they can reinforce what students are learning at school.

Evaluation:

Observe student participation in class activities. Students can practice saying the alphabet to each other in pairs. As students learn to print the letters, you can have them write them as dictated.

SAFE Lesson No. 7

TITLE: CHARTING FIRST DAY AT SCHOOL

DIFFICULTY LEVEL: GRADES K–4

OBJECTIVES:

Students will:

1. Learn useful words and concepts related to the classroom activities
2. Practice using context clues and phonics skills
3. Be successful in reading meaningful text

DESCRIPTION:

Young students enjoy reading about their experiences. Prepare a chart about the first day of school. Tell the day, date, temperature, room number, teacher's name, and a message. For example:

September 7, 1989
Welcome to First Grade.
Today is a happy sunny day.
We will have a good year together.
Mrs. Green

PROCEDURES:

Stimulus:

Place the chart in the window or on the outside of the door if the students will be waiting there for school to start. Those who have it read to them by their parents will be able to help the group read it. Place the chart on a holder or on the board when you are ready to discuss it. Ask the students if anyone knows what the first line tells about.

Activity:

Show students how to use phonics and context clues to help decode words they do not know. After each line is decoded, discuss it and have the group read it. When the whole chart has been read, divide the class into two groups and have each group read it.

Follow-Up:

The next day have a new chart prepared. Ask if the group can remember how to read the first chart. Then use the same procedure for the second chart.

Evaluation:

Do the students show any interest in reading? Were they successful? Can they use context clues and phonics? If you keep a class list handy during the lesson, you can note next to the students' names any strengths and weaknesses you observe, or special information you want to remember.

MORE LESSONS TO DISCOVER SOUND-SYMBOL RELATIONSHIPS

Try these additional ideas for promoting students' knowledge of sound-symbol relationships. Notice that these activities can benefit older students as well as beginning readers and writers.

- Picture Presents: Talk about presents that begin with a given phoneme. If you choose /b/, for example, students might name: *bird, blue ribbon, bracelet,* or *baby buggy.* At first, avoid using phonemes that have more than one common spelling, as in /f/.

- Comparing Spellings: As students learn more about spelling, you might deliberately focus on these more complex phoneme-grapheme relationships, compiling lists of words. For example:

fur	phone
fuzzy bear	pheasant
flashlight	photograph
flower	phosphorescent

- Wordlists: Encourage students to write words they know how to spell or interesting ones they can find out how to spell. For a period of time you might assign as homework the making of a list of words that begin with a given blend of letters, for example, /bl/. Students can share their words at school, which adds interest to spelling and to vocabulary growth.

- Listening to Sounds: For older students, dictate interesting words that they are not likely to know, for example, *flamboyant, blustery, gruesome.* Challenge them to write the first two letters of each word. As students gain ability with this relatively simple auditory task, Challenge them to write the whole word, spelling it as it sounds to them. Have someone write the word on the board and discuss the correct spelling. Note that auditory work with sound-symbol relationships helps some students particularly.

- Visualizing Words: Help students become aware of spelling patterns by encouraging the visualization of words. Display on a transparency a list of words that students might have a need to know how to spell. Cover all but one at a time. Tell students to look carefully at the patterns of the letters in the word shown, for example, *vacation.* Say the word aloud slowly, pointing to the three syllables as you say them. Then have students close their eyes as they visualize the patterns of the letters. Have them write the word. Repeat this exercise periodically to demonstrate the process that students can do individually. Have students talk about how this exercise helps them spell words more easily (for some, this is a real help).

- Process Analysis: Have students write in their Learning Logs about how they discover what an unfamiliar word is when they are reading. What do they do specifically? Read these entries to gain insight into modes of learning encoding-decoding skills.

Extending Reading/Thinking/Writing Abilities

Once students have been exposed to the sound-symbol relationships (phonemes and graphemes), they need to practice applying these understandings in varied contexts. They will learn to read by reading frequently and will learn to write by writing frequently. Note, too, that children also learn to read by writing and learn to write by reading. Therefore, we will continue to reinforce their awareness of the reading/writing connections.

We can guide students to an awareness of the thinking that goes on as they engage in classroom learning experiences. As they discriminate between words that begin with different sounds and compare those that sound alike, children are using thinking skills. They are recalling, listing, and sequencing as they retell or act out a story together. Your questions will lead them to conjecture, to predict, and to infer as you share a good book you are reading aloud. Thinking skills introduced orally are the same ones students will use as they read what an author has written and also as they write their own "thinking" so others can read it.

In the early stages of learning to read, to think, and to write, students need support. They need to feel successful. The following activities are designed to develop self-esteem as young learners apply the new concepts and abilities involved in reading and writing.

A USEFUL STRATEGY: LANGUAGE EXPERIENCE

Young students come to school ready to read. They can be very successful readers if they read stories that they have written. Activities should develop meaning for words and provide early reading and writing material. Students can start writing as soon as they know how to write the letters of the alphabet. With very young students nursery rhymes and every day experience provide the material for the lessons.

SAFE Lesson No. 8

TITLE: BEGINNING WRITING ACTIVITIES
DIFFICULTY LEVEL: GRADES K–2
OBJECTIVES:

Students will:

1. Learn to write easy words and short sentences
2. Illustrate and be able to read the sentences

DESCRIPTION:

Read a story to the group. Choose an important word from the story and use it for the beginning sentence writing.

PROCEDURES:

Stimulus:

Read a story to the group. *Babar,* by Laurent de Brunhoff, is a good example. Choose an important word from the story and discuss it. Write it on the board. For example, if the story is about an animal, you might use the size, or the shape, or the feel of the animal as the word. If the story is about an elephant, you might use the word *big.*

Activity:

Write the word *big* on the board. Ask the students to name the letters as you write them. Put a circle around the word *big.* Read it together.

Ask students to name other big objects. Each time that one is named, write it on the board. Illustrate it and enclose it in a circle. Underneath it write a sentence: "A_____is big." Have the class read the sentence.

Connect the circle around the picture and the word. Ask for the name of another big object. Illustrate it and write a sentence on the board. Have the students read the sentences as you write them. When three or four sentences have been completed, ask the students to choose one, draw the picture, and write the sentence on their paper.

Use the first few lessons as oral activities if writing is a difficult task for your students.

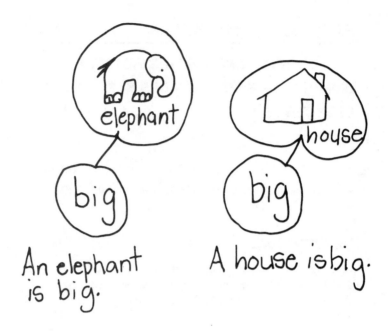

Follow-up:

Share the pictures and sentences in class. Staple the pictures together for a class book. Use other stories and words. Ask the students to cluster, illustrate, and write a sentence. As students become more capable, ask them to write two or three sentences.

Evaluation:

Note the ability of the students to copy the sentences, illustrate them, and read them. Make a list of the letters of the alphabet that are difficult for the students to form and use them as a handwriting lesson.

SAFE Lesson No. 9

TITLE: INCLUDE STUDENTS IN THE STORY

DIFFICULTY LEVEL: GRADES K–4

OBJECTIVES:

Students will:

1. Be motivated to learn what the chart says when they see their name or names of their friends in print
2. Enjoy reading a chart story
3. Practice using phonics and context clues

DESCRIPTION:

Write a chart story about the class. Use the names of many students. Be sure to include the names of some who are less excited about reading. For example:

Bill likes to read stories about dogs.

Helen has two new books.

Jan will ride home on the bus.

We will have a surprise today.

Luis knows what the surprise will be.

PROCEDURES:

Stimulus:

Reread old charts.

Activity:

Show the new chart. Discuss the words that are names. Can the students find their names and underline, circle, or frame them with their hands? Read the names. Help the group use phonics and context clues to decode. After each line is decoded, discuss it and have the group read it. When the whole chart has been read, divide the class into two groups and have each group read it. During the day and before the group goes home, read the chart again. *Tell the students that they are reading.*

Follow-Up:

The next day, have a new chart prepared. Ask if the group can remember how to read the first chart. Then use the same procedure for the second chart.

Evaluation:

Do the students show an interest in reading? Were they successful? Can they use context clues and phonics? If you keep a class list handy during the lesson, you can note next to the students' names any strengths or weaknesses you observe or special information you want to remember.

SAFE Lesson No. 10

TITLE: STORY CHARACTERS FOR BEGINNING WRITING LESSONS

LEVEL OF DIFFICULTY: GRADES K–3

OBJECTIVES:

Students will:

1. Write simple sentences about characters in the stories
2. Learn more about the characters in the stories
3. Be able to read the sentences

DESCRIPTION:

When the students have finished a story in their reading book, discuss the characters in the story. Ask the students to list the characters as you write them on the board. Later, give each student a sheet on which you have drawn the characters from the story. Ask them to write a sentence about each character. Work as a group until you are sure the students are able to write independently.

PROCEDURES:

Stimulus:

When the group has finished reading a story in the reading text, list and discuss the characters in the story. Ask the students what they can tell you about the characters. Write the sentences on the board, for example:

> The rabbit is hungry.
>
> Jack likes to play.
>
> Buffy made a surprise for her father.

Read the sentences together.

Activity:

Give each student a duplicated copy of pictures of characters from the reading book with lines underneath where a sentence may be written.

 Andrew saw a bear.

Ask the students to write a sentence about each picture. Work as a group until you are sure the students can work independently.

 Badger put stars in the sky.

Follow-up:

As the students become more capable, increase the number of sentences they will write. Use characters from other stories and ask the students to write about them. Ask the students to choose their own characters, draw the pictures, and write the sentences.

Evaluation:

If you go slowly, all students can experience success in these beginning lessons in writing. Be sure there is enough discussion preceding the writing so that students will understand the assignment.

A USEFUL STRATEGY: COMPARING

Young students gain a great deal from discussions following the reading of a story. Comparing characters helps the student better understand the story.

Students can learn to compare characters by listing descriptive words, using these words in sentences, and later writing paragraphs telling about the characters. Students can learn to use inference as they describe characters and tell why characters act as they do and how they may change. The same technique can be used to compare settings for stories or the plot.

SAFE Lesson No. 11

TITLE: COMPARING CHARACTERS
DIFFICULTY LEVEL: GRADES K–5
OBJECTIVES:

Students will:

1. List descriptive words about a character
2. Use these lists to write comparisons

DESCRIPTION:

Students will learn to compare characters in a story by comparing lists of descriptive words or phrases. After reading a story, they will select words that describe each character and write a comparison of the characters using the words on the list.

PROCEDURES:

Stimulus:

Read *Where the Wild Things Are* (Maurice Sendak) aloud. Discuss the characters. Ask the students to help you list the names of the characters on the board.

Activity:

Ask the students to tell you words that describe the main character in the story. If the students are beginning readers, work as a group. Older students may work independently. When a student describes a character, ask the student to read the part of the story that gave him or her that information. List the descriptive words under the names of the characters. Then list adjectives for classmates, thus:

John	*Lionel*	*Jeanne*
friendly	cross	afraid
kind	unfriendly	shy

Ask the group to write a sentence or tell you about the characters or class members using the words under their names.

> John is friendly.
> Lionel is cross.
> Jeanne is afraid.

Ask them to put two sentences together to compare two characters using the word *but* or *and.*

> John is friendly and Lionel is cross.
> John is friendly but Jeanne is afraid.

Older students will have longer lists and can write a second sentence giving evidence from the story.

> John is friendly. He helps new children feel at home.
> Jeanne is afraid and doesn't speak to many people.

Follow-up:

Ask the students to write another sentence telling how they feel about the two characters, such as:

John is friendly, but Lionel is unfriendly.
I would rather have John for a friend.

Evaluation:

Using the events in the story, evaluate the ability of the students to describe and compare characters.

SAFE Lesson No. 12

TITLE: FOLLOWING A PATTERN

DIFFICULTY LEVEL: GRADES K–2

OBJECTIVES:

Children will:

1. Listen to a patterned story
2. Follow the author's pattern to create new ideas

DESCRIPTION:

Children will listen as you read *Brown Bear, Brown Bear* by Bill Martin. They will help "read" the story after observing the pattern. They will then apply this pattern to create pages for a class book.

PROCEDURES:

Obtain one or more copies of *Brown Bear, Brown Bear* by Bill Martin.

Stimulus:

Read this simple story aloud as children listen. As the pattern becomes evident, encourage children to join in saying the lines with you.

Activity:

Have students draw pictures to suggest new animals to include in a class book. They can dictate the words that should accompany their pages.

Follow-Up:

Fasten the pages together with brads to create a book that children can read to each other. Allow children to sign the book out to take home to read to their families.

Evaluation:

See that each child completes a page for the class book. Make positive comments about the class product and the contribution of each student to its production.

SAFE Lesson No. 13

TITLE: WHAT MAKES IT HUMOROUS?
DIFFICULTY LEVEL: GRADES 2–8
OBJECTIVES:

Students will:

1. Enjoy listening to a humorous story
2. Learn that unexpected outcomes and misunderstandings often produce funny situations
3. Experiment with writing humorous material

DESCRIPTION:

Students will listen to a humorous story. They will borrow the methods used by the author of this story to write their own humorous story.

PROCEDURES:
Stimulus:

Read a humorous book to the class, such as *The Stupids Step Out* by Harry Allard and James Marshall.

Discuss the events in the story. Ask why the students laughed when the Stupid children sat on the bannister and wanted to move up.

Why was the bath scene funny? (All the Stupids are in the bathtub wearing their clothes. They don't use water because it would get their clothes wet).

Continue discussing the scenes in the story, deciding whether or not they are funny. If they are, what makes them funny?

Activity:

Draw the following chart on the board. Fill in the chart as students recall incidents in the story.

Incident in story		Was it funny?	Why?
Stupids go to bed	All in one bed Feet on pillows Heads under covers	yes	Things were in the wrong place What happened?
Children on banister expecting to slide up	They don't slide	yes	Confusion as to how things work

Discuss with students the fact that unexpected events and mis-understandings often create humorous situations.

Ask students to describe everyday situations and tell how they can be made humorous. List ideas on the board.

1. You get a hair cut.   1. You send a friend to get it for you.

2. Buy a house plant.   2. Buy a house plant to grow a house.

3. Buy new tires before   3. Buy tires when you get back from your

   you go on a trip.   trip so they won't get worn out on the trip.

Ask students to choose one of the examples on the board (or think of one of their own) and write sentences about the situation. Have them illustrate it. Then have them change the situation so that it is funny, write sentences about it, and illustrate it.

Make a bulletin board like the one below:

Do you need a house? Buy a house plant and grow your own.

Have students add sentences and illustrations.

Follow-Up:

Read other stories to the class. Have students fill in the chart, or discuss events in the story, and decide whether or not they are funny.

Evaluation:

Give each student two cards. Have them write "Funny" on one and "Not Funny" on the other. When stories are read from the board, have the students vote with these cards as to whether or not the stories are funny and to decide if the stories have been placed on the board under the proper heading. Note whether or not students are developing skill at identifying and writing humorous material.

SAFE Lesson No. 14

TITLE: COMPARING STORIES
DIFFICULTY LEVEL: GRADES 1–6
OBJECTIVES:

Students will:

1. Discuss the stories to be compared and list descriptive words
2. Use their list of descriptive words to write sentences and paragraphs comparing the stories

DESCRIPTION:

Students who have finished reading a story can tell you what they did and did not like about it. When they describe a story and compare it to another, they are learning more about the stories and about themselves.

PROCEDURES:

Stimulus:

Discuss two stories the students have read with the group, for example, *Madeline* or *Make Way for Ducklings*. Ask the students to help you list descriptive words under each title, for example, *funny, silly, spooky, boring*. Ask for evidence from the story that the word does describe it.

When the lists are complete, ask the students to use some of the words to write a sentence about the story. For example,

Where the Wild Things Are is a scary, funny story.
Curious George is a funny story.
Little House on the Prairie is a sweet, old-fashioned, happy story.
Dear Mr. Henshaw is a real, modern, sad, and funny story.

Have students write two sentences using *but* or *and* to compare the stories. For example:

Where the Wild Things Are is a scary story, but *Curious George* is a funny story.

Note that as they compare and evaluate, they are developing thinking skills. Discuss this with students, making them aware that they are thinking.

Follow-Up:

Ask the students to decide which story they like better and add that sentence. Use the same procedure with other stories, lessons, poems, or games.

Evaluation:

Evaluate the ability of the students to judge the quality of a book and to compare the quality of one book to another.

Still More Ideas to Try

It was reported recently that 80 percent of the students in second grade today will have jobs as adults for which we do not now even have names. It is important that we teach our children thinking skills so that as adults they can use their knowledge and skills to cope with an ever-changing environment.

- Put the Story in Order: Read a story to the class. Have the students help you recall the events of the story. Write the events in random order on a ditto and give each student a copy. Ask them to cut up the ditto, put the events in the proper order, paste them on paper, copy the words, and illustrate them.
- Cloze Stories: Write a story and omit words. Adjust the difficulty level according to that of the students. Ask the students to fill in the words to complete the story, for example:

Once there was a _____. He was big and _____. He liked to scare people on _____. One night he decided to have a party. He made punch for the party. He put in five _____, two _____, and three cups of _____. They drank the punch, played the games, and said it was a _____ party. He was _____.

- Stump the Teacher: Ask the students to find words that you may not know. They must be able to pronounce, spell, and define the word. If you cannot spell the word, the students receive a "Teacher Stumper" certificate.

- Favorite Words: After reading a story, ask the students to choose their favorite words from the story. Write these words on cards and give them to the students to learn.

- All Area Favorites: Ask the students to find favorite words in any subject area and write them on cards telling why they like them. Share these words with the group. Later make a "Class Favorite Word Book."

- Secret Commercials: Have the students choose a television commercial and tell it to the group. Say: "Don't tell us the name of the product. Tell us as much as you can about the product and see who can guess what it is."

- Mystery Personality: Ask the students to write or tell a description of another student in the class in twenty-five words or less, and have students guess who it is.

- Mystery Word: Put a word on a card in a box. Give the students clues and see who can guess the word. The first student to guess the word correctly takes the box home and puts in a word for the students to guess the next day.

Developing a Thematic Module:
Self-Esteem

Success in school enhances the students' self-esteem. Self-esteem helps students achieve success. A primary concern of all teachers, therefore, should be to enhance the self-esteem of each student.

Children who are treated as valuable members of their home come to school with a positive self-image. Usually successful, they seldom create discipline problems. Self-esteem can be enhanced or damaged through experiences at school. The following unit is recommended for the beginning of the school year.

SELF-ESTEEM

Objectives:

Through working with this unit, students will be able to:

1. Compare their learning mode with that of other students
2. Compare an evaluation of their progress in school with the teacher's evaluation of their progress
3. Evaluate the progress they have made in writing and reading during the year
4. Know and appreciate other members of the group
5. Understand that their uniqueness makes them a valuable member of the group

Getting Started:

The materials you will need are the following:

1. Tape recorder
2. Activity sheets described in the unit
3. Copies of blank report card
4. A class list

These activities can be used at all grade levels to show students that each is a unique and valuable member of the group.

Have students keep a Learning Log in which to record ideas.

Learning Activities for the Students:

- Writing Pretest: During the first week of school, have each student write a paragraph about the previous school year. Ask them to tell what they like best, what was the hardest work for them, who their friends were, and how the teacher helped them. This information will be recorded in individual Learning Logs.

  For kindergartners and other nonwriters, ask questions orally and note the answers. Instead of a paragraph, you may have students complete such sentences as the following:

  1. School was _____last year.
  2. _____ and _____were my best friends.
  3. I learned how to _____.
  4. The hardest work to do was _____.

5. My teacher helped me to ———————————————.

6. At recess I ——————————————————.

Keep this writing as a pretest for each student's self-esteem. When the unit is completed, use the same exercise as a posttest for comparison.

- **Partner Introductions:**   On the first day of school, assign each student a partner. Ask them to interview each other for about two minutes. You may want to list questions that each will ask on the board or on a sheet of paper on which students can take notes. For younger students, keep the questions simpler, for example, the person's name and his or her favorite kind of ice cream. After the introductions, see how many names children can remember.

- **Pictures for Attendance:**   When taking roll, ask about those students who are absent. Young children may draw pictures of themselves to place on a chart with two columns: "At School," and "At Home." Pictures will be moved to the appropriate column. Thus, the group is aware of students even when they are absent. This adds to the group cohesiveness.

- **What Kind of Learner Am I?:**   Tell students that people learn in many ways—feeling, seeing, hearing, and doing. Some people prefer to hear about things, whereas others learn better when they see or read about them. Guide students to follow this activity to decide how they learn best. You will learn the different modalities students favor.

Procedure:

On a large paper, write this list in very large letters that can be seen easily by all students. Show the list to the class for about thirty seconds. Then turn it over and have students write as many words as they can remember. Use the following words for the lists.

Grades 1–3	Grades 4 and Above
cat	toothpaste
man	shoelaces
bag	envelope
hat	hairbrush
fan	wristwatch
rat	sandwich

Discuss the results with the students. Ask how many thought it was easy, who remembered them all, and who thought it was hard. Have students write individual responses in their Learning Logs. (For K–1 students, you may use pictures and oral responses.)

For the second part, given on a second day, read the list to the students.

Grades 1–3	Grades 4–6
ball	rollerskates
tree	bandaid
book	sidewalk
dog	windmill
pan	pocketknife
room	cowboy

Discuss the results. Have students write their reactions to this experience in their Learning Logs. (For K–1 students, you may use pictures and oral responses.)

On the third day, ask students to write as you dictate this list.

Grades 1–3	Grades 4–8
duck	green pencil
pool	yellow shirt
lamp	three stamps
gum	coffee cup
paper	little dog
cup	white house

When you finish, ask students to turn over the paper and to write as many of the words as they can from memory. (K–1 students can draw pictures.)

When these learning experiences are completed, ask students to write their reactions in their Learning Logs. Discuss how this learning about themselves and their learning styles might help them when studying.

Note information about individual learning styles for each student in your roll book.

- Student of the Day: Without letting the students know what you are doing, choose one student each day to observe, closely noting process, problems, friends, special interests, and abilities. Ask that student to give you special help. Note your observations. You will get to know your students more quickly and in greater depth.

- Special Interest Clubs: Form one or more clubs around a special interest (books, math, science) and meet before or after school. You might develop these clubs as a whole school so that all students have a chance to be in a special grouping, interacting with different students and teachers in a less formal setting.

- All about Me: Have students bring pictures of themselves to paste on a large sheet of heavy paper or cardboard. Have each one write a few sentences about herself or himself, such as:

I like to __Swim__ .   I hope to __be on__   My friend is __Joe__.
__a football team__.

I would like to __go__   I was born in _____   I am __8 years old__.
__to London__ .   __Korea__ .

Young children can dictate sentences to older students who visit from an upper grade.

Put the completed charts on the wall. (This is a good display for Open House.) After taking them down, staple the pages together for a class book students can read.

- Conversations on Tape: Have a tape recorder available for students who would like to talk with you. Listen and answer their part of the dialogue.

- Bulletin Board: For a bulletin board, fasten plastic sleeves on the wall and have each student in turn fill one with special stories or pictures, whatever he or she desires.

- Report Cards: When it is time for reporting to parents, give each student a duplicated copy of the report card form. Ask them to fill it out for themselves. Have a conference with each student to talk about their personal evaluations. Students should also attend parent-teacher conferences. They can be responsible for leading the conference. They can present their grades and discuss what they intend to do about maintaining or improving them. You might record these conferences.

- Hobby Show: Hold a hobby show for the class. Each student will have an assigned time during the year to bring in his or her hobby to share with the other students.

- Books for Self-Esteem: Choose books to read aloud that especially feature problems and successes children have with which your students can identify. For example:

Yashima, Taro. *Crow Boy*. Viking. Story of an elementary school boy who remains an outsider until an understanding teacher gets to know him.

Lionni, Leo. *Swimmy*. Pantheon. Cooperation leads to the solution of a community problem.

George, Jean C. *Julie of the Wolves*. Harper. Julie manages to survive the cold of the tundra by using her head.

Taylor, Theodore. *The Cay*. Doubleday. Phillip and an elderly black man help each other when marooned on an island.

Such books provide food for thought as children respond to the ideas of the author and discuss their reactions to the behavior of characters portrayed.

Resources for the Teacher:

Canfield, Jack, and Well, Harol. *100 Ways to Enhance Self-Concept in the Classroom*. Prentice-Hall, 1976.

Fischer, Carl. *Dimensions of Personality*, 1972.

Paulus, Trina. *Hope for the Flowers*. Paulist Press, 1972.

Rogers, Carl. *On Becoming a Person*. Houghton Mifflin, 1961.

Williams, Frank. *Classroom Ideas for Encouraging Thinking and Feeling*. D.O.K. Publishers, 1970.

Houston, Jean. *The Possible Human*. Houghton Mifflin, 1982.

Berger, Terry. *I Have Feelings*. Behavioral Publications, 1971.

Lecker, Sidney. *Who Are You?* Simon and Schuster, 1980.

Baldwin, Christina. *One to One: Self Understanding through Journal Writing*. M. Evans, 1977.

Maslow, Abraham. *Motivation and Personality*. Harper, 1954.

Exploring Further

Graves, Donnald H. *Writing: Teachers & Children at Work*. Heineman, 1983.

Johnson, Ferne. *Start Early for an Early Start: You and the Young Child*. American Library Association, 1976.

Kroll, Barry M., and Vann, Roberta J., eds. *Exploring Speaking-Writing Relationships: Connections and Contrasts*. NCTE, 1981.

Tiedt, Iris, M. *The Language Arts Handbook*. Prentice-Hall, 1983.

4

Gaining Power Through Reading/Thinking/Writing

Once children begin to discover basic literacy concepts, they need to reinforce their growing knowledge by applying it in the context of working with written language. They should have time to read a variety of books for fun and information, and they should have time to express their ideas in writing. The old adage, "Practice makes perfect," is restated today as "time on task." Children learn to read by reading and to write by writing.

At the same time, however, we are concerned about the quality of the learning experiences we plan for the classroom. We want students to think about what they are doing, to question, and to grow. Discussions, small group work, and opportunities to share what they are reading and writing will stimulate student interest and lend purpose to classroom learning experiences.

As students engage in learning, they use all of the language skills. Thus, we stress activities that integrate thinking, listening, and speaking with reading and writing, selecting learning experiences that strengthen student language and literacy competencies. Studies around a theme or issue, for example, involve students in purposeful work that leads to increased proficiency with both oral and written language.

The activities described in this chapter are grouped under the following headings:

Developing Reading/Thinking/Writing Fluency

Thinking about What We Read

Sharing Reading Orally and in Writing

Focusing on a Theme: Love

Implementing the Program

Research related to the growth of fluency and power over the written language focuses chiefly on how students spend learning time. The implications for teaching suggest a changing role for us, as teachers.

1. In order to learn to read and write successfully, students need to read and write frequently; and if we want children to learn to think, we must provide opportunities for them to use thinking abilities. Students need to spend quality time on the tasks to be learned.

2. Students need to engage in the full reading and writing processes, working in whole language contexts. (Many drill or workbook activities do not add to the child's reading or writing abilities. They may actually have a negative effect, particularly on attitudes toward reading and writing.)

3. Children should discover the joy of reading good literature, making transactions with authors. Talking about books, getting to know authors, and responding to books in writing provide positive support for the literacy program.

4. We can supply stimuli, positive reinforcement, and opportunity for reading, thinking, and writing, but motivation must come from within the student. Students need opportunities to make choices in selecting books to read, topics of study, and forms of writing in which to present their ideas.

5. Being aware of student interests enables us to plan a more effective literacy program. For example, we can let students plan integrated studies around topics of their choice.

6. In order to become independent thinkers, students need opportunities to discover, to question, and to solve problems. We need to step back and avoid giving the "right" answer and overcorrecting student speech, reading, and writing. Children need time to think.

Selected Resources

You may wish to explore the following resources from which we have drawn the information presented above.

California State Department of Education. *Handbook for Planning an Effective Literature Program: Kindergarten through Grade Twelve*. The Department, 1987.

California State Department of Education. *Handbook for Planning an Effective Writing Program: Kindergarten through Grade Twelve*, 3rd ed. The Department, 1986.

Goodman, Kenneth. *What's Whole about Whole Language?* Heineman, 1986.

Julie Jensen, ed. *Composing and Comprehending.* NCTE and ERIC, 1984.

Moffett, James, and Wagner, Betty Jane. *Student-centered Language Arts and Reading, K–13,* 2nd ed. Houghton, 1981.

Petersen, Bruce T., ed. *Convergences: Transactions in Reading and Writing.* NCTE, 1986.

Tiedt, Iris M. *The Language Arts Handbook.* Prentice-Hall, 1983.

Developing Reading/Thinking/Writing Fluency

Fluency means flowing smoothly and easily—the easy flow of ideas onto the paper, ease with reading, and approaching problem solving and brainstorming ideas with enthusiasm. For the language arts teacher, developing fluency presents a challenge to plan a classroom environment filled with purposeful activities and stimulating opportunities so that students can and will read, think, and write frequently. In this section of the chapter, we share strategies that give you the confidence to create a student-centered classroom—one that encourages students to read, to think, and to write.

A USEFUL STRATEGY: TIME ON TASK WITH READING AND THINKING

When planning lessons, allow time for silent reading. Suggest that students read materials that are not part of the regular basal program. Fluency is your target, so encourage them to read a variety of materials daily. Set up a classroom environment where students see reading and talking about books as important. Reward them with points for their involvement with reading during class time. Become a provider of stimulating reading materials and a facilitator of a comfortable, quiet environment for reading. Schedule time for talking about the books students are reading.

SAFE Lesson No. 1

TITLE OF LESSON: UNINTERRUPTED SUSTAINED SILENT READING (USSR)

DIFFICULTY LEVEL: GRADES 2–12

OBJECTIVES:

Students will:

1. Display confidence and fluency in reading
2. Increase interest in reading

3. Recognize different purposes for reading
4. Analyze feelings about what was read

DESCRIPTION:

Every day, students will select materials to read during class time.

PROCEDURES:

Stimulus:

Share guidelines for the USSR program with students.

1. Bring a book of your choice to class.
2. The ringing of the bell signals when to read.
3. Read the first fifteen minutes of class.
4. Do not talk—read!
5. Everyone reads, including the teacher.

Define the terms *uninterrupted* and *sustained* to the class so that they understand the need for a quiet, ongoing time for reading.

Activity:

Take students to the library and have them select any book that they would like to read. Have them bring these books to class every day.

Since students will read each day, fill the classroom with magazines and newspapers. If a student forgets a book, have her or him read articles from the newspaper and magazines. Tell the children that their reading materials must be "in hand" at the start of the USSR period so that they do not disturb others who are reading.

Set a kitchen timer for the end of the USSR period.

Follow-Up:

Set up a classroom library of magazines, books, and newspapers. Encourage students to browse through the library to select reading materials for the sustained silent reading program.

Make a "Reading Power" bulletin board where students recommend exciting books they read. By placing the title and summary of the book in the Reading Power section, they are evaluating the book as being superior, and they are recommending it to their classmates.

Encourage students to maintain Reading Logs (see page 16) of the books read during the USSR period. Set up a reward system for students who read the most books.

Develop school spirit by setting up a USSR period throughout the school. Encourage all staff members, the principal, students, and visitors to read during the USSR time.

Evaluation:

Display a chart that reflects the number of books read by each student. Assign student monitors to maintain the chart. Reward students twice a month for the quantity of reading. Make the requirements achievable for all.

Bimonthly, assign students to small groups and have them tell classmates about their favorite books. Have classmates rate their interest in these books. (See page 262 for more book-sharing ideas.)

SAFE Lesson No. 2

TITLE OF LESSON: READING CENTER

DIFFICULTY LEVEL: GRADES K–8

OBJECTIVES:

Students will:

1. Select books from different categories
2. Synthesize directions to make their own books
3. Recognize different kinds of reading materials
4. Analyze fluency in reading

DESCRIPTION:

Students will organize a reading center to include books, magazines, and newspapers from their homes. In addition, students will add student-made books and anthologies. This strategy can be extended to junior and senior high levels using library space.

PROCEDURES:

Stimulus:

Talk to students about organizing a Reading Center. Tell them that they will help decide how and when to use the Reading Center. Include a variety of books (children's classics, poetry, young adult novels, and nonfiction) and a variety of magazines (*Writers' Digest, Sports Illustrated, Highlights,* and *Readers' Digest).* Seek help from a librarian when choosing the books for your grade level. As a challenge, however, include books that span a variety of reading levels.

Here are sample categories and suggested books for each category.

- Folktales

    Ambrus, Victor G. *The Sultan's Bath.* Harcourt Brace Jovanovich, 1972. (Hungary)

    Berson, Harold. *The Boy, The Baker, The Miller, and More.* Crown, 1974. (France)

    Jameson, Cynthia. *The Clay Pot Boy.* Illustrated by Anita Lobel. Coward-McCann, 1973. (Russia)

- Realism

    Bartoli, Jennifer. *Nonna.* Harvey House, 1975.

    Jordan, Julie. *New Life: New Room.* Thomas Y. Crowell, 1975.

    Williams, Barbara. *Kevin's Grandma.* Dutton, 1975.

- Wordless Books

    Alexander, Martha. *Bobo's Dream.* Dial, 1970.

    Carl, Eric. *Do You Want to Be My Friend?* Thomas Y. Crowell, 1971.

    Krahn, Fernando. *A Flying Saucer Full of Spaghetti.* Dutton, 1970.

- Fanciful Tales/Picture Books

    Ayme, Marcel. *The Wonderful Farm.* Harper, 1951.

    Bianco, Margery. *The Velveteen Rabbit.* Doubleday, 1926. (See new edition)

    Lionni, Leo. *Frederick.* Pantheon, 1967.

- Fanciful Tales/Older Children

    Cleary, Beverly, *Runaway Ralph.* Morrow, 1970.

    Sleigh, Barbara. *Carbonel: The King of the Cats.* Bobbs-Merrill, 1957.

    Stolz, Mary. *Maximilian's World.* Harper and Row, 1966.

- Science Fiction/Younger Children

    Brooks, Walter. *Freddy and the Men From Mars.* Knopf, 1954.

    Cameron, Eleanor. *Wonderful Flight to the Mushroom Planet.* Little, Brown, 1954.

    Todd, Ruthven. *Space Cat.* Scribner, 1952.

- Science Fiction/Older Children

    Bradbury, Ray. *S Is for Space.* Doubleday, 1966.

    Clarke, Arthur C. *Dolphin Island.* Holt, 1963.

    Martel, Suzanne. *The City Under the Ground.* Viking, 1964.

- Search for Identity/Younger Children

    Caudill, Rebecca. *Did You Carry the Flag Today, Charley?* Holt, 1966.

Turkle, Brinton, *The Adventures of Obadiah*. Viking, 1972.
Zolotow, Charlotte S. *A Father Like That*. Harper and Row, 1971.

- Search for Identity/Older Children

Buck, Pearl. *Matthew, Mark, Luke, and John*. John Day, 1967.
Clymer, Eleanor. *My Brother Stevie*. Holt, 1967.
Sachs, Marilyn. *Amy and Laura*. Doubleday, 1966.

- Peer Relationships/Young Children

Cohen, Miriam. *Will I Have a Friend?* Macmillan, 1967.
Sherman, Ivan. *I Do Not Like It When My Friend Comes to Visit*. Harcourt Brace Jovanovich, 1973.
Zolotow, Charlotte, *Janey*. Harper, 1973.

- Peer Relationships/Middle School

Coles, Robert. *Dead End School*. Little, Brown, 1968.
Little, Jean. *One to Grow On*. Little, Brown, 1969.
Smith, Doris B. *Tough Chauncey*. Morrow, 1974.

Additional lists appear in the Appendix. *Multicultural Teaching* by Pamela L. and Iris M. Tiedt (Allyn and Bacon, 1986) is an excellent source for additional book lists that focus on muticultural education.

Activity:

Assign students to small groups of three or four. Have them decide what materials could go into the Reading Center. Within student groups, have them list categories and then think of ways to get materials donated. Suggestions may include:

Asking neighbors

Going to thrift stores

Starting a "used book drive" at school

Asking friends and relatives

Looking for discarded books at libraries

Talking to the student government board

After you involve the students in supplying the Reading Center, have them write the guidelines for the center. Suggest that they include:

Who should use the Center?

What should be included?

When should it be used?

Where can it be placed in the classroom?

How can we arrange the reading materials?

After they decide on the guidelines, have one person report the group's decisions to the class. Involve the students in a class discussion of the effective use of the Reading Center in the classroom.

Follow-Up:

After involving students in setting guidelines and in getting materials for the Reading Center, see that the Reading Center is used. Use the center in conjunction with the USSR program when students are selecting something to read. Use the Reading Center to ensure time on task by allowing students who finish early to spend time in the center.

Show students how to make books (see Chapter 5, page 183). Require all students to put one book in the Reading Center. Award extra credit to students who choose to contribute more of their books to the Center. Encourage cross-grade activities by asking students in other grades to contribute student-made books to the Reading Center.

Add variety to the Reading Center by including videotapes and cassette tapes that are commercial or student-made (see page 109). These tapes could coincide with books students want to read.

Evaluation:

Invite "dignitaries" (principals, other teachers, students from other classes) into your classroom to evaluate the materials in the Reading Center. Have them offer suggestions for additional sources to be added.

Have students evaluate the materials in the Reading Center and its use. Have them determine whether the Reading Center gets enough attention from the class by collecting answers to these questions:

How often do you use the Reading Center?

What materials are needed in the center?

Where can our class get more materials?

Does the center distract from instruction?

Does the center add to instruction?

Does the center help your classroom performance?

Should the teacher expect more from you?

What should the teacher expect?

What materials can you add to the center?

Have students keep logs of their involvement in the Reading Center, recording the date, title of reading material, summary, and personal reaction. Use the logs to assess how much and how well students are using the center.

MORE LESSONS TO PROMOTE FLUENCY

Anything you can do to get students to read, think, and write promotes fluency. Look around you and gather any object, record, videotape, cassette tape, film, or book to bring to the classroom. Make the students focus their senses to see and hear all that surrounds them. Help develop thinking skills by getting them to express opinions and feelings. By developing fluency when reacting to their surroundings, they become articulate speakers and writers.

SAFE Lesson No. 3

TITLE OF LESSON: VIDEO READING
DIFFICULTY LEVEL: GRADES K–10
OBJECTIVES:

Students will:

1. Read poetry orally on the videotape
2. Write their own poems
3. Prepare an anthology of poetry (theirs and others)
4. Critique poetry readings
5. Evaluate poetry anthologies
6. Practice oral interpretation while reading orally

DESCRIPTION:

Students will write poems. They will collect favorite poems and their own poetry to make an anthology. While being videotaped, they will read a few poems.

PROCEDURES:
Stimulus:

Read a number of poems aloud to students. Focus on a theme so that they all hear a series of poems on one topic. When reading aloud, select a series of poems that include varied forms, such as song lyrics, classics (Shakespeare, Tennyson, Longfellow), and limericks.

Bring several anthologies to class. Tell the students that they will be putting together an anthology of their favorite poetry.

Activity:

Have students brainstorm topics for poetry. Have them start with abstract words, such as *love, hate, joy,* or *friendship.*

Put them into groups according to similar topics. For instance, all the "love" students work together to list specific examples for the word. They can share the combined list.

Assign a recorder in each group to compile the list on a blank ditto master. Since the list was compiled on a ditto master, you can make the list available to the entire class. Students will use the lists to write poetry.

Have students look through the books to select poetry they would like to include in a booklet of their own. Give them a minimum requirement of ten poems in addition to three poems of their own. As a homework assignment, have them compile these poems into an attractive anthology.

Put students into groups to practice reading poetry orally. Have them work on voice intonation, inflection, volume, eye contact, and gestures. After students have had time to practice, videotape each student reading two poems.

Follow-Up:

After each student has been videotaped, invite other classes to view the tape. Use the videotape as a stimulus for cross-grade-level interest in poetry.

Invite a poet into the classroom to read poetry and to talk about the writing process.

Evaluation:

Use this checklist to evaluate the poetry readings. Next to each word, write 5 for outstanding, 3 for average, and 1 for poor. Add the total points for the final score.

_____ volume

_____ enunciation

_____ voice intonation

_____ voice inflection

_____ eye contact

_____ gestures

_____ facial expressions

_____ content

_____ TOTAL POINTS

Have students view the videotape and complete the checklist for each student. Pause the videotape after each reading and ask students to discuss the merits of each presentation. Write notes about the discussion and include these notes on the evaluation sheet, which will be given to each presenter.

Put students into small groups and have them read the poetry anthologies. Have them give each booklet a pass or fail grade, based on the number of poems and the quality of the student-written poems.

SAFE Lesson No. 4

TITLE OF LESSON: MEMORY ASSOCIATION

DIFFICULTY LEVEL: GRADES 3–8

OBJECTIVES:

Students will:

1. Describe experiences of their childhood
2. Write associations for objects
3. Discuss the importance of memories
4. Synthesize experiences into a story

DESCRIPTION:

Students will be reminded of a personal experience by looking at an object and associating that object with a memory. They will write about that memory.

PROCEDURES:

Stimulus:

Remind the students of the word-association game in which students give the name of the very first word that comes to mind when another word is said to them. For example, when you say, "blue," the response is often "skies."

Play this game but use objects instead of words. Have students visualize a memory (a complete scene) after they see each object.

Select five objects taken from a toy box, medicine cabinet, or kitchen drawer. Hold the objects up, one by one, and give students time to write the name of the object on the paper. Give them time to jot down a phrase that captures a memory each object suggests. They should write the first memory that the object suggests, as in these examples:

1. bandage   I fell off the bike at Aunt Sue's.
2. toy cycle   A policeman pulled Dad over.
3. chalk   I could never do math problems when Mrs. Grimm sent me to the board.
4. ski cap   no ski cap; I never took my baseball cap off in fifth grade.
5. rose   Dad gave me one when I graduated from sixth grade.

Activity:

After students complete this memory association chart, have them write about one memory. As they write about the experience, have them use action verbs and descriptive details. Their writing should aim at re-creating the experience.

Discuss the enjoyment of sharing personal memories. Tell students to be more sensitive to their own memory banks by associating objects with memories. Students who internalize this attitude will wean themselves from the teacher as a source for writing ideas as they search within themselves.

Follow-up:

Have students read their stories in small groups and select the best story from the group. Read the best story from each group aloud as the students listen for action verbs and descriptions.

Instead of using objects, read stories aloud that will evoke personal experiences. Use children's stories which deal, for example, with self-concept, such as:

Brown, Margaret Wise. *The Important Book*. Harper, 1949.

Charlip, Remy. *Fortunately*. Parents, 1964.

Krasilovsky, Phyllis. *Shy Little Girl*. Houghton Mifflin, 1970.

Mayer, Mercer. *Just for You*. New York: Golden, 1975.

Silverstein, Shel. *The Giving Tree*. Harper, 1979.

Zolotow, Charlotte. *Do You Know What I'll Do?* Harper, 1958.

Evaluation:

Observe the students completing the memory charts. Reward students who use key phrases correctly.

As you listen to the "best" story from each group, pay attention to the class discussion and give points to students who are actively involved. Have the class help you pick the "best" paper in the class. Award that paper with an A, and give all group members an A grade. Grade the other selected papers and assign that grade to all group members. (Most groups will receive an A grade for their work.)

Still More Ideas to Try

- Solve the Mystery: Have students read puzzling stories and write their own endings to these stories. Collect the stories from newspapers, magazines, radio, or television.

- Dear Abby: Have students write their own solutions to Abby letters. Have them get into groups and discuss the different solutions they may have for the same problem. Use role-playing techniques.

- Mom or Dad-a-Gram: Have the students send messages to their parents, explaining what and how they are doing at school.

- Rhyme Ending: Have students write another stanza to a nursery rhyme. Try to arrange for them to read these to primary students.

- Booklets of Love: Have students write a poem for a loved one and put this message in a booklet. (Refer to Chapter 5 for instructions on bookbinding.)

- Round Table Write: Have students sit in a circle and write one line per person to a story they share. Give them each a timed five-minute period. Have them share the finished stories with the class.

Thinking About What We Read

Through language, the child begins to communicate and to understand. Oral language development occurs without dittos, without labeling parts of speech, and without laborious copying of the same sentence. It happens because the child is motivated to think about and to use language. Language development is stimulating and fun as long as the child is comfortable in a stress-free learning environment. It makes sense that the classroom teacher would strive to re-create the same enjoyable, nonjudgmental environment for literacy instruction. This can be done when thinking, reading, and writing are learned naturally, through meaningful experiences for students.

A USEFUL STRATEGY: TRANSACTION LOGS

Transactions occur when students have a chance to think about what they are reading or hearing and enter into a transaction with the speaker or author. Two kinds of transaction logs, reading and learning logs, can be used in the classroom.

The learning log functions as a process journal that gives students an opportunity to write about what they are hearing or reading as a way of making meaning. With the log, they process knowledge, asking questions, noting assumptions, interpreting based on their personal knowledge.

The reading log also gives students a chance to react to what they are reading. In reading logs, they can write summaries or note the use of language as well as offer opinions and feelings as they react to what they read.

Both the reading log and the learning log give students the means they need to become involved in the learning process. They offer a real transaction and help students make connections between reading, thinking, and writing.

SAFE Lesson No. 5

TITLE OF LESSON: LEARNING LOGS
DIFFICULTY LEVEL: GRADES 5–10
OBJECTIVES:

Students will:

1. Make daily entries in their learning logs
2. Write reactions to reading assignments
3. Summarize their notes
4. Critique the class assignments
5. Interpret class discussions

DESCRIPTION:

Students will use learning logs in specific content areas. Students will write the summary of the lesson, including their reactions.

PROCEDURES:

Stimulus:

Encourage students to discuss the difficulty they are having in some classes. Ask them to write a few sentences about the specific problems they are having in one subject. They can share their comments in small groups with their peers.

Then ask them if they would like to join you in an experiment that may help them improve their study skills and their grades in the subject they wrote about. Most will be at least semi-enthusiastic.

Activity:

Have each child make a chart like this:

Instruct them to use this chart during that subject period. Have them write key words in the columns as they participate in the class. They will do this on Tuesdays and Thursdays.

On alternate days, have the students keep a log of the information learned in this class. They can answer such questions as:

What are new words I learned?

Can I write my own definitions?

Can I explain this lesson to someone else?

Can I use this information in my personal life?

Do I have an opinion about something I learned?

Awareness of these questions forces students to think about the lesson being taught. The questions challenge them to interact with the teacher and the lesson, and make significant gains in critical thinking.

Note that thus far, the log is being kept without any interaction with the content-area teacher. Students simply keep the logs and bring them to your class, along with the charts that they are keeping.

Follow-Up:

After the students have kept logs and charts for two weeks, put them into response groups to discuss the advantages of the log versus the chart. In the response groups, have them brainstorm other questions that could be entered into the logs.

Then have students share logs with the content-area teachers, and solicit reactions from the teachers by finding out if they were aware that students had been taking notes as well as writing reactions. Ask the content-area teacher to comment on any improvement in class performance.

Initiate a staff development meeting to try to have staff members agree to use the log in their classrooms. Show them samples of logs that have been kept. Have the teachers brainstorm questions that would be effective for their classes. Develop a chart to help teachers or students keep track of which method helped them learn.

Evaluation:

Analyze the quality of classroom instruction and student learning after the use of the log for two weeks. Answer these questions:

1. Do students have a better understanding of content?
2. Are students more responsive (oral participation, deadlines met, enjoyment during discussions)?
3. Are you closer to students (understanding of opinions, feelings)?
4. Has the log affected your methodology? Does the information in the log suggest you reteach, give practice time, introduce additional concepts, use small or large groups?
5. Have test scores, especially on essay tests, improved?
6. Are students better able to apply what they learned?
7. Are students taking more responsibility for their own learning?
8. Has your relationship with the students changed?

Evaluate the students' reactions to the use of the log by having them answer the same questions.

SAFE Lesson No. 6

TITLE OF LESSON: READING LOG

DIFFICULTY LEVEL: GRADES 3–12

OBJECTIVES:

Students will:

1. Summarize what they read
2. State opinions about what they read
3. Describe their feelings after they read
4. Keep a cumulative record of how much they read
5. Analyze a transaction between reader and writer

DESCRIPTION:

Students will use the reading log to write feelings, opinions, and summaries about the reading material.

PROCEDURES:

Stimulus:

Talk about the relationship that exists between the reader and the writer of a book. Discuss the unspoken dialogue that occurs as the reader "thinks" while reading. Define the reading log as a method to record their thoughts.

Give each student a composition book, or require them to bring a notebook to class.

Activity:

Have students react to a book. Tell them that this information gathering can also apply to magazine and newspaper articles.

Have each student make a list of these subheadings:

1. Book Information

   Write this information:

   Title of Book:_____
   Author:_____
   Place of Publication:_____
   Publisher:_____
   Date of Publication:_____

2. Book Summary:

   Record a statement about these details:

   Characters:
   Setting:
   Conflict (problem):
   Rising action (trying to solve the problem):
   Climax (conflict is solved):

3. Ideas in the Book:

   Think about what you may have read "between the lines" that reveals the author's opinions. Answer these questions in your log.
   What are two opinions stated by the writer?
   Do you agree with these opinions?
   Do you disagree with anything else the author wrote?
   Have any of your opinions changed since reading the book?

4. Feelings about the Book:

Write about any feelings you experienced while reading the book. Consider these thoughts:

How do you feel now that you read the book?
What is at least one emotion you felt while reading the book?
Did your feelings change about any of the characters?
Have you shared any of the same feelings the characters may have had?
What made you most upset in the book?
What made you most satisfied?

Make sure all students understand how to respond to these sub-topics. Suggest that these questions appear at the beginning of their reading logs so that they can refer to them as they think about what they read.

A reading log page can be set up as such:

Title:_____

Author:_____

Publication information:_____

Summary of the Book:

Reactions to Ideas Presented in the Book:

My Feelings After Reading the Book:

Have students organize the reading log pages in a notebook. A well-organized reading log records how many books and magazine and newspaper articles a student has read. Students can reflect on their growth and what they have learned by rereading their responses.

Follow-Up:

Have students share the contents of the reading logs by discussing the thinking and feelings they expressed in the logs. Put students into groups and have them discuss one entry in their reading logs. Monitor this discussion by listening for summaries, opinions, and feelings about the books.

Use the reading log in conjunction with the Uninterrupted Sustained Silent Reading program (page 103) and the Reading Center (page 105). Soon, students will increase their fluency, and they will recognize the transaction between the reader and the writer. In addition, they will be more prepared to think, talk, and write about what they read. They will see that reading gives them information to think, talk, and write about.

Evaluation:

Use the list of questions under each subdivision as a checklist to evaluate how well the reading logs were written.

Put students into small groups and have them read each other's reading logs. Tell them to ask these questions of the writer of the reading log:

Did the writer summarize the book?

Did the writer express opinions taken from the book?

Did the writer express feelings after reading the book?

After reading the logs, have students react by answering these questions:

Do you want to read this book?

Did this summary evoke any feelings within you?

Do you have any differing opinions?

Did this entry in the reading log make you think?

MORE LESSONS TO PROMOTE THINKING ABOUT WHAT WE READ

By sharing in small groups, students speak, write, listen, and think together. They have the opportunity to brainstorm together. The size of the groups (three to five members) gives them a better chance to express what they are thinking. They are "on task" as they work within the guidelines set by you, and their self-esteem and articulation skills are enhanced. Working in small groups gives them an opportunity to express feelings and opinions that may have otherwise stayed locked within them.

SAFE Lesson No. 7

TITLE OF LESSON: ROLE PLAYING AND RECORDING

DIFFICULTY LEVEL: GRADES K–10

OBJECTIVES:

Students will:

1. Role play situations with conflicts
2. Compare solutions to conflicts
3. Write solutions to problems

DESCRIPTIONS:

Students will role play problem situations, and they will write solutions.

PROCEDURES:

Stimulus:

On 3″ × 5″ filecards, write short descriptive summaries of typical situations. Within groups of three or four, have the students read the information on the card. Have them plan a role-playing situation that offers solutions to the problem, such as:

> Your parents are angry because you came home at 5:30.
> You were told to be home at 4 P.M.

Assign characters (mother, father, son or daughter, friends, relatives). Decide who will say what. Practice acting out the skit.

Activity:

After the students have been given time to practice, have them role play the situation in front of the class. As classmates listen and watch the skits, they should think of alternate solutions to the same problem.

Instruct them to write their alternate solutions in script form or paragraph form. Have them share their solutions within small groups. Have each group reach a consensus on the "best" solution and give their reasons for this choice.

Follow-Up:

Vary this activity by having the students write a situation that has the same problem but different characters, for example, the mother is an hour late and the children are worried.

Bring copies of *TV Guide* to class. Have students read the program listings and the summaries. Tell students to find *TV Guide* program summaries that could be used in role-playing situations.

Have students work in groups to brainstorm other conflicts. Have the recorders of the group write each situation on 3 × 5 notecards. Tell students that these situations can be used for other brainstorming, role-playing, and writing assignments.

Evaluation:

Watch the skits then ask these questions:

Was the acting believable?

Did the students communicate the problem and offer realistic solutions?

Did the class offer good alternate solutions?

Read the student-written paragraphs about the conflict and evaluate whether the students presented the problem accurately and offered realistic solutions.

SAFE Lesson No. 8

TITLE OF LESSON: LANGUAGE GAMES

DIFFICULTY LEVEL: GRADES K–8

OBJECTIVES:

Students will:

1. Critique humorous examples of a play on words
2. Write paragraphs
3. Discuss the varied meanings of language
4. Contrast literal and figurative language

DESCRIPTION:

Students will listen to words used humorously. They will then create their own messages by "playing with words."

PROCEDURES:

Stimulus:

Read the book, *The King Who Reigned,* by Fred Gwynne, aloud to the class. Show the pictures while you read so that the class can appreciate the humor of the homonyms. The cover of the book has a picture of a king lying in midair with rain pouring from his back. Have the students discuss the humor of the play on words of *rain* and *reigned.* List two examples from the book on the board:

frog in your throat
Mom's friends are playing bridge.

Introduce two words, *literal* and *figurative.* Literal is the exact definition, whereas figurative is the hidden meaning of an expression. Tell students that these expressions are referred to as *idioms.* Label the literal and figurative meanings of these expressions and have them note that the literal interpretation is humorous, as in the sample:

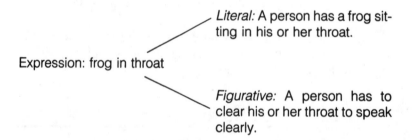

Literal: A person has a frog sitting in his or her throat.

Expression: frog in throat

Figurative: A person has to clear his or her throat to speak clearly.

Tell students that words can have a double meaning. The meaning of the word or phrase is derived from the context (how it is used.) It is humorous when you visualize the word "out of context."

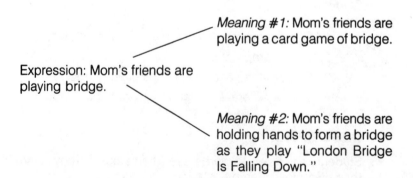

Meaning #1: Mom's friends are playing a card game of bridge.

Expression: Mom's friends are playing bridge.

Meaning #2: Mom's friends are holding hands to form a bridge as they play "London Bridge Is Falling Down."

Activity:

Have the students brainstorm phrases or words that could have double meanings. Have them select idioms, such as:

heart of gold

two left feet

pea brain

all thumbs

green thumb

broken heart

sticky fingers

In groups of three, have students write the literal and figurative meanings of these expressions. Have them draw the humorous (literal) interpretations. Help students make a class book similar to *The King Who Reigned.*

Follow-Up:

Have students invent the names of businesses that would specialize in a product. Have fun using the literal meaning of the words in the title, such as:

Sticky Fingers Security Systems

Green Thumb Pest Control Co.

All-Thumbs Carpentry School

Two-Left-Feet Dancing School

Broken Heart Video Dating Corporation

Have them share these titles in groups of five and compile a group list.

Tell students to write a paragraph about one of these companies. Challenge them to incorporate idioms within the paragraph by awarding points for every "double meaning" word used.

Evaluation:

Have students read the paragraphs and put a check in the margin for every idiom that is used correctly. Count the number of checks and give points according to the number of idioms found.

Read the company slogans to the class. Have the class vote "Yes" if the slogan has a double meaning. Listen to the class discussions and give an "A" to all acceptable slogans.

Have students read the student-made books. They should evaluate how well the illustrations match the phrases. (Caution them not to grade the quality of the illustrations; they're evaluating the students' knowledge of double meaning.) Have students discuss the success of this class project.

SAFE Lesson No. 9

TITLE OF LESSON: PUTTING LIFE INTO SHARING BOOKS

DIFFICULTY LEVEL: GRADES K–8

OBJECTIVES:

Students will:

1. Read books independently
2. Present a review of the book to the class
3. Critique book reviews
4. Analyze a book

DESCRIPTION:

Students will read books. Instead of a book report, students will be given a variety of ways to tell classmates about a book they read.

PROCEDURES:

Stimulus:

Show your students a variety of creative ways to share a book with classmates. (Tell them that standing in front of the class and telling about the best parts of the book will not be permitted.) Give them this list of suggestions for sharing books and have them brainstorm other methods of presentation.

1. Write a poem about a character in the book.
2. Write your feelings for the book in a letter.
3. Read parts of a book aloud to a younger child. Ask the child what he or she liked best about the book. Write the responses as advertising on the book jacket you make for the book.

4. Write a short play about the book. Recruit class members to be in your play, and present the play to the class.

5. Pretend you are a reporter. Select a key event in your story and write a news story about it. Find other classmates who read the same book. By working in groups, write a complete newspaper based on characters and events in the book. List newspaper parts: local news, obituaries, ads, and the like. Make sure it looks like a newspaper with headlines and columns.

6. Write a diary of one of the characters in the book. Make sure the dates and events match events in the book. Keep the diary at least a week.

7. On a day designated as Character Day, dress up like one of the characters in the book. During the "social hour," mingle with the characters and describe your role in the book.

8. Make paper-bag puppets of characters in your book. Recruit classmates to give a puppet show of the book.

9. Make a cassette tape of a commercial for your book.

10. Make a television from a box. Put slots on the sides of the box and draw scenes on rolled paper (such as shelf paper). As you roll the scenes across the TV screen, tell your classmates about the book.

Activity:

Tell students to read the list of book-sharing suggestions. After they read a book, have them select one way to share the book with classmates. Have the students schedule the book-sharing experience with you so that you can register the date, the kind of presentation, and the amount of time needed.

Follow-Up:

Have the students write reactions to these book-sharing experiences by listing the pros and cons of the activities. Compare the variety of book sharing experiences to the usual method of giving a book report. Have them tell why they may or may not have enjoyed these methods more.

Ask students to think about one of the book-sharing experiences. Tell them to select one of the books which was shared with them and write a summary of the book. Have the student who originally shared the book with the class read the summary and accept it or amend it.

Evaluation:

When listening and watching the book-sharing experiences, evaluate the accuracy of the details in the book, the creativity, and the effectiveness of the presentation (voice volume and intonation).

Still More Ideas to Try

- Recipe Recital: Have students write a favorite recipe and then read it to the class. Try having them use words from vocabulary lists as they follow the recipe format to create recipes for the following: an American, happiness, spring, creativity, a fraction, or an invention.

- Song Lyrics Limbo: In groups, have students brainstorm lists of song titles. Have students mix their own words with the lyrics of songs to create an original story, poem, or script. Challenge them to make the song lyric original coincide with a current national event.

- Idiom Dictionary: Have students compile a comprehensive class dictionary of idioms. Make sure they give both the literal and figurative definitions. Encourage them to use illustrations.

- Dictionary Diaries: Have students keep a dictionary of their own definitions for content areas. Include both the dictionary definitions and the students' interpretations of the definitions.

- Predict-a-Plot: Prior to reading a story, give students the title of the story and have them predict the plot. List all responses on butcher paper and post them in the room. Then, as you read the story, mark any statements that are accurate.

- Jeopardy: Similar to the TV game show, have students prepare a list of questions and answers that could be used in a Jeopardy game. Keep the set of questions and answers relevant to one of the difficult subjects. After groups are finished with their lists, set up team competition within the class.

Sharing Reading Orally and in Writing

When students share reading and writing, they use language in a meaningful way. Sharing reading and writing gives the students an opportunity to go beyond the classroom to use language with a variety of audiences. These audiences should represent real-life situations. Writing for the teacher, for example, is not a real-life situation, whereas writing to the editor of a newspaper is meaningful. In this section, you will find strategies that make it possible for students to share reading and writing in meaningful ways.

SAFE Lesson No. 10

TITLE OF LESSON: PERFORMING LITERATURE

DIFFICULTY LEVEL: GRADES K–8

OBJECTIVES:

Students will:

1. Read children's picture books
2. Synthesize reactions to children's books by writing scripts
3. Interpret literature before a live audience
4. Analyze the conventions of writing a play

DESCRIPTIONS:

Students will read children's picture books, discuss the stories, write scripts, and perform. They will perform before a live audience.

PROCEDURES:

Stimulus:

Bring in copies of children's picture books. Tell students that they will work in groups to rewrite the stories into play form, and they will perform this literature for primary students.

Divide the class into groups and tell each group to select a story and discuss how they could "perform" this story. Have them list characters and the number of speaking parts. Have them identify who said key speeches, as in these examples:

Snow White and the Seven Dwarfs

"Mirror, mirror on the wall; who's the fairest of them all?"

"Would you like a poison apple?"

Three Little Pigs

"I'll huff and I'll puff and I'll blow your house in."

"Little pig, little pig, let me come in."

"Not by the hair of my chinny, chin chin."

Activity:

Give students copies of a play. Have them identify the conventions followed in writing a play. Have the students write a script for the story they selected. Except for the key speaking parts, they should write the rest of the story in their own words. They can pattern the original story, but unlike a readers' theater script, they should use their own words when writing the script.

After the script is written, direct students to discuss how to perform this literature script. Have them discuss voice intonation and characterization of the characters in the story. Have them make a list of the props and costumes needed to perform for their classmates. These props and costumes should be simple for the in-class performance.

Next, the students perform for their classmates. As they perform, have classmates critique the skit by making suggestions for these criteria:

Accuracy of stories (plot)

Characterization

Voice intonation

Voice volume

Body movements

Props

Costumes

Videotape the skits so that the groups can see themselves and can take part in their classmates' evaluations of the skits.

Follow-Up:

After viewing the videotaped skits and discussing them, have the students rehearse together with their groups to make improvements. Then invite classes of primary students to your classroom stage and have the students perform for the younger children. After the performance, ask the audience to evaluate the performers, and ask them if the performances made them want to read the stories or perform the plays themselves.

Send student performers to the primary classes to perform and to act as coaches as they help the primary children perform the picture book scripts.

Evaluation:

Observe the students as they work in small groups. Complete a checklist of individual student performance in the group discussions and preparations.

While the students are giving suggestions for improving the videotaped skits, grade the skits. Base this grade on the accuracy of the plot, the acting ability, and the voice volume and intonation.

Ask the teachers of the primary students you invited to your classroom to evaluate the effectiveness of the skits presented to the primary students.

A USEFUL STRATEGY: READERS' THEATER

Readers' theater is an exciting strategy that integrates reading, thinking, oral expression, and writing. Students have fun as they take a new look at printed literature, think about its mood and messages, consider how to convey that mood through oral expression, prepare a script from the reading material, and practice reading the written words to an audience. Readers' theater encourages group participation in discussion and decision making as students plan their presentations. Students use the music of their voices to present literature to the classroom audience.

SAFE Lesson No. 11

TITLE OF LESSON: READERS' THEATER WITH DR. SEUSS

DIFFICULTY LEVEL: GRADES 3–8

OBJECTIVES:

Students will:

1. Read literature and discuss the purpose
2. Plan oral presentations of literature
3. Interpret stories read
4. Write scripts for a readers' theater presentation

DESCRIPTION:

Students will read a picture book and will write a readers' theater script based on that book. They will make an oral presentation of that script.

PROCEDURES:

Stimulus:

Bring a Dr. Seuss book to class to model how to write and present a readers' theater script. Read the story aloud to students so that they can hear it read by one person. Then show them how to write a script. Follow this format:

Narrator 1:	*The Cat in the Hat*
Narrator 2:	by Dr. Seuss
Narrator 1:	The sun did not shine. It was too wet to play.
Narrator 2:	So we sat in the house All that cold, cold, wet day.

Select students from the class and assign speaking parts for the characters. Make sure the cat, Sally, I, and the fish have lines written in dialogue form. Encourage them to experiment with oral interpretation by chanting, choral reading, and varied intonation when reading the script in their groups.

Activity:

Bring a number of Dr. Seuss books to class. Have students form groups of three or four. As a group, have them select one book. Within that group, assign a recorder, a reader, and a discussion leader. Tell each group to write a readers' theater script and to practice the voice presentation of the script. Have them present these to the class.

Follow-Up:

Have the class listen to scripts being presented by the groups. After all groups have presented, challenge the groups to exchange their script with one different from theirs and rewrite it so that it is in a different script format, as in this sample:

Narrator 1:	*The Cat in the Hat* by Dr. Seuss
Narrator 2:	The sun did not shine.
Narrator 1:	It was too late to play.
Narrator 2:	So we sat in the house
Narrators 1 & 2:	All that cold, cold wet day.

Have the groups perform the readers' theater scripts for the class.

Evaluation:

Observe how well students assume their roles within the groups. Watch and reward active involvement. Rate the oral presentations by asking the students to give an overall rating of "Yes" or "No" for the reading of the readers' theater scripts.

Read the scripts and grade how well they followed the model of script writing. Mark punctuation as well as content accuracy.

SAFE Lesson No. 12

TITLE OF LESSON: FABLES AS SCRIPTS

DIFFICULTY LEVEL: GRADES 3–10

OBJECTIVES:

Students will:

1. Read fables and discuss their morals
2. Write a readers' theater script
3. Synthesize the stories into an oral presentation for an audience

DESCRIPTION:

Students will listen to and read Aesop's Fables. They will write scripts and present these as readers' theater scripts.

PROCEDURES:

Stimulus:

Read the fable "The Fox and the Crow" aloud to the class. As you do so, use intonation and expression so that the fable comes alive for them.

The Fox and the Crow

A Fox once saw a Crow making off with a piece of cheese in its beak and made up his mind he was going to get it. "Good morning, friend Crow," he called. "I see your feathers are as black and shining and beautiful as ever. You are really a beautiful bird. It is too bad your voice is poor! If that were lovely too, you would, without question, be the Queen of Birds."

The Crow, rather indignant that the Fox doubted the beauty of her voice, began to caw at once.

Of course, the cheese dropped; and, as the Fox put his paw on it, he yelled, "I have what I wanted—and let me give you a bit of advice—Don't trust flatterers."

Show the students how to write this into a script format:

Narrator 1:	The Fox and the Crow
Narrator 2:	An Aesop Fable
Narrator 1:	A fox once saw a Crow making off with a piece of cheese in its beak and made up his mind he was going to get it.
Fox:	Good morning, friend Crow. I see your feathers are as black and shining and beautiful as ever. You are really a beautiful bird. It is too bad your voice is poor. If that were lovely too, you would, without question, be the Queen of Birds.
Narrator 2:	The Crow, rather indignant that the Fox doubted the beauty of her voice, began to caw at once.
Crow:	Caw, Caw.
Narrator 1:	Of course the cheese dropped, and the Fox put his paw on it.
Fox:	I have what I wanted—and let me give you a bit of advice—Don't trust flatterers.
All:	Don't trust flatterers.

Activity:

Select students to read this script orally to the class. Have them discuss how well the readers used voice intonation and expression. Have them get into groups of three or four and write scripts based on another fable, "The Hare and the Tortoise."

A Hare was once boasting about how fast he could run when a Tortoise, overhearing him, said, "I'll run you a race."

"Done," said the Hare, laughing to himself, "but let's get the Fox for a judge." The Fox consented and the two started. The Hare quickly outran the Tortoise, and knowing he was far ahead, lay down to take a nap.

"I can soon pass the Tortoise whenever I awaken." But unfortunately, the Hare overslept; therefore, when he awoke, though he ran his best, he found the Tortoise was already at the goal.

He had learned that "Slow and steady wins the race."

Ask them to try different methods to write this script. When the groups have finished writing the scripts, have the students read them to the class.

Follow-Up:

Have students compare the differences in the way they wrote the scripts and presented the same fable. Have the students vote to select the most entertaining readers' theater script presentation.

Bring in other fables and have the students write scripts and present them. As an added treat, have classmates guess the morals of the fables. They can also state the moral in different ways, for example, "The race does not always go to the swiftest."

Evaluation:

After several fables have been demonstrated by using readers' theater scripts, check whether the students remember the moral of each. Evaluate by giving a teacher-directed test. Read the beginning of a fable and have the students write the ending of the fable. Point out that these morals are often stated as proverbs and are widely known, part of our cultural literacy.

Give students another fable and have them write it into a script form. Grade the script for accuracy of content, form, and punctuation.

As the groups give their readers' theater presentations, have students make suggestions for improving voice intonation, volume, and expression. Students can plan a schoolwide assembly program featuring fables.

SAFE Lesson No. 13

TITLE OF LESSON: STORYTELLING
DIFFICULTY LEVEL: GRADES 4–10
OBJECTIVES:

Students will:

1. Interpret a story
2. Block out a story to tell to an audience
3. Visualize a story and tell it

DESCRIPTION:

Students will read a story and will block it out so that they can tell it to an audience.

PROCEDURES:

Stimulus:

Invite a colleague, parent, or librarian into your room to act as a storyteller. Have the storyteller tell a well-known fable or fairytale. Tell students to listen to the familiar story, paying attention to the voice intonations and gestures, which add to the effectiveness of the storytelling. Have them write what makes this experience different from listening to the story being read.

Videotape a storyteller and have students make suggestions, pro and con, after they view it, as to the effectiveness of the storyteller. Encourage them to rely on their natural feelings about what makes the storytelling interesting. As students suggest ideas, write these tips on the board:

Know the content of the story very well.

Know the characters.

Understand the conflict of the story.

Visualize the characters in the setting.

Know key sentences (dialogue) that should be repeated exactly.

Think about how body movements would enhance the story.

Activity:

Have students select a fable, children's picture book, fairytale, or personal story that they would enjoy sharing with classmates. Using notecards, have them block out the story by writing scenes, characters, conflict, and setting for the story. (When telling the story, they will not use the notecards.)

Put students into groups of four where they can practice telling their story to a small group. Have the group members help the storyteller by listening for the following:

Accuracy of story

Voice intonation

Voice volume

Creativity with story

During a second telling of the story, have them watch the presentation for the following:

Facial expressions

Body movements

Tell them to make concrete suggestions to their classmates about each of these criteria.

Follow-Up:

Have each group select its best storyteller to speak in front of the whole class. When selecting the "key" storyteller for the group, direct students to use these questions:

Did the storyteller make you think?

Did the storyteller get involved (body language)?

Did the storyteller tell the plot?

Were you able to visualize the setting and characters?

Did the storyteller seem natural?

Did the storyteller's voice enhance the story?

Were the gestures appropriate?

Did the storyteller involve the audience?

Did the storyteller establish eye contact?

As a variation of this activity, have students use slang and everyday settings to enhance such well-known nursery tales as "The Three Little Pigs." Require them to keep the original plot, but have them change the settings and characters to make it a modern tale.

Have the storytellers travel to the primary grades to tell their stories to the younger children.

Evaluation:

Observe the storytellers in the small groups. Complete a checklist for each student.

Have students respond to the list of questions given above when evaluating the "key" storyteller from each group. Complete these questions and award a grade for the students' effectiveness. The grade given to the "key" person will be given to every member of that group since the group acted as an evaluator or coach for that person.

When traveling to the primary grades, ask your colleagues to evaluate the storytellers' effectiveness with the younger audience. Have both students and colleagues use this checklist and mark "Yes" or "No" after each word as they rate whether the storyteller can tell a story in front of a large group.

Story accuracy

Creativity with story

Body movements

Facial expressions

Voice intonation

Voice volume

MORE LESSONS TO PROMOTE THE SHARING OF READING AND WRITING

Gifts of writing are excellent ways to share reading and writing. Because students are expressing their love, they are especially careful in editing to find errors and correct them. Students take an active, caring part because they want the finished product to look attractive enough to display. This interest heightens motivation and strengthens the bond between the writer and his or her audience.

SAFE Lesson No. 14

TITLE OF LESSON: MOTHER'S DAY BOOKLETS (ADAPT FOR FATHER'S DAY)

DIFFICULTY LEVEL: GRADES 3–8

OBJECTIVES:

Students will:

1. Write a paragraph, poem, or letter to a mother, a grandmother, or friend
2. Synthesize written material into a booklet
3. Edit their writing to correct errors in punctuation, grammar, spelling, and usage
4. Bind the book created

DESCRIPTION:

Each student will write a paragraph, letter, or poem. The written work will be edited, revised, and rewritten in ink or typed. It will be presented in a booklet.

PROCEDURES:

Stimulus:

Talk to the students about their need to tell their parents and loved ones that they appreciate them. Have them think of special moments they shared. Here are samples:

- Dad and I had breakfast downtown together after we took José to a soccer game. That was the first and last time we spent time alone together. I really had a good talk with Dad.
- Once a month I visit Grandmother so we can spend the day together—shopping, dining, seeing a play, or going to an amusement park.
- Mom and I clear the table and do dishes. At first I mumbled that boys should do the dishes. Now, I love the time we spend together because we talk about the day's happenings.

Tell students that they will write a poem, letter, or paragraph to a loved one. Then they will write or type it neatly in a booklet.

If possible, use a computer, as described here. Bring xeroxed sheets of Mother's Day greetings that you made by using the Print Shop for the Apple computer. This software gives you the option of creating greeting cards, stationery, and banners. Use the greeting card option. To save printing costs, make a few master copies. Cut and paste so that the design is on the front and back. Thus the design should be on all sections of the paper.

Run several copies of this design on regular 8½″ × 11″ paper. Cut these in half (4¼″ × 5½″). The students can use several half-sheets to write their messages. Bring to class a set of 4¼″ × 5½″ sheets of wallpaper. When the student-written Mother's Day sheets are sewn down the center to wallpaper, an attractive booklet comes to life. (Directions for bookbinding are in Chapter 5.)

For students who have written a short verse (six lines or fewer), use the regular greeting card you create with the software. Again, use the computer to make the master copy, and xerox sheets for classroom use.

Activity:

Have students make their own lists of special moments spent with someone they love. Have them write a paragraph or poem by using the details on that list.

When all students have written, put them into editing groups. Use several different techniques so that as many persons edit as possible during class time (see Chapter 5 for editing strategies).

Have students make a dummy booklet so they can determine how many half-sheets of xeroxed pages they will need to make their booklets. Have students write the paragraph, letter, or verse neatly in ink on the xeroxed sheets. Then have them sew the booklet to the wallpaper to complete the booklet.

Follow-Up:

If students have access to an Apple computer and the Print Shop software, they can make their own greeting card designs.

After the first booklet is completed, have students make booklets to share with other special people. Students might take a set of booklets to a convalescent hospital near the school.

On the students' return to school after giving the booklet to someone, have them answer the following questions:

How did your mom (the recipient) react to this gift?

How did the other family members react?

How do you feel about yourself?

Had you ever told your mom (anyone) how much you care about her before making this gift?

When could you give "gifts of writing" again?

Evaluation:

Look at the Mother's Day booklets and evaluate the neatness of the booklet (binding and handwriting or typing). Read the content of the paragraph, letter, or verse, noting specific details about that child's relationship with his or her mother. Help students eliminate such trite statements as:

You brought me into this world.

You're so special to me.

You're the best from all the rest.

SAFE Lesson No. 15

TITLE OF LESSON: FATHER'S DAY STATIONERY (ADAPT FOR OTHER PURPOSES)

DIFFICULTY LEVEL: GRADES 3–8

OBJECTIVES:

Students will:

1. Write a letter
2. Use editing techniques to analyze spelling, usage, grammar, and punctuation errors, and correct them
3. Construct a "gift of writing" for someone special

DESCRIPTION:

Students will write a letter to their fathers.

PROCEDURES:

Stimulus:

Tell the students that they will write a letter to express their love and appreciation. Have them brainstorm special moments they share with their fathers (or another man who is important to them).

Have students use the Print Shop software to make stationery. Xerox several different pattern choices and make these available to the students. Tell the students that they will write their letters on this stationery in ink after their letters have gone through the editing process. Tell them that the letter will either be framed or mounted on a wall plaque.

Activity:

Have the students list special moments that they spend with their fathers or have them write a letter to a man they admire. Have them incorporate specific details in the letter.

Use several editing strategies so that the letter is read by as many classmates as possible. Then have the students rewrite the letter in ink in their best handwriting on the stationery.

After the letter has been checked for neatness and correctness, have students mount the letter on a wall plaque by using decoupage glue, or frame the letter in an 8″ × 10″ frame.

Follow-Up:

Have the students listen to the letters being read aloud and point out sentences or ideas they think are effective. Send the best letters to the local newspaper for possible publication in the Father's Day edition.

Have students suggest other ways to present their letters to a loved one.

Have students write letters to other special people in their lives. Students could write to elderly people in a nearby convalescent hospital or a Senior Citizens' Center.

Evaluation:

After students write the letter in ink on the stationery, approve the letter for neatness and correctness of content. Have a student rewrite the letter before it is framed or mounted on wood.

Have the students report how their fathers reacted when they received the gift of writing.

Still More Ideas to Try

- Choral Chanting: In groups, students will read and compose lines that can be chanted. Have them chant these lines to other groups in the class before they perform for the whole class.

- Visualization: Tell students to close their eyes and think about something that happened yesterday. Have students write what they see, using action verbs only. This should be a list of verbs or verb phrases. Then they can write complete sentences.

- Creative Dramatics: Have the students freeze their bodies into positions that stimulate conversation and dialogue writing. Have two people freeze at the same time, but do not let them plan their moves. Have them freeze independent of each other. When the student writers look at them, they will look like a pair who should be conversing with each other. Have the students write the conversation. Have students observe the punctuation of dialogue in a story and check their dialogues for correct punctuation.

- Frame-a-Story: Have students mount their favorite story with a corresponding photo in a picture frame.

- Children's Literature Grab Bag: Have students talk about the familiar ending of a story. After they have had a chance to brainstorm possible endings, have them write a different beginning for the same ending.

- Poetry Pocket: Read humorous limericks and have students write their own. Before they write, have them tell you the humorous endings.

- Enacting Characters: Have students dressed like nursery rhyme characters chant the rhyme. Dressed like a character in a children's picture book, they can tell key passages from the book. For example, if a student is dressed like the cat in *The Cat and the Hat* by Dr. Seuss, then the story will be told from the point of view of the cat.

- Design the Stationery: Have students volunteer to draw designs for stationery.

Resources:

Lissner, Rupert, and Apple Computer Inc. *Appleworks Integrated*. Software, Apple Computer, v. 1.22. USA. 1983.

Balsam, David, and Kahn, Martin. *The Print Shop*. San Rafael, CA: Broderbund Software Inc., 1984.

Balsam, David, and Kahn, Martin. *The Graphics Library*. San Rafael, CA: Broderbund Software, Inc., 1984.

Tchudi, Stephen and Susan. *Gifts of Writing: Creative Projects with Words and Art*. New York: Charles Scribner's Sons, 1982.

Focusing on a Theme: Love

Why teach a theme unit on love? Answer that question by looking at the confused messages young people get by watching sex and violence on television. Teaching a unit on love will give the students an understanding that there is a peaceful way to interact in this world. A unit on love will expose them to movies, books, and songs that show different kinds of love: love of country, love of family, love of peers, love of self, love of life, and love of nature.

Students need to clarify the role of "love" in their own lives. They need strategies to help them identify, as well as express, their love. The following unit will give you materials, learning activities, and resources to help you guide students in clarifying the value of love in their own lives. This theme is suitable for all levels.

LOVE

Objectives:

By working with this unit, students will be able to:

1. Define the different kinds of love
2. Write letters, paragraphs, or poems to express their love
3. Read stories about love
4. Discuss the meaning of love with peers
5. Listen to song lyrics and view movies about love
6. Make "gifts of love"

7. Tell each other the meanings of love

8. Compare and contrast the kinds of love

9. Think about the experiences of fictitious characters as they deal with conflicts of love

10. Discuss fictitious situations about love and compare their own circumstances

11. Use role playing in impromptu problem-solving situations

Getting Started:

The materials you need are the following:

1. Children's picture books

2. Literature books (anthologies)

3. Records

4. Tapes

5. Films

6. Video cassettes

7. Arts/crafts supplies: glue, pens, decoupage glue, wall plaques

8. Stationery

9. Video equipment

Use one of these methods to motivate student interest:

1. Tell the students that you want them to explore the theme of love. Begin by introducing stories that present conflicts concerning love. Scour the literature anthologies. Go to the library and use the *Book-finder* (two volumes), which categorizes children's literature according to subject. Summaries are included as well as recommended age levels. Another recommended source is the *Children's Catalog*, which prints bibliographic information, summaries, and prices of children's book. Sharing literature and discussing its contents are two strategies that lead the students to read, write, discuss, role play, and think about love.

2. Ignite discussions about love by using video cassettes, films, and song lyrics. Stir student expressions of love with student-made projects. Keep your eye on the TV and your ear to the radio as you look and listen for videos or songs that fit the "love" theme. Inspire students to be "scavengers of love" as they recommend songs or videos about love. (Make sure you preview everything before sharing with students.) Once the classroom climate is set so that they talk openly about love, involve them in student-made projects: framed letters on stationery,

greeting cards, wall plaques, and booklets. Model arts and crafts projects by asking each student to give a "how-to-make-a-gift-of-love" speech.

The length of time required for this unit is two to three weeks (with demonstration speeches, five weeks). This unit can be adapted for all grade levels.

Learning Activities for the Students:

- Real Toys: Read *The Velveteen Rabbit* by Margery Williams (Doubleday, 1926; Simon and Schuster, 1983). Discuss the love this boy had for his toy rabbit and the wisdom shared by the skin horse. Talk about how the concept of loving the stuffed animal until the fur rubs off relates to humans. The following concepts should come from the discussion:

  New friends are like new toys; they seem exciting, but you don't know how long they will last.

  People rush to get the latest gadget, yet they disregard what they know is "good."

  Like the toys in the toyroom, there are many different people in this world—some snobs and "plastic." How do you deal with them?

  Take comfort that you may feel insignificant and commonplace, because if you have the "real" love of one, you have treasured love.

  As these are listed on the board, have the students write them and then place a number by each concept. On another paper, have them write the number and write how this "insight" from the book relates to experiences they have had with people.

  Write on the board these powerful sentences, spoken by the velveteen rabbit as he lies in the sack with the rest of the junk:

  "Of what use was it to be loved and lose one's beauty and become Real if it all ended like this? And a tear, a real tear, trickled down his shabby velvet nose and fell to the ground."

  Introduce the words *vulnerability* and *risk* to students. Have them list reasons why we need to take risks in order to love someone, especially when we could get hurt.

  Give these writing assignments:

  Write about a toy you loved as a child.

  Write about a time when you shared the same experiences as the velveteen rabbit.

Write about whether your ideas about love have changed after reading this story.

Compare a child's love to an adult's love.

Let the students get into groups to discuss these topics. As they prepare to write, tell them they need to select specific lines from the story and include them in their paragraph. Also tell them to support any ideas with personal experiences.

- Giving Tree Love: Read Shel Silverstein's *The Giving Tree* (New York: Harper, 1964) aloud to the students. Assign them to groups and have them list questions for writing and discussion, such as the following:

    Was the tree's love for the boy like a mother's love?

    Was the man looking for love?

    Is the ability to give a major part of loving?

    What were ways that the tree showed love?

    Do you show love or take love?

    Are you a giver or a taker?

    Why do we travel away from our homes?

    Once we leave home, do we lose the love that is there?

    How are giving and loving related?

    Do you need to show love more?

- Song Lyrics Love: Have the students form groups and have them brainstorm titles that have the word *love* in them.

    I Just Called to Say I Love You

    Love, Love Me, Do

    Precious Love

    Love Makes the World Go Round

    All You Need Is Love

Have them string these titles together to form a paragraph or use one title as the topic sentence about which to write a paragraph. Have them create song titles that reflect different kinds of love (lost love, vulnerability of love, love of country, love of parents).

- Videos: Although there are complaints that children watch too much television, selective viewing of video cassettes can be a worthwhile experience. Many movies that present conflicts about love are very touching and carry a powerful message; they are contemporary. A trip to a video rental store will provide you with an endless list of movies that relate to love. Ask the clerk for suggestions and then preview the tapes. After the students have seen the movie, have them work in groups to discuss the conflict. Have them draw their own conclusions about how they would have solved the problem. Have them role play different solutions to the conflict which they viewed.

- Stationery Love: Encourage students to express the love they feel for their parents. Have students make stationery decorated with gadget printing or other designs. Tell the students that they will write a poem, paragraph, or letter to a loved one. Tell them they will do this in their very best handwriting so that the message can be framed and placed in the family's home with pride.

- Teacher Thank You: Have students think of one teacher they love because that teacher really touched their lives. Have them make a list under the words *Thank You*. Make sure they list specific reasons they felt that teacher's love, such as:

> He smiled at me every day.
>
> She had us dress up like prairie people.
>
> He took us on field trips.
>
> She helped me with math after school.

Have them express their love and appreciation to that teacher by writing a letter.

- Mothers: Bring in the book, *The Way Mothers Are* by Miriam Schlein (Whitman, 1963). This story helps the anxious child understand that, although a parent may not like what the child does, the parent still loves the child. Put students into small groups and have them discuss how they would deal with the anxious feelings this child had. Have them list how they know their parents love them. Ask them to write a paragraph about love between children and parents.

More Books to Explore:

These books can be used by teachers for modeling lessons.

Waber, Bernard. *Nobody is Perfick*. Houghton Mifflin, 1971.

Anglund, Joan W. *A Friend Is Someone Who Likes You*. Harcourt, 1958.

Brown, Margaret W. *The Important Book*. Harper.

Bulla, Clyde Robert. *White Bird*. Thomas Crowell, 1966.

Cifford, Ethel Rosenberg. *The Year of the Three-Legged Deer*. Houghton Mifflin, 1972.

Eyerly, Jeannette Hyde. *More Than a Summer Love*. Lippincott, 1962.

Gripe, Maria Kristina. *The Night Daddy*. Delacorte, 1968.

Hall, Lynn. *Stray*. Follett, 1974.

Howard, Moses L. *The Ostrich Chase*. Holt, 1974.

Kerr, M. E. *If I Love You, Am I Trapped Forever?* Harper, Row.

Killilea, Marie Lyons. *With Love From Karen*. Prentice-Hall, 1963.

Raskin, Ellen. *Figgs and Phantoms*. Dutton, 1974.

Schlein, Miriam. *The Way Mothers Are*. Whitman, 1963.

Stinetorf, Louise Allender. *A Charm for Paco's Mother*. Day, 1965.

Zolotow, Charlotte, *Big Sister and Little Sister*. Harper, 1966.

Evaluation:

The learning activities can be evaluated as follows:

- Group Checklist: Complete a checklist of behaviors observed while students participate in discussion groups. Observe for active participation by all students.
- Rally in the Alley: Use a "check in the margin" method for evaluating the stationery projects. Students cannot prepare these as a gift until the writing (content, form, and handwriting) on the stationery is perfect.
- Finished Projects: Grade the overall appearance of the projects (neatness, clarity of the written assignment, creativity.)
- Others: Use the editing techniques and suggestions for evaluation (Chapter 5) for grading student writing.

The whole unit can be evaluated by students. Ask them to write about what they learned through this focus on love. Have them include a final paragraph discussing the value of the study and what they thought was the best activity.

Exploring Further

In addition to the resources listed in the research summary, these materials will provide more ideas to use in your classroom.

Brown, Rosellen, et al. *The Whole Word Catalogue 1: A Handbook of Writing Ideas for Teachers*. Teachers & Writers Collaborative, 1983.

Christensen, Jane, ed. *Your Reading: A Booklist for Junior High and Middle School Students*. NCTE, 1983.

Lamme, Linda, ed. *Learning to Love Literature: Preschool through Grade 3*. NCTE, 1981.

Moss, Joy. *Focus Units in Literature: A Handbook for Elementary School Teachers*. NCTE, 1984.

Sims, Rudine. *Shadow and Substance: Afro-American Experience in Contemporary Children's Fiction*. NCTE, 1982.

Sloyer, Shirlee. *Readers' Theatre: Story Dramatization in the Classroom*. NCTE, 1982.

Tiedt, Iris, et al. *Teaching Writing in K–8 Classrooms*. Prentice-Hall, 1983.

Tiedt, Pamela, and Tiedt, Iris. *Multicultural Teaching: Activities, Resources, and Information*, 2nd ed. Allyn and Bacon, 1986.

5

Strengthening Reading/ Writing Connections

Reading and writing are closely interrelated in many ways. As we have already noted, both depend on a strong thinking and oral language foundation. Both also involve the relationships of sounds and symbols that children learn in beginning reading and writing instruction. In addition, reading and writing are connected through literature. As we teach students to read and write with increasing competence, it makes sense to help them take advantage of all of these relationships.

In this chapter, we emphasize helping students learn to read like writers as they observe how writers use language. Students can then apply their observations to their own writing—their production of literature. We stress the transaction between reader and writer as both engage in making meaning.

The activities presented in this chapter are grouped as follows:

Writing Begins with Thinking and Leads to Reading

Learning to Write by Reading

Writing to Be Read

Implementing the Program

Early research has more commonly related reading to listening and related writing to speaking. Currently, however, researchers are finding that strong relationships exist between reading and writing and that making these connections clearer to students may facilitate their engaging in more thoughtful transactions as they play the alternate roles of reader and/or writer. Pertinent findings include:

1. Reading and writing abilities are correlated; generally, good readers are good writers and good writers are good readers.
2. Better writers tend to read more books than do less able writers.
3. Better readers and writers see themselves as being good at reading and writing; therefore, they engage in reading and writing independently.
4. Additional reading may be as effective in improving writing as actual practice in writing.
5. Using children's literature as a prewriting stimulus improves students' free writing.
6. Writing activities assist students in retaining and understanding instructional material.

Selected Resources

The following resources add to our understanding of the relationships between reading and writing and the acquisition of literacy.

Loban, Walter. *Language Development: Kindergarten through Grade Twelve*. National Council of Teachers of English, 1976.

Petersen, Bruce T., ed. *Convergences: Transactions in Reading and Writing*. National Council of Teachers of English, 1986.

Stock, P. *Forum: Reflections on Theory and Practice in the Teaching of Writing*. Boynton/Cook, 1983.

Stotsky, Sandra. "Research on Reading/Writing Relationships: A Synthesis and Suggested Directions." In *Composing and Comprehending*, ed. Julie Jensen. National Conference on Research in English, 1984.

Writing Begins with Thinking and Leads to Reading

Getting started—filling that blank page with meaningful words—can be the most difficult task for a writer. You, the teacher, have the opportunity to motivate students to trust their innermost thoughts—a challenging task, indeed! You possess the skills needed to make students believe in themselves so that they want to write. No, this is not an easy task, but once you arm yourself with a positive attitude and exciting materials, your students will do the thinking and the creating.

Begin by collecting interesting pictures, books, and clippings; become a scavenger of stimuli. In other words, you need to gather reading and listening materials, visual objects, and problem-solving strategies to stimulate student thinking and to make them want to write. You need to equip the students with strategies for attacking that threatening blank page. This section presents ideas designed to help students begin writing successfully.

A USEFUL STRATEGY: CLUSTERING

Clustering is a prewriting technique that helps the writer discover his or her ideas about a topic and to begin to organize them. Students write as many associations as possible related to a specific topic so that they see their thoughts on paper. As their ideas begin to cluster, they can choose from the "bubbled ideas" and write about some of the ideas generated. Most writers are surprised to find that they have many more thoughts about a given topic than they realized. This is an excellent strategy for helping students become aware of their thinking processes (metacognition).

SAFE Lesson No. 1

TITLE OF LESSON: CLUSTERING AROUND A ONE-WORD STIMULUS

DIFFICULTY LEVEL: GRADES 2–10

OBJECTIVES:

Students will:

1. Write associations for a one-word stimulus
2. Select words to group around a given word
3. Write a story or paragraph after they have clustered
4. Discuss associations for a given word
5. Interpret the associations

DESCRIPTION:

Students look at a given word. Together, on the board, they write associations for that word. As they develop a cluster about this word, they discover varied meanings and experiences associated with the word. Then students cluster independently about their own word. Finally, they write a paragraph or story based on the clustering.

PROCEDURES:

Stimulus

Tell the students that they have many ideas in their heads about which to write. Before they start writing, they can help themselves by getting all their ideas about the topic on paper first. They can then look at all the ideas and pick one idea or a group of closely related ideas to write about.

First, ask the students to contribute ten words. List these words on the board as the students call them out.

stone	clothes
blue	rock
store	grass
house	teacher
school	parents

Select one of these words and put a circle around it. Have the students think of that word and tell you anything they associate with the word. Students might think of any ideas triggered by the given word, such as:

Another word similar to the one selected

An experience

A phrase

Synonyms or antonyms

Proper nouns associated with it

Any memory association

As soon as a student gives you an association, write the word on the board, drawing a circle around the new word and hooking it to the center word. Your clustering design will resemble this example, which began with *blue*.

Whenever a student gives you a word that is related to a word that was already circled, then you connect it to that word. Have the classmates contribute to the cluster.

As they continue clustering together, students will realize that some clusters may have only a few links in them because they cannot think of other examples, whereas other clusters will include several ideas as they enthusiastically add more and more to that idea. This indicates to them that they have identified a clustering of ideas they could write about because they have a lot to say about that topic, whereas less developed clusters reflect a lack of information or interest.

After the students have completed the clustering on the board, have them select one of the other words and cluster ideas around that word on paper at their desks.

Tell them to look at their notes and the example on the board and follow the same procedure. Walk around the classroom to monitor completion of the cluster correctly.

Activity:

After students have identified a cluster that is significantly interesting to them, have them put a box around the set of ideas so they know which cluster will be written in paragraph form. Have them look at the set of ideas and write a paragraph.

Follow-Up:

After you have given enough time for students to cluster and write, put them into pairs so that they can check each other's work. Have them discuss with each other what they plan to write about and how the cluster helped them pick a topic.

While in pairs, the students should check to see that they have put word groups in the appropriate cluster. For example, the common strand that is pulling the cluster of words together may be *songs.* Thus, all the phrases on that particular cluster should be excerpts from songs that have something to do with the word *blue,* as in this example:

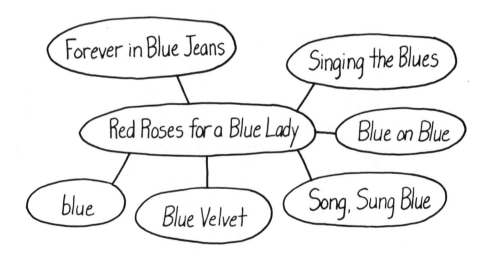

Evaluation:

This exercise helps students learn how to categorize and organize their thoughts. In addition, they have enough related examples, incidents, or facts to write a well-organized paragraph. Read the students' clusters and put a check by any associations that are not in the appropriate cluster.

While the students are working in pairs and groups, observe their active involvement while completing the cluster. Tell them that each group member must have a chance to contribute associations for the center word.

Read the individual paragraphs and compare them to the cluster that is submitted with the paragraph. Tell students that they will be evaluated on whether the ideas belong with the paragraph.

SAFE Lesson No. 2

TITLE OF LESSON: WRITING A PARAGRAPH AFTER CLUSTERING

DIFFICULTY LEVEL: GRADES 4–8

OBJECTIVES:

Students will:

1. Put key concepts into categories
2. Write a paragraph
3. Compare clusters
4. Synthesize associations into one cluster

DESCRIPTION:

Students use clustering as a brainstorming and organizational strategy. Then they build an expository paragraph around one of the clusters of ideas.

PROCEDURES:

This lesson builds on the preceding lesson.

Stimulus:

Have students observe the clustering they did about the color *blue* in the preceding lesson. Have them identify the different categories of ideas developed through making free associations.

Help them identify the characteristics of the words that fit into one cluster or category. For example, the words are closely related, and you can identify a key word that ties them together.

Have them check this cluster to see if it has been completed satisfactorily.

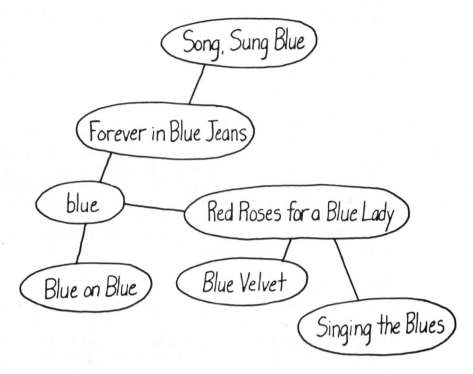

Ask the following questions:

Are all the words closely related? (Yes)

What key word/words tie the cluster together? (Songs)

Then ask students to compose a topic sentence about this cluster. The words *song* and *blue* should be in the topic sentence. The cluster consists of examples of songs that have the word *blue* in them.

Write the topic sentence on the board; for example:

Many song titles contain the word *blue*.

Now tell the students that writing the paragraph is just a matter of using sentence structure and mechanics to talk about the ideas included in this specific cluster. Have students suggest sentences as you write them on the board beneath the topic sentence. Make sure all ideas are included.

Activity:

Have students number off by 5 or 6, with each number being assigned a topic around which to cluster. Print the following list of topics on the board.

1. grass
2. kitchen
3. school
4. book
5. mother
6. television

Each person clusters around the word assigned to his or her number. After clustering, each student checks the associations written to see that they are related. Then they examine one of the clusters that is more fully developed. After determining the key word that ties the ideas together, each student writes a paragraph about the cluster. They should begin with a topic sentence that includes the assigned word and the key word they identified.

Follow-Up:

Have students form groups according to the word assigned. Those who clustered around the word *school* would form one group, and students who used the word *grass* would form a different group.

While in their groups, have students look at each other's clusters and compare the variety of clusters that spin out from the key word. Have them discuss each other's clusters, noting ideas that they had not thought of for their own clusters. Have them read their paragraphs aloud to each other. Have each group select one student to read his or her paragraph aloud to the class.

Evaluation:

Have each group's paragraph read aloud to the class. After hearing the paragraph, students should give the paper an "A" if it followed the organization that was indicated in the cluster that was submitted with the paragraph.

When students hear a paragraph that did not follow the cluster, have them identify the ideas that did not belong to the cluster. Write those words on the bottom of the paper and have the author of the paragraph remove the words that do not belong. Have that individual write another paragraph that does follow the cluster.

A USEFUL STRATEGY: VENN DIAGRAM

The Venn Diagram is another useful strategy to get students started in writing about a topic. This diagram is an organizational tool designed to help students separate the similarities and differences between two topics. As a prewriting device, it helps students think and organize before they decide what they will write.

SAFE Lesson No. 3

TITLE OF LESSON: INTRODUCING THE VENN DIAGRAM

DIFFICULTY LEVEL: GRADES 3–8

OBJECTIVES:

Students will:

1. Select key words
2. Set up a Venn Diagram
3. State the similarities and differences between topics
4. Compare information in the Venn Diagrams

DESCRIPTION:

Students will use a Venn Diagram to help them organize their thinking. This procedure will help them list similarities and differences.

PROCEDURES:

Stimulus:

Sketch a Venn Diagram on the board.

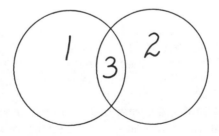

Tell the students that the place where the two circles overlap (3) is where we list the similarities between two topics. The individual circles (1 and 2) represent the examples, incidents, facts, or reasons that are unique only to that topic.

Have the students suggest pairs of words that have similarities and differences. Here are some examples:

dog   cat
fall   summer
teacher   student
car   bike
Mother   Dad

Direct the students to work in pairs. Tell the pairs to select any two words and put them into a Venn Diagram. Caution each pair to think specifically about the unique characteristics and similarities of the two words, as in this example:

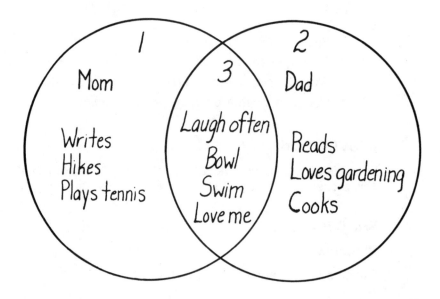

Activity:

Have the students form groups of four and compare their Venn Diagrams. Tell them to check the accuracy of the information within the spaces. They might, for example, tell a classmate if a word is supposed to be in the "overlapped" space. Tell the students to write three paragraphs from this diagram that show the comparison and contrast of the two words. Paragraph 1 will be about Topic 1, paragraph 2 will be about Topic 2, and paragraph 3 will be about both, using ideas in the "overlapped" area.

Follow-Up:

Have the students form teams of six members each. From within the team, decide which Venn Diagram should be put on the board. Have the team captain sketch the Venn Diagram on the board. All team captains should be at the board at the same time so that all teams have a Venn Diagram on the board. At the signal, any team can challenge a Venn Diagram. If the diagram is perfect and all teams agree that it is, then the team gets ten points. Other teams can pick up additional points (two for each idea) for any other ideas they can add to the diagram.

After the scores have been tabulated for the accuracy of the Venn Diagram, have the teams enter their three-paragraph essays into competition. Have each team select one essay that reflects the best work of the team. Have each team select one member who will read this essay aloud to the class. The class will award points based on the content of the essays.

Evaluation:

Observe the teams and give them a grade for their performance. Listen to how the teams awarded points for the essays and tell the students how your evaluation of the essays compares with their remarks. Give each essay a grade which will be shared by all team members.

SAFE Lesson No. 4

TITLE OF LESSON: VENN AND HEROES

DIFFICULTY LEVEL: GRADES 3–10

OBJECTIVES:

Students will:

1. Review the characteristics of heroes in social studies
2. Complete a Venn Diagram for two different personalities
3. Identify similarities and differences between two personalities
4. Write comparison and contrast paragraphs

DESCRIPTION:

Students will read about social studies personalities. They will use the Venn Diagram to organize their thinking about the similarities and differences between two different personalities. They will then write a comparison/contrast essay.

PROCEDURES:

Stimulus:

Have the students check the index of a social studies book to find historical figures in the book. Have them list at least ten personalities to discuss and write about.

Give students five notecards on which to write the names of personalities whom they think they know after having read the textbook. Collect the notecards and shuffle them together.

Pick two cards out of the stack and write the names on the board. Model the Venn Diagram with the students by having the entire class participate in completing this diagram together.

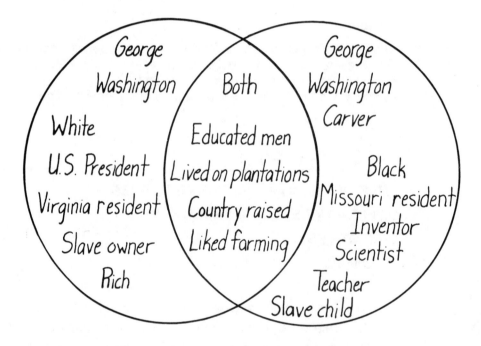

Activity:

After the class successfully completes the Venn Diagram together, put the class into groups of three and have each group select four note-cards from the stack. From those four notecards, tell the group to select two personalities and complete a Venn Diagram together.

After the classroom activity has been completed, instruct the students that their homework assignment is to take any two social studies personalities and complete a Venn Diagram for them. Then ask them to write a three-paragraph essay:

Paragraph #1:   Write about personality #1 only

Paragraph #2:   Write about personality #2 only

Paragraph #3:   Write about the similarities between #1 and #2

Follow-Up:

Make this a competitive activity by challenging the groups to finish and race to the chalkboard to put their Venn Diagrams on the board. The team's Venn Diagram is evaluated by the classmates who give the team two points for each accurate informational item placed in the correct space of the diagram.

Once a team's diagram has been evaluated and scored by the classmates, the other teams can earn points for any additional information that is accurate.

Collect the students' three-paragraph essays. At random, select a few to read aloud to the class. Have the classmates rate the paper according to these criteria:

- Paragraph #1: Was this paragraph about one social studies personality? Did the writer include at least four characteristics about the person? (Count the details and award one point for each new detail. Keep track of the points for that paragraph.)
- Paragraph #2: Use the same criteria as Paragraph #1.
- Paragraph #3: Does this paragraph include information about the two personalities in paragraphs 1 and 2? Are the personalities being compared? (Count the details—what is similar and different between the two persons.)

Evaluation:

Add the total points for the essay. These points are awarded for details that would be a direct result of using the Venn Diagram accurately.

Award ten bonus points if the paper is enjoyable to listen to (the language is colorful).

Score the essays and give that score to the entire team of the person who wrote the paper. Continue to select papers at random until all teams have one paper representing a team. If you randomly choose another paper for a team that has already received a score, return the paper to your stack.

Observe the individual performance in the group activity. Give an "active participation" grade for each team member.

Still More Ideas to Try

The above lessons should illustrate that getting started requires brainstorming. Although the Venn Diagram and clustering are two useful strategies, anything a writer does to get a "stream of ideas" on paper prior to tackling a specific form (such as story, paragraph, or letter) is a necessary prewriting activity. Here are other suggestions for getting started.

- President Game: Have students select two presidents. Tell them to work independently to complete a Venn Diagram for the two presidents. After they have finished, have them tell the names of the presidents they selected. Then group them according to similar presidents. Within the groups, have them talk about whether they had the same characteristics about that person in their Venn Diagrams even though they had not worked together prior to completing the diagrams. Have them write a three-paragraph essay about these presidents.

- Career Comparison: Place the students in groups of three and have them think of the various careers at the school site (custodian, cook, secretary, teacher, principal, aide). Tell them to select two different careers and complete a Venn Diagram, then write a three-paragraph essay about these careers.

- Peanut Cluster: Give each student a small paper cup full of peanuts. Tell each student to look at the peanuts and cluster the word *peanuts*. Remind them to include similar words, experiences, or ideas that the key word brings to their minds. Allow them to eat while they work.

- Shoe Sale: Ask students to bring a shoe to class. Tell them to look for an unusual shoe (unusual in color, shape, style, or size). Have the students form groups of three or four. As a group, have them prepare an advertising campaign or a commercial where they sell two or more of these shoes.

- Poster Pull: Have students pull out ideas for a writing assignment by looking at a poster of scenery. You can use posters several times to stimulate writing by narrowing the assignment. For example, have them look at the poster and use only the scene in the poster. Have them put themselves in the scene in the poster and write about their own adventures there. Another use of the poster is to have them pull out two or three objects in the poster and write about those objects.

- Sound Effects: Bring in instrumental music that creates a mood. Dim the lights and have the students make a list of what they are feeling. Turn on the lights, stop the tape, and have students describe a setting.

- Song Title Tilt: Use song titles to get students thinking and writing. On the board, have the students write as many song titles as possible in a timed five-minute segment. After the board is full of titles, have each student pick one title and cluster all words, experiences, and memories associated with the title. Then have them write a paragraph about the title. After everyone has completed the paragraph, take a poll to find out how many of them wrote paragraphs that had nothing to do with songs or that song. This will demonstrate that the title is an interesting stimulus that takes them beyond the song itself.

Learning to Write by Reading

This section shows you useful strategies for helping your students learn to write by reading. Reading is an excellent springboard for the act of writing because reading serves many functions. First, reading gives your students necessary information so that they can form an opinion. Once that opinion is formed, they should write. Students can use information gathering as a primary reason to read, and their writing will be filled with more details.

Second, reading provides an environment for brainstorming, which makes the students "active learners" who strive to share opinions and attitudes that may have been buried in their subconscious prior to the reading and brainstorming.

Third, by reading, students are exposed to excellent models of form and style in language. The conventions of language (capitalization, punctuation, etc.) are learned more easily as the students imitate a writing style that is very similar to the style they read. Reading is one of the most powerful prewriting activities.

A USEFUL STRATEGY: PATTERNING

Patterning is imitation. Reading materials to be patterned are numerous. Every time you pick up something and say, "Wow, I wish I had written that!" you are selecting material that could be patterned. For classroom use, patterning can be an effective way to teach anything from descriptive settings in a short story to the proper use of a semi-colon. With patterning, you could be imitating the style, the mechanics, the grammar, the dialect, the usage, and the consistent spelling. The reading material you select will dictate how you can use it as a patterning tool. The following lessons demonstrate patterning methods.

SAFE Lesson No. 5

TITLE OF LESSON: COMMAS, JUST FOR YOU

DIFFICULTY LEVEL: GRADES 2–8

OBJECTIVES:

Students will:

1. Use the comma correctly with compound sentences
2. Write a compound sentence pattern
3. Give an oral response to the beginning of a compound sentence
4. Recite the pattern of a story
5. Critique each other's compound sentences

DESCRIPTION:

Students will use the comma correctly in compound sentences after they pattern the sentences from Mercer Mayer's *Just For You.*

PROCEDURES:

Stimulus:

Bring a copy of Mercer Mayer's *Just For You* (Golden Press) to class. Involve the students in oral language by having them listen to the story.

Next, have them participate. Read the first part of the sentence. Stop reading right after the conjunction *but.* Wait for classmates to contribute another sentence to form a compound sentence. Here are some student samples:

> This morning I wanted to make breakfast just for you, but *the eggs were too slippery.*

> This morning I wanted to make breakfast just for you, but
> I overslept.
> my alarm clock didn't go off.
> the cold cereal was stale.
> the school bus was waiting for me.

Continue this procedure until you have completed the book.

Activity:

Have the students work in pairs as they write endings for each sentence. To assure that they are imitating a pattern correctly, make sure they write the complete compound sentence, including the comma. If they follow the pattern already set in the book, they will write compound sentences automatically.

> Mayer's:
> I wanted to wash the floor just for you, but the soap was too bubbly.

Student's:
> I wanted to wash the floor just for you, but I didn't wear my sponge roller skates.

Follow-Up:

Have the class divide into three teams. Tell the team captains to write the compound sentences on the board. Give them a five-minute time limit. Each team will have ten points awarded for a well-written sentence, and five points awarded for the accurate use of a comma. When a team challenges the accuracy of a sentence, they must give the correct answer themselves before they can earn the points.

Evaluation:

Ask the students to write a paragraph about doing something special for a person they love. Tell them that you will award ten points each time a compound sentence is used correctly.

SAFE Lesson No. 6

TITLE OF LESSON: RHYMING PATTERN

DIFFICULTY LEVEL: GRADES 2–8

OBJECTIVES:

Students will:

1. Chant a rhyming story
2. Write a rhyming pattern of their own
3. Categorize different objects
4. Analyze each other's rhyming patterns

DESCRIPTION:

Students will listen to a rhyming story. They will repeat the rhyme orally. Then they will pattern this story by writing their own rhyming story with a different category.

PROCEDURES:

Stimulus:

Read the book *"I Can't" Said the Ant* written by Polly Cameron (Scholastic). The story is about a teapot that fell off the counter and broke. All the objects in the kitchen work together to return her to the counter. The rhyme is so interesting that the students enjoy imitating it. Here is an excerpt.

> "What's all the clatter?" asked the platter.
> "Teapot fell," said the dinner bell.
> "Teapot broke," said the artichoke.

After you have read this to the students a few times, let them repeat the rhyme in unison.

Activity:

Arrange the class into groups of four and have them rewrite some of the rhymes, for example:

Original: "Is she dead?" asked the bread.

Student: "Lost her head?" asked the bread.

For this exercise, make sure they change the dialogue and not the speaker.
Have the students list the speakers in this book:

platter	dinner bell
artichoke	mop
bread	steak
trout	kettle
glass	knife

These are just a few. After they have listed the speakers, tell them to write the common category for these words (kitchen items). Let the students discover this for themselves.
In their small groups, have them use the clustering method with a new category. Cluster objects or food that belong to that new category.

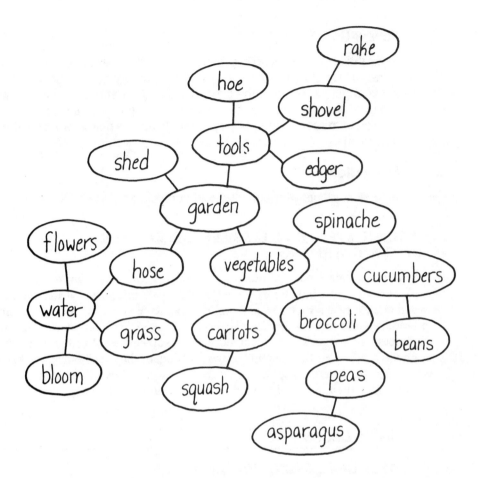

These clustered objects become the speakers of the new rhyme book the students will write. Before they can begin, they need to have a tragedy appropriate to that category. (In other words, a teapot would not be in the garden.) Have the whole class brainstorm together. On the board, list suggestions made by the students, such as:

Break in the rake

Slow hoe

Holey hose

Zits on the zuchinni

Now ask each group to follow the pattern in *"I Can't" Said the Ant* and have them write their own rhyming story.

Follow-Up:

Since the class is working in groups, you will have six or seven rhyming stories. Have students read their books to primary grade students. Ask the youngsters to select the best rhyming story and then reward that group by sending them to that classroom as "tutors for the day." Their mission is to read to the primary students and to help them write their own rhymes.

Evaluation:

Give all students who participate in compiling a book a grade of A.

A USEFUL STRATEGY: LITERATURE MODELS FOR GOOD WRITING

Selecting excellent models of literature stimulates students to write what they read. Your role is to find literary models that provide imagery, stylistic devices, varied grammatical structures, and different points of view. Involving students in reading these literary models enhances writing skills. Plan your lessons to encompass the author's style included with the objectives of your lesson. For example, if you want the students to write dialogue, they read dialogue; if you want them to write description, they read passages of excellent imagery. In essence, give them a model to read, and they will learn to write.

SAFE Lesson No. 7

TITLE OF LESSON: WRITING DESCRIPTIONS

DIFFICULTY LEVEL: GRADES 4–12

OBJECTIVES:

Students will:

1. Read literary passages aloud
2. Analyze stylistic devices in the passages
3. Compare and contrast styles
4. Write descriptive paragraphs
5. Identify metaphor

DESCRIPTION:

Students will read a passage and will model that style in their own writing.

PROCEDURES:

Stimulus:

Read the following descriptive passage of Ichabod Crane from Washington Irving's *Legend of Sleepy Hollow*. Give students a copy of this passage and have them read along with you as you read aloud.

> He was tall, but exceedingly lank, with narrow shoulders, long arms and legs, hands that dangled a mile out of his sleeves, feet that might have served for shovels, and his whole frame most loosely hung together. His head was small, and flat at top, with huge ears, large green glassy eyes, and a long snipe nose, so that it looked like a weathercock perched upon his spindle neck, to tell which way the wind blew. To see him striding along the profile of a hill on a windy day, with his clothes bagging and fluttering about him, one might have mistaken him for the genius of famine descending upon the earth, or some scarecrow eloped from a cornfield.

Activity:

Have students work in groups of four to list phrases that evoked imagery. Start with these two examples and have them list the rest.

> hands that dangled a mile out of his sleeve
>
> feet that might have served as shovels

Have the recorder of each group write the reasons why the phrases on the list were selected.

Define *metaphor,* a direct comparison, and *simile,* a comparison using *like* or *as.* Have the students underline the metaphors and similes in the Ichabod Crane passage. Have each group write the similes or metaphors, such as

> nose like a weathercock perched upon his spindle neck
>
> feet that might have served for shovels
>
> Have students pay attention to the verb forms in the passage:

dangled

striding

bagging

fluttering

descending

eloped

perched

Have each student borrow one or two phrases to describe a character of their own. In addition, have them use similar verb forms and descriptions as in this example:

> My hand quivered over the Macintosh apple as the store manager towered over me. He glared at me over his nose, which looked *like a weathercock perched upon his spindle neck.* My clutched right hand slowly peeled open to show the rolled, sweaty five-dollar bill to Mr. Grimm, *who looked like some scarecrow eloped from a cornfield.*

Have them read the passages within groups to select one paragraph from the group to read to the entire class. (Hence, if you have six groups, you now have six papers to read aloud to the class.)

Follow-Up:

Have students exchange the student-written paragraphs. Tell them to draw illustrations to accompany the written passages. Make a class book of descriptive paragraphs with illustrations.

Evaluation:

Collect the descriptive paragraphs to read aloud to the class. Tell the students that they will be editors as you read. Instruct them to listen for the following:

Exciting verb forms—Lots of action; movement

Imagery—When you hear the words, you see . . . (a setting, movement, characters)

Descriptive words

Comparisons—Metaphor and simile

Tell them to raise their hands when they hear excellent examples of imagery (verb forms and description).

Position one student in front of the room to keep a tally using a calculator. Instruct him or her to count the number of times hands are raised.

Vary this technique by having each group select one outstanding paper. Reproduce the selected papers and have the groups underline excellent examples of metaphor, similes, and imagery. Award an A to the group whose paper has the most words and phrases correctly underlined.

Still More Ideas to Try

Teaching your students how to write by reading will broaden their world. They will begin to read with the eye of a writer, looking for reading materials that stimulate their own writing. By doing this, you have put them in control of their own learning.

- Paper Chase: Have students bring newspaper stories to class and block off an interesting segment of a story. Then have students exchange the stories and add to the beginning, middle, and end of the story.

- Storybook Blues: Have students read a children's story. Many times these stories have happy endings. In groups of three or four, have them read a story and decide if the ending is happy or sad. Whatever the ending, have them write the opposite of the original story. For example, Sleeping Beauty lives "happily ever after," but have your students write about the real life that the prince and princess share.

- Add Ads: Tell students to bring in copies of advertisements. Have them read the ads and list all the words and phrases they like. They should then use the list of words to write a different advertisement for another product.

- Adjective Sandwich: After students bring in advertisements, put them into groups of three to scour the ads for adjectives. List the adjectives and use them to write a descriptive paragraph about an object in the room.

- Classified Paragraph: After students bring in the classified sections of the newspaper, have them look through the ads to list categories: cars, trucks, jobs, houses, and so on. Have them list specific details about what they read in the paper. Then they write paragraphs using these details.

- Novel Notions: Have students copy two or more paragraphs directly out of a novel. Have them write their own paragraphs following the style of the novel. Follow this procedure in writing a book review by using the vocabulary and style of the author.

- Hallmark Style: Have students read the verses from greeting cards and pattern their own verses. Styles from Mother's and Father's Day cards will help students write their own verses for parents. Other cards will suggest remembrances for birthdays, graduation, anniversaries, friendship, and holidays.

- Lyric Limbo: Ask students to bring in favorite song lyrics. Have them copy a verse from the song and write a second verse by trying to imitate the writer's style.

Writing to Be Read

A significant motivational tool is the students' excitement of seeing their name in print. Writing to be read stimulates students to do their very best writing because they know it will be read by others. Opportunities for student writings to be read can occur within the classroom or school in the form of a newspaper, in the community by being published in local newspapers, and in the form of personal journals or historical books for the family. As a teacher, you are challenged to try any strategy that will get your students' names in print.

In addition to seeing their names in print, students need to discover a "sense of audience." Discourage them from writing only for the teacher. Involving students in peer-editing groups gives them a reason to use spelling and punctuation correctly. Awareness of their peers as an audience and editors heightens their motivation to write well. Writing to be read paves the way for a change in attitude and an improvement in skills.

A USEFUL STRATEGY: EDITING SKILLS

What better way to promote reading, thinking, and writing than by having students read, make revisions, and rewrite writing of peers? This is not an isolated task, however. Editing is a process where students are reading to find their errors and then writing to improve the paper. The following lessons demonstrate editing as a process that involves the interaction of your students as they learn to write by reading their own writing, as well as the writing of their classmates.

SAFE Lesson No. 8

TITLE OF LESSON: READING ALOUD FOR SENTENCE STRENGTH

DIFFICULTY LEVEL: GRADES 3–12

OBJECTIVES:

Students will:

1. Edit their writing by reading aloud
2. Identify revision needed on their own paper as it is read aloud
3. Select alternative ways to make revisions
4. Compare each other's papers

DESCRIPTION:

Students will listen to their own written work and make revisions. Students will work alone, in small groups, and then in large groups.

PROCEDURES:

Stimulus:

When assigning a writing assignment, it is helpful and fair to the students to tell them that it will be shared with their peers. Have them bring one of their writing assignments to class. Tell them that the written work will be read aloud, evaluated for content, and revised.

Reading aloud for content can begin with the large group. Brainstorm the specific skills by having the students tell you what they need to listen for as they are listening to a student's paper. This brainstorming method gets the students actively involved in preparing guidelines, and it serves as a review of the lesson. The key to setting up a rubric (criteria for evaluating a paper) is that you limit the list to only a few items. In other words, concentrate on a few skills at a time. For example:

- Action Verbs Instead of Telling Verbs
  As I listen to the story, does someone or something do something?
- Descriptive Words
  As I listen to the story, can I see something?

Begin by reading a few papers aloud. Select these papers at random. Model the editing technique by involving the class in a discussion about one or two sentences in that paper. For example:

Student writes: I think it is raining.

Editing: Can someone or something do something? (no)
Can a place or thing do something? (no)
Can I see something? (yes, rain)

Revision: The pounding of the rain slapped my bedroom window.

Editing: Is someone or something doing something? (Yes: slap, pound)
Can I see something? (Yes: bedroom window, rain pounding, slapping)

Activity:

Have the students bring two copies of their writing to class. Collect one copy and have the students keep the other copy in front of them at the desk. Ask them to correct their copy at their seats when it is used with the class. Follow this procedure:

- Large Group:
  Model one paper on an overhead transparency. (Take the sample from a previous assignment or make your own model. The student sample is more effective.)

- Small Groups:
  Form groups of four students each. Have the students read the papers and put stars (**) by any sentence that needs improvement. The student writing is circulated to everyone in the group. Tell the students to follow this procedure:

  1. Select one group member to be the oral reader. This person will collect all the student papers and will read at least one of the "starred" sentences from each paper.

  2. Select two recorders. These two people will take turns writing the comments on the paper. They must use the procedure that was demonstrated in the large group. (It would be helpful if you prepare editing sheets that have these questions on them.)

  3. All group members will react to a sentence after it is read. The recorder will write the suggestions directly on the paper.

- Individual:
  Have the students return to their seats. If class time is still available, have students read their own papers and make additional corrections. Direct them to follow the same procedure that was used in the large and small group activity.

Follow-Up:

Give students an opportunity to show you that they learned this editing process by giving two assignments.

1. Rewrite the paper that went through the editing process. (Make this optional; give it extra-credit grading.)

2. Write a new paragraph in which they ask themselves as they write: Can I do it? Can I see it?

Evaluation:

Observe how the students responded in the editing groups and give them a participation grade. Collect their paragraphs and write "Can I see it?" in the right margin at the top and "Can I do it?" in the left margin at the top, as shown:

Can I do it?   Can I see it?

Write "Yes" under the appropriate column on the same line where you noticed the "doing" and "seeing." Find the paper that has the most number of "Yes" responses and give that paper an A. Base the rest of the grades on that A.

SAFE Lesson No. 9

TITLE OF LESSON: READING IN REVERSE
DIFFICULTY LEVEL: GRADES 4–8
OBJECTIVES:

Students will:

1. Identify a paragraph, story, or poem
2. Analyze spelling errors
3. Evaluate sentence structures

DESCRIPTION:

Students will write a paragraph. They will edit in small groups and individually to find spelling and sentence (grammar) errors.

PROCEDURES:

Stimulus:

Tell the students that they will be editing, so they need to bring a written assignment to class. Explain to them that they will help each other find spelling errors and sentence structure errors. Give each person in the row a job of either looking for spelling errors or sentence errors, thus: The first person in the row and odd-numbered persons look for spelling errors. The second person in the row and even-numbered persons look for errors in sentence structure.

Give them these directions:

1. Hand your paper to the person behind you.
2. Remember your assigned job (spelling or sentences).
3. Spelling Editors: When the paper comes to you, read in *reverse sequence* (start with the last word and read to the first word.) Sentence Editors: Read in *reverse sequence* (start with last sentence and read to the first).
   (Note: Reverse sequence slows down eye movement; thus, the students are less likely to glide over errors.)
4. When you find an error, underline it on the paper. Do not erase or change the original.

Activity:

After these papers have been edited within the rows, tell the class that they will form groups of four persons per group. Tell them that they cannot be in a group that contains someone from the original editing group (the row).

Once they are in groups, have them switch editing roles (spelling editors are now sentence editors). Pass the papers around the group by using the reverse sequence approach again. Tell students to mark any errors that may have been missed by the first editing group.

Follow-Up:

When the editing group work is completed, have each student find a partner. Tell them to review their papers with the partner. Have them seek a third opinion if the two of them cannot explain the corrections. (You want to train them to come to you as a last resort. Students need to learn to edit among themselves and to trust their judgment).

Have the partners assess how accurately the editors found all errors. Tell the students to write any errors they discovered that were missed by the editors. Also have them write anything that may have been marked wrong, although the original was accurate.

Have the students go back to the original editing group and share their papers with the group. Tell them that as a group they must agree on the corrections.

Make sure all group members sign their names to the writing assignment. Tell them that they will receive a grade based on how well they edited.

Evaluation:

Observe the group interaction, and grade the students on how well they work in the editing group. Your grade will not be based on how many mistakes were found, but on how well the students stayed on task and looked for errors.

Collect the papers after they have been rewritten. Grade the papers, and since the partner was the last person in the editing process, give the grade to both the writer and his or her partner.

SAFE Lesson No. 10

TITLE OF LESSON: USING THE HOLISTIC METHOD

DIFFICULTY LEVEL: GRADES 4–8

OBJECTIVES:

Students will:

1. Analyze a sense of "wholeness" (beginning, middle, end) in a story
2. Evaluate corrections on their own papers

DESCRIPTION:

Students will write a story and read it aloud to listen for a beginning, middle, or end.

PROCEDURES:

Stimulus:

Have students bring a narrative writing assignment to class. Write these three words on the board:

beginning

middle

end

At random, select three student-written papers. Tell the students to listen to the story as another student reads it. Have the students raise their hands if the story had a beginning, middle, and end. Have students tell you which part/parts are missing if they do not raise their hands for a particular paper.

Prepare the following editing checklist and have the students write "Yes" or "No" for each question:

1. Is there a beginning?
2. Do you understand everything in the story?

3. Is everything in the right order?

4. Were there enough descriptive words?

5. Is there an ending?

Collect the students' papers and have the class form groups of four. Distribute the papers so students and their own writing are in different groups.

Activity:

Within the editing groups, have the members appoint a reader and a recorder. Have the reader read the whole story aloud to the group. Have the recorder ask the questions on the checklist and circle according to the group's reaction to the story.

After the students finish the checklist, have them give suggestions for improving the story, following this format:

Strong points:

Suggestions:

Have the recorder write these comments on the paper.

Follow-Up:

Return the papers and have the students work in pairs as they go over the suggestions that were made in the editing groups. Have them write any suggestions the partner makes regarding the paper by using this form:

Revisions

I agree with the following corrections:

I disagree with these suggestions:

I learned:

Evaluation:

Observe the roles of the students in the editing groups and grade their performance. Grade information on the Revision Form by comparing the students' reactions to the paper that was edited. For example, if the student and partner write, "I disagree with the use of the semi-colon on line 6" and they are correct, then that person and his partner should get a high evaluation.

SAFE Lesson No. 11

TITLE OF LESSON: READING ALOUD FOR OMISSIONS AND INSERTIONS

DIFFICULTY LEVEL: GRADES 3–8

OBJECTIVES:

Students will:

1. Read their writing aloud
2. Analyze omissions and insertions in their own writing
3. Correct insertion and omission problems

DESCRIPTION:

Students will read their own writing aloud. They will listen for omission or insertion errors and they will correct these errors.

PROCEDURES:

Stimulus:

Have students bring a written assignment to class. Tell them that they will be reading each other's papers for omissions and insertions.

On the board, write an example of an omission.

John and I went to store.

Then write the correction:

the
John and I went to/store.

Write an example of insertion.

We went to the the store.

Write the correction:

We went to the store.

Tell the class that you expect to hear a "hum" in the classroom because you would like them to read their own writing aloud (each student can read in a low tone.) Give them approximately ten minutes to read their writing aloud. Have them listen for a word that they left out (omission) or a word they inserted (insertion.)

Tell them to mark the paper with the correction.

Activity:

Have the students work in pairs to check this reading-aloud method. Have the partner read the paper aloud and mark any insertions or omissions that may have been overlooked.

Follow-Up:

Have the students exchange papers and write the following on the bottom of the page:

# of omissions   # of insertions

Have students read these aloud and write the number of insertions or omissions they may have found. During this stage, many or all should have been found previously.

Use this grading scale:

Total # of insertions/ omissions	Grade
0	A
1	B
2	C
3	D
4+	F

Evaluation:

Compare the editing sheet the students completed in the Follow-Up to their papers now. Grade the accuracy of the editing paper for their written compositions.

MORE LESSONS TO PROMOTE WRITING TO BE READ

By writing for different audiences, students' interest in the composing, editing, and revising process is heightened because they feel a purpose for writing. This interest in their writing captures a lasting value when they learn to bind books and publish their personal writing.

SAFE Lesson No. 12

TITLE OF LESSON: POSTER MANIA

DIFFICULTY LEVEL: GRADES 4–8

OBJECTIVES:

Students will:

1. List key ideas from their reading
2. Write to a person and explain these key points
3. Read and discuss each other's papers
4. Critique each other's papers

DESCRIPTION:

Students will list review terms from their textbook. They will look at a poster and write a letter or a paragraph to the person in the poster. In that writing sample, they will explain the concepts they read.

PROCEDURES:

Stimulus:

Bring in a selection of four posters to class. Select posters of the "heroes" of the class (Garfield, a rock star, a TV personality, a classic character such as Dracula, Godzilla, or Wizard of Oz). Tell students that they will write to one of these characters when they review their reading assignment.

Place the posters so that they are visible to all students. Tell each student to select one character who will receive the letter.

Put students into groups of four. Have them share the vocabulary words from the assigned chapter reading. Collectively, the group should make a list of words and definitions. Here is a sample list of science words:

electricity

ions

valence

electrolysis

ionization

Have them return to their desks and write a letter to their poster personality. Tell them to explain the vocabulary words to this personality. Here is the beginning of a letter written to Big Bird.

Dear Big Bird,

I am writing to tell you about solutions that conduct electricity. Its touch can be deadly. Negative ions in it take away your electrons. But, if you get a positive ion, it will give you electrons. If the valence is in the negative stage, it takes away ions.

José

Activity:

After the letters are written, have the students get into groups of four (composed of different classmates than their initial group). Have them circulate their papers and put a check in the margin where there is an error with the use of the vocabulary word.

Have the students read the papers aloud within the groups. If there is an error in the use of a word, have them discuss that within the group so the writer of the paper can make the necessary revision.

Follow-Up:

While the papers are being read aloud, have the students listen for one paper from the group that represents the best paper from that group. This selection will be based on:

Originality

Clarity

Correctness of vocabulary words

Number of vocabulary words explained

Evaluation:

Have students read these papers aloud to the class and have the students select the best of these by using the same criteria. Award this outstanding paper a purple ribbon shared by every member of that group. If the other papers were very good, then give those papers a blue ribbon.

Give an objective test of these vocabulary words the next day. Check to see if they know these words because of the writing activity.

SAFE Lesson No. 13

TITLE OF LESSON: BINDING A BLANK BOOK

DIFFICULTY LEVEL: GRADES 3–8

OBJECTIVES:

Students will:

1. Bind a book
2. Interpret directions
3. Follow directions
4. Organize materials

DESCRIPTION:

Students will use blank sheets of paper to bind a book. They will assemble their own books.

PROCEDURES:

Stimulus:

List the equipment and materials needed.

Paper cutter

Electric iron (for dry mounting)

Heavy stapler (If the book is to be stapled together, the stapler must reach to the center fold of the book.)

Needle and thread (heavy darning needles and button thread)

Sewing machine (With parent volunteers and supervision, the book can be sewn directly on the machine.)

Cloth or paper—Recommended: wallpaper samples, wrapping paper, lightweight decorative paper, cotton fabrics (Book covers are cut one inch larger on all sides of the cardboard. Inside covers are cut the same size as the inside pages.)

Pages of the book

Step 1:   Give each student five 8½″ × 11″ sheets of paper to use as the inside pages for the book. This paper can be inexpensive typing paper, onion skin, lined composition paper, or whatever kind of lightweight paper you have available. Students fold these sheets in half horizontally.

Step 2:   Each student also needs a 9½″ × 11½″ sheet of lightweight colored paper to serve as the inside cover of the book. Decorative wrapping paper works well. This sheet is also folded in half.

Step 3:   Assemble the folded white pages inside the slightly larger cover sheet. When folded together, the unattractive side of the inside cover will be seen. This will be ironed to the covered cardboard so it will not be seen. The decorative side will be seen since it is right next to the inside of the book. This inside sheet is 8½″ × 11″ before it is folded. After it is folded, it is 4¼″ × 5½″.

Step 4:   Use the sewing machine or a darning needle with button thread. Sew the crease of the folded book pages to the crease of the decorative inside sheet. When you do this correctly, the "rough-looking" side of the wrapping paper should be facing you when the book is closed.

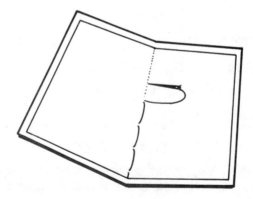

Assembling the Outside of the Book:

Step 1:   Cut out cloth and dry mounting the same size (10″ × 12″). Place the cloth first (decorative side down) and put the dry mounting section directly on top of the cloth.

Step 2:   Place the cardboard sections (two sections: 4¼″ × 5½″) on top of the dry mounting paper and cloth outside cover. Leave a section between the two pieces of cardboard and use the piece of masking tape to secure the cardboard to the cloth.

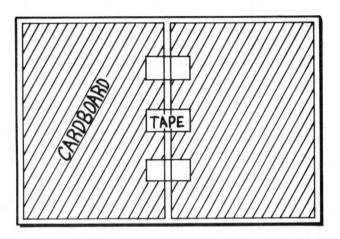

Step 3:   Use the iron to press the four corners down. Then press the four sides down. (Heat applied to the dry mounting will hold the paper and cardboard together like glue.)

To protect the iron, place a sheet of newspaper between the iron and the cardboard.

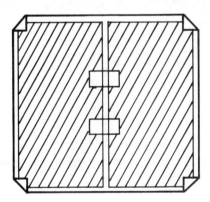 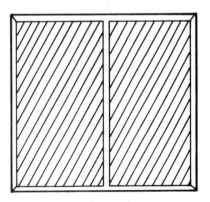

Step 4:   Cut out a section of dry mounting that is the size of the inside "book" when it is opened up (8½″ × 11″).

Lay the smaller sheet of dry mounting paper over the covered cardboard (the front cover of book).

Step 5: Iron the inside "book" to the outside of the book (the covered cardboard). Line up the crease of the inside "book" to the crease of the covered cardboard. (Make the outside cover form the shape of an "L" before you line up the creases.)

Step 6: Iron. Close the book. Congratulations! You have made a blank book.

Activity:

Use parent volunteers or student monitors to help assist you when the students begin following the procedures to make the book. Have all materials available. Bring two or three irons, a sewing machine, and needles and thread. Then be ready to walk around the classroom as your students make books.

Have your students use this book in a variety of ways, such as:

Autograph Book

Journal

Baby Book

Things I Want to Do

Picture Book

With the students brainstorm other ways to bind books. Try these ideas for covers:

Using polyester fiberfill

Using leather or vinyl

Using felt and cutting out objects

Drawing on cardboard and laminating it

Follow-Up:

Have the students share their bound books with each other. If a book doesn't "hold together right" then ask the student if he or she can tell you why. Be prepared to give students another try if they didn't produce a perfect book the first time.

Evaluation:

Grade the book on the overall appearance, content, illustrations, binding, and clarity.

SAFE Lesson No. 14

TITLE OF LESSON: HOW TO MAKE A DUMMY
DIFFICULTY LEVEL: GRADES 4–8
OBJECTIVES:

Students will:

1. Write legibly or type a story
2. Make the "dummy" for a book
3. Illustrate their own book
4. Bind and cover their book

DESCRIPTION:

After students have taken a selected story through the editing process, they will make a "dummy" (a mock-up) book. Then, they will write, illustrate, and bind a book.

PROCEDURES:

Stimulus:

Have students discover the different parts of a book so that the students will include these in the books. Tell them that they want to make a book seem real.

Book Cover

Title Page

Table of Contents

Dedication

Content

Art Work

End Sections

Have the class brainstorm what specific things would go under each of those book parts. Add to the list:

Book Cover
    design (art work)
    inside cover
    the binding of the book

Title Page
    arrangement of title, author, and publishing company
    copyright information (on back)
    design (art work)

Table of Contents
    list of chapters
    list of illustrations
    page numbers
    (not needed for all books)

Dedication
    friends, loved ones
    persons who helped

Content
    fiction or nonfiction
    number of pages
    organization
        how much is placed on each page
        where sections are placed
    illustrations

Art Work
    photos (color or black and white)
    kind of art
    organization (where placed)

End Sections
    index
    glossary
    information about the author
    picture of the author

Activity:

Tell the students to write the contents of the book in ink on white-lined paper. (This paper has already gone through the editing process and it is ready to be published in the book.)

Show them how to mark papers and number them so that they can create a "dummy." First, have them look at the list from the Stimulus section of this lesson. If any of those sections are going to be in the book, then have them put each section on a separate sheet of paper so that it can be numbered easily. Look at how a student's paper can be marked to determine the layout of the book.

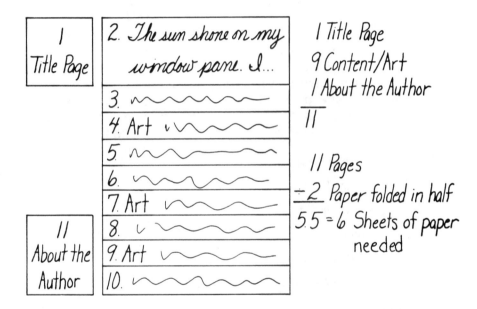

Have the students add the section pages with the number of pages they will need for a table of contents and the illustrations. Have them add these pages together.

Tell them this number will be divided in half to determine how many sheets of paper are needed. (If the student's number is 11, then he or she needs 6 sheets of paper since 11 ÷ 2 = 5½).

Once the students receive the number of papers they need, have them write or type their books. Sometimes it helps to have them make a miniature book (1" × 2") where they can use phrases and numbers to remind them what will be on each page.

Tell them that they can disassemble the miniature book as they are working on their larger book so that they'll always know where to place the pages of the book. Here is a sample of a miniature book.

After the book is written or typed, they will sew it to the decorative inside cover and bind the book as shown in the above lesson.

Have the students use this same method to write, illustrate, and bind books on their own concerning the following topics:

Younger years

Original poetry

Family history

Family culture

Ways of coping

Greatest joys, fears, plans (etc.)

Follow-Up:

Begin a Book Fair within your school or district so that these books can be displayed for the public.

Evaluation:

The books can be evaluated for the following:

Creativity

Content

Mechanics/Grammar/Usage

Illustrations

Organization

Resources

Althea. *Making a Book.* Dinosaur Publications, 1980.
Bechtel, Judith. *Improving Writing and Learning.* Allyn and Bacon, 1985.

Still More Ideas to Try

- Class Binding: Make class books for any writing project that focuses on a theme. If everyone writes a paragraph on freedom, then have all class members collect magazine pictures that highlight the paragraphs. Bind all paragraphs and illustrations into one book.

- Study Skills: Have students prepare units of study. In groups of four, have them brainstorm subdivisions for the book: preface to the students, important key concepts, sample test questions, sample paragraphs, and a dictionary. Combine this information into a book that can be used with another class. Send a group of students to the other class to serve as tutors with sample finished books.

- Interview Brief: Invite the principal, custodian, cook, nurse, secretary, and other staff members to class. Help students interview them and collect data about their jobs and personal interests. Have them write a personal letter to one of the staff members, seeking additional information than what was acquired during the interview.

- Pen Pal Help: Set up an anonymous pen pal relationship with students from the same grade level. Ask them to write about personal concerns. Have them pattern the letters from the Dear Abby column. Encourage serious responses to these letters.

- Publishing Company: Develop a publishing company. Set up the room with a binding machine, sewing machine, iron, paper cutter, and typewriter. Let older students help primary students publish their writing. Set up a system so that a sixth-grade class (or any upper elementary class) will tutor a primary class on the writing process and then will help them publish a book of the writing.

Exploring Further

Bechtel, Judith. *Improving Writing and Learning*. Allyn and Bacon, 1985.

Brown, Rosellen, et al. *The Whole Word Catalogue: A Handbook of Writing Ideas for Teachers*. Teachers and Writers Collaborative, 1983.

Christensen, Jane, ed. *Your Reading: A Booklist for Junior High and Middle School Students*. NCTE, 1983.

Lamme, Linda, ed. *Learning to Love Literature: Preschool through Grade 3*. NCTE, 1981.

Moss, Joy. *Focus Units on Literature: A Handbook for Elementary School Teachers*. NCTE, 1984.

Sims, Rudine. *Shadow and Substance: Afro-American Experience in Contemporary Children's Fiction*. NCTE, 1982.

Sloyer, Shirlee. *Readers Theatre: Story Dramatization in the Classroom*. NCTE, 1982.

Tiedt, Iris M. *Writing: From Topic to Evaluation*. Allyn and Bacon, 1989.

Tiedt, Iris, et al. *Teaching Writing in K–8 Classrooms*. Prentice-Hall, 1983.

Tiedt, Iris, and Ho, Nora. *Lessons from a Writing Project, Grades K–3*. David Lake, 1987.

Tiedt, Iris, and Johnson, Lisa. *Lessons from a Writing Project, Grades 2–4*. David Lake, 1987.

Tiedt, Iris, and Williams, Mary Young. *Lessons from a Writing Project, Grades 4–6*. David Lake, 1987.

Tiedt, Pamela, and Tiedt, Iris. *Multicultural Teaching: Activities, Resources, and Information,* 2nd ed. Allyn and Bacon, 1986.

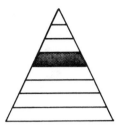

6

Learning Advanced Thinking Skills

As students grow in their ability to read and write, they are also continuing to develop listening and speaking skills. In addition, they are learning to think, for thinking is an integral part of every learning experience. A major focus for instruction should be to make students aware that they are thinking and how the process works for them (metacognition).

Just as with the other language skills, students require direct experience in thinking if their thinking skills are to progress. We need to plan lessons designed to involve students in thinking that gradually becomes more sophisticated as they delve beneath the surface of what they read. We can show students how thinking moves from factual or literal levels to inference, evaluation, and synthesis. We begin with data collecting, an essential first step in any thinking process. Then we introduce various ways of processing the data—analyzing, categorizing, comparing, and prioritizing. The best instructional strategies engage students in using a number of thinking skills as part of a purposeful learning activity.

We can help students become aware of their own thinking, which they can express orally or in writing, and lead them to extend their creative (or right-brain) thinking abilities. We can also show them that what they read reveals the thinking of other people. Focusing on thinking in your classroom will make teaching and learning more exciting!

The ideas in this chapter will help you teach students more about the thinking processes inherent in all of learning. Lessons presented are grouped as follows:

Gathering Data at the Knowledge Level

Working with Data in Varied Ways

Integrative Thinking

Implementing the Program

Thinking is the foundation of all learning. Therefore, it is essential that we be aware of the thinking processes that students engage in as they listen, speak, read, and write. Our teaching should reflect this awareness as we select strategies that reinforce the development of thinking skills.

1. Thinking and language develop together. The child acquires thinking skills in much the same manner as he or she acquires language in natural situations that involve the use of language. Complex thinking skills are used in order to acquire facility with spoken language.

2. Schools have stressed left-brain (linear) thinking—drill, rote memorization, and answers based on facts. We need to provide opportunities for right-brain thinking that encourages children to make creative leaps, to synthesize information.

3. We can plan lessons that make children aware of thinking processes. We can help them move from basing thinking only on factual data collected as they process the data, making inferences, and using critical thinking abilities.

4. Thinking skills are involved in the comprehension process as children listen and read. Their thinking is revealed through what they say and write.

5. We can guide students to acquire data-collecting skills through observation using all their senses, and show them how to use specific techniques that probe into their own knowledge base. We can then plan opportunities to process the data collected in various ways to gain interesting insights beyond the factual level.

Selected Resources

If you want to know more about theory and research related to thinking, you may want to examine these resources and those at the end of the chapter.

Almy, Millie, et al. *Young Children's Thinking: Studies of Some Aspects of Piaget's Theory*. Teachers College Press, 1966.

Berthoff, Ann E. *The Making of Meaning*. Boynton/Cook, 1981.

Bogen, Benjamin. *All Our Children Learning: A Primer for Parents, Teachers and Other Educators*. McGraw, 1981.

Bogen, Joseph E. "The Other Side of the Brain VII: Some Educational Aspects of Hemispheric Specialization." *UCLA Educator,* 17 (1975):24–32.

Costa, Arthur. *Developing Minds.* ASCD, 1985.

PAR Thinking Skills Resource Panel. "Thinking about the Teaching of Thinking." *Practical Applications of Research: Newsletter of Phi Delta Kappa's Center on Evaluation, Development, and Research,* vol. 3, no. 1 (September 1980).

Tiedt, Iris M., et al. *Teaching Thinking in K–12 Classrooms.* Allyn and Bacon, 1989.

Gathering Data at the Knowledge Level

Comprehension of speech or reading begins with unlocking meaning at the surface level. This ability is linked to close reading for the facts or close observation and involves the base level of thinking—data collection. Students display their ability at this level by listing, locating, naming, recalling, recording, or reciting orally or in writing. Answers can be easily checked against the text or the subject observed.

The strategies in this section first deal with recall of factual knowledge. The process of checking students' ability to read at the surface level is basic to the building of higher level thinking skills. These lessons help students learn to unlock surface meaning with activities that are not monotonous drill—learning experiences that lead to the next stage of processing the data collected.

A USEFUL STRATEGY: MAPPING

Mapping is a strategy that will help students categorize or list in an organized fashion the ideas they comprehend from their reading. This strategy may be applied later to higher level thinking skills, but is especially helpful for recording information gathered from close reading. Although mapping is spontaneous and random, compared to formal outlining, it does promote logical and organized arrangement of information. Mapping has no one format, so it leaves you and your students free to explore the possibilities of the strategy creatively.

Mapping promotes thinking about reading and thinking about thinking. Students will develop their thinking abilities as they identify their own thinking patterns and levels of thought. Teach mapping to the students as a means of recording data they have collected. Begin by asking them to read a selection from a textbook or a piece of literature. At the beginning, give them the main topic and categories. Later, the students may arrive at these on their own. Whatever pattern you choose, the students are asked to place facts in appropriate classifications, not just at random.

The following simple example of a map classifies levels of thinking and presents vocabulary approriate for each. This map shows the vocabulary that will be presented in each section of this chapter. Mapping is useful for organizing information gathered by the students and it also gives the teacher a means to assess the students' ability to unlock meaning.

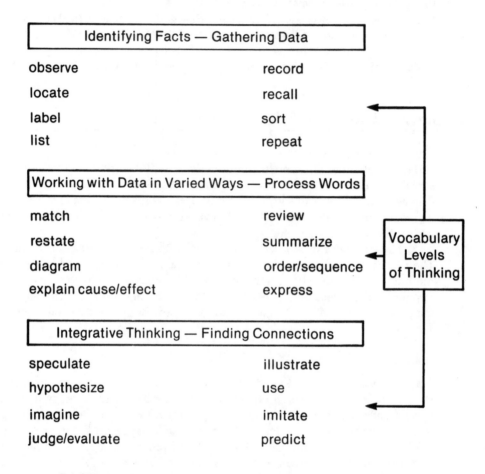

Identifying Facts — Gathering Data	
observe	record
locate	recall
label	sort
list	repeat

Working with Data in Varied Ways — Process Words	
match	review
restate	summarize
diagram	order/sequence
explain cause/effect	express

Integrative Thinking — Finding Connections	
speculate	illustrate
hypothesize	use
imagine	imitate
judge/evaluate	predict

Vocabulary
Levels
of Thinking

SAFE Lesson No. 1

TITLE OF LESSON: NEWSPAPERS AND GATHERING FACTS BY CLOSE READING

DIFFICULTY LEVEL: GRADES 2–8

OBJECTIVES:

Students will:

1. Identify facts (who, what, where, when, and why) in a news story
2. Record the data or information

DESCRIPTION:

The students will read a newspaper to find the 5 Ws. They will gather the data according to one type of mapping. They will check their work for accuracy, redo it if necessary, and learn to recheck the source.

PROCEDURES:

Stimulus:

Before the lesson begins, write the 5 Ws on the board. Also make copies of a report from a local newspaper so that students have a copy of the same article.

Write the word *fact* on the board and discuss the meaning. Discuss where we can find facts. Have the students make factual statements. For example:

That desk is brown.

Activity:

Direct the students to read the report looking for the 5 Ws (Who? What? Where? When? Why?). Have students fold a piece of binder paper into sixths. As they read, they should fill in the spaces. Note with the students that the sixth space contains not a fact but a statement of the main idea drawn from the 5 Ws that they identified. For example:

Who?	What?	Where?
When?	Why?	Sentence: Main Idea of Article Directly Derived from Facts

For some classes, this activity might be best modeled or done on the board together before the students try it on their own. Some students might try it first in small groups. When recording data, students should be as specific as possible. (They should not just answer *"When?"* by writing "recently"; but by stating *"July 4, 1989."*) The sixth space will read something like this: "On July 4th, 1989, Fred Smith sold fireworks illegally at his home in order to make money." No opinion from the reader is inserted at this point.

Follow-Up:

Have students share their findings. Record findings on the chart or board so that all students may check their work. They should be encouraged to change answers when they verify that the answer offered by others is the fact according to the text of the article.

Students should be encouraged to offer differing answers, referring to the text for support. This establishes the idea of surface level or factual thinking and encourages those with differing answers to reread more closely.

Evaluation:

Have the students work in pairs to check the accuracy of their maps. In this exercise the answers are the same for each person. Give the students another article to map individually. Have students work in pairs to check accuracy again. Have students turn in corrected maps to receive ten points each for the completed task.

Notes: Variations in this lesson are possible. The first news article might be totally analyzed as an oral activity, practicing the sentence summaries by recording several variations on the board. The students may find their own articles on any topic to practice the activity. Students might discuss a school activity and write an individual or group report modeling the inclusion of the 5 Ws. Students might respond to peer news stories by asking the basic questions and identifying the 5 Ws on a map.

SAFE Lesson No. 2

TITLE OF LESSON: MAPPING THE ELEMENTS OF A SHORT STORY

DIFFICULTY LEVEL: GRADES 3–8

OBJECTIVES:

Students will:

1. Identify the parts of a story
2. Practice mapping these elements

DESCRIPTION:

The students will read a folktale and learn through mapping to identify the parts of a story. Students will verify facts and use the map to retell the story. Students will record the facts as they are presented in the story, not as they appear on the map. A folktale will be shared in a manner that may be adapted to any book or novel.

PROCEDURES:

Choose a folktale to read aloud to the class.

Stimulus:

Read "Cinderella" (or any other folktale) aloud. You may use a story from the basal reader so that all have copies.

Activity:

Give the students a map pattern to follow when identifying the basic elements of the story.

Setting	Plot
Place	Situation
Time	Problem/Conflict
	Title
	Author
	Turning Point
Characters	
Major	Conclusion/Resolution (How problem is solved)
Minor	

Fill in the major categories as a class. Ask them to label the map as it is done together. Direct students to identify verifiable facts and specifics and fill in the map.

Follow-Up:

Have the students share their maps in small groups. Ask them to discuss variations and improve their maps. Have the group share the mapping of a story by retelling the story using only the map, not the text.

Evaluation:

Direct the students to map a different short tale. Tell them to practice with partners, retelling the story using only the map. Partners should be able to read the story using the map.

Notes: This mapping pattern can be used with any story or novel that students read. Mapping can also be used as a way of planning a story that will be written.

SAFE Lesson No. 3

TITLE OF LESSON: MAKING A THINKING PROCESS LOG

DIFFICULTY LEVEL: GRADES 3–8

OBJECTIVES:

Students will:

1. Identify words associated with factual thinking
2. Label the kind of thinking needed to answer a question
3. Identify the factual level of thinking in their logs

DESCRIPTION:

Students will use the key words that will unlock surface meaning of written material. During this lesson, the students will draw on information unconsciously known by them and learn to identify what kind of thinking they are doing. They will begin to share ideas about thinking and become more aware that knowing how to answer a question is just as important as knowing the answer. This lesson is the beginning of developing an individual student thinking log in class as well as vocabulary that will help them become better learners.

PROCEDURES:

Stimulus:

Ask the students a question that they can answer readily, for example:

What are the names of the planets?

What are the parts of a short story?

What color can a rose be?

Discuss with the students how they knew the information. Brainstorm and record on the board words for the kind of thinking they are doing. Let them use resource books to help.

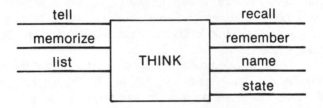

tell		recall
memorize	THINK	remember
list		name
		state

Ask the students to think about experiences in and out of school when they use the processes or skills identified. They will probably recall a lesson you have recently taught during which they were asked to identify characters, count items, or label parts.

Activity:

Have the students take a piece of binder paper or use a notebook that will become a thinking journal. (This might be binder paper stapled into packets.) Tell the students to put the words *experiences with factual thinking* in the middle of the map. Allow students to use any form of mapping they are familiar with but model one example on the board. They are to categorize times when they use surface level or factual thinking.

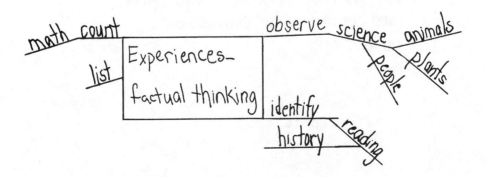

Follow-Up:

In groups, students can share the results of their individual mapping. They may add to their maps. Encourage them to explain or defend why they think a certain experience uses the surface level of thinking. After the group sharing, discuss the source of thinking based on memory and facts.

Evaluation:

Ask the students to write in a notebook about one experience that day or recently during which they solved a problem, answered a question, or asked a question involving surface-level thinking. Observe student participation.

Notes: Students should continue making entries in their thinking log. This log is private but will be read by the teacher periodically. Tell the students it will be read to see how they and the class are progressing. Let them know it is nongraded. Ask students to write in their logs several times a week as they learn more about their own thinking processes.

MORE LESSONS TO PROMOTE SKILL IN DATA GATHERING

The following lessons will promote thinking at the factual level and help students to unlock meaning. They should continue to write in their thinking logs as this will help them continue to be aware of their own skills. The following lessons make use of strategies other than mapping.

SAFE Lesson No. 4

TITLE OF LESSON: IDENTIFYING SUPERSTITION IN *HUCKLEBERRY FINN*

DIFFICULTY LEVEL: GRADES 6–10

OBJECTIVES:

Students will:

1. Read to locate specific ideas in a piece of literature
2. Retell part of a story
3. Identify superstition

DESCRIPTION:

After a class has read *Huckleberry Finn,* they may focus on the amount of superstition present in the novel. After brainstorming examples of superstition from the story, students will practice retelling an incident accurately, using superstition as the focus.

PROCEDURES:

Stimulus:

Write the word *superstition* on the board. Draw a circle around the word and ask for examples of superstitions in our daily life. Cluster these around the circle.

broken mirror   13   black cat

superstition

spilling salt   ladder

Ask the students to define *superstition* for themselves. Share definitions by listing them and identifying several definitions or characteristics of superstition.

Activity:

Have the students brainstorm superstitions present in *Huckleberry Finn.* Cluster these around the name of the novel.

Huckleberry Finn

Ask students to think about the situation in the story when a specific superstition was displayed. Share a few of these with the whole class so all are sure what it means to retell a situation or incident rather than the whole story.

Follow-Up:

Have the students work in pairs as they each choose the incident and superstition they like best in the novel. Ask the partners to take turns retelling the incident.

Evaluation:

Have each pair choose one incident to write and publish for the class. Use peer editing and responding to judge whether it is truly one incident and one superstition. Students may also illustrate the superstition or scene from the novel identifying the superstition. Display these on a bulletin board.

SAFE Lesson No. 5

TITLE OF LESSON: IDENTIFYING LITERAL AND FIGURATIVE MEANINGS

DIFFICULTY LEVEL: GRADES 1–8

OBJECTIVES:

Students will:

1. Define the term *idiom*
2. Define the words *literal* and *figurative*
3. Unlock the meaning of idioms

DESCRIPTION:

This lesson focuses on idioms, which often appear in stories and novels, especially in dialogue. The students will first identify idioms common in daily language, then discuss both the literal and figurative meanings. The students will move from a prewrite activity to a written or oral assignment.

PROCEDURES:

Stimulus:

List some common idiomatic phrases on the board.

He blew his top.

Get lost.

Don't roll your eyes at me.

Ask the students to offer examples of phrases of this type that they use in daily language. Add these to the list. Discuss the literal meaning of one of the idioms. Ask the students what they mean in dialogue when they tell someone to "cool it." Identify the dictionary meaning of the same idiom.

Activity:

Ask the students to choose one favorite idiom to explain to a partner. Direct them to explain both the literal and figurative meanings. Ask each pair to write a paragraph in which they explain the literal and figurative meanings of one idiom.

Follow-Up:

Students next illustrate the idiom in picture form, showing the literal and figurative meanings. Bind the student pages into a class book.

Evaluation:

Check the students' paragraphs and pictures for accurate literal and figurative interpretation of an idiom. Give help to those having problems and reward them with the publication of idiom in the class book.

Notes: This activity can be pursued on an oral basis for younger children. They also enjoy listening at home and asking parents for idioms popular before the present time. Prizes can be given for the longest list of idioms. Older students can identify idioms from conversation and reading and enjoy researching the meaning.

SAFE Lesson No. 6

TITLE OF LESSON: RETELLING THE NEWS WITH PUPPETS

DIFFICULTY LEVEL: GRADES 2–8

OBJECTIVES:

Students will:

1. Read newspapers for factual information

2. Recall items reported in the news accurately
3. Sequence events logically

DESCRIPTION:

After students have practiced reading literature or the newspaper for the 5 Ws, they need to perfect the skill. In this lesson, they will identify the 5 Ws, write about events logically, and use puppets to give a newscast about the incident.

PROCEDURES:

Review the 5 Ws with students.

Stimulus:

Discuss a current event from the school or local newspaper. Draw and display a finger puppet, which is easily made out of construction paper. Have each student make a puppet and draw a face on it that represents a newscaster. In pairs, have the students retell the current event discussed, but use the hand puppet as the newscaster. Direct them to practice identifying the 5 Ws in their presentation.

Activity:

Give each student a day to be a newsperson. They are to retell a current event as if they are on TV or radio. They should name their puppet and be that newscaster.

Follow-Up:

Discuss the newscasts and put together a team to present a full production for the whole class or another class.

Evaluation:

List the attributes of a good newscast. Have a panel of students judge the newscast for accuracy, clarity, and logical sequence.

Still More Ideas to Try

These lessons continue to focus on factual thinking skills. They involve recall and comprehension at the surface level. As students become more proficient at unlocking the factual meaning and gathering data, they will find answering questions with accuracy an easier task.

- Labeling the Basic Elements of a Story: Give the students a map of a simple story. (The story should be well known by the students, for example

"The Three Little Pigs.") Leave out the words *character, setting,* and *plot,* and have the students identify or label the map.

- Retelling Old Tales in New Ways: Direct the students to read a folktale or legend like "Johnny Appleseed" or "Paul Bunyan." Have the students use mapping to identify the 5 Ws: Who, What, Where, When, and Why? Ask the students to rewrite the tale using modern language. These should be shared in response groups. Older students may change the plot to a modern theme, for example, "Johnny Appleseed" might be concerned about conservation.

- Test Writing: After completing a unit or story, allow the students to write the test. Be sure the key words are available for reference either in the student's thinking log or on a classroom chart. Have them use the recall level words to write five questions. Exchange papers and give students an opportunity to take the test. The evaluation is the test taker's ability to understand the questions and recall the facts.

- Current Issues: Have the students choose a current problem that they would like to see resolved, for example, the need for more dances at school or a local issue such as preserving public parks. Have students follow the problems in the local newspaper. Ask them to keep a log of facts noting who is for and against the proposed solutions and what is involved in the solution or proposal. The log should be shared with the teacher or a peer to be checked. Look for facts recorded, not opinions or reactions to the opinions. This log can later be used to write a report, give a speech, or conduct a debate.

- Character Study: After reading a story from the basal reader or an anthology used by the students, discuss the characters in the story. Have the students find and record any physical description of the character. From a randomly chosen number of papers, read the physical description and have the students identify the character. A game may be played using groups to see which one recalls the most characters accurately. If a series of stories are read, this may be used as a review of characters.

- T-Shirt Parade: Have the students create their own clever phrase for a T-shirt. Give them construction paper on which to draw a shirt to display their original phrase. Instruct the students to use figurative meanings. The shirt might be related to a current event or personality. Display the drawings. In partners or individually, ask the students to pick a T-shirt other than their own and write the literal and figurative meanings. You might even have students attempt to guess the maker.

- Focus on a Category: Divide the class into groups of three to five persons. Give each group a large sheet of newsprint on which they can write and several colored felt pens. Each group will brainstorm a list of interesting words related to the category you assign them. These word lists can be shared and displayed around the room. Students can refer to the lists during writing periods.

Give the students a category, for example, the color green. Have them think of words related to *green*, such as, *chartreuse, celery, mint, apple, lime, kelly, emerald, olive,* and *pistachio*. Another category might be *movement*, with related words as *walk, creep, crawl, plod, tiptoe,* and *amble*.

Other categories might be *shapes, loud words, smell,* and *sound*. Create large charts for students to use in their written work.

• Making New Creatures: The skill of labeling can be practiced by using prefixes and suffixes to create a strange creature. First, give or illicit from the students the prefixes related to numbers: *uni, bi, tri*. Have the students practice combining these prefixes with body parts. An example is *bi-headed* or *tri-eyed*. After practice, to be sure students have many prefixes and are able to add suffixes like *-ed*, let them draw an animal and write a sentence of description. For example, "This is a uni-bodied, tri-eyed, biped."

Later, sentences may be covered or reproduced and a game played matching the description to the animal.

• Modeling Writing: Put a sentence on the board:

Jean came out of the kitchen carrying a bowlful of apples.

Next, rewrite the sentence showing only the structure:

_____came out of the _____carrying a _____
_____of cookies.

Have students suggest various ways of completing this sentence framework. Sentences can be taken from reading material and focus on skills to improve writing. One might be a passage using active verbs. An example is to omit every fifth word of a passage from Kenneth Grahame's *Wind in the Willows:*

The Mole had been _____very hard all the _____, spring-cleaning his little _____. First the brooms, then _____dusters; then on ladders _____steps and chairs, with brush and a pail _____ whitewash; till he had _____in his throat and _____. . . .

This cloze technique fosters good reading and discussion of grammar as students decide on words to fit the blanks.

Working with Data in Varied Ways

After students practice gathering factual material, they need practice using the knowledge. Although thinking through a problem involves all levels, the students need guided practice as they work with the data. Inferences, explanations, applications, and summaries are but a few of the processes used in the classroom. Some students will reach these levels on their own; others will need more structured guidance from the teacher. Students who create a new game, write an original essay, or editorialize succinctly on a subject on their own are in our classrooms. It is important that all students be given the opportunity to reach for these levels of thinking. Conscious effort on the part of the teacher must be made to plan lessons that involve all students in all levels.

Many strategies have already been discussed. Peer editing itself asks students to judge/evaluate a written piece or project. Self-evaluation asks the student to judge the unique quality of a given contribution. Our world will demand these high-level skills. The ability to solve problems is becoming more and more important.

Everyday life asks people to apply what they already know to new situations. The creative solution comprises originality and flexibility. The creative thinker is willing to risk being different or divergent. This person must also be willing to be convergent or flexible enough to adjust to new ideas. Whatever the demands, they will be greater in our technological society.

A USEFUL STRATEGY: PLANNING QUESTIONS

Planning questions is an integral part of lesson planning. It is the part we often take for granted. We teachers have not consciously thought about what level of thinking we are asking of our students when we pose a question. Although all types of questions are necessary, the teacher must be aware of the level of thinking demanded. Your task is to develop relevant questions that begin with recall of factual material, but move to higher levels of thinking. The way the child is questioned becomes as important to the learning process as the material set in front of him or her. Questions should lead the learner to wonder, to make connections, and to move from recall to application and evaluation.

Teacher behaviors are important to the questioning process. Besides awareness of the key words that initiate different types of thinking, the teacher must practice responses to the students' answers. After a recall question, some students will answer with specifics; others will relate only general information; still others will not answer at all. Teacher behaviors can foster thinking from more students; these are based on the teacher's responses.

If the teacher asks a question, calls on the first person to raise his or her hand, then moves to the next question when given a correct response, the remainder of the class becomes lazy and relies on a certain few to give this basic information. On the other hand, if the teacher asks a question and waits ten to twenty seconds before calling on any student, more hands will go up. Next, if the teacher makes no immediate response to the first answer given, but calls on other students to share their ideas, the class must continue to think. With the first question and answer, there may well be only one opinion. By waiting and not confirming correctness, various divergent and creative opinions develop. The strategy of questioning for higher and more creative, involved class participation is a skill to be practiced. It can make the classroom a lively place for discussion, wonder, and exploration.

SAFE Lesson No. 7

TITLE OF LESSON: QUESTIONING TO ELICIT HIGHER ORDER THINKING

DIFFICULTY LEVEL: GRADES 6–12

OBJECTIVES:

Students will:

1. Predict the author's purpose from biographical information
2. Practice predictions based on factual support
3. Apply biographical facts to the purpose or theme of a piece of literature

DESCRIPTION:

The students will read about the life of an author after having read a piece of literature by that author. They will hypothesize the connection between the author's life and the message of the literature. The students will use reading and thinking skills and express their ideas in writing.

PROCEDURES:

Stimulus:

Assign the students a piece of literature by a chosen author, for example, Conrad Richter's *Light in the Forest*. Refer to lists in Chapter 10 for more ideas. Tell the students that the novel has a message that is based on a childhood experience; therefore, the purpose is linked to the author's life.

Activity:

After the students read and discuss the novel, have them go to the library to use a biographical dictionary or encyclopedia. Depending on student age and ability, you might choose to read the information to the class. Older students should use research skills. Have students take notes, using the following questions as guides:

Who/What did the author like?

What experience is related to the situation in the novel?

What belief is related to the theme?

Direct the students to write the answers to these questions.

Follow-Up:

Brainstorm with the class ideas about the author's experiences and the novel. Discuss what message they feel the author is attempting to convey. List different expressions of this message on the board.

Evaluation:

Have the students write an explanation connecting the author's attitudes with the message of the novel. Encourage them to support their ideas with examples from the book. Read these quickly for clarity and logic, but especially for connection between the author's experience and theme.

SAFE Lesson No. 8

TITLE OF LESSON: TEACHING VOCABULARY FOR PROCESSING DATA

DIFFICULTY LEVEL: GRADES 4–8

OBJECTIVES:

Students will:

1. Identify key words for thinking processes
2. Describe the level of thinking they are using

DESCRIPTION:

This lesson will help both students and teacher add to their thinking vocabulary. They will identify added key words and know what they ask of the thinker. Students will continue to add to their thinking log and make entries that show they are aware of the level of thinking demanded by a question.

PROCEDURES:

Stimulus:

Ask students to review their log list of factual words. Note that these processes include the gathering of and simple listing of information. Tell students that they will now add key words that demand a higher level of response to questions. Ask students to think about words that suggest what they can do with information (data) they have collected.

connect		compare
summarize	INFORMATION	order
conclude	COLLECTED	explain

Activity:

Ask students to think about experiences in and out of school when they use the strategies clustered around "information."

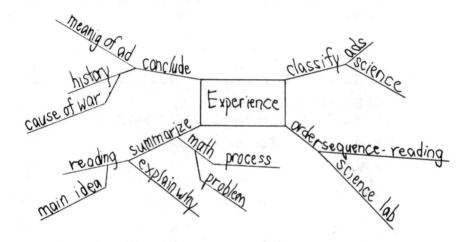

The map of the experiences with data processing skills may look something like the one above. The student will find many other examples to add. During the clustering process, ask students to explain why the experience demands more than gathering facts. Next, have the students think of questions that ask for higher level thinking skills. For example, "In science we were asked to: Compare the alligator to the crocodile."

Follow-Up:

In groups, share the results of the individual mapping. Encourage students to add to their maps. Ask them to write five questions using words from the map.

Evaluation:

Direct the students to make an entry in their logs describing a time when they used different thinking skills. Collect and check the log and questions to see if the students are correctly identifying higher level processes. Give an A+ if the student is on target. Confer with and guide any student who needs help.

SAFE Lesson No. 9

TITLE OF LESSON: LEARNING THE VOCABULARY OF HIGHER ORDER THINKING

DIFFICULTY LEVEL: GRADES 4–8

OBJECTIVES:

Students will:

1. Add to their thinking log
2. Make a chart showing thinking vocabulary
3. Recognize the level of thinking asked of a question

DESCRIPTION:

This lesson culminates in the presentation of thinking vocabulary. The students will add to their log and have a chart that will help them identify the process asked for in a question. Therefore, they will know more easily how to proceed with a task.

PROCEDURES:

Stimulus:

Ask the students to look at their logs and add the following words to it: *forecast, speculate, predict, imagine, judge, apply,* and *hypothesize.* Brainstorm with the students what these words demand of them when they are asked to use them in the classroom. Responses may include ideas such as create a model, draw a conclusion, compare past to present, tell about the future. Next, illicit from students some characteristics of the work developed through one of these processes. Help students see that these processes result in products that are not all the same, do not demand the same correct answer, or are unique to the individual.

Activity:

Put students in groups of three or four and ask them to develop a chart, showing the words in their journals in a symbolic way. They might think of them as building blocks and list the words on them. A tree might be a symbol. Have each group report their idea to the class. Decide on one to be used in the room for all students. Individuals may develop and turn in their own or keep it in their thinking logs.

Evaluation:

Students should write in their journals soon after developing the chart. You can note reactions to the process of developing a thinking chart and whether this demanded a higher level skill. Give the students questions and have them identify which key word from their chart is expected.

Notes: Younger children might be given a thinking vocabulary chart. They can use it in the classroom to identify orally the type of thinking that certain assignments demand of them and the action that should follow.

MORE LESSONS TO PROMOTE WORKING WITH DATA

The following lessons expand on the theme of teaching higher level thinking skills. Finding causes, summarizing, or diagramming are ways to express thinking beyond the factual level. Using the facts properly helps students to seek and see deeper meaning.

SAFE Lesson No. 10

TITLE OF LESSON: UNDERSTANDING BIAS

DIFFICULTY LEVEL: GRADES 3–10

OBJECTIVES:

Students will:

1. Recognize that advertisers use words that are biased or slanted
2. Recognize the unstated meaning in key words of ads

DESCRIPTION:

Students will recall current ads and recognize the "catch" word or phrase. They will become familiar with some of the techniques used to sway a consumer and will identify what the advertiser is promising.

PROCEDURES:

Stimulus:

Ask students to recite the main line of familiar TV ads or radio commercials. List some of these on the board.

Activity:

Give the students a list of terms used to describe advertising techniques. These might include: *exaggeration, generality, bargain price, promise of free gifts, promise of a better life,* or *being one of the group.* Ask students to look at the first ad line that they remembered and identify which technique catches the consumer. Write the technique next to the line. Continue for several of the lines on the board. Allow for the identification of more than one technique. Students may notice that the inferred message can also often be read from the picture as well as the words. For example:

> Greeting Card Commercial: promise of better life—"If you care enough, you'll send the best."

> Inference: You don't care unless you send cards made by this company.

Follow-Up:

Cut advertisements from magazines. Give each student one ad to underline the key words and write the technique being employed or the idea inferred.

Evaluation:

Direct students to hand in their ad. Check to see if they have accurately identified the key line or word. Award an A+ if the work is well done. Ask students to choose a partner if they need added help.

SAFE Lesson No. 11

TITLE OF LESSON: SHOW ME, DON'T TELL ME

DIFFICULTY LEVEL: GRADES 5–10

OBJECTIVES:

Students will:

1. Write for the purpose of showing a statement, not presenting facts

2. Practice responding techniques

3. Infer what is being described from the vividness of the description

DESCRIPTION:

Students will read a description that is vivid. They will identify what is being said and the words that make the description clear. The students will begin by using inference in their own writing style.

PROCEDURES:

Stimulus:

Bring into class a well-written description, such as the following from Rose Wilder's writing in *Prairie Winter*:

> Three days and nights the winds did not cease to howl, and when Caroline opened the door, she could not see the door ledge through swirling snow. How cold it was she could not guess. At the sight of clouds earlier, she had hurriedly crammed every spare inch of the dugout with hay. Twisted hard, it burned with a brief, hot flame. Her palms were soon raw and bleeding from handling the sharp, harsh stuff, but she kept on twisting it. She kept the dugout warm.

Read the description to the class or with the class. Ask the students to identify in one sentence what is being described, such as:

It was a cold night.

The prairie winter was long and cold.

The girl feels cold.

Accept all the answers.

Activity:

Give each student a sentence or give the whole class the same sentence. Tell them to write a description showing the idea, but not saying it. Suggestions might be:

The room was warm.

The fire was hot.

The dinner smelled good.

Follow-Up:

Direct the students to share their descriptions with a partner. Ask the reader to underline the words that are especially descriptive. Give the writer an opportunity to add more words to make the writing more vivid.

Evaluation:

Ask each pair to choose one description to share with the class. Have the writer read it and the partner say why it is vivid. Check that they understood how to show, not tell. At the end, identify that the writers used inference skills in reverse to hide meaning beneath the surface.

SAFE Lesson No. 12

TITLE OF LESSON: CHARACTER COMPARISON

DIFFICULTY LEVEL: GRADES 2–8

OBJECTIVES:

Students will:

1. Make a Venn Diagram showing the comparison between two characters
2. Summarize the similarities and differences between the two characters

DESCRIPTION:

After reading a story, the students will use the Venn Diagram to compare two characters. They will identify the major differences and write a summary.

PROCEDURES:

Stimulus:

Have the students read the story *Light in the Forest* by Conrad Richter. (Use *Sound of Sunshine, Sound of Rain* by Florence Heide for grades 3–6.; see page 226.)

Activity:

As students read the novel, start them on a Venn Diagram. They should do this at the beginning as a class activity, but add to it after you are sure they understand it. They are to find and record similarities and differences as labeled on the diagram below.

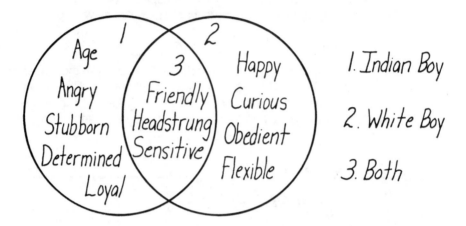

Follow-Up:

Let the students discuss their diagram with a partner. They may add to their diagram or delete from it. Direct the students to underline the major differences and then write a comparison of the two characters. They should express similarities and differences.

Evaluation:

Use student response groups to evaluate whether the student expressed both similarities and differences. Evaluate the work with a plus sign or a checkmark. Help students rewrite by giving positive direction.

Still More Ideas to Try

These lessons provide more ideas from which to build "thinking beneath the surface" skills in students. The ideas continue to build the skills necessary to move children to the highest levels of thinking. The lessons also continually make the link between reading and writing and encourage the student to be aware of what kind of reasoning process they are using.

- Distinguishing Fact from Opinion: Ask students to read an article on a current issue in which the author gives or implies opinion. Have the class read the article together. First, list the fact and have the students underline these on their copy of the article. Have the students discuss in small groups what they think is the writer's opinion about the issue. Have each group share their ideas and write these on the board. Finally, discuss these opinions in terms of their validity. Determine if they are based on facts from the article.

- Similes: Write several similes on the board. These may be taken from literature or the writing of students. Observe that the word *like* or *as* is present in similes. Ask students to decide what is being compared and how the two objects are alike and different. Students may also use poems for this lesson. Note that the reason for the similarity is based on inference. Have students identify similes in a piece of literature. They may also write their own.

- Reading Pictures: When introducing a story from the student's text, have them first look only at the pictures. Discuss what is happening, the setting, and a possible problem. A story that has good pictures is "To Build A Fire" by Jack London. (You might also use the film with the sound off.) List on the board the problems or conflict that students guess or predict are going to be present in the story. Have the students read the story to verify the accuracy of their predictions. This method of introducing a story can be used with any age group, and often motivates reluctant readers to find out what really happens. It gives children purpose for reading and sends them from an inference to verification of their reasoning.

- Creature Fun: Have the students draw a picture of the worst monster they can imagine. Tell them to keep their picture secret. Next, have the students write a description of their creature, including physical characteristics. Tell them to be accurate about size, color, and shape. Put students into pairs to share. Tell them first to give the partner their picture. Have the partner write a description using only the picture as reference. This ensures that the students try to conclude what the creature is like. Have the partners compare written descriptions with the original writing. Tell them to look for size, shape, and colors that have been missed. They will note that the problem might have occurred from faulty inference or from inaccurate information given in the writing. To draw accurate inferences, one must be given accurate information.

- Symbolism: After reading a story, discuss the major characteristics of the character. Choose one character on which to focus attention. You might use mapping or a Venn Diagram to help students record their findings.

  After a discussion of the character, have students create a symbol of the character. For example, if the person liked to ice skate and that was the focus of his or her life, have the students make an ice skate and write on it or draw other words or pictures that tell about the character. They may quote words from the story. For example, they might write the word *strong* or draw a picture of a strong person.

- Mapping: Have the students map the plot development of a story, getting as complex as they wish (see page 195). After completing the map, have students write a summary of the story. They should include important incidents and the necessary elements of a story. Have the students also include in their summary the way one event led to another. For some classes, this might need to be practiced orally first. The important part of the summary is that the students see that a well-written story has connections between events and that they must often read between the lines to find these connections.

- Metaphor: This lesson is much like the one on similes, but focuses on metaphor or the implied comparison. In a poem such as "Fog" by Carl Sandburg, the metaphor is easily distinguished. This poem is an easy one to begin with for students who are unfamiliar with metaphor. After students have discussed orally several metaphors and are able to distinguish what is being compared and how, give them a metaphor to explain or summarize in their own words.

  Common metaphors like "the party was dead" might be a starting point. In the explanation, the key is that the student infers why the two unlike things are said to be the same.

  A variation of this lesson is to have students write poems. Give them a word (colors are easily used to write poems). Their major focus is to compare *white* to _____. For example:

  > White is in the sky's sunlight,
  > It's in the mountain high,
  > And in a stream as it rushes by.
  > White is fate or a frozen pond. . . .

This poem exemplifies a student's use of metaphor and inference to make meaningful verse.

- If Animals Could Talk: Students love to infer or imagine what an animal is saying. Excellent sources of pictures of animals are *National Geographic* or *National Wildlife*. Tell students to look at a picture and decide what the animal might say. This is asking for an inference or thought about what is not stated. You might introduce or review (as appropriate) the use of quotation marks. Have the students write sentences quoting the animal. Publish these on a bulletin board with the pictures. On another day, move the pictures to a different area and ask the students to match quotes with the animal. Older students will write more, but all elementary students can enjoy this activity either orally or by writing simple sentences. Carried another step, the students might make up dialogue between animals. Again, this can be accomplished orally or in writing.

- Questions to Develop Inference Skills: A very direct way to give students an opportunity to develop inference skills is to have them read a selection and give them a set of questions focused on inference. Multiple-choice questions work well. Give the students a question based on a certain paragraph. Ask them such questions as:

     In the first paragraph, the author implied:_____

     In the second paragraph we can infer that:_____

  If the exact time of a story is not given, ask:

     The time of year in which this story takes place is _____

  Give them a choice not directly stated.
     This strategy can also be used to focus on cause and effect questions. Students should be able to make entries in their thinking logs after these exercises. They should be aware that the word *implies* asks for an inference and *why* connotes a cause-effect relationship.

Integrative Thinking

The final section of this chapter deals with the concept that thinking skills often cannot be taught in isolation. Most lessons move beyond the recall level and involve a variety of thinking skills at one time. Making an inference leads to seeing cause and effect and comparison. Summarizing demands that the child see relationships. The final goal for the student is to integrate the processes and apply knowledge creatively to new situations. Consciousness of one's own thought processes or method of problem solving is important.

A USEFUL STRATEGY: JOURNALS

Journals can be kept to compile records. These records can consist of thought analysis, as introduced earlier in this chapter. Journals can also be an opportunity for the student to write without the threat or worry of "grading." In this section, journals are presented as a means of recording the stream of one's thought while reading, after writing, or just as a diary that helps the student become aware of how they think. Once individuals understand how they solve a problem, they can refine their methods, correct problems, and use this to approach new challenges. A journal can be used after a field trip, as in Chapter 7, or to develop written pieces. They are used in this chapter to clarify thinking, think about thinking, and help the student to become a better thinker.

SAFE Lesson No.13

TITLE OF LESSON: KEEPING A READING LOG

DIFFICULTY LEVEL: GRADES 6–12 (ADAPT FOR GRADES 2–5)

OBJECTIVES:

Students will:

1. Record their feelings and questions as they read
2. Think about what they read
3. Read with purpose

DESCRIPTION:

Each student needs a notebook in which to write while silently reading a short story such as *The Legend of Sleepy Hollow*. Give the students a list of questions to answer while reading. The notebook will also be set up so that students can record their own questions and thoughts about the reading.

PROCEDURES:

Stimulus:

Introduce the basic problem of the story. In this case, was there a headless horseman or a ghost? Were these just country stories or was the major character imagining the ghosts? Were these superstitions? Read the first paragraph to the students. Ask them to identify the name of the town, who gave it its name, how far away the valley was, and what kind of birds were mentioned. Explain to the students that this basic information must be specifically recalled to understand the character. The questions given the students should demonstrate different levels of thinking. For example:

Why did the school teacher come to this village?

What do you think caused the women to like the school teacher?

Do you think the headless horseman was superstition, a trick by the enemies of the school teacher, or a real ghost?

After the questioning, introduce a basic guide for students to follow in writing responses to other questions as they read. Give them a model to use to set up their notebook.

Activity:

Students read silently to answer the questions you give them. They record their answers in the log. Have the students move part of the way through a longer piece. Fifteen minutes of quiet reading is a good beginning. Be careful not to move too far before checking for thinking and sharing answers. The following is a suggested way to have students set up their reading log or journal.

Teacher Questions	Student Answers to Questions or Their Thoughts and Observations
What did the major character do in the village?	
Did the women of the village like the character?	
What problem do you think will confront the character?	
How does the school teacher compare to teachers today?	

Note that these questions require higher level thinking. Have students leave space for brief notes or evidence. Emphasize that lengthy answers will interrupt the reading of the story. Model an example of an observation that a student might record that is not illicited directly by the questions. For example:

"I wonder why the character lived in the homes of the villagers."

"Could that happen today?"

Tell the students that these observations or questions will receive answers or discussion as well as basic questions asked by the teacher.

Follow-Up:

After the period of quiet reading, divide the students into groups of three or four to discuss their answers. They may change or add information to an answer. Ask them to identify the reason for the change. For instance, "I disagree with my answer" or "My answer was not complete." If time allows in one period, the groups should share their answers while the teacher takes notes. Discuss any variations and help the students use the text for verification. Recognize especially when there is more than one reasonable answer.

On another day, share in groups any observation or questions from the nondirected part of the journal. Again, record these for the class and discuss variations. Keep in mind your response behaviors to questions that have many answers.

Evaluation:

The students turn in their journals after the first attempt. These need not be evaluated for accuracy as much as procedure. Check to see if students are recording answers both individually and from group discussion. The process of thinking while reading is as important as the answers given. Respond with comments rather than grades for this activity. Let the students know they are using thinking skills while reading and give constructive ideas that will make their recording more valuable.

Notes: Possible ways to guide thinking while reading are included in the following suggestions for reading journal questions. Emphasize that these ideas are not the only ones to use nor must the reader include any of these as others come to mind while reading.

1. I like this character because _____.
2. I have had a similar experience _____.
3. This character reminds me of myself in this way _____.
4. This character reminds me of another character from _____ (name of other book or story) because _____.
5. On page _____, the words _____ seemed especially significant.
6. I wonder why the character did _____.
7. I do not understand the word _____.
8. The next thing that the character will do is _____.
9. I can just visualize that scene _____.
10. I thought the relationship between _____ and _____ was unusual/usual or like _____.

Note: To adapt this lesson for younger students, select literature appropriate for the grade level.

SAFE Lesson No. 14

TITLE OF LESSON: IDENTIFYING CAUSE FOR ACTION FROM A CHARACTER

DIFFICULTY LEVEL: GRADES 6–10 (ADAPT FOR YOUNGER STUDENTS)

OBJECTIVES:

Students will:

1. Identify the reasons for a character's actions
2. Identify when a character acted within the expectations of his or her personality or the related causes

DESCRIPTION:

This lesson uses the journal to focus on one aspect: cause and effect. The students evaluate the characters' actions according to the description of the personality of the characters. They ask themselves if the author prepared the reader for the actions and if the causes were clear. Journals are used to record thoughts.

PROCEDURES:

Stimulus:

Ask students if they have read stories that demanded decisions from the main characters. Summarize the story of *The Leaf* by O. Henry. Have the students read the story. Direct them to record in their journals reasons why the man painted the leaf for the girl.

Activity:

Ask the students to share their ideas. List these on the board and ask the students to summarize the reasons for the answer given. Students may read a section aloud or retell part of the action. Encourage students to refer to their journal notes.

Evaluation:

Ask students to write the best answer given in their journals. Tell them to choose the answer that presented the best reasons. Collect student journals and check the entries, giving credit indicated by a plus sign or checkmark.

Note: To adapt this lesson for younger students, select literature appropriate for grade level.

SAFE Lesson No. 15

TITLE OF LESSON: IDENTIFYING PERSONALITY TRAITS

DIFFICULTY LEVEL: GRADES 1–12

OBJECTIVES:

Students will:

1. Identify words that give clues to the personality of a character in a story
2. Compare the traits of two characters
3. Summarize the data collected on a Venn Diagram

DESCRIPTION:

Students will listen to a story. They will list the characters in the story and compare two contrasting characters by using a Venn Diagram. They will summarize the information in a three-paragraph report.

PROCEDURES:

Obtain a copy of *Sound of Sunshine; Sound of Rain* by Florence Heide (Parents).

Stimulus:

Read *Sound of Sunshine, Sound of Rain* aloud to the class. Discuss the story, noting the boy's handicap (blindness) and his way of coping with his life. Map the characters, settings, plot events, and themes to review the content of the story. Discuss the development of the character, the sister, and why students' feelings may have changed about her as the story progressed. Use a Venn Diagram to compare the sister and another character, Abram, the ice cream man, thus:

Activity:

Ask students to write one paragraph about the sister, one paragraph about Abram, and one paragraph about both.

Follow-Up:

Point out that they have written a three-paragraph report. They have compared two characters, showing how the two persons were alike and how they were different. Have students read their reports aloud to each other in groups of four to five to see how they presented the information in sentences for each paragraph. Have each group choose several sentences that they consider particularly well written to share with the whole class.

Evaluation:

Students are participating in evaluating the writing done by selecting well-written sentences. Discuss the qualities that make these sentences stand out. Have students begin a list of "What Makes Good Writing" that will serve both as a guide and a checklist as students write. Add to this list after each writing experience, guiding students to discover varied aspects of good writing and to begin editing their own writing by using their class-generated checklist.

Have students place this writing in their individual portfolios. Repeat this lesson by having students place themselves in one of the circles, comparing themselves to a character. Have students use the class checklist to score each other's writing holistically, giving papers

5 for Terrific!, 3 for Pretty Good, and 1 for Could Be Better. Have students rewrite to obtain a score of 5.

MORE LESSONS TO PROMOTE INTEGRATIVE THINKING

The following activities incorporate integrative thinking and engage students in interaction with other students. All of these ideas can be adapted across grade levels and subject areas.

SAFE Lesson No. 16

TITLE OF LESSON: PLACING CHARACTER IN A NEW SITUATION

DIFFICULTY LEVEL: GRADES 3–8

OBJECTIVES:

Students will:

1. Predict how a character will react to a modern problem
2. Identify the point of view of a character in order to predict his or her attitudes

DESCRIPTION:

The students will decide on the point of view of a character from the facts given by the author. They will then predict how that character might react in a different society. The students will move from reading to writing.

PROCEDURES:

Stimulus:

Read the students a folktale or have the students read a folktale such as "Johnny Appleseed." Ask the students what Johnny's goal was. Next, read or duplicate for students an article about pollution or ecology.

Activity:

Through class discussion, identify the point of view of Johnny Appleseed. Possible questions might include:

Why did Johnny plant seeds?

How did he feel about nature?

Ask the students what point of view is being expressed in the news article. In partners, have the students discuss how Johnny might feel about the current problem. Have them write their answer in the form of a letter to the editor signed by Johnny Appleseed.

Follow-Up:

Have the partners share their letter with a larger group. Form groups of four or six. Let the others respond to the accuracy or validity of Johnny's viewpoint to the modern problem based on his attitudes from the original folktale.

Evaluation:

Ask the partners to polish their letters. Collect and read these for accuracy of point of view. Respond with comments or a plus sign or checkmark.

SAFE Lesson No. 17

TITLE OF LESSON: RECOGNIZING AND WRITING PERSONIFICATION

DIFFICULTY LEVEL: GRADES 3–8 (ADAPT FOR K–2)

OBJECTIVES:

Students will:

1. Identify personification
2. Imagine what an inanimate thing might say or do if human
3. Write personification

DESCRIPTION:

The students will read a piece of literature chosen for their ability. The piece will show good use of personification. The students will judge the effectiveness of the technique, recognize it, and practice it in their own writing.

PROCEDURES:

Put the definition of *personification* on the board.

Stimulus:

Read the poem "Silver"* by Walter De La Mare to the students.

> Slowly, silently, now the moon
> Walks the night in her silver shoon;
> This way, and that, she peers, and sees
> Silver fruit upon silver trees;
> One by one the casements catch
> Her beams beneath the silvery thatch;
> Couched in his kennel, like a log,
> With paws of silver sleeps the dog;
> From their shadowy cote the white breasts peep
> Of doves in a silver-feathered sleep;
> A harvest mouse goes scampering by,
> With silver claws, and silver eye;
> And moveless fish in the water gleam,
> By silver reeds in a silver stream.

Ask the students to identify the examples of personification.

Activity:

Give the students a copy of the entire poem. Ask them the following questions about the lines above.

In the poem who or what is walking?

Can the moon walk?

Does the moon wear shoes? (Explain that in Old English *shoon* is *shoes*.)

Identify this as imagery or personification. Ask the students what image they visualize when reading these lines and how the moon might be walking. Ask the students to find other examples of personification.

Follow-Up:

Ask the students to bring an object to class. This can be anything from a stuffed animal to a kitchen utensil. Ask the students to write a short story from the point of view of the object. They should include abilities to walk, talk, feel, and so on.

---

*"Silver." From *Collected Poems, 1901–1918*, by Walter de la Mare. Copyright, 1920, by Henry Holt and Company, Inc. Copyright, 1948, by Walter de la Mare.

Evaluation:

Exchange papers among peers. Have the reader respond to the paper by writing:

> You showed good use of personification when you had the character _____.
>
> You could use more personification when _____.

SAFE Lesson No. 18

TITLE OF LESSON: IMAGINING A CHARACTER IN A NEW SITUATION

DIFFICULTY LEVEL: GRADES 4–10 (ADAPT FOR K–3)

OBJECTIVES:

Students will:

1. Practice identifying the personality of a character
2. Recognize that setting and details should fit the character
3. Identify actions that fit the character

DESCRIPTION:

The students will read a piece of literature and identify the major personality characteristics of the main character. They will also identify the clothes of the person and the place that the person is as being compatible with the character. The room in which they live and the type of situation should fit the personality. The students will discuss the actions of the character. They will then make some logical predictions and construct a new setting that will fit the character.

PROCEDURES:

Stimulus:

Have the students read "To Build a Fire" by Jack London found in *Counterpoint,* an anthology published by Scott Foresman. (This story is available in many other anthologies.) Brainstorm words that would describe the main character, for example: *stubborn, independent,* and *inflexible.* Note that the character disregards the advice of experts and takes the journey. Help students identify the outcome of this decision and how it fits his personality. Note with students other places that the character ignores clues that he should not take this journey.

Activity:

Have the students identify the attitude of the dog. Ask them to imagine that the dog could talk and to write what the dog might say to the man. Include how the man might have reacted. This might be done in form of a dialogue. Give the students a new situation, such as a desert or high mountainous territory. Ask them to write a description of the man's actions.

Follow-Up:

Have the students exchange their new ideas with a partner.

Evaluation:

Have students comment on the validity of the reaction of the man as related to his personality. Did the actions fit the personality? Ask each group to share one new idea.

Still More Ideas to Try

The following lessons continue to use the integration of several levels of thinking. They can be adapted for different ages.

- Telling the Story through Different Eyes: Share a story, such as *The Leaf* by O. Henry, and discuss the elements of the story. Have the students retell the story from the point of view of the leaf. The students will have to speculate about the leaf's observations of the man and the girl. Any story can be retold in this manner.

- Predicting Outcomes: Read or share a well-known story with the students, for example "Little Red Riding Hood." Have the students suggest words that fit the characters in the story, for instance, the wolf is mean, sneaky, and clever. Now have them suggest the opposite meaning of each word, the opposite of *mean* being *kind,* the opposite of *sneaky* being *trustworthy,* and so on. Have the students change the character into a new personality using the opposite traits listed. The wolf now would act differently to Red Riding Hood. Have the students share their new characters with the group or class.

- Using Controversial Issues: Have the students identify various issues having two sides. Examples might be the death penalty, off-shore oil drilling, gun control, stricter drunk-driving laws, or toxic wastes. Have the students interview a variety of people about one selected issue. After discussion in small groups, have them choose one point of view to defend.

They should choose the best reasons for their position. Have them write an argument for that point of view.

- Rewriting Nursery Rhymes: Review familiar nursery rhymes such as "Simple Simon." Recite several of these. Choose one to recite as if you were a salesperson, then a politician, then a storyteller. The voice interpretation with younger children can be used to suggest a type of person they might recognize. Ask the children to recite the poem using the voice of a certain character.

   Older children might reword the rhyme putting in modern issues or facts. They could choose to be a politician, school principal, or parent. They might be discussing or entertaining. As the children read their rhyme, let the others guess the chosen character. (See *Inner City Mother Goose* by Eva Merriam.)

- Creating a New Game: Using higher level thinking skills can make sharing books a unique experience. After reading a book, have the students list the main action in sequence. Ask them to develop a game board using the events of the story. They may even use the character to make the moves.

   If necessary, first brainstorm a game made by the class based on a well-known tale or fable.

Focus on a Theme: Understanding Our Diversity

Cultural diversity is a major part of America's heritage. Throughout its history, this nation has drawn enormous strength from the contributions of immigrants and it continues to do so. Therefore, it is incumbent upon education to reflect our multiethnic origins so that each child knows that he or she is important.

Part of developing this understanding is to foster through work in the classroom a positive self-concept and pride. Each person needs to know that his or her heritage is rich. Students also need to recognize the importance of individual differences as well as our commonalities. We should foster an atmosphere of understanding in our classrooms that will enhance learning and group dynamics. These are especially important as we emphasize peer responses to ideas, whether in written or oral language. It is also important as students offer solutions to problems and learn to accept divergent thinking.

UNDERSTANDING OUR DIVERSITY

Objectives:

By working with this unit, students will:

1. Describe their own heritage
2. Compare their life with that of another person in their family

3. Think about their heritage as rich and important
4. Understand that all have made contributions to our society
5. Compare their heritage or family culture with that of others
6. Explore the contributions of immigrants
7. Judge the theme of a piece of literature and relate its value to understanding and accepting others
8. Write a theme or story that shows understanding of others
9. Use a variety of thinking skills

Students can begin learning about themselves and members of their classroom. They can then broaden their investigations to include the many groups that make up our national population, for example:

- Racial groups:
  Black Americans
  Asian Americans
  Caucasians
  (Have students check on the meaning of *race*)
- Ethnic groups based on:
  Religious beliefs
  Sex
  Age
  Special needs (blind, retarded, deaf, aids victims)
- Persons from other countries living in America:
  Mexicans, Cubans, Canadians
  Any immigrants from other countries—history

An international study fits nicely with this thematic unit. Students can become acquainted with the many people who populate the world. Use some of the following activities:

Learning Activities for Students:

- Human Bingo: This is a game that can be shared, adapted, and played in the classroom. The children are given the sketch of a bingo card on a ditto. Each square has a question or description. Students move around the room finding students who can answer the question. The students fill in the answer and initial it. At the end of a designated time limit, give out prizes and discuss what they learned about each other.
- Guess Who?   This activity is best done at the beginning of the unit. It helps students realize that we can't judge just by what is seen. Have the students sit in groups of three or four. They are to write two "Guess Who" questions about people in their group. Examples might be:

Who has eight brothers?

Who has been to four countries?

Who has flown a plane?

Who likes to cook?

The questions should be those that cannot be readily answered by looking at people in the group. They also should not rely on physical characteristics. The class tries to answer the group's questions and then discuss whether they inferred information, judged by looks, or simply guessed. Perceptions and misperceptions is the theme. Discuss how judgments are made (e.g., clothes, neatness, color, sex, and size). Direct the students to write a short explanation of the saying, "You can't judge a book by its cover."

- Interviews: Have each student interview a member of his or her family and write a biographical sketch about the person. The following questions might be asked:

    What toys did you have?

    What games or hobbies were available?

    How long did you go to school?

    What special trips do you remember?

    How did you travel? (car, train)

    What clothes were in style when you were _____?

    What utilities did you have in your house?

- Family Tree: On a large piece of paper, outline a family tree for yourself. Try to determine a place that someone immigrated from outside the United States. Do only one side of the family if that is all the information that is available. If you prefer, find a family tree of a famous American like Benjamin Franklin, John F. Kennedy, or John Rockefeller. Have students begin a family tree with help from their families. Invite parents to come to school to share family stories on a special "Celebrating Our Families" day.

- Holiday Project: Have students pick a favorite holiday and find out how it is celebrated in other countries. You might like to choose a holiday we do not celebrate. Describe the activities and the meaning of the festival. Students may add illustrations or artifacts when they report to the class. They might bring a type of food to share with the class.

- Text Reading: In your class history text and other books, have students find information about immigration. They should take notes, using good mapping skills, and find out why the group came, when, and how. They might also include legislation such as that related to the American Indian. Students can make a timeline to illustrate this information.

- Graphing: Using the information found in texts, have students make graphs showing when immigration was great and when it was low. Write a description of reasons for the changes. Pay attention to world events that affected immigration.

- Famous Immigrants: Ask students to research famous immigrants, including what they did for our country and how they did it. You might prefer to feature a group of immigrants and where they settled, what skills they brought, and how they succeeded in our country. What problems did they encounter? Use the "I Search" form for this paper (see page 240).

- Literature: Read multicultural novels. Have the class choose individual books about immigrants or, if possible, choose a book available as a class set, perhaps *Farewell to Manzanar* or *Dragonwings*. Read the book for setting, plot, characters, and theme. For the unit, have students write an analysis of the book related to the accuracy of historical data.

- Story Writing: Read the story *Crow Boy* to the class. Discuss why the boy was not accepted at first and how he finally was. Brainstorm with the class reasons for both. Discuss the message or theme: Get to know someone before judging them. Have the students write their own story using this theme or a related one.

Resources for the Teacher:

Weitzman, David. *My Backyard History Book*. Little, Brown, 1975.

NCSS How To Do It Series. "Family History." 1981.

Leathers, N. *The Chinese in America*. Series. Lerner.

Tiedt, Pamela, and Tiedt, Iris M. *Multicultural Teaching*, 2nd ed. Allyn and Bacon, 1986.

See Chapter 10 for more ideas.

Evaluation:

- Writing an Essay: One of the best methods to evaluate understanding of this unit is through a written activity. Give the students the quote, "Never judge another man until you have walked a mile in his moccasins" (North American Indian proverb). Ask the students to explain what this means to them and how it can be practiced in their daily life. They may include examples at their school where misjudgments have caused conflict. Have them suggest methods for overcoming such problems. These essays should express ideas they've learned from the interviews, the readings, and writing of the unit.

- Personal Artifacts: Invite the students to present a poster board collage of artifacts from their family and other experiences. This should include pictures, realia, paintings, or drawings. Have the students label each item as to why it is important. These labels provide the substance of whether the students have appreciated the unit and learned more about themselves and their family.

- Cultural Influences: Ask the students to do a final project that is a collection of pictures from magazines or newspapers showing other varied cultural ideas, names, items, and foods still present in our environment. Students may draw, if able, but pictures from magazines are effective. If the students understand the point of the unit, they will dig for word origins, brand names, and other everyday things that surround us that reveal cultural influences. They should present this as a poster, diagram, or large mural.

Exploring Further

Bossone, Richard. *The Fourth R: Reasoning*. New York City University, 1983.

Educational Testing Service. *Focus 15: Critical Thinking*, 1984.

ERIC Clearinghouse on Reading and Communication Skills. *Thinking Skills in English— And Across the Curriculum*. 1985.

Hays, Janice, et al. *The Writer's Mind*. NCTE, 1983.

Jensen, Julie, ed. *Composing and Comprehending*. NCTE, 1984.

Lewis, David, and Greene, James. *Thinking Better*. Rawson, Wade, 1982.

Kirby, Dan, and Kuykendall, Carol. *Thinking through Language. Book I*. NCTE, 1985. (Teacher Guide available.) See Stanford, Barbara below.

Moffett, James, and Wagner, Betty Jane. *Student-Centered Language Arts and Reading: A Handbook for Teachers,* 3rd ed. Houghton Mifflin, 1983.

National Assessment of Educational Progress. *Reading, Thinking, and Writing*. NAEP, 1981.

Phi Delta Kappa. *National Forum: Critical Thinking*. Winter, 1985.

Purves, Alan, and Niles, Olive (Eds.). *Becoming Readers in a Complex Society*. Yearbook of the National Society for the Study of Education. University of Chicago, 1984.

Smith, Frank. *Comprehension and Learning*. Holt, 1975.

Stanford, Barbara, and Stanford, Gene. *Thinking through Language. Book II*. National Council of Teachers of English, 1985. Teacher Guide available. See Kirby, Dan above.

Tiedt, Iris M. *The Language Arts Handbook*. Prentice-Hall, 1983.

Tiedt, Iris M., et al. *Teaching Thinking in K–12 Classrooms*. Allyn and Bacon, 1989.

7

Reading/Thinking/Writing Across the Curriculum

Reading, thinking, and writing are basic processes of learning that are not limited to the reading or language arts class. These processes are essential in every study that we undertake at any stage of our lives.

Thus, using reading, thinking, and writing to enhance learning across the curriculum not only makes sense, it is essential. Each teacher can reinforce growth in these skills by providing meaningful purposes for their application. Students will improve their abilities to read, think, and write as they grapple with the content of social studies, math, and science. The same skills will be strengthened in learning about art and music, too. Your job is to plan lessons that challenge students to apply these language skills in ways appropriate to the subject they are studying.

Most of the ideas presented in preceding chapters are applicable to instruction across the curriculum. In this chapter, we present a few selected strategies that are especially recommended for these major subject areas:

Social Studies

Science

Mathematics

Art

Music

Implementing the Program

As we focus on reading, thinking, and writing across the curriculum, we should be aware of the following understandings drawn from current research:

1. Reading, thinking, and writing skills are foundational for all of learning. They are not taught only in the English classroom, but are developed throughout the curriculum.

2. Borrowing strategies from the language arts enhances instruction in all classrooms.

3. Literature can be used to enliven and enrich instruction across the curriculum. Students need to become aware of writing in different fields of study.

4. Global and multicultural education are most effectively taught as part of studies across the curriculum rather than as separate subjects.

5. Writing is one way of expressing thinking in any field. Students begin by gathering data through observation or reading, and then they process the data in some way. Students write "thinking" based on the information they have collected and how they have processed it.

Selected Resources

Explore these sources for additional information about the ideas summarized above:

Fulwiler, Toby, and Young, Art, eds. *Language Connections: Writing and Reading across the Curriculum*. NCTE, 1983.

Julie Jensen, ed. *Composing and Comprehending*. NCTE, 1984.

Squire, James, ed. *The Dynamics of Language Learning: Research in Reading and English*. National Conference on Research in English, 1987.

Tiedt, Iris M. *The Language Arts Handbook*. Prentice-Hall, 1983.

Tiedt, Pamela, and Tiedt, Iris M. *Multicultural Teaching*, 2nd ed. Allyn and Bacon, 1986.

Reading/Thinking/Writing in Social Studies

Learning the facts and concepts in the social studies class can provide the natural environment for practice of reading and writing skills. Reading and thinking provide the means or skills necessary to function in this discipline.

Combining all three, reading, thinking, and writing, can make social studies exciting. Rather than pure memorization of facts, the class time becomes a time when the past and present come alive. Students can discover social studies data and process it through speaking and writing.

When a student reads about the past, thinks about its meaning, and writes to clarify thinking, the study of the past becomes alive in the imagination of the learner. These lessons provide ideas that stimulate thinking.

A USEFUL STRATEGY: THE I-SEARCH PAPER

One of the biggest problems teachers face when assigning research is motivating the students to do more than copy facts and rewrite the encyclopedia for the teacher. We all know that this results in little or no student thought, but becomes an exercise in copying strategically so that the teacher is not sure what book is being copied. Little or no thought or appreciation for the subject matter results. Retention of new ideas or exploration of new connections between facts is lost.

The I-Search paper is one method that fosters more thought and presents the student with choices of topics. The learner searches for information about a selected problem. The personal I-Search method involves searching in different places for information, comparing facts, and then drawing conclusions. This involves reading, thinking, evaluating, deciding what else needs to be known, and analyzing facts until some conclusions are reached. The students are not just copying facts but telling the teacher what they learned, how they learned it, and why it is important to know.

Although the subject for such a paper can be as simple as which brand of jeans to buy for a special purpose, it can also be as complex as which group of Indians seems personally the most interesting, or why a cultural group is attempting to gain more recognition and rights. It can focus on a current problem as well as analysis of why a culture turned to a certain economic or political system.

The format of the I-Search paper is much like the traditional research paper. An introduction explains what will be sought; the procedure section relates what was discovered and where; the body of the report makes connections between facts and how they relate to what is sought; and the conclusion, or final analysis, summarizes what all this means to the researcher. A bibliography includes books, history texts, interviews, periodicals, or any other human or written source that the student utilized for gathering information.

The evaluation of such a paper can be based not only on the conclusions made by the student, but on the sources that they chose to find facts and the logic of the conclusions drawn. In other words, the thought process becomes the focus as well as the clarity of the writing and understanding of the facts read.

SAFE Lesson No. 1

TITLE OF LESSON: GETTING READY TO WRITE THE I-SEARCH PAPER

DIFFICULTY LEVEL: GRADES 5–10 (ADAPT FOR GRADES 2–4)

OBJECTIVES:

Students will:

1. Identify a topic they would like to know more about
2. Discuss a variety of sources for locating information
3. Explain the problem to be investigated and the questions to which they will seek answers

DESCRIPTION:

This lesson will get the students started on their search for information. They will know what and why they want to investigate a subject that is related to the unit identified by the teacher of social studies. The lesson focuses on student choice and knowledge of how to pursue an investigation.

PROCEDURES:

Stimulus:

Review with the students the unit, era, or concept that the class has selected to focus around. Brainstorm ideas of what they want to investigate; for example, one concept might be *revolution*. Brainstorm meanings of revolution and examples of different revolutions.

Activity:

Have the students write questions about "revolution" based on the cluster of their ideas, for example:

What were the causes of the Renaissance?

What is the connection between political and economic revolution?

What is the result of the computer revolution in our daily lives?

Why did the colonists seek independence from a powerful nation like Britain?

How would revolution change people's daily lives?

Have the students continue to write questions. Share these in small groups. One person's thoughts stimulate others.

Follow-Up:

Have the students identify one question that they would like to know the answer to. Ask the students to give this question to the teacher.

Evaluation:

Although variations are possible, the best evaluation of this lesson is the student's enthusiasm about the subject. Another criterion is the student's ability to identify the question that they want to research.

SAFE Lesson No. 2

TITLE OF LESSON: HELPING STUDENTS BEGIN THE INVESTIGATION

DIFFICULTY LEVEL: GRADES 5–10

OBJECTIVES:

Students will:

1. Identify the best sources for their topic
2. Explore several types of sources
3. Read with purpose and take notes directly related to their topic

DESCRIPTION:

After the students have identified the question to be answered, it is extremely important that they know where and how to begin to look for an answer. They need to understand that they may not find specific answers, but several clues or facts that can be used to infer information and make conclusions. Methods of keeping notes and recording sources should be taught or reviewed. Research skills are easily taught through the discipline of social studies because students are using them within a meaningful context, not in isolation. The following are some methods that are easy for students at a variety of grade levels.

PROCEDURES:

Stimulus:

Take the students to the school library and show them where the various resource books are. Include:

Encyclopedias

Atlases

Reader's Guide to Periodical Literature

Almanacs

Books on the subject (e.g., American Revolution, Renaissance artists)

Picture files

Filmstrips and VCR recordings

Identify other sources of information:

Letters to experts

Interviews of history teachers or parents with special interests

Interviews of people in business that have relevant experience

Activity:

Have the students make a list of sources best for their topic. Share this list in groups and allow others to make suggestions; revise the list. The list should then be handed in to you.

Follow-Up:

Respond to the list, including adding suggestions or deletions. Give the student an outline to follow during the investigation, such as:

Part I   Statement of the problem—what you plan to investigate.

Part II   Describe where you went for information and what you found.

Part III   Describe information that you found about your topic.

Part IV   Conclusion or answer to your question.

Part V   Prepare a bibliography for your paper.

Evaluation:

Set a date on which to examine students' notes. Suggest that they include each source on a different sheet of paper. Evaluate each student's success in finding information.

SAFE Lesson No. 3

**TITLE OF LESSON: WRITING AND
SHARING THE I-SEARCH PAPER**

DIFFICULTY LEVEL: GRADES 5–10

OBJECTIVES:

Students will:

1. Present a logically developed written report that includes information and sources
2. Discuss and share information
3. Evaluate other research according to its clarity and purpose

DESCRIPTION:

Reports should not be written just for the teacher but for other students. Peer response can be one of the best ways to save you hours of grading and, more importantly, to share information in the social studies class. Through sharing reports, students learn new information and learn to value the ideas of others. They also readily respond to good writing as well as help those who need to know they are not communicating ideas clearly. This lesson focuses on this process and changes the audience for the report to other students. It also stimulates class discussion.

PROCEDURES:

Stimulus:

Let students know that they will be sharing their reports with others in the class. Although they are reporting on a question that they chose, sharing different ideas is itself a learning process.

Activity:

Divide students in groups of three or four and have them read their papers to the group. This means the responses will be to ideas—not just handwriting or spelling. Have the members of the group each give a positive response and also some suggestions for improvement for each paper. Have the writer record these on a response sheet like the following and attach them to their paper.

Responses (positive)
1.
2.
3.

Suggestions for change
1.
2.

I will work on _____

Follow-Up:

Have the students turn in their reports with the response sheet that includes a statement of what they feel they need to work on. This can be used for reference for another paper or given back to the students so that they can revise their paper. A place on the response sheet for teacher comments can also be added.

Evaluation:

The group process is one form of evaluation; the teacher response is another. The students' recognition that they have answered the question they asked is the best evaluation. This can be judged by both you and the student. A plus sign or checkmark can be used to indicate the evaluation.

Note: Although these lessons are labeled for fifth through tenth grades, the concept is easily adapted to lower grades. This is especially true of the beginning research.

Still More Ideas to Try

The following lessons are short summaries of thinking, reading, and writing connections made within the social studies discipline. The various levels of thinking are involved. Students use discussion to stimulate writing and reading, and reading to inform writing. These ideas are adaptable for a variety of age groups and levels of ability.

- A Pioneer Letter: After spending time on a unit about the westward movement, read examples of actual letters written during this period. Excerpts can be found in some history texts or in J. S. Holliday's book, *Fools Rush In*. Students should analyze the basic mood and message found in these letters.

  Assign the students a letter-writing activity. Give them a friendly letter format to follow. They should write to an imaginary character about the sights and experiences of being a pioneer. Follow the writing with

with paired students responding to the letters, giving the writer constructive suggestions for improvement and positive responses about the effectiveness of the letter. Have the students rewrite the original letters, making corrections and additions. Have students hand in the letters with an illustration, just as a person might send with an actual letter of the time.

- "Paul Revere's Ride" and News Reporting: Students can write a newspaper account from either the British or colonial point of view based on Paul Revere's midnight ride. They can use this technique after discussing any incident in history. For this activity, provide the students with a copy of the poem by Henry Wadsworth Longfellow.

  Oral reading is an effective way to present the poem. Divide the poem into chronological parts based on the setting in the poem. For example, start at Old North Church, move to the Charleston shore, Medford town, Lexington, Concord, and Middlesex. Have groups of students read their assigned parts in order. Encourage dramatic interpretation. After the reading, discuss the incidents from the point of view of the British and the colonists. Help students see that "hero versus traitor" depends on one's point of view.

  Brainstorm headlines that might have appeared in either side's newspaper. Assign a news article. Have the students write from a definite point of view and relate the incident as it might have appeared in the newspaper of that time. Newspaper articles based on various historical incidents can be collected during the school year, bound, and placed in the school library. The evaluation of the article is based on the writers' ability to convince the reader of their point of view. Encourage students not to state this too pointedly but to imply it by the words they choose for their article.

- Analyzing Attitudes toward Conflict: Any war studied in social studies can be discussed from various attitudes. Some people are for the war and others are against it. Some feel any war should be averted. Attitudes are also colored by whether one is a soldier doing the fighting or a civilian hearing reports about the war. This concept can be used to discuss any conflict. Assign the reading of *Red Badge of Courage*. Discuss the main character's attitudes toward war. An effective means is to look at what the character does, what he says to himself and/or others, and how he is described by other characters in the novel. During the discussion, emphasize that the character's feelings might be the same as a soldier's during any war. Have the students research articles written recently about the draft. Assign an essay, "If I were drafted, I would. . . ." This assignment asks students to evaluate their feelings and leads them to gain insight into different points of view.

- Teaching Economics through Commercials: By listening to and reading commercials, students increase their knowledge of language as well as their ability to recognize biased language. Have the students read several magazine ads and note the key words used to grab the attention of the consumer. Record a common commercial and play it for the children. Discuss what advertisers are trying to do and how they go about doing it. After careful analysis and identification of key words in several kinds of ads, have the students write their own commercial or present their own ad to the class. Encourage recording, role playing, or other creative methods of presentation. Insist on catch words that sway the consumer. Older children might look at careers in advertising and the relationship between effective ads and the profits of various companies.

- Understanding Historical Setting: The reading of history will be more meaningful when the student can visualize the setting of that time. Understanding human feelings can aid this process and increase the students' ability to understand people's reactions to current problems. Students will write about a fictional character in an historical setting; this requires a full understanding of that period. The first step is to have students read historical novels or short stories. These are most effective when they focus on a universal theme such as imprisonment, poverty, or separation. Books that are excellent resources include: *South Town* by Loren Graham (New York: Crowell, 1969) or *Farewell to Manzanar* by Jeanne Wakatsuki Houston and James D. Houston (Houghton Mifflin, 1972). Engage students in a discussion of human reactions to separation, prejudice, or personal disappointment. Identify fear, loneliness, and confusion. Brainstorm a time or several periods of history when such feelings were prevalent. Have the students choose a period and relate the character and setting. The students can write a story, dialogue, play, or character sketch about a person and his or her place in a particular setting. Valid human emotions in a factually based setting is the basis for evaluation.

- Creating a Country: After a study of geography, lifestyle, economics, politics, and daily life in any country, students can create their own fictional country. They should present written as well as visual material. Maps of various types might display landforms, bodies of water, and other geographical characteristics. Illustrations of shelter, clothes, and ceremonies can also be included. A written description of the people and their rules is important. Creating a new country can be a group or individual project. It makes clear whether children understand what common elements are present in a country or culture.

- Reading for Historical Accuracy: Have the students read an account or description of a historical character (e.g., Abraham Lincoln). Have the students brainstorm adjectives that describe the character, such as kind, freed the slaves, honest, studious, rugged, persistent, determined. Next, have the students list settings that are associated with Lincoln (e.g., battlefield, school room, White House, Ford Theater). Now have the students divide into groups, select one setting, and role play Lincoln in that setting. Encourage the use of a variety of resources for information so that the role playing is historically accurate.

Reading/Thinking/Writing in Science

By its very nature, science involves students in the process of hypothesizing or moving from idea to proof. This is the process used by famous scientists to substantiate ideas so that they will be accepted as fact. The student of science can clarify thinking that is based on data gathered from observations and reading materials through the process of writing. Using the scientific method is easily connected to writing.

A USEFUL STRATEGY: THE LEARNING LOG

The learning log is an excellent way for students to express their findings or their questions. They can clarify concepts, ask questions of the teacher, or set goals for learning. The log is usually kept in a notebook or paper in a folder. In it the students summarize what they learn after a lecture, a laboratory period, or a class discussion. They may also express frustrations and ask specific questions of the teacher. The teacher reads the logs to evaluate the effectiveness of a lesson as well as to identify students who need specific help. The teacher may ask to see the student or respond to questions in the log itself. This method establishes the atmosphere of trusted communication between teacher and student.

SAFE Lesson No. 4

TITLE OF LESSON: USING A LEARNING/ READING LOG

DIFFICULTY LEVEL: GRADES 3–8

OBJECTIVES:

Students will:

1. Record thoughts while reading a scientific description
2. Understand that writing and reading can clarify learning

DESCRIPTION:

This lesson helps the students to take notes while reading. It focuses on the skill of finding key words—not writing everything in the text. It helps students to synthesize what is read or to read with purpose.

PROCEDURES:

Stimulus:

Assign students a section of a text or periodical to read. Tell them to use a notebook to take notes.

Activity:

Model the process of writing about what was read. Ask students to read a section or paragraph that has a heading. After reading, put the main words of the heading on the board, for example: "Circulation." Under the main subject have the students first list the key words related to the topic (e.g., *arteries, veins*). Do this with the class as they read. Next, ask the students to add a phrase of clarification after the key words.

Follow-Up:

Give the students a few more pages to read in class or for homework. Have them follow the same procedure for each section. Emphasize that they are picking out key words and reading for a definite purpose.

Evaluation:

The next day or during a subsequent time period, have the students share their notes with a partner. They should compare their choice of main ideas and come to some conclusion. Both may be right or one person may clarify what the main topics are.

Collect the reading notes and check them for key ideas. Be sure students are not copying the entire chapter.

SAFE Lesson No. 5

TITLE OF LESSON: RECORDING THE RESULTS OF A LAB EXPERIMENT

DIFFICULTY LEVEL: GRADES 4–8

OBJECTIVES:

Students will:

1. Write to clarify for themselves what they have observed
2. Ask questions immediately after the lab period
3. Write in science class

DESCRIPTION:

This lesson provides an example of using the learning log immediately following a lab experiment. It provides an opportunity for you to have the students express what they have learned from the experiment.

PROCEDURES:

Stimulus:

Have students observe a demonstration in the science lab. They will participate in whatever activities are outlined for the particular units.

Activity:

Following the lab experiment, the students record their findings in their learning log, which is set aside for this purpose. Encourage the students to connect new learning to old, express discoveries, ask questions of the teacher, and express any frustration related to the lesson.

Follow-Up:

Read the logs or have the students exchange their logs with someone in the class. The latter should be announced ahead of time.

Evaluation:

Respond or have a classmate respond in writing to the individual. (This may be a quick comment.) Comments can be a note saying that the concept will be reviewed since several students asked the same question. Peers may offer answers to student questions.

SAFE Lesson No. 6

TITLE OF LESSON: RECORDING OBSERVATIONS FROM A FIELD TRIP

DIFFICULTY LEVEL: GRADES 1–8

OBJECTIVES:

Students will:

1. Use writing to set goals for the field trip
2. Write in a journal about their observations after a field trip

PROCEDURES:

Stimulus:

Tell the students that, related to the study of reptiles, they are going to visit a local museum or exhibit on that subject. Brainstorm questions the students would like to have answered during the trip.

Activity:

Have each student record the questions that they individually most want answered as a result of the trip. Have the students label a section: "Observations during my trip to _____"

Follow-Up:

After the trip or during the field trip (whichever is more convenient), have the students record observations or discoveries. They might focus on new information or information that substantiates what has been read or discussed prior to the trip. Direct the students to answer the questions they asked before the trip whenever possible.

Evaluation:

You may collect the logs for reading as a means of evaluating the effectiveness of the field trip or planning future lessons. Or you may have students exchange journals among peers so that they can discuss observations.

Still More Ideas to Try

- Letter Writing: Letters can be a useful technique for obtaining information. Have the students write to organizations for information related to a field of science. The Sierra Club, Department of Forestry, and Audubon Society are good resources. Students may write to the editor of a specific magazine. If an inventor or scientist is available, writing directly to the person can be rewarding. Students should be given a format to follow for their letter and some guidance so that they write to places or people who might answer. Teach them to have a specific question in mind. They may also want to write to a senator or representative about a scientific issue such as the extinction of wildlife or conservation.

- Newspapers in Science: Just as newspapers related to social science can be used to synthesize information, they can also be a creative mode in the science class. The students might write a description of a classroom experiment as if it were a scientific discovery.

- Storywriting and Science: Students love to imagine themselves as some other being. If they are studying personification in literature, they might like to apply this to science. A fourth grader studying reptiles might find it more interesting to write about a day in the life of a tortoise rather than writing a report. The life of a raindrop can become exciting when told as if the person were the raindrop. This assignment involves students in making judgments based on fact rather than relating information memorized from reading.

- Poetry and Science: Students might make up their own limericks or riddles based on a science unit. This is an excellent tool used to review information for a test. The riddle can be used to test peers. Give the students a model to follow and a list of words to use as the subject. For example:

> I am in your head.
>
> I help you think.
>
> I help you get good grades.
>
> I am your _____.

- Symbolism in Science: After the study of a unit, brainstorm with the students some symbols related to the subject. If they have studied circulation, they might think of the heart, the roots of a tree, the branches of a river, and so on. Have the students choose a symbol and diagram the main elements of circulation. Ask them to present this to the class, well illustrated, and labeled. Have them give an oral presentation.

- Taking Notes in Science: Mapping, described earlier in this text, can also be used to help students organize their notes. Have them find the key elements of the subjects to use as the main parts of the map. Have the students take notes, categorizing as they read. They may work together to decide what is important and discuss their thoughts. These notes might be used to have the students make a crossword puzzle for class review or a practice test for others.

Reading/Thinking/Writing in Math

Calculating and solving problems might at first be considered far removed from reading and writing. Most of us who have struggled in math, however, are well aware that thinking logically is extremely important in solving word problems. More recently, emphasis has been put on the relationship between the ability to read and the ability to solve written problems. Finding the main ideas, key words, and making inferences are often involved.

This section focuses on solving word problems. It models the use of reading and writing skills to unlock the meaning of a math problem and writing thoughts and ideas to clarify thinking in math.

A USEFUL STRATEGY: IDENTIFYING KEY WORDS IN A PROBLEM

Reading a word problem can become easier if the reading skill of identifying key words is employed. The basic decision the mathematician makes is what determines the process employed to solve a problem. No matter how well the student adds or subtracts, if he or she uses these functions at the wrong time, the answer will be incorrect. To identify key words have students simply underline or make note of the words that indicate a function. *More than, less than,* and *how much* are keys to word problem solution. The student should first underline or identify these before proceeding to any calculation. The teacher can model this process by asking students to do this as a class, helping to clarify misunderstandings.

The next step before calculating might be to write the problem using different words and exchanging these with peers. Students can evaluate whether the peer has correctly analyzed the problem.

SAFE Lesson No. 7

TITLE OF LESSON: DEFINING MATHEMATICAL VOCABULARY

DIFFICULTY LEVEL: GRADES 2–8

OBJECTIVES:

Students will:

1. Identify the correct meaning of key math terms
2. Use the definitions to direct their choice of solutions to a word problem
3. Practice reading (word attack) skills in math class

DESCRIPTION:

This lesson helps the student use strategies learned in reading class in math class. Context clues, main idea, and use of synonyms will help the student identify the correct process to solve a math word problem.

PROCEDURES:

Stimulus:

Write a word problem on the board. Have the students record in their logs, journals, or on a piece of binder paper the words that are key to the problem. Tell students that getting the right mathematical answer is not the objective at this time.

Activity:

Discuss in class the clues in the word problem that help the student know the meaning of key words. *More than, less than,* and *compared to* are examples. Underline the context clues and main ideas in the problem on the board.

Follow-Up:

Have the students find another problem in their text and follow the same process. Have them do two more problems for homework. Do not have the students calculate the answer, but write only terms and clues.

Evaluation:

Share the homework with a peer to see if partners agree on the key words and can identify the mathematical process. You may collect and evaluate the students' ability to find the key words.

SAFE Lesson No. 8

TITLE OF LESSON: REWRITING THE WORD PROBLEM

DIFFICULTY LEVEL: GRADES 3–6

OBJECTIVES:

Students will:

1. Write the word problems clearly, but using words other than those of the math text
2. Substitute synonyms and phrases that convey the same meaning as the original problem
3. Write a clear math problem

DESCRIPTION:

By rewriting a problem for another student, the learner will clarify their own understanding of a word problem. They will think logically about the problem and practice using synonyms and other context clues in math.

PROCEDURES:

Stimulus:

Write a math problem on the board. Brainstorm with the students two or three ways that the problem might be expressed.

Activity:

Have the students write a math problem from the text and ask them to rewrite it in other words.

Follow-Up:

Have the students exchange problems and solve the rewritten problem. Compare the answer to the correct answer of the original problem.

Evaluation:

The successful solution of the problem would indicate that the rewritten problem was written clearly. It would also indicate that the students did understand what they read.

SAFE Lesson No. 9

TITLE OF LESSON: THE PROCESS JOURNAL

DIFFICULTY LEVEL: GRADES 4–8

OBJECTIVES:

Students will:

1. Describe the process method of solving a word problem in a journal
2. Identify the correct procedures and be able to put these in their own words

DESCRIPTION:

This lesson is essentially the use of a learning log in math class. The students record their thinking and questions. By reading their process journal, they may become aware of inaccurate patterns of thought. If students can identify how and why they have used a process, the chances of true understanding are greater.

PROCEDURES:

Stimulus:

Have the students solve several problems from their text. Identify with students the basic concept being emphasized in the problems.

Activity:

Have the students record their feelings, their frustrations, and their questions in their learning log. They must describe how they arrived at the solution to a problem. For example:

> To solve this problem, I added X and Y because of the words
> _____
>
> I proved my answer by _____because I know that _____ means _____.

Follow-Up:

Have the students check to see if their answers were correct. Have them share logs to check if the choice of process was correct.

Evaluation:

Collect only the journals of the students not getting the correct answer. Check the process for accuracy.

Still More Ideas to Try

- Introducing New Vocabulary: To introduce a new word to the class, the method of clustering might be useful. Put the new word in a circle and cluster around it other words associated with it. Relate the general definition or understanding to the specific definition to be used in math class. The teacher might define the word and then elicit class responses to compare/contrast definitions. Have the students write a definition of the word introduced, for example, *fraction*.

- Songs and Rhymes in Math: The song "Ten Little Indians" can be used to help children learn addition and subtraction facts. Have the students stand in a line and point to each one as you sing. As you go from ten to zero, have each one sit down. Next, put the children in groups, say the following rhyme as the students act it out.

> Ten little children sitting in a line;
> One went away and then there were nine.
> Nine little children said, "It's getting late."
> One went away and then there were eight.

Eight little children talking about heaven;
One went away then there were seven.
Seven little children doing funny tricks;
One went away then there were six.
Six little children learning how to dive;
One went away and then there were five.
Five little children sitting on the floor;
One went away and then there were four.
Four little children happy as can be;
One went away and then there were three.
Three little children had nothing to do;
One went away and then there were two.

Ask the children to think of a rhyme that will finish the poem to zero. They might also write their own poem from zero to ten.

- Writing Jingles in Math: Students love jingles. "One, Two, Buckle My Shoe" is a popular example. Give each child ten markers and yarn to make a circle. Ask them to put two markers in the circle and then two more markers in the circle. Write on the board: $2 + 2 = 4$. Help students to write a jingle about this fact. For example:

    If you have 2, and I have 2,
    And we put them on the floor,
    I'll bet when we count them,
    They'll add up to 4.

    I had 4 and,
    I put one on my knee.
    Then I counted and,
    There were only 3.

Keep a chart of these jingles in the classroom. The students love to watch their jingles grow and will chant them as math and language practice.

- Letter Writing in Math: Often students will find mistakes in the math text, especially in the answer section. Have them write a letter to the editor suggesting that the mistake be corrected. Give the students the correct business letter format for this activity. The letter may be written individually or as a group project. Keep track of responses.

- Evaluating the Use of Calculators and Computers: This might be a personal narrative about how the students feel the calculator or computer will influence their use of math. Have them interview people in careers (e.g., checkers at the supermarket) about what math is needed as they use the new machinery. They might ask what happens when the computer breaks down. This activity makes use of research, interviewing, and writing skills. It also helps students evaluate and judge new developments.

Reading/Thinking/Writing in Art

Thinking creatively when writing is an important skill. The artist is also challenged to be creative. The processes are linked. The two disciplines can be fused to help students read, write, and think with skill.

Art is a form of communication. One must be able to interpret the ideas of the artist and clarify these through writing. Bringing all disciplines together elicits a communication in harmonious unity. It breaks down any stereotype that the artist need not read or write or that the writer need not understand art.

A USEFUL STRATEGY: PUBLISHING BOOKS

Many of us secretly dream of fame. The future writer visualizes his or her first best seller. This dream need not be limited to the gifted. Writing will be a gratifying experience if our one word, phrase, poem, story, or description is appreciated by a wide audience. If writing is communication, then it should be shared at the local school level through student-made books. These can be enjoyed by another class, by parents at open house, as gifts for special occasions, or by students of another grade level.

Adding illustrations or making an exciting cover for class or individual writing is important to the author. Writing can also be used within the art class to bring meaning to the art. This also gives credibility to the fact that reading and writing are used by many in all disciplines. It is important across the curriculum.

SAFE Lesson No. 10

TITLE OF LESSON: PUBLISHING FOR OTHER GRADE LEVELS

DIFFICULTY LEVEL: GRADES 4–8

OBJECTIVES:

Students will:

1. Identify an audience and write for it
2. Illustrate or choose illustrations to fit their story
3. Make books to be enjoyed by another grade

DESCRIPTION:

Students will review, then write their own story for a younger grade level. This lesson focuses on the various methods for publishing a book.

PROCEDURES:

Stimulus:

Have students evaluate books for students of a lower grade, identifying the qualities that attract them. Next, have students read and share favorite books written for a grade level below them.

Activity:

Have students share stories they have written. Ask them to identify the setting, characters, and scenes key to understanding their story. Next, students list the possible illustrations necessary to make their story come alive. They may draw, make collages, trace, or create designs that will fit the story they have written.

Follow-Up:

Students will share the illustrations they have made for their story.

Evaluation:

Students respond to peers' illustrations and suggest changes or give positive input. They complete their books and place illustrations where they belong.

SAFE Lesson No. 11

TITLE OF LESSON: SHARING CLASSROOM WRITING

DIFFICULTY LEVEL: GRADES 3–12

OBJECTIVES:

Students will:

1. Choose a favorite piece of writing to be published in a class collection
2. Draw an illustration or choose an illustrator for their story

DESCRIPTION:

This lesson focuses on publishing writing for the class itself to enjoy. Although these may be shared with parents, other classrooms, or other grades, the prime purpose is to have each student have a class magazine or anthology that includes one of their writings and an illustration.

PROCEDURES:

Stimulus:

Show the students a magazine or collection of stories or poems. Discuss the kind of art used to enhance the collection.

Activity:

Have the students choose one piece of writing they have done. This might be a poem, description, or story. Have them decide on an illustration.

Follow-Up:

Have each student submit a final copy of their writing and an illustration. Let the class decide on a cover design or symbol for their class anthology of literary works. They may choose or vote on an artist to do the work or do this as a group. They might all submit an illustration for the cover and vote on the best.

Evaluation:

Reproduce the writings with the cover for the class. The evaluation will be the satisfaction expressed by all the students when they see their writing in print. Students may also choose to do a publication for a special season or time of the year. This may be given as gift or shared with other peers. Most important, it should represent the entire class.

Note: A variation is to use this method to publish a cookbook for a home economics class, computer work, or directions for favorite projects in an industrial arts class.

SAFE Lesson No. 12

TITLE OF LESSON: EASY ART

DIFFICULTY LEVEL: GRADES 1–4

OBJECTIVES:

Students will:

1. Follow directions
2. Use art lessons to lead to writing

DESCRIPTION:

Students will follow directions with the teacher demonstrating. They will create an elephant.

PROCEDURES:

Stimulus:

Display pictures of animals. Ask the group if they would like to be able to draw an elephant or other animal. Draw with the group.

Activity:

Work on the chalkboard. Tell the group to make each part as you demonstrate.

1. Draw a big mountain.

2. Curl the front.

3. Come right on the same line as the curl and stop at end of curl.

4. Draw a line toward back of elephant.

5. Draw a line down to ground.

6. Draw a line to back of elephant.

7. Draw a tiny eye on nose.

8. Draw a big "C" for ear.

9. Draw a little tail on back.

Have the students share their animal.

Follow-Up:

Have the students write a sentence or paragraph about the elephant. Then tell them to combine their art and story or paragraph in a finished booklet.

Evaluation:

Observe the students' willingness to share their writing.

Still More Ideas to Try

- Journal Writing in Art: Have the students record observations about color or design in their writing journals. These entries may be related to a unit under study. The journal entries may take the form of accomplishments or frustrations, much like the learning log. Allow five minutes for writing at the end of a class or on days that it seems to be needed. The teacher response will be to answer questions, give positive feedback, or evaluate class progress.

- Letter Writing in Art: Students will need supplies. As they need special or unusual supplies, letters to distributors can be used. Give the students a model business letter for this activity. The letter might also be one of complaint about the quality of an item, or it may inquire about an art exhibit. Students may also write to a museum requesting information or complimenting it on an exhibit.

- Biographical Sketches: Art students need to be aware of great artists. Researching the contribution of a person and writing a sketch of him or her is a valuable writing activity as well as one that enhances art appreciation. The sketch should include where and when the artist lived and his or her major contribution.

- Personal Reaction to a Piece of Art: After a field trip, students may write a review of the exhibit or of one favorite piece of art. This might be published by the school newspaper or just shared with the class. Students might also tell the history of a piece of art and why they think it has stayed in the realm of great art.

- Color and Form in Poetry: Students can write their poems in an artistic format. An example is to write the word *wave* in the shape of a wave. Another use of poetry is using the color as the key word in a poem. An example of a poem using a color is:

  > Blue is the endless sky.
  > Blue is rough waters.
  > Blue is the ocean calm.
  > Blue is worn-out jeans.
  > Blue is flashing eyes.
  > Blue is scribbling on a blank piece of paper.

- Sharing Books through Art: Book reports and summaries become mundane and often result in copied material, which does not really tell whether a student has appreciated or understood what was read. Art can be incorporated to make this a more meaningful classroom activity. Dioramas, mobiles made on a coat hanger with yarn and symbols from the story, as well as charts are art forms used to express understanding. Building a structure based on the novel or making a clay figure is also a creative way to integrate art and reading.

Clustering can also be used as a report form. The reader might begin with a picture, either drawn or cut from a magazine, that represents the main character or a scene from the book. Have them draw lines from the picture on which to place verbs, adjectives, or whatever part of speech decided on. These words should be related to the action of the book, or the description of character or setting. At the end of each line, place another picture illustrating the word. This clustered chart can be used as the center of an oral presentation.

Mapping can also be employed. The students might use symbols to represent the character or setting in each of the blocks of the map. Constructing a relief map of the setting of a story employs artistic talents of the students.

Reading/Thinking/Writing in Music

As with art, music is a form of communication. The mood of a piece of music can correspond to the mood of the listener. Music can soothe or irritate, excite or inspire. The words to the music enhance the meaning. Music is used by the dancer, the writer, the skater, or the person wanting to relax. Music is often used in the classroom to calm worried test takers. Our world, filled with noise, needs to make greater use of music. It needs to look at the part music can play in our ability to produce or our ability to relax.

This section focuses on the use of music in the classroom. Reading and listening to the words, writing our own lyrics, and evaluation of mood are all aspects of the thought process.

A USEFUL STRATEGY: SONGS AND MOOD

Many of our children listen to songs, repeating the words yet comprehending little of their meaning. The words of songs are poetic and often carry a message lost on the listener. The classroom teacher can help the listener to be a reader of words, to evaluate their message, and to become aware of the mood they create for the listeners. As consumers, we want people to be aware of the quality of the product.

Music can create the mood for learning. Music can be used to teach sounds and as an inspiration for new words. Music is communication; therefore, it is related to writing, reading, and thinking processes.

SAFE Lesson No. 13

TITLE OF LESSON: COMPARING THE MOOD OF A POEM AND SONG

DIFFICULTY LEVEL: GRADES 6–12

OBJECTIVES:

Students will:

1. Read a poem and recognize the theme
2. Listen to a song and recognize the theme
3. Write a comparison between the themes of the poem and song

DESCRIPTION:

Students will listen to a poem and the words of a song. They will analyze them according to the theme. This lesson will develop a need to listen to the words of a song. Through writing, the students will express the similarities.

PROCEDURES:

Stimulus:

Share the song "Eleanor Rigby" (or any song you choose) with the class. Hand out a copy of the words and discuss the theme. (In "Eleanor Rigby," the theme is loneliness.)

Activity:

After the class identifies the theme and key words that express it, have them search for a poem with the same theme. Poems expressing loneliness are readily available in classroom anthologies. Have the students underline the words in the poem that they feel add to this mood.

Follow-Up:

Have the students write a description of why they feel the song and the poem create the mood of loneliness. They should be encouraged to quote words and phrases to prove their point.

Evaluation:

Have the students share their writing in groups. Evaluation should be based on whether they have shown that both the song and the poem have the same theme.

SAFE Lesson No. 14

TITLE OF LESSON: ANALYZING THE CHARACTER PRESENTED IN SONG

DIFFICULTY LEVEL: GRADES 5–12

OBJECTIVES:

Students will:

1. Listen to the song and recognize the description of a character
2. Analyze the description of the character and draw conclusion about this person

DESCRIPTION:

The students will listen to the song "Richard Cory" sung by Simon and Garfunkel. They will discuss the character, using the skills used in comprehending the personality of a character from a story or other piece of literature. Students will discuss the character and move from the musical poetry to prose.

PROCEDURES:

Stimulus:

Play the song "Richard Cory." Give the students a copy of the words and listen a second time.

Activity:

After hearing the song and reading the words, have the students list characteristics of Richard Cory that are obvious, such as:

He is rich.

He has political connections.

He was born rich.

He was born to a banker.

He was an only child.

Next ask the students to list the qualities of the unnamed character, the narrator. For example:

He is a worker.

He wants to be like Richard.

He is poor.

He does not like being poor.

Students might use a Venn Diagram to compare these two characters.

Follow-Up:

Ask the students to infer the question that the narrator might be asking about Richard Cory. (Is he happy?) Brainstorm possible answers. Have students write on the theme of material possessions and happiness. This can be a paper in which they give their opinion, or they might prefer to write a description of Richard Cory based on the song.

Evaluation:

Students will relate to the song and be able to discuss ideas or character after reading the words. Students will share their writing with peers and give responses related to comprehension of the words of the poem.

Note: As a follow-up to this lesson, provide a copy of E. A. Robinson's poem on which this song was based. Compare the two interpretations of the same person.

SAFE Lesson No. 15

TITLE OF LESSON: WRITING LYRICS

DIFFICULTY LEVEL: GRADES 5–8

OBJECTIVES:

Students will:

1. Write lyrics that have rhythm and rhyme patterned after a song
2. Discuss the meaning of the song and understand that the new song should also have meaning

DESCRIPTION:

Students will read the words of the song "There's a Place for Us" from the musical *West Side Story.* They will note the rhyme and rhythm as they listen, then discuss the song. They will express the ideas or meaning of the poem or song. This song might be the song of any teenager hoping for their future. The song that the student writes should show an understanding of the elements of poetry as well as the meaning of the song.

PROCEDURES:

Stimulus:

Play the song "There's a Place for Us." Tell the story or, with the help of the students, review the story of *West Side Story.*

Activity:

Analyze the rhyme of the poem at the end of the lines. Note the rhythm. Brainstorm the theme or meaning and ask students to write down hopes they might have.

Follow-Up:

Have the students think of a first line that is a statement of their hope. Ask them to list words that rhyme with the last word. Then have the students complete their own poem.

Evaluation:

Let students share their poems and get peer response concerning their message as well as their use of rhyme.

Still More Ideas to Try

- Mood and Music in the Classroom: Music can create a quiet mood in the classroom. Play a variety of music, asking the children to identify the specific mood created: love, hate, anger, quiet, or strangeness. Have the students find other music that creates a mood and share this with the class. Have the students find a poem that has the same mood. They can share this with the class in small groups, write their own mood poetry, or present a booklet of mood poetry. Another activity related to this would be to have students write the lyrics for the song and try to present the mood through the lyrics.

- Folksongs: Find a folksong, such as "John Henry," "Erie Canal," or other historically set song. Have the students analyze the setting and identify the time described by the song. Students might then choose a different time and pattern a new poem, using the words of a different time, yet keeping the original pattern.

    This activity can help children understand setting and music as well as the fact that music often makes a statement about the attitudes and values of a time in history. Patriotic songs, songs of war and soldiers, and songs about historical figures are examples of this.

- Understanding Composers: Writers of music often have a message to convey about the time in which they live. After studying a particular period in history or a culture, the students may profit from hearing and analyzing the message of music from that time. They might choose a representative composer and research the historical setting of his or her lifetime. Understanding why a piece was written can help students understand history as well as music.

- Patterning: Have the students sing a song such as "Make New Friends." They enjoy singing this as a round. Have the students make up added verses of their own to be sung by the class. This activity combines writing and oral work.

- Using Music to Reinforce Sound and Spellings: Display pictures of objects beginning with the sound to be taught. Have the students sing "Mary Had a Little Lamb." Sing it together once or twice, then have them sing just the first line but use the name of something in one of the pictures, such as:

> Mary had a little duck, little duck, little duck
> Mary had a little duck
> Downy, downy duck.

These new words are suggested by the students as they add lines to the songs. Notice they are repeating the /d/ phoneme. Students may want to think of other songs to use with pictures, for example "Old MacDonald." Let the students compose in groups and share their songs with the class.

Exploring Further

Lystad, Mary. *At Home in America as Seen through Its Books for Children*. Schenkman, 1984.

Moffett, James. *Active Voice: A Writing Program across the Curriculum*. Boynton/ Cook, 1981.

Pellowski, Anne. *The Story Vine: A Source Book of Unusual and Easy-to-Tell Stories from around the World*. Macmillan, 1984.

Tchudi, Stephen and Tchudi, Susan. *Teaching Writing in the Content Area: Elementary, Middle School/Junior High, Senior High School*. National Education Association, 1983.

Tiedt, Pamela, and Tiedt, Iris. *Multicultural Teaching: Activities, Resources, and Information,* 2nd ed. Allyn and Bacon, 1986.

Tway, Eileen, ed. *Reading Ladders for Human Relations,* 6th ed. American Council on Education and National Council of Teachers of English, 1981.

8

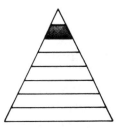

Reading and Responding to Literature

A major reason for learning to read is to be able to read literature—to know and appreciate our literary heritage. At each level, we introduce books, films, and other forms of literature that will engage students in thinking, questioning, and responding. We open the doors to the great variety of literature available and share the joys of exploring the offerings of a good library.

As students read, they respond, thinking about what they have read and expressing their thinking orally and in writing. We talk about their role as readers in transaction with the author—a shared responsibility for the communication of meaning. We help them see authors as real people, putting words on paper, writing to communicate to an audience just as they do. We guide them to make connections between their own reading and the writing that they read as they learn to write by reading. Our aim is to involve these students with books so that reading becomes an integral part of their lives and they will be lifetime readers.

Here are many ideas for working with students as they expand their knowledge of literature, their ease with reading for information and enjoyment. Activities are grouped in these categories:

Learning to Read/Think/Write with Literature

Exploring Literature Concepts and Forms

Experiencing Drama: Process and Product

Developing a Thematic Module: Freedom

Implementing the Program

Why use literature in a reading program? Literature, the wonderful *trade books* written especially for young people over the years, offers exciting content—stimulating information to answer students' questions, well-written narratives to lead children into the worlds created by skilled authors, inspiring poetry and drama that speak to these growing human beings as they begin to read the world around them. Literature, then, can:

Increase students' self-awareness, their sense of identity

Transmit our cultural heritage

Share the thinking of great minds with young learners

Help students understand other people in our society

Expose young writers to excellent writing styles

Stimulate the enjoyment of reading

Present examples of literary concepts and forms

If literature is not an integral part of our literary program, when will children have an opportunity to meet Maurice Sendak, Beverly Cleary, and Judy Blume? Shouldn't every child know Madeline, Charlotte and Wilbur, the Borrowers, Pippi Longstocking, Homer Price, and Robin Hood? We have a responsibility for bringing children and literature together. We need to lead them to the works of Robert Frost, Barbara Tuchman, and Toni Morrison.

As we plan a holistic language and literacy program in which literature plays an important role, we rely on theory and research to provide such guidelines as these:

1. Student interests vary widely. Not all students enjoy the same literature selections. Therefore, we know that we need libraries that offer a wide variety of fiction and nonfiction, poetry and prose, books for young people of all ages. We need books to satisfy every child's needs.

2. Children learn to think as they read. They learn to discover the hidden meanings that authors hide "between the lines." They use higher order thinking skills as they evaluate what they read in terms of content and quality of writing.

   Students need to read many different kinds of books. They need to hear the thinking of authors who share their ideas about historical events, how families get along, and the beauties of our country. Children need grist for their active brains to grind as they create meal—the ideas that will be shaped and reworked as they learn.

3. Positive experiences with reading and sharing literature motivate students to read literature independently. The classroom offers many opportunities for children to have positive experiences with literature as they read in a pleasant setting, supported by an enthusiastic teacher. A selected collection of enticing books, a cozy book nook, and time for reading and sharing good books—these are the elements of a classroom in which reading takes place.

4. Students who read frequently tend to write better than those who do not read well. Students learn much about writing through reading. We can help students become aware of the connections between reading and writing. They can begin to perceive themselves as authors writing for specific audiences as they create original books that we display with those of more famous authors. Children are interested in observing the writing of authors whose books they enjoy reading, and they may choose to imitate an author's way of writing. As they read, they also notice the use of mechanics, acquire new vocabulary, and encounter new ideas that they may want to talk about in their writing.

5. Drama involves students with literature through acting out activities as well as reading and writing. We can introduce students to literature presented in play form, and we can also help them dramatize other forms of literature, such as role playing, readers' theater, story theater, and puppetry.

6. Children learn to read by reading. We want to be sure that the time they spend in reading includes quality activities that engage them with the very best of literature. Children should not be bored by "watered down" reading material or fill-in-the-blank activities that present words out of the context of whole language. They should be challenged and motivated to read because the story is so exciting they cannot put it down! Students need a chance to choose books that interest them. Through reading, they will learn to read more fluently; they will learn ways to unlock meaning by working with words and ideas in the context of whole language in whole books.

Selected Resources

For more information about the above topics, you may want to refer to the following resources:

Cullinan, Bernice. *Literature and the Child*. Harcourt, 1981.

Egoff, Sheila. *Thursday's Child: Trends and Patterns in Contemporary Children's Literature*. American Library Assn., 1981.

Huck, Charlotte. *Children's Literature in the Elementary School*. New York: Holt, 1982.

Nilsen, Aileen, and Donelson, Kenneth. *Literature for Today's Young Adults*. Scott, Foresman, 1985.

Somers, Albert B., and Worthington, Janet E. *Response Guides for Teaching Children's Books*. NCTE, 1979.

Sutherland, Zena, et al. *Children and Books*. Scott, Foresman, 1984.

Tiedt, Iris M. *The Language Arts Handbook*. Prentice-Hall, 1986.

Tiedt, Pamela L., and Tiedt, Iris M. *Multicultural Teaching: A Handbook of Activities, Information, and Resources*, 2nd ed. Allyn and Bacon, 1986.

Learning to Read/Think/Write with Literature

From the time children crawl into their parents' laps and listen to stories, they hear the beautiful language of literature. The pictures painted by the words help them develop creative thinking and visualization abilities. Books present the natural flow of language, varied structures of sentences, and different styles, which in turn help expand student reading and writing abilities. We can encourage this continued growth by sharing books with children in school.

Because literature is readily available in school libraries, it can be one of the least expensive, yet effective, teaching tools. Patterned excerpts from stories suggest interesting and provocative writing experiments. Poetry stimulates thinking, focusing on sensory language and introducing imagery. After reading fables, myths, and tales, children can invent their own, following the ancient traditions of folklore. Don't overlook literature as a rich, satisfying resource for teaching reading, thinking, and writing.

A USEFUL STRATEGY: LA DICTÉE

Are you looking for a technique that will improve listening abilities, serve as a stimulus for learning writing skills, yet stimulate the enjoyment of literature? By using a multisensory method, called La Dicteé (Iris M. Tiedt, "La Dictée: A Dictation Method for Learning to Write," ERIC, 1983), you achieve that and you also enhance enthusiasm for writing, listening, and thinking. This technique can be adapted for any age level and ability.

First, choose a good book and find an interesting, well-written paragraph from the book that you can dictate to your students. This paragraph should illustrate one or more aspects of composition, such as capitalization, parallelism, or punctuation of dialogue. The next step is to introduce the book to the students and tell them that you are going to read a selection to them.

After reading the paragraph, ask appropriate questions about the characters or plot and introduce vocabulary words, discussing the meanings. Write difficult words on the board to relieve students of the anxieties they normally feel about dictation and spelling.

Now dictate the paragraph one sentence at a time. Read each sentence twice, once in its entirety, and a second time in phrases of reasonable length. Caution students not to ask questions during dictation so as not to disturb others. Once you have finished, slowly read the paragraph again, stressing word endings and pauses. During this reading, students check for accuracy.

The final important step is correcting the dictation on the board, sentence by sentence, pointing out the author's style, grammar features, punctuation, and various spelling patterns. Students make corrections on their own papers.

Subsequent lessons reinforce composition skills presented in the dictated paragraph. When students see composition conventions used correctly, they are learning to write by reading. In their own compositions they more readily experiment with style, reinforcing newly learned techniques and expanding their thinking.

SAFE Lesson No. 1

TITLE OF LESSON: LA DICTEÉ, AN INTRODUCTION

DIFFICULTY LEVEL: GRADES 6–10 (ADAPT FOR GRADES 1–5)

OBJECTIVES:

Students will:

1. Observe punctuation used in a literature text
2. Write from dictation to see if they can punctuate correctly
3. Apply rules for using commas in a series

DESCRIPTION:

Students learn how to use commas in a series. They will follow a La Dicteé presentation of a paragraph from *Treasure Island.* They will not only learn this specific punctuation skill, but they will also develop listening ability, new vocabulary, and an interest in reading a classic.

PROCEDURES:

Bring in multiple copies of *Treasure Island* so that students can read independently after you complete this lesson.

Stimulus:

Begin this lesson with a brief introduction of the author, Robert Louis Stevenson (1850–1894). He came from Scotland, but he traveled throughout the world. Sporadic illness confined him to bed throughout his life, causing him to write from his bedside. He spent his last ten years in the South Seas, learning to know the people and creating his famous book, *Treasure Island.* He was awarded the title, Tusitala (Teller of Tales), by the Samoans.

Present a brief introduction to the book. *Treasure Island* is a tale about a young boy, Jim Hawkins, who goes to sea after his father dies. He meets Long John Silver and Blind Pew who are searching for Captain Kidd's treasure. Tim encounters hair-raising adventures while on the island and battles the pirates for the treasure. He becomes a hero and grows to love the island.

Activity:

Dictate the following paragraph after first reading the paragraph to them.

> The cold evening breeze, of which I have spoken, whistled through every chink of the crude building, and sprinkled the floor with a continual rain of fine sand. There was sand in our eyes, sand in our teeth, sand in our suppers, sand dancing in the spring at the bottom of the kettle, for all the world like porridge beginning to boil. Our chimney was a square hole in the roof: it was but a little part of the smoke that found its way out, and the rest eddied about the house, and kept us coughing and wiping the eye.

Before dictating the paragraph, ask:

Who is the "I" in the story?

Where is he? Who else might be there?

How did the people feel?

What were the living quarters like?

After dictation, make corrections on the board. Then discuss the use of commas in the series of phrases and the use of the colon. In this paragraph, Stevenson uses *commas* differently than we do today in two sentences (before *and* + a phrase). Use that as a source of lively discussion.

Follow-Up:

The next day, repeat the paragraph as a lead-off lesson to the repetition of the *sand* phrases. Discuss the effect of this parallel structure on the scene. Develop a sentence using parallel structure for snow:

Looking through the car window I could see snow on the passing fences, snow on the trees, snow on the road, snow on the hood of the car.

Compare that sentence to *I could see snow everywhere.*
Have the students pattern sentences for:

Peanut butter on a baby

Fire on an object

Litter at a ballgame

Spilled paint in a room

Toilet paper in a yard

Make sure you emphasize the use of commas. You could also include a lesson on the use of commas with the dependent clause "of which I have spoken," and have the students pattern that as well.

Evaluation:

Students recognize the use of commas in a series as a means of connecting ideas. They use commas and parallel structure when writing.

Their ability should greatly improve in listening and in taking dictation. Students should show improved writing skills with this technique if used often enough, and they will probably start experimenting with other types of punctuation besides the comma.

SAFE Lesson No. 2

TITLE OF LESSON: LA DICTÉE: VARIED GRAMMATICAL PATTERNS—SHOWING, NOT TELLING

DIFFICULTY LEVEL: GRADES 6–10 (ADAPT FOR GRADES 1–5)

OBJECTIVES:

Students will:

1. Analyze more sophisticated sentence patterns
2. Associate commas with intonation
3. Observe how the author shows emotion

DESCRIPTION:

Students will listen to a paragraph dictated from *Farewell to Manzanar*. They will discuss the use of commas in a more complex sentence structure, and they will learn to show, not tell.

PROCEDURES:

Bring a copy of *Farewell to Manzanar* to share. Give the following lesson.

Stimulus:

Introduce the book *Farewell to Manzanar* by Jeanne W. Houston and James D. Houston (1974). Born just before World War II, Ms. Houston was learning to integrate her Japanese culture with the American society until her family was moved to a war camp. This story is about that move and their camp life.

Read the following paragraph:

Mama took out another dinner plate and hurled it at the floor, then another and another, never moving, never opening her mouth, just quivering and glaring at the retreating dealer, with tears streaming down her cheeks. He finally turned and scuttled out the door, heading for the next house. When he was gone she stood there smashing cups and bowls and platters until the whole set lay in scattered blue and white fragments across the wooden floor.

Discuss the emotions mentioned. Talk about the reaction of Mother, the dealer, and any witnesses that might have seen this. Discuss the vocabulary words *hurled, quivering, glaring, retreating, scuttled, smashing, scattered,* and *fragments.*

Activity:

Dictate the paragraph. After correcting the paragraph on the board, discuss the use of commas and the intonation involved. Use choral reading. Then have students underline all active verbs. Have them discover how the author shows rather than tells. Let students read aloud those phrases that allow people to visualize actions.

Assign students the task of finding other "showing" sentences in the story as a means of evaluating success.

Follow-Up:

On the following day, cluster words that demonstrate specific emotions, as in these examples.

Have students write "showing" paragraphs for each clustered emotion.

Evaluation:

Use response groups to select effective student examples of "showing paragraphs" to display.

Note: Benefits of La Dictée are many. Grammar and the mechanics of writing become more meaningful when observed in the context of literature. Students apply conventions and pattern the various authors' styles. Their own writing becomes more sophisticated and interesting.

Besides the improved writing skills, students show more enthusiasm for reading and sharing books. They participate in class discussions, asking questions about the passages. More readily responding to the emotions and reactions of the characters, they can learn to think and write from the point of view of the characters.

Another advantage of this way of connecting reading and writing is improved listening skill. The quietest periods are those involving La Dictée. Students learn to listen and remain quiet during the dictation process even though they may not particularly enjoy having to follow the procedure. They learn how to keep on writing while listening, how not to interrupt, and how to listen for intonation.

MORE LESSONS TO TEACH READING/ THINKING/WRITING WITH LITERATURE

SAFE Lesson No. 3

TITLE OF LESSON: RETELLING OLD TALES

DIFFICULTY LEVEL: GRADES K–3

OBJECTIVES:

Students will:

1. Retell events in sequence
2. Collectively create a story
3. Read the story written in their own words

DESCRIPTION:

Students will create their own easy-reading stories by retelling old stories.

PROCEDURES:

Read aloud an old story such as *Jack and the Beanstalk, The Three Little Pigs,* or *The Little Red Hen.*

Stimulus:

Introduce a picture book presentation of an old story. Relate the idea that stories like this were not originally written down, but rather told from one generation to the next. Thus, many different versions exist. If students have heard other versions of the story you read, allow them to relate their version. Compare stories.

Activity:

After students listen to the story, have them retell the story in their own words. Write their version on a chart similar to the one below, based on *Jack and the Beanstalk.*

> Jack has to sell the family cow for food.
> A man offers him some magic beans for the cow.
> His mother throws away the beans.
> The beans grow and grow and grow.
> Jack climbs the beanstalk and finds a strange land.
> He discovers the giant's castle.
> He explores the castle and finds a goose.
> The goose lays golden eggs.
> Jack steals the goose and runs down the beanstalk.
> The giant chases Jack.
> Jack chops down the beanstalk and the giant falls.
> The giant creates the Grand Canyon when he falls.
> Jack keeps the goose and lives happily ever after.

Have students read their story. Number the sentences and assign each student a sentence. Each student writes that sentence and illustrates it. Erase the sentences on the board and group the students so that all of the story can be retold from their sentences.

Have them arrange themselves in the proper order to retell their stories while showing their illustrations.

Follow-Up:

Put the story in a Big Book of Stories that will grow with the children through the year.

Evaluation:

Students will listen to each other read in pairs or small groups. Each one can have someone sign a Reading Achievement form like this:

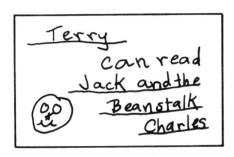

This activity is also recommended for slow readers and ESL students.

SAFE Lesson No. 4

**TITLE OF LESSON: IDENTIFYING
CHARACTERS AND PATTERNING
SENTENCES**

DIFFICULTY LEVEL: GRADES K–3

OBJECTIVES:

Students will:

1. Identify the different speakers in a poem
2. Interpret who is speaking
3. Pattern sentences introduced

DESCRIPTION:

Students will listen to poem "Sh" by James S. Tippett and identify who is speaking. This will pattern his sentences.

PROCEDURES:

Have a feltboard character for mother, father, and Mrs. Grumpy Grundy. Duplicate pictures of a mother, a father, and a grumpy person. Put the poem on strips of tagboard.

Stimulus:

Introduce the poem "Sh" by James S. Tippett. After sharing the poem, ask the students who the people are in the story poem. Introduce the feltboard characters. Ask the children what each person said. *Note:* Mrs. Grumpy Grundy never speaks and there may be some disagreement as to who said the "running . . . , who lives down below . . . , can't you play. . . ."

Reread the poem, displaying the tagboard strips as you speak.

Activity:

Give the students copies of mother, father, and Mrs. Grumpy Grundy. After cutting out the pictures, students are to hold up the appropriate picture for each speaker when you reread the poem a third time. Mrs. Grumpy Grundy's picture should be displayed when she is mentioned.

Give the tagboard strips to various children. When you again read the poem, have them place their strip on the felt.

Follow-Up:

Have students pattern the sentence strips. Use these suggested beginnings:

"Sh!" says _____.

"_____ down the _____is a very great bother."

"Mrs. _____, who _____, will _____."

"Can't you _____?"

Evaluation:

Look for sentences that appropriately use nouns, gerunds, and phrases as used in the poem. Copy these examples to share with the students.

Students can share their patterned sentences in response groups. The response groups can evaluate the effectiveness of the sentences produced.

SAFE Lesson No. 5

TITLE OF LESSON: USING QUOTATION MARKS

DIFFICULTY LEVEL: GRADES 3–8

OBJECTIVES:

Students will:

1. Observe the use of quotation marks in literature selection
2. Apply acquired knowledge of quotation usage
3. Work in pairs to create a dialogue

DESCRIPTION:

Students will learn how to use quotation marks by observing their use in a poem, "Pirate Captain Jim." They will write an original dialogue verse patterning the given poem, including proper usage of quotation marks.

PROCEDURES:

Obtain a copy of Shel Silverstein's *Where the Sidewalk Ends* (New York: Harper, 1974). Make a transparency of "Pirate Captain Jim."

Stimulus:

Share the poem "Pirate Captain Jim." Then project the transparency and read the poem aloud together. Discuss what the pirate and the little boy say. Ask students how they can tell who is speaking. Discuss the use of quotation marks to differentiate between speakers.

Activity:

Have the students work together in pairs, having one student write a "pirate" (or other devious person) part and the second student write the response. Each part must be enclosed in quotation marks.

Have the pairs write their dialogue poem on a chart which they will share with the rest of the class.

Follow-Up:

Have the students display their poems around the class or in the central hall.

Evaluation:

Choose three "editors" to check if students remembered to use quotation marks. Have students make necessary corrections.

SAFE Lesson No. 6

TITLE OF LESSON: USING LITERATURE TO TEACH IMAGERY

DIFFICULTY LEVEL: GRADES 7–8

OBJECTIVES:

Students will:

1. Observe the imagery in poetry
2. Analyze the inferred meaning
3. Pattern sentences
4. Learn new vocabulary

DESCRIPTION:

Students read the poem "The Highwayman" to analyze the imagery presented. The vocabulary words *highwayman*, *'ostler*, *galleon*, *casement*, *writhed*, and *moor* will be presented. Students compare the imagery to "telling sentences" and develop their own imagery.

PROCEDURES:

Make a transparency of "The Highwayman" by Alfred Noyes.

Stimulus:

Present the poem "The Highwayman" orally to the students. Project a copy and allow the students to reread silently. Have the following portions, used as a source of study, underlined on the transparency:

> The wind was a torrent of darkness among the gusty trees,
> The moon was a ghostly galleon tossed upon cloudy seas.
> The road was a ribbon of moonlight over the purple moor,
>
> Where Tim the 'ostler listened. His face was white and peaked.
> His eyes were hollows of madness, his hair like mouldy hay,
>
> But she loosened her hair i' the casement. His face burnt like a brand
> As the black cascade of perfume came tumbling over his breast;
> And he kissed its waves in the moonlight.
>
> She writhed her hands till her fingers were wet with sweat or blood!
> They stretched and strained in the darkness, and the hours crawled
>   by like years,
>
> Back, he spurred like a madman, shouting a curse to the sky,
> With the white road smoking behind him. . . .

List the vocabulary *galleon, 'ostler, moor, casement,* and *writhed* on the board. Discuss how they are used. Analyze the underlined portions of the poem. Describe the visual images.

Activity:

Ask the students to paraphrase the images. Some possible responses are:

> The wind blew through the trees.
>
> The moon moved across the sky.
>
> The curvy road ran past the moor.
>
> He had angry eyes and his hair stuck straight out.
>
> When her black hair fell to his shoulder, he kissed it.
>
> Time dragged on and on.
>
> The dust rose off the road as the horse galloped.

Compare these responses to the original images in the poem. Create new images for "wind blowing through the trees" or the "moon moving across the sky."

Have the students work in pairs to develop other visual images for the paraphrased statements. Have them pattern Noyes' style when using their images in sentences.

Follow-Up:

Each pair presents their sentences to the class. Select effective examples to post on the board next to the original pattern.

Evaluation:

Students help select effective examples for a bulletin board. They should learn to create imagery and use it in their writing.

Still More Ideas to Try

This potpourri of suggestions should trigger additional ideas that you can use in your classroom for teaching reading, thinking, and writing skills based on literature lessons.

- Duplicate a page of dialogue from any story that students have (even stories in the basal reader). Give each student a copy of the page. Choose one paragraph to copy together. Have a student read the first sentence and then spell it aloud, *including the punctuation marks*. Then ask the students to copy the sentence, saying each letter aloud as well as the punctuation marks. Have them check each other in assigned pairs for accuracy based on the copy they have. After this initial practice, have them copy a second portion of dialogue independently. They can check this in pairs again. Follow up with a discussion of how authors use quotation marks and why (to inform the reader).

- After reading any story aloud, ask the students to write questions based on the story, but specify the kind of thinking required: fact, inference, evaluation, or creativity. Begin orally so all understand what you are doing. If they read, for example, *Little Red Riding Hood*, have them generate such questions as:

  1. Where was Little Red Riding Hood going? (The answer is given factually. This answer requires close reading.)

  2. Why did the wolf ask her so many questions? (The answer is there, but hidden between the lines. The reader must use inference.)

  3. Do you think Red Riding Hood was a smart girl? (The reader must make a judgment that can be substantiated. Students might complete this frame for an answer: I think she was or was not smart because _____.)

4. How would Little Red Riding Hood tell her mother about this incident? (The reader must create something new, using imagination and creativity.)

- Create a newspaper that reports such events as Paul Revere's ride or the activities of Johnny Tremain. Make literature come alive as students relate real events to novels and poetry.
- Provide students with a sheet of haiku poetry. Have them read the poems and compose a description of this poetry form based on the examples. After discussing these characteristics, students can write original haiku.
- After observing imagery in poetry or prose, ask students to complete these similes:

as white as _____

as busy as _____

as quiet as _____

Generate a list of similar well-known expressions. Explain that these comparisons once were fresh but now are overworked. They are trite expressions or cliches. Ask students to compose new comparisons.

- Discuss paragraphing in expository prose compared to narrative prose. Note that we use the term *start a new paragraph* in dialogue even if a speaker says only "Yes." This word hardly constitutes a paragraph! Have students use the term *indent* as we do when we begin a new paragraph. (Indentation and paragraphing are not synonymous.)

Exploring Literature Concepts and Forms

Students need to be exposed to all varieties of writing, including:

Poetry—free verse, quatrain, haiku, cinquain

Prose—fairytale, myth, fable, short story, dialogue, diary, novel

Drama—skit comedy, dialogue tragedy, parody

Exposition—biography, autobiography, essay, article

Since the setting, mood, point of view, theme, and plot affect the outcome of stories and the way students interpret them, they need to study these elements. The character development of the antagonist and protagonist provides insights into humankind. If there is an anticlimax in the story, can students discover its purpose?

Literature provides many opportunities to develop critical thinking skills while allowing students to observe the author's skilled use of language. Literature not only stimulates students to speak, think, and read, but it also leads them to write with increasing ability. Developing a chart with students that looks something like this helps them define the elements of literature:

A Sense of Story

Question?	Literature Term	Other Ideas	
Who?	Characters	Protagonist	
		Antagonist	
		Dialogue	
Where?	Setting	Place	
When?		Time	
		Mood	
What?	Plot	Sequence	Hook
Why?		Theme	Problem
		Point of View	Transition
		Climax	Unity
How?	Conclusion	Solution	
	Dénouement		

A USEFUL STRATEGY: WORKING WITH POINT OF VIEW

In order to evaluate the validity of what they read, students need to identify the point of view of the narrator, for the author's perception influences the interpretation of a story. By identifying attitudes, prejudices, opinions, values, and judgments, students can define the author's viewpoint.

Most stories can be written from several different angles. Students are helped to understand point of view by reading and discussing first-person narratives. Introduce students to different points of view early. Start with simple tasks, such as describing action pictures as if they were one of the participants. Having students retell schoolground incidents from their opponent's point of view provides empathy.

Another benefit of working with point of view is to check students' comprehension of stories, situations, or activities. As they retell an event from a different point of view, students not only clarify facts and information about a given subject, they also become aware of their own feelings, opinions, and insights.

SAFE Lesson No. 7

TITLE OF LESSON: ASSUMING THE VIEWPOINT OF AN OBJECT

DIFFICULTY LEVEL: GRADES 2–10

OBJECTIVES:

Students will:

1. Compare different points of view from the same scene
2. Identify the point of view in a written sample
3. Write a similar essay in the first person

DESCRIPTION:

Students hear an example of student writing in the first person. After identifying the role the writer is assuming, they write short I-statements from a specific point of view. (This activity can be completed orally in K–1 classrooms.)

PROCEDURES:

Find a large mountain (or other landscape) scene that can be displayed so all students can see it. You may prefer to use one or more slides instead.

Stimulus:

Present the mountainous landscape. Ask the students to describe the picture. Write on the board key words that describe colors, textures, moods, and actions.

Ask them if the picture would look different to various objects in the picture. Discuss the differences.

Share this paragraph written by a student. Discuss who is describing the scene and how they know.

Guardian

I look down upon the green valley filled with tall, stately trees that tickle my belly. The soft, white clouds brush against me and provide me with a crown. I love guarding this valley and watching the gentle stream flow down the middle. Sometimes after a hard rain, that stream becomes a rushing torrent and floods the valley floor. I don't mind though because it's always so green and beautiful afterwards.

Sometimes I see people sitting on the big boulders that line the stream. Sometimes people even try to climb my steep cliffs, but I usually start a rockslide so that they can't get to the top. By the time people get to the top, I've run out of trees because I'm so high I reach way up into the sky.

Tony

Activity:

Give each student a landscape picture. Discuss the types of pictures and write related words on the board. Encourage students to talk about their pictures to develop new vocabulary.

Have the students write I-statements about their picture, describing the scene and including sensory detail.

Follow-Up:

Display all the pictures in the front of the room and have the students read their descriptions, seeing if other students can select the matching picture.

Evaluation:

Have students self-evaluate their writing by underlining all sensory details. Give five extra points if the other students select the paired description.

SAFE Lesson No. 8

TITLE OF LESSON: ASSUMING ANOTHER ROLE

DIFFICULTY LEVEL: GRADES 6–8

OBJECTIVES:

Students will:

1. Interpret the narrator of an incident
2. Contrast the varying points of view
3. Write dialogue assuming a specific role

DESCRIPTION:

Students read paragraphs describing an incident and discover the writers' point of view. After contrasting the attitudes and opinions of the narrators, they describe the same scene from different viewpoints.

PROCEDURE:

This lesson uses *Roll of Thunder Hear My Cry* by Mildred D. Taylor. Any book containing "an incident" involving several characters can be used.

Stimulus:

Read aloud the book *Roll of Thunder* by Mildred D. Taylor. After reading the chapter to the students that involves the bus accident, discuss the various activities leading up to the accident. Use La Dicteé for the paragraph on page 54 about the bus accident. Talk about the accident and how the various people might have interpreted the accident, stressing that the bus driver, as an adult, would have a different perspective than either the white children or the black children.

Activity:

Duplicate the following student-written paragraphs and distribute them:

> I could hardly wait to get even with those kids. They always stick their tongues out at us when they drive past us every morning. They think they're such big shots! You just wait and see! They won't even know what hit them, and I'll just laugh and laugh. . . .
>
> Vicky

> Honest, Boss, I don't know what happened. All of a sudden the bus just fell into this hole. I couldn't budge it or anything. Of course, I took care of the children. None of them was hurt. I done my job, just like I'm supposed to. . . .
>
> James

> All morning I had that feeling of doom about me. I couldn't shake that awesome feeling that something was about to go wrong. From the time I ambled over the low hill I felt that a dark cloud hung over my head. Even when the late bus arrived I couldn't shake that terrible feeling of

doom. I saw those black kids in the bushes but I never thought that it meant anything. Oh, no, the bus is turning over, kids are screaming. I can't see. I can't breathe. It's dark in here.

Vic

Guess what, Mom. I had to walk to school today! Yes, I got all wet. That's what happens when it's raining! Can you believe it? The bus got stuck and nobody would come pick us up. I can't believe that those teachers made us walk.

Tonya

I was so scared. I couldn't believe what we had done. I didn't really want anyone to get hurt. I was so afraid that someone would get hurt when I saw that bus toppling on its wheels. I said my prayers real fast and hid my face. I was so frightened.

Darlene

Have the students read the paragraphs and determine who might have written each statement. Compare the paragraphs, pointing out the differences as a result of change in narrator. Analyze the attitude of each writer.

Divide the class into small groups. Assign each group a different viewpoint. Each student within the group writes a description of the accident.

Follow-Up:

After writing is completed, students share in response groups. Members of the response groups listen for opinions and value judgments. Each group picks one dialogue that best expresses the assigned point of view to share with the class.

Evaluation:

There are *no* right or wrong answers in this activity. Students interpret incidents according to the assigned point of view, leaving preconceived ideas aside. They gain understanding about differing points of view and can select effective examples for each viewpoint.

MORE LESSONS TO TEACH LITERATURE CONCEPTS

The following lessons are similar to those on point of view. Notice that a good piece of writing provides a text to assist you in teaching literature. You have only to find an example of what you want to teach—metaphor, hyperbole, or personification (as in the example that follows).

SAFE Lesson No. 9

TITLE OF LESSON: EXPERIMENTING WITH PERSONIFICATION

DIFFICULTY LEVEL: GRADES 6–8

OBJECTIVES:

Students will:

1. Analyze a poem
2. Identify what is being personified and how
3. Use personification in an original essay or poem

DESCRIPTION:

Students read a portion of "The Cloud" by Shelley to see how the poet assumes the voice (point of view) of a cloud. They also note how he gives the cloud human characteristics and personality—the kind of imagery we call "personification."

PROCEDURES:

Copy the following portion of "The Cloud" on a transparency.

Stimulus:

Read an excerpt from the poem, "The Cloud" by Percy Bysshe Shelley, having the students listen for signs of a personality. Ask students to determine who the "I" is and to observe how the poet makes this thing (cloud) human (verbs).

> I bring fresh showers for the thirsting flowers,
>   From the seas and the streams;
> I bear light shade for the leaves when laid
>   In their noonday dreams.
> From my wings are shaken the dews that waken
>   The sweet buds every one,
> When rocked to rest on their mother's breast,
>   As she dances about the sun.
> I wield the flail of the lashing hail,
>   And whiten the green plains under,
> And then again I dissolve it in rain,
>   And laugh as I pass in thunder.

Underline the verbs that give the cloud personality. Cluster the personality traits on the board from student responses.

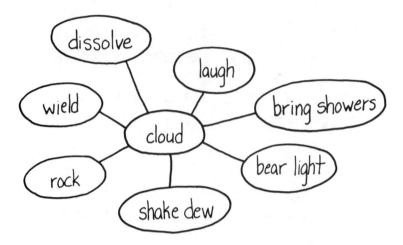

Talk about personalities and what makes people different. Can things in nature have personalities?

Activity:

Have the students identify the personality qualities of some natural phenomenon (rainbow, ocean, grass) by clustering. Stress that they are to consider the life cycle and to infer some type of personality for this object. They are to write a poem or essay in first person. Following is an example:

Personality of the Wind

I am the wind. I have many different personalities. I'm the wind that gently blows branches back and forth, but sometimes I'm violent and rip the branches off the trees. I'm also the wind that steals balloons from helpless kids. I provide entertainment for those with kites and entertain myself by breaking the strings.

I am the sweet summer breeze, peaceful, warm, and refreshing. I bring smiles to many different people. My special moment is when young love is in the air; I help spread it to all the congenial inviting hearts.

At times I'm wicked and savage. I blow down trees, destroy houses, and instill a scary feeling. I rampage my way through towns and cities, destroying everything in my path. I blast through desert sands, reconstructing the dunes as I move.

I am the power of the world. I move through time creating different realities. I have no beginning or ending. I'm evil; but good. You can feel me, but you can't see me. You can't catch me because I'm free. I am the never ending, ever-changing wind.

Steve

Follow-Up:

Have the students share their compositions in Response Groups. Direct the students to think of questions to ask about the life cycle that might not have been included. Have students research their "I" and revise their compositions with the new information.

Evaluation:

Have students create a checklist for evaluating their personifications. Give each student a copy or post the list on the wall to guide them as they write. A suggested checklist might be as follows:

Checklist for Personification Assignment

1. Include the life cycle of the object personified.
2. Develop a personality for the object.
3. Use verbs to indicate personification.
4. Include sensory detail.

SAFE Lesson No. 10

TITLE OF LESSON: EFFECTIVE REPETITION AND PATTERN

DIFFICULTY LEVEL: GRADES 2–6

OBJECTIVES:

Students will:

1. Recite a poem
2. Observe the rhyme scheme
3. Compose a poem patterning the rhyme and repetition

DESCRIPTION:

A humorous poem is used to help students become aware of how repetition can be effective. They enjoy saying the poem in a chorus and recognizing the interesting visual effect the poet achieves in putting the poem on the page.

PROCEDURES:

Put the poem "There Once was a Puffin" by Florence Page Jaques on a transparency. (If possible, obtain a picture of a puffin.)

There Once Was a Puffin
by Florence Page Jaques

Oh, there once was a Puffin
Just the shape of a muffin,
And he lived on an island
In the
  bright
    blue
      sea!

He ate little fishes,
That were most delicious,
And he had them for supper
And he
  had
    them
      for tea!

But this poor little Puffin,
He couldn't play nothin',
For he hadn't anybody
To
  play
    with
      at all.

So he sat on his island,
And he cried for a while, and
He felt very lonely,
And he
  felt
    very
      small.

Then along came the fishes,
And they said, "If you wishes,
You can have us for playmates,
Instead
  of
    for
      tea!"

So they now play together
In all sort of weather,
And the puffin eats pancakes,
Like you
  and
    like
      me.

Stimulus:

Read the poem aloud. Discuss how rhyming enhances a clever poem and adds to its humor. Have the students recite the poem in chorus. As students chant the poem, emphasize the staggered lines as they speak them. Note how the last line of each stanza is naturally slowed down and spoken more quietly, influenced by the physical presentation.

Discuss the last line of each stanza. Within each stanza the first two lines rhyme, the middle does not, and the last line rhymes with the last line of the stanza preceding or succeeding it.

Make a list of the words that rhyme. Show the students how to make rhyme lists when they need rhyming words for their poems. For example:

hand	wing	look
band	bring	shook
canned	sing	book
fanned	spring	cook
land	ring	hook
sand	swing	nook
stand	fling	crook

Rhyming reinforces knowledge of sound and symbol relationships while spelling common word families.

Activity:

Have the students create imaginative poems patterned after the puffin poem with the last line staggered. Students can follow any rhyme scheme as long as they are consistent.

Follow-Up:

Have students work in pairs to help each other improve their poems. Observe that poetry needs to be read aloud to test the rhythm.

Share some of the students' poems. Display their poems next to the original poem on the bulletin board.

Evaluation:

Discuss the criteria for completing the patterned poem successfully. Write the criteria on the board as students list them. For example:

Use a clear rhyming pattern.

Make the poem imaginative and humorous.

Tell a story.

Create a rhythm to the poem.

Have the students work in pairs to help each other meet these criteria.

Still More Ideas to Try

These ideas will add to your repertoire of interesting ways to present literature concepts to students.

- Use *Happiness Is* by Charles Shultz or *A Friend Is* by Joan Anglund to introduce metaphor. Let students extend the lists suggested by one of these books. For example:

  Happiness is . . .
  finding a ten dollar bill.
  lying on the beach.
  smiling at your mother.

- Ask students what animal they are. Then have them write adjectives to describe this animal, as in this example:

  I am a cat . . .
  independent, proud;
  soft, yet strong;
  loving and purring.

- Help students observe the various ways of beginning sentences used in literature. Using their books, begin a list on a chart.

- Use the Cloze technique to help students become aware of the author's choice of words. Prepare several paragraphs from literature. Omit every few words for students to fill in the blanks. (You may select nouns, verbs, or adjectives, but be consistent in the selection.) This example is from *Little Women* by Louisa May Alcott.

  Amy's delight was an _____cabinet full of _____drawings, _____pigeonholes, and _____places in which were kept all sorts of ornaments, some _____, some merely _____, all _____or _____antique. To examine these things gave Amy satisfaction, especially the _____cases in which on _____cushions reposed the ornaments which had adorned a belle of _____years ago. . . .

Experiencing Drama: Process and Product

Students enjoy dramatizing literature. They are motivated to read the part, to memorize their lines, and to interpret the character's personality. In turn, when they write plays, they will provide personalities for their characters, develop a plot involving some conflict, and derive a logical conclusion.

Other types of dramatization, such as story theater or creative dramatics, stimulate students' thinking abilities and provide a natural outlet for creativity. Pantomiming titles of songs, books, and common sayings encourages students to think on their feet. Drama should not be overlooked as a method of learning.

A USEFUL STRATEGY: CREATIVE DRAMATICS

Creative dramatics can be enjoyed by people of all ages. A good activity when students are forced to stay inside and need to vent some of their energies, creative dramatics allows students to act out life's experiences and to internalize stories by becoming part of the scene.

Begin simple drama by having students pantomime their impressions of some common task or behavior. They can depict anything from waking up in the morning and getting dressed to a simple activity in a story. There are no wrong interpretations, so it helps students feel good about themselves and their abilities.

Introduce and follow up every creative experience with discussion. Half of the class may act as observers who analyze and appreciate the portrayals. The group discussions allow input from both sections. By discussing and evaluating their activities, the students develop critical thinking, which can be further sensitized by writing about their experiences.

SAFE Lesson No. 11

TITLE OF LESSON: INTRODUCING CREATIVE DRAMATICS
DIFFICULTY LEVEL: GRADES K–3
OBJECTIVES:

Students will:

1. Identify characters in story
2. Imagine characteristics and endings
3. Plan actions and settings

DESCRIPTION:

As you read a simple story or describe an incident, students act out the scene. Free movement and interpretation are allowed. All students are involved in critiquing and interpreting behaviors. This can be used with ESL groups.

PROCEDURES:

Tell the story, discuss the four scenes, and have students volunteer for parts. The seated portion of the class will critique the performers.

Stimulus:

Ask students what happens when they go to bed at night. List some of their responses on the board. Introduce the following story as something that might happen.

Tell this story, having students listen for scenes:

Once a little girl and a little boy were going to bed, and they said to their dolls and toys, "Now you lie down here and go to sleep, too." The dolls and toys were lying on the bed, but as soon as the children went to sleep, they jumped up, began jumping on the bed and clapping their hands and laughed.

The father in the family heard the noise and came into the room. He turned on the light and looked around, but he didn't see anything but the toys lying still on the bed, so he went back to bed. As soon as they were sure he was asleep, the toys began playing and clapping again.

This time the noise awakened the mother. She creaked open the door, looked around and listened. All she saw was the toys lying still on the bed. So she went back to bed. As soon as the toys thought she was asleep, they jumped up, danced, and played with each other.

Finally the family dog awakened. He came into the room and saw all the dolls and toys lying still. He took his big, wet tongue and kissed each toy. He said, "Oh, I just love you dolls and toys." Then he went back to his corner and went to sleep. The Teddy Bear sat up and said, "Do we want that big, wet tongue to kiss us again?" "No!" said all the dolls. "Yuk," said the toys. "Well, I guess we'd better go to sleep or he will be back. Good night."

Activity:

Discuss what happened, scene by scene. Set the scene for interpretation. Allow students to volunteer for parts—children, toys, parents, and dog. Have students construct the setting before starting the first scene. Discuss what happens next after each scene is completed.

Follow-Up:

Critique how various students interpreted the story. Ask how the story could have ended if (1) the parents found the toys playing, (2) the dog played with the toys, or (3) the toys marched through the house. Have students imagine other endings and act out those scenes. Plan to share the play with other classes.

Evaluation:

Choose one set of performers to present the play to another class. Determine the qualities of a good performance, such as:

Demonstration of comprehension

Expression of emotion

Coordination of scenes

Clarity of actions

Encourage students to compliment their peers and to learn from each other.

SAFE Lesson No. 12

TITLE OF LESSON: DRAMATIZING A POEM
DIFFICULTY LEVEL: GRADES K–6
OBJECTIVES:

Students will:

1. Identify the characters in a poem
2. Recall the sequence of events
3. Interpret the emotions of characters

DESCRIPTION:

After students listen to a poem, they act out the scenes when you reread it. Movement and interpretation are determined by students. Half of the class watches and critiques the other half.

PROCEDURES:

A good introductory dramatic activity, this poetry interpretation can be used with children of all ages. Read the poem "The Tree Stands Very

Straight and Still" to students who interpret the characters' actions. All students participate and discuss roles.

Stimulus:

Introduce the poem by Annette Wynne, "The Tree Stands Very Straight and Still."

> The tree stands very straight and still
> All night long far on the hill;
> But if I go and listen near
> A million little sounds I hear,
> The leaves are little whispering elves
> Talking, playing by themselves,
> Playing softly altogether
> In the warm or windy weather,
> Talking softly to the sky
> Or any bird that dartles by.
> O little elves within the tree,
> Is there no word to tell to me?

Discuss the elements mentioned—the tree, the hill, whispering elves, warm wind, the sky, and darting birds. Ask students how these elements could be portrayed.

Activity:

Have half of the class interpret what it is like to be a tree. Have the wind (2–4 students) blow gently through the "trees." Have the wind increase in volume.

Have the elves chop wood or dance and have the birds fly. (Note that students can choose the type of bird.) Tell the birds to land beside the "trees." Have students dramatize animals that might be found in a tree.

Follow-Up:

Discuss the interpretations of being elves, birds, and other animals. Discuss the perceptions and emotions the actors felt. Encourage students to make positive comments about their peers.

Evaluation:

Have students evaluate the interpretation of trees, elves, birds, plants, and animals. Were they able to observe the emotions?

SAFE Lesson No. 13

TITLE OF LESSON: DRAMATIZING A FAIRYTALE

DIFFICULTY LEVEL: GRADES 3–6

OBJECTIVES:

Students will:

1. Analyze the parts of a fairytale
2. Plan a dramatic presentation
3. Interpret the mannerisms and behaviors of characters

DESCRIPTION:

After hearing a fairytale, students plan scenes and act them out. They add movement, mannerisms, and behaviors to fit the plot. Students volunteer for character parts.

PROCEDURES:

Read "The Mouse Princess" or substitute any fairytale and follow the same procedure. Allow time for planning and organization. Students imagine the settings.

Stimulus:

Introduce the story, "The Mouse Princess" from *French Legends, Tales and Fairy Stories* by Barbara Leonie Picard (Henry Z. Walck, Inc.) Map the story on the board by placing the name of the story in the center and the subgroups above and below. Students supply missing elements in blanks. (See Chapter 6, page 195, for more mapping experiences.)

Discuss characterizations of the brothers. Allow students to demonstrate how arrogant brothers or haughty brides might behave. Designate area for various settings.

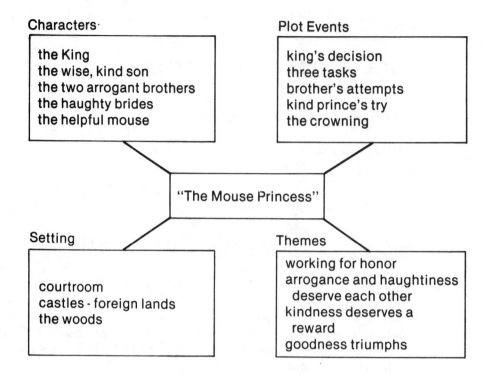

Characters·
- the King
- the wise, kind son
- the two arrogant brothers
- the haughty brides
- the helpful mouse

Plot Events
- king's decision
- three tasks
- brother's attempts
- kind prince's try
- the crowning

"The Mouse Princess"

Setting
- courtroom
- castles - foreign lands
- the woods

Themes
- working for honor
- arrogance and haughtiness deserve each other
- kindness deserves a reward
- goodness triumphs

Activity:

Have half of the class plan the scenes so that all members of the group are involved as friends, bystanders, or soldiers. Each student interprets the assigned role freely.

The other half of the class serves as an active audience. Their task is to observe and list mannerisms and behaviors that interpret characters well. They are to offer suggestions for improving the scenes.

The observers then become the actors, incorporating observations and suggestions for improvement. The first actors become the observers and are charged with listing mannerisms and comparing behaviors.

Follow-Up:

The class selects individuals to portray specific roles in the play for presentation to another class. You may wish to develop this presentation to include painted scenery and other props so it can be shown in the multipurpose room for several classes.

Evaluation:

Develop criteria for interpretations, as in the following example:

All students are involved.

Observers evaluate actors who then switch roles.

Interpretations are up to individuals.

Audience approval is final evaluation.

The success of the experience will be revealed when students choose to work with another story in the same manner.

MORE LESSONS TO PROMOTE THE USE OF DRAMA

Varied approaches to drama can be used in all classrooms. Here are additional ideas to try.

SAFE Lesson No. 14

TITLE OF LESSON: EXPANDING VOCABULARY

DIFFICULTY LEVEL: GRADES 2–4

OBJECTIVES:

Students will:

1. Compare subtle differences in word meanings
2. Interpret meanings of through actions
3. Synthesize connotations of words

DESCRIPTION:

Students will use dramatization as a way of furthering the understanding of varied words. They will learn the vocabulary words *see, notice, glance, glare, look, peek, observe, stare,* and *search.* They will learn the subtle differences in these actions and be able to use the words correctly.

PROCEDURES:

Display a picture of an eye on the board or on a flannelboard.

Stimulus:

Ask the students what an eye does. Discuss its ability to interpret color, size, and mood. List on the board words students give you that suggest seeing. Hint at others, as necessary, to include these:

stare	search
glare	glance
peek	observe
look	notice

Ask the students if these words mean the same thing.

Activity:

Discuss how these actions might be portrayed. Using creative dramatics, create a scene for each word:

Have some of the students peek at an object

Have others glance around in a store

A third group searches for some lost object

The fourth group stares at treasure chest

Compare each action and its affect. Were the students able to create the total scene?

Follow-Up:

Ask the students to tell you a sentence for each of the words. Write the students' sentences on the board. Have a student underline the "seeing" word. Then have several students read the sentences you have written on the board. Again, discuss the meanings of the words.

Make a chart of "Seeing" words.

Evaluation:

Students have learned new vocabulary: *stare, glare, peek, glance,* and *search.* They can explain the difference between the actions by writing sentences that are checked by peers.

SAFE Lesson No. 15

TITLE OF LESSON: UNDERSTANDING IDIOMS

DIFFICULTY LEVEL: GRADES 6–8

OBJECTIVES:

Students will:

1. Expand their knowledge of how language works
2. Enjoy acting out meanings of common English idioms
3. Begin to understand the concept of *idiom*

DESCRIPTION:

Students will use dramatization as a way of furthering the understanding of common idioms that we use in English. (Notice that this lesson builds on one in Chapter 6; see page 121.)

PROCEDURES:

In this lesson, students will learn to interpret common idioms through dramatization. They pantomime the expressions to their peers.

Stimulus:

Discuss how idioms, such as "give me a break," come into existence. Encourage students to imagine how certain idioms may have developed. Brainstorm a list of idioms. For example:

eat a horse	Don't rattle me.
raining cats and dogs	He's ripped.
in one ear and out the other	I bombed out.
crazy as a cuckoo	What a rat!
stomach in my mouth	He turns me on.
white as a sheet	What a nerd!
up to my neck in trouble	I flipped out.
quiet as a mouse	Buzz off!
pretty as a picture	Give me some bread.
stiff as a board	He's got my goat.
like a frightened puppy	higher than a kite
an airhead	up against a wall
eat one's words	fit to kill

Ask the students to read the phrases and to explain the meaning as used in conversation in their own words. Point out that they add interesting statements to stories, but they can mislead people who are learning the English language.

Identify the literal meanings and compare them to the figurative meanings.

Activity:

Divide the class into small groups to brainstorm other terms, writing these expressions on narrow strips of paper. Each group puts the idioms in a box or bag. Using the idioms as cue directions, play team charades.

Before the game starts, the class decides whether they want to act out the figurative or the literal meaning of the expressions. Both variations can be played on alternate days.

Encourage all members of the team to be the "actor." In each game, discuss the actual meaning before a new expression is drawn.

Follow-Up:

After the game, discuss the idioms used and what students have learned about the English language. Have students collect idiomatic expressions on a card catalog displayed in the classroom.

Evaluation:

Even though a few students may complain about having to act out the expressions, their laughter indicates that they really enjoyed the lesson. Students can evaluate the accuracy of portraying the literal or figurative meaning of the idioms. They can suggest other ways of expressing these idioms.

SAFE Lesson No. 16

TITLE OF LESSON: USING STORY THEATER WITH NURSERY TALES

DIFFICULTY LEVEL: GRADES K–8

OBJECTIVES:

Students will:

1. Define folklore, our literary heritage
2. Retell a familiar nursery tale
3. Demonstrate understanding through dramatization

DESCRIPTION:

Students use dramatization in responding to a story. They will see story theater as yet another way of enjoying literature. This method can be used with varied literature selections. (Note this lesson relates to Chapter 2, page 38.)

PROCEDURES:

Story theater involves role playing along with a story as it is being told. All students have a purpose for listening. You need a copy of "The Three Little Pigs" or a similar tale. This activity is a good method to bring in childhood literature that older students may have missed.

Stimulus:

Ask the students if they know the story of "The Three Little Pigs." Have the students tell the story as a group. Share your published version of the story. Make a chart of the story similar to this.

Characters	Scenes	Dialogue	Actions
Three pigs			
Man with straw			
Man with wood			
Man with brick			
Wolf			
Houses (three students interlock fingers)			

Activity:

Use a portion of the classroom as the stage. Assign roles and tell the actors that they will stay off stage until they hear their parts being read. Caution the students not to "invent their own lines," but encourage them to grunt, squeal, or act frightened.

As you or a student rereads the story, check to see that the "straw" pig walks up to the man selling the straw. Then, have the pig pretend to build the house. See that the children portraying houses interlock their fingers while the pig hides. The wolf should approach the house and pretend to knock on the door.

Once you are sure they understand how to role play, continue reading the story. Read at a natural pace, stopping as needed for the students to "follow" the script.

Vary this activity by allowing students to make up their own lines as they role play.

Follow-Up:

Talk about the experience after all students have had a chance to participate.

As an art project, have students make face masks for the parts they are playing. Older students can make their own props, costumes, and dialogue for a skit to be presented to primary classes.

Evaluation:

Appoint three students to observe and evaluate correct body language. Ask the students to write their reactions to this experience and then to share these reactions. Students in K–1 classrooms can "write" these responses collectively with the teacher as an experience chart. Ask students if they would like to demonstrate story theater for another class (which can participate with them) or for the Parent-Teacher Association.

Still More Ideas to Try

These suggestions will help you bring drama as a form of literature into your classroom.

- Have students act out various poems that have narrative content, for example:

  "The Elf and the Dormouse" by Oliver Hereford

  "A Visit from St. Nicholas" by Clement Moore

  "Lewis and Clark" by Rosemary and Stephen Benet

  "The Owl and the Pussycat" by Edward Lear

  "You Are Old, Father William" by Lewis Carroll (2 persons)

  "The Walrus and the Carpenter" by Lewis Carroll

  While some students act out the poem, the rest of the class can read or say it from memory.

- Have students work in small groups to write skits for humorous real-life situations. They can begin by listing the characters, outlining the plot, and deciding on a setting by preparing a map of the drama as on page 195. Each group can present its short play to the rest of the class. The audience responds in writing by pointing out what they liked about the skit.

- Divide the class into groups of five or six students. Each group selects a folktale to present in play form. They write dialogue based on that in the story, but they can add whatever they like to increase interest, action, and to provide a role for each person in the group. (Point out that most folktales are retold and rewritten and that they change during the process over the years. You might bring in several versions of a story, for example, *Johnny Cake* and *The Runaway Pancake*.)

- Bring in books of plays from your library, for example: *One Hundred Plays for Children: An Anthology of Nonroyalty One-Act Plays* (A. Burack, ed. Plays, Inc., 1970) or *Christmas Play Favorites for Young People: A Collection of Traditional and Modern One-Act, Royalty-free Plays for Celebrating Christmas in Schools and Drama Groups* (S. Kamerman, ed. Plays, Inc., 1982).

    You might like to subscribe to *Plays, The Drama Magazine for Young People* available from: Plays, Inc., 8 Arlington St., Boston MA 02116.

    Students will enjoy reading the plays. They may work in groups to present a selected play for the class or as part of a school-wide assembly.

Developing a Thematic Module: Freedom

Freedom can be defined as that civil liberty given by the government that allows individuals to have certain privileges, such as freedom of speech, freedom of religion, and freedom of the press as stated in our Bill of Rights. It is also the personal liberty that allows us to determine our own destiny or actions. It is the ability to make choices and accept the responsibilities that go along with those decisions.

Students need to be exposed to the other ideas that go along with freedom: rights and responsibilities, loyalty and trustworthiness, honor and morality, dependability and reliability. The poem by Emma Lazarus, "The New Colossus," that is inscribed on the pedestal of the Statue of Liberty embodies many of these principles and can be used to foster discussion to begin this unit on freedom.

> Not like the brazen giant of Greek fame,
>   With conquering limbs astride from land to land;
>   Here at our sea-washed, sunset gates shall stand
> A mighty woman with a torch, whose flame
> Is the imprisoned lightning, and her name
>   Mother of Exiles. From her beacon-hand
>   Glows world-wide welcome; her mild eyes command
> The air-bridged harbor that twin cities frame.
>   "Keep ancient lands, your storied pomp!" cries she
>   With silent lips. "Give me your tired, your poor,

> Your huddled masses yearning to breathe free,
>   The wretched refuse of your teeming shore.
> Send these, the homeless, tempest-tost to me,
>   I lift my lamp beside the golden door!"

FREEDOM

Objectives:

1. Students will study the Bill of Rights and relate these to the responsibilities that one should accept with these rights. They will devise a Bill of Rights for the classroom.

2. Students will study the words of Martin Luther King and relate them to all civil liberties regardless of sex, color, or religion. They will write letters to the editor from the point of view of someone who has been deprived of some of these basic freedoms, and they will respond as the editor to someone else's letter.

3. Students will study the songs of the 1960s and compare them to some of Neil Diamond's and Bruce Springsteen's songs about America. By contrasting the turbulence of the sixties with the nationalism of modern day, students will develop a better understanding of our freedoms. Students will create "songs" about freedom.

4. After studying some of the plays about key moments and personalities in America's past, students will learn how these people had to make decisions. They in turn will study decision-making strategies. Then students will write and present a play about personal freedoms and decisions.

Getting Started:

Gather the following materials:

A picture of the Statue of Liberty, Martin Luther King, immigrants, and other symbols of freedom (Liberty Bell); pictures of Americans enjoying their natural rights and freedoms (Norman Rockwell)

A copy of the Bill of Rights, and the Statue of Liberty's inscription

A copy of Martin Luther's famous speech and other stories about him; articles from the Suffrage Movement and from the current ERA movement

Recordings of songs from the sixties (Neil Diamond and Bruce Springsteen)

Short plays about American history personalities (Opportunities for Learning, Inc., 20417 Nordhoff St., Chatsworth, Calif. has some listed in their catalog or similar plays)

Worksheets on decision making

Use the poem by Emma Lazarus as an opener to motivate the students. Discuss the centennial celebration and the efforts of students to help the Statue of Liberty get her "facelift." Discuss the role she has played in our history and in freedom itself. Cluster all the words that students associate with *freedom*. Have them write a paragraph from that cluster and share the results of their writing. Discuss appropriate phrases and thoughts.

Classroom organization: small group, resource group, and classroom discussions.

Length of time: Each objective will take about one week or more. Grade level can be modified as low as third, but most lessons are designed for sixth through ninth grades.

Learning Activities for Students:

1. Introduce the students to the Bill of Rights by providing historical information about it: Thomas Jefferson wrote most of it; they are the first 10 amendments to the U.S. Constitution; and the constitution was not to be ratified until these were added. Discuss each amendment and relate each to individual freedoms that students have today.

   Have students role play how it would be without each of these freedoms. For the first amendment, they might act out not having freedom of religion, freedom of speech, freedom of the press, and the right to convene for meetings. For the fifth amendment, students might act out the inability to have a trial and have property seized. Discuss the effects of not having these rights.

   Draw up a chart to show which freedoms are guaranteed by each amendment. Discuss the responsibilities that people have with these rights. Discuss why these responsibilities are as important as the rights. Make sure you discuss some of the other ideas that are suggested by these freedoms. Have the students create a classroom Bill of Rights:

   Students have the right to disagree courteously.

   Students have the right to work quietly, undistracted.

   Students have the right of privacy.

   Students have the right to defend themselves against false accusation.

   Students have the right to have their own property without fear of loss.

   Teachers have the right to instruct.

   Teachers have the right to expect assignments to be turned in on time.

   Teachers have the right of privacy.

2. Deliver Martin Luther King's address. Relate the civil rights movement to the rights guaranteed in the constitution. Read other stories about Martin Luther King and civil rights.

Read stories about suffrage and the women's movements. Relate these stories to the rights guaranteed.

After having discussed these rights, guarantees and actualities, list some of the things that are really happening today. Discuss how people feel when some of their basic rights and privileges have been taken from them. Discuss responsible behavior in obtaining their rights.

Have the students write a letter to the editor from the point of view of someone who has not been given a guaranteed right. Share these letters in response groups and discuss appropriately. Have the students exchange papers with some member of their response groups, taking on the role of the editor who is writing an editorial for that letter.

Dear Editor:

I recently was driving down highway 85 in my brand new corvette, when a cop pulled me over for no reason whatsoever. I wasn't even speeding. He looked over my car and asked how a kid like me could afford such a nice car. Before I could even respond, he started cursing me and calling me all sorts of names—ones that I don't care to repeat. It's not my fault I'm black!

Then he told me to get out of the car. I didn't even call him all the names I know! Then would you believe it—he climbed in the car and started to drive off! I ran after him, calling him all the names I know and he just grinned. He spun my wheels and covered me with dust before he got out of the car and handed me a ticket. He said I was speeding and attempting to escape.

I protest this treatment because the judge wouldn't believe my story. What can I do?

Confused,
V. Hudson

3. Share recordings of songs from the 1960s. Hand out copies of the words so students can read and discuss them. Study about the turbulence of the sixties and the influence made on these songs. Have students write stories in response to such songs as, "Where Have All the Flowers Gone?"

Bring in recordings of the songs by either Neil Diamond or Bruce Springsteen about America. Compare the feelings of nationalism seen today—flags proudly displayed at the Olympics, camouflaged clothing, willingness to join the service, Goodwill Games, and fundraising for the Statue of Liberty, for farmers, and for flood victims. Discuss how the songs relate to nationalism.

Ask the students what it means to them to have the freedoms

that are guaranteed to them. Discuss how they could create songs to display those feelings. Have them write poems or songs to show their happiness in having those freedoms.

4. Read a mini-play or short play, such as "Abe's Longest Walk," about one of the personalities in American history. Discuss the decisions that they had in determining their behaviors. Discuss how things might have been different if some of their freedoms had not existed.

Review the basic freedoms that we have and how they relate to decision making. Do some decision-making exercises. Then have students divide into small groups and create plays that involve some sort of decision making. Have each play presented to the whole class and to parents.

Resources for the Teacher:

Dewey, R. *Freedom: Its History, Natures and Varieties*. Random House, 1970.

Fast, Howard. *The Immigrants*. Houghton-Mifflin, 1977.

Glazer, T. *Songs of Peace, Freedom & Protest*. 1970.

Guerney, T., and Alden, J. *Harper's Pictorical History of the Civil War*. The Fairfax Press.

Heller, Nancy; Williams, Julie; and Watson, Guptill. *Painters of the American Scene*. Houghton-Mifflin, 1976.

Lewis, David L. *King: A Critical Biography*. Pelican Books, 1970.

McKenzie, R. *Bound to be Free*. Random House, 1982.

Stratten, Joanne L. *Pioneer Women*. Touchstone, 1981.

VHS Movies:

The Cotton Club; And Justice for All; Absence of Malice

Resources for the Students:

Brink, Carol Ryrie. *Caddie Woodlawn*. Collier MacMillian, 1970.

Cooper, Ilene. *Susan B. Anthony*. Impact Biography, 1984.

de Kay, James T., *Meet Martin Luther King*. Random House. (for younger children)

Hunt, Irene. *Across Five Aprils*. Tempo Books, 1983.

Steine, Emma G. *I Have a Dream*. Alfred Knopf, 1965.

Washington, Booker T. *Up from Slavery*. Dell.

Computer Software:

"Famous Names in American History" (MicroLearning Ware) for Apples, TRS, and Commodore.

"American, An Early History" (Aquarius), for Apples and TRS.

"The Factory" Strategies in Problem Solving for Apples, Commodores, IBM, TRS, and Atari.

"The Pond: Strategies in Problem Solving for Apples, Commodores, IBM, TRS, and Atari.

"The Time Tunnel: American History Series" (Focus Media) for Apples, TRS.

Filmstrip/Cassettes:

"400 Years: Black History in America," ED-410.

"The American Woman: A Social Chronicle," RH-51002.

"The Bill of Rights: Foundation of Our Liberties," GU-6139, Opportunities for Learning.

"The Woman's Movement: Suffrage and Beyond," MM-3012.

Interact Games:

"Equality, Her Story," Gateway (Interact, P.O. Box 997D, Lakeside, Calif. 92040)

Multimedia Kits:

"Freedom and the Law" PO49, Resources for the Gifted, Inc.

"Risk-Taking, 9883, Resources for the Gifted, Inc.

"Simulations" 0662, Resources for the Gifted, Inc.

VHS Movies:

Sounder; The Jazz Singer; The Bostonians

Evaluation:

Design a point system for the unit, such as:

> 30 for Bill of Rights activities
>
> 15 for letter to editor/editorial response
>
> 20 for poem/essay about freedom
>
> 30 for decision-making activities
>
> 5 for extra contributions students bring in

Have students evaluate role playing of constitutional freedoms and responsibilities. Display their poems/essays written in response to songs studied. Critique the plays on role playing and choose one to be presented to the whole school.

Exploring Further

Baskin, Barbara, and Harris, Karen. *More Notes from a Different Drummer: A Guide to Juvenile Fiction Portraying the Disabled*. Bowker, 1984.

Bauer, Caroline. *This Way to Books*. Wilson, 1983.

Butler, Francelia, and Rotert, Richard (eds.) *Reflections on Literature for Children*. Shoe String Press, 1984.

Leonard, Charlotte. *Tied Together: Topics and Thoughts for Introducing Children's Books*. Scarecrow Press, 1980.

Rees, David. *Painted Desert, Green Shade: Essays on Contemporary Writers of Fiction for Children and Young Adults*. Horn Book, 1984.

Roser, Nancy. *Children's Choices: Teaching with Books Children Like*. International Reading Assn., 1983.

Rudman, Masha. *An Issues Approach to Children's Literature*. Heath, 1984.

White, Mary Lou. *Adventuring with Books: A Booklist for Pre-K–Grade 8*. NCTE, 1981.

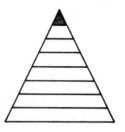

9

Developing a Student-Centered Curriculum

Inherent to the success of implementing the language and literacy program described in this book is the development of a student-centered curriculum. We need to use methods that involve students actively in learning so that they experience growth and an understanding of themselves and the world around them. We should examine our methods and teaching behaviors closely to see if we are teaching effectively.

We need to examine all aspects of our program: the curriculum, the methods, and the instructional materials. If we begin with our goals and objectives, we can evaluate our teaching to see if we are meeting these aims. We can then select different strategies that increase student involvement in learning and evaluation, if we are not already doing so.

Ideas in this chapter are presented in these groupings:

Designing the Curriculum

Characteristics of a Strong Program

Objectives for Student Learning

Skills of a Good Teacher

Communicating with Parents

Involving Students in Learning

Working in Small Groups

Holistic Scoring of Student Writing

Evaluating Progress

Publishing Student Work

Implementing the Program

A student-centered program focuses on the welfare of the students: their individual needs, involvement, and progress. Concern for student learning reflects on all the decisions we make about teaching, including instructional strategies, materials, and methods of evaluation. As we implement this program, we should be aware of the following understandings about teaching reading, thinking, and writing, keeping the student clearly in mind as we plan.

1. Positive evaluation is more effective than negative evaluation in improving student performance. Although we have known this concept in theory, in practice we have noted the number wrong at the top of a spelling paper and marked all errors with a red pencil on student compositions. We have hastened to correct each mispronounced word as students read aloud. In the classroom, we can involve students in evaluation methods that truly help them improve their own writing and remove the teacher from the role as the "ogre who wields the red pencil." We can give students time to comprehend as they read and to make their own corrections based on the sense of what they read.

2. Engaging students with the total language process stresses thinking and making meaning through composing and comprehending. Evaluation based on meaningful experiences and performance in a larger context for varied purposes reflect real learning. Holistic methods of scoring student compositions, for example, are quick, efficient, and can be easily understood by students. Reading for varied purposes can result in a Readers' Theater presentation that clearly demonstrates comprehension.

   Using holistic methods for evaluating compositions introduces both teachers and students to the use of a rubric (set of criteria) for establishing scores (grades) for student writing performance. Students and teachers are becoming more aware of what good writing is. Stress in on content and organization, not only the conventions of writing or usage. The same approach can be used with evaluating reading activities.

3. The goal of reading is to gain meaning and comprehension. Comprehension skills involve students in higher order thinking skills. Con-

versely, thinking is an integral part of composition, so we look to the meaning expressed, the ideas, before critiquing the form.

Evaluation of reading abilities should reflect this understanding as we engage students in responding to literature, interacting with the author, and thinking about what the author is saying. Evaluation can take forms other than paper-and-pencil exams. Students can act out a story, contrasting characters, role playing the situation, and extending the action. They can retell stories to younger students; map a story as they analyze the plot, characters, and setting; or keep a reading log as they record their reactions, questions, and related ideas. Thus, evaluation is a positive learning experience, not just proof to the teacher that the student really did read a book!

The same ideas are used in teaching composition. Students are directly involved in editing and evaluation as they progress in a writing program. They become aware of the levels of thinking they are revealing through writing.

4. Evaluation should take varied forms and it should be an ongoing part of the learning process. Self-evaluation is more meaningful than is teacher evaluation if students understand the objectives and take responsibility for their own learning. Teacher-student conferences encourage individual interaction between the teacher and each individual student.

5. Effective communication with both parent and student clarifies objectives and the rationale on which we base our teaching. Thinking through your philosophy of teaching enables you to communicate your thinking to students and to their parents. You can justify practices you use in the classroom and yet are open to consideration of questions that may suggest alternatives.

Selected Resources

California State Department of Education. *Handbook for Planning an Effective Reading Program*. The Department, 1979.

California State Department of Education. *Handbook for Planning an Effective Writing Program*, 3rd ed. The Department, 1986.

Tiedt, Iris M. *Writing: From Topic to Evaluation*. Allyn and Bacon, 1989.

Tiedt, Iris M., et al. *Teaching Thinking in K–12 Classrooms*. Allyn and Bacon, 1989.

Carrying Out the Reading/Thinking/ Writing Literacy Program

In order for any reading/thinking/writing program to be effective, the curriculum presented must be centered in the student's own experiences and needs. Reading and writing must emerge as a natural result of speaking and thinking, and be supported throughout by oral language growth. Teachers' enthusiasm and knowledge of motivational techniques enable them to implement a strong student-centered language and literacy curriculum effectively.

Any good framework outlines sequential skill development for both comprehension and fluency skills and suggests literature appropriate for children of all ability levels. Students are encouraged to apply these skills as they build up pleasure and purpose in learning through reading, thinking, and writing. The integration of these areas needs to begin in the primary grades and continue throughout all school years.

Following are checklists that will help you determine the strengths and weaknesses of your language arts program, especially in terms of whole language approaches to reading, writing, and thinking. We begin with characteristics of a strong reading/thinking/writing program and then focus on objectives for student learning and the behaviors of a good teacher. We conclude with a section on communicating with parents, since that is a supportive aspect of effective teaching.

CHARACTERISTICS OF A STRONG READING/ THINKING/WRITING PROGRAM

The ideas included in this list will stimulate your thinking as you meet with curriculum committees. Keep in mind that any areas not included can be added, but the listed items are essential in developing a well-rounded program.

Does the program provide . . .

A curriculum that:

Develops a logical sequence for instruction?

Identifies the skills and level of performance of individual students?

Adapts itself to meet student needs?

Uses various resource material and strategies in order to reach all students?

Integrates reading/thinking/writing instruction?

Student activities that:

Provide lessons appropriate to their skills and abilities?

Allow them to move at their own speed?

Continually identify success and acknowledgment?

Reading instruction that:

Provides students with ways to independently attack a text?

Works toward different levels of comprehension?

Develops a meaningful vocabulary based on the student speaking and listening vocabularies?

Provides many opportunities to read, think, and write?

Provides opportunities to observe and use figurative language?

Writing exercises that:

Develop writing fluency without fear of evaluation?

Provide prewriting activities to motivate students and to build in success?

Utilize writing to express thinking in all curriculum areas?

Thinking skills that:

Require students to predict, to compare, to sequence, and to infer?

Show students that they are thinking and guide them to observe the process?

Encourage students to look beyond the text and to analyze the author's intent.

OBJECTIVES FOR STUDENT LEARNING

Your objectives state what you, as a teacher, want the students to learn. Your expectations and instructional strategies will influence their achievements and lend excitement to learning. The following objectives form a checklist that you can use.

After reading, do the students:

Identify the theme, plot, character traits, and supporting details?

Sequence ideas, events, and character developments?

Interpret content by restating it in their own language?

Make generalizations about given events?

Comprehend literature that is spoken or read aloud?

Read for pleasure and respond through a variety of media?

In thinking activities, can students:

Interpret nonverbal language and symbolic behaviors?

Apply knowledge of past experience to present lessons?

Predict outcomes and identify the author's purpose, mood, and theme?

Draw conclusions and make reasonable judgments?

Identify varied levels of thinking, moving from simple to more complex?

Use both right-brain and left-brain thinking processes?

Use the inquiry or discovery method, inductive as well as deductive thinking?

In writing exercises, do students:

Write for a variety of audiences and purposes?

Identify characteristics of styles and pattern these authors?

Become involved in the process of responding, revising, and editing?

SKILLS OF A GOOD TEACHER

The ideas listed below may reinforce some of the strategies you already use or encourage you to make changes in your methods of teaching. Remember that you are the single-most influential model in the classroom—perhaps in the students' lives—and your attitude and enthusiasm are contagious.

In initiating and presenting lessons, do you:

Structure lessons so that students understand what they are to do and can respond successfully?

Relate lessons to previous learning?

Select literature for students' listening and reading pleasure so that students can see the effect of good word choice and of the flow and rhythm of the language?

Create lessons that promote quantity at times and quality at others?

Utilize oral language and thinking as an integral part of the reading/ writing process?

Select varied media for instruction to integrate reading/thinking/writing as a naturally related process?

Model the anticipated behavior?

While interacting with students, do you:

Provide some meaning to their lives?

Provide opportunities for students to write about their own experiences and interests?

Allow students time to reflect and to develop their stories?

Interact with students frequently?

Provide positive experiences for personal satisfaction of students and development of self-esteem?

Foster a spirit of cooperation and allow students to assume responsibility for learning?

As follow-through of achievement, do you:

Utilize positive feedback through human interaction, answer keys, computer responses, peer responses, and self-evaluation activities?

Recognize the students for achieving, for quietly working, and for succeeding at individual levels?

Display or publish student work on bulletin boards, in class books, and in school newspapers?

COMMUNICATING WITH PARENTS

Invite parents to join you in promoting the learning process with their children. Let parents hear from you early in the school year. A letter sent home informs them of your expectations and how you plan to implement your program. When parents have received a letter before Open House or Back to School Night, they can be prepared to ask questions they might have about your program; they will also have a better understanding of your attitudes toward reading, thinking, and writing, and will tend to support you. You can adapt this sample letter:

Dear Parents,

Your child has been assigned to my Reading class. I hope to make this year exciting and full of learning experiences. Your child will be exposed to various types of literature with many writing exercises because I strongly feel that reading teaches writing and writing increases reading skills. The only way to be a better reader or writer is to read and write frequently.

I emphasize reading and thinking about good literature. I plan several activities in association with the books we shall be reading so that students can learn to attack a book on their own, without my guidance. I want them to be able to go beyond the text by learning how to critique and to analyze the author's style and theme. Most importantly, I want them to learn to love reading.

Good grammar and good punctuation are inherent parts of good writing. I stress having your child discover and correct his or her own mistakes through the revision and editing process. Students will share their compositions in response groups and, in turn, receive positive feedback and helpful suggestions from peers. This process should help your child develop confidence in his or her ability.

Students will be encouraged to participate in oral discussions and to evaluate what they have read and written. I encourage them to be creative in their responses and to be constructive in their criticism. In most cases there will be no wrong answers, so encourage them to "speak up."

Students will maintain a portfolio of their compositions; therefore, you will not be receiving these papers home on a weekly basis. Periodically, each student will pick selections to be revised and duplicated for a classbook which will be given to you. Please share your satisfaction with your child when you have the opportunity to read the compositions.

Thank you for your involvement and encouragement in this learning process.

Respectfully,
Mary Jane Smith

A letter home is not only good public relations, it also provides a method of communication that pays off for everyone.

Involving Students in Learning

New directions in teaching emphasize individual achievement and self-appraisal, use of response groups, and involving students in evaluation. Gradually, we are moving away from the traditional report card and ABC grading. The most effective teachers plan strategies that include more time on task, students working in cooperative learning groups, and individual student conferencing with teachers.

In this section you will find ideas for encouraging group cooperation and interaction through small group work. Of course, you must provide direction for student group work, but the students themselves do most of the responding, revising, and evaluating. Our ultimate goal is to have students edit their writing, which is a wonderful learning process that also removes the heavy paperload from the teacher's shoulders. Holistic scoring, a widely used technique for evaluating student writing and competencies, can be used with students, as described here.

Also included is a section on recording and evaluating progress, with suggested methods for involving students in considering individual growth. Publishing student work, for example, communicates the message of success to the students. The feedback from parents also will reward your efforts.

WORKING IN SMALL GROUPS

Students must be taught how to work effectively in small groups. From the time they enter kindergarten, they can work in pairs. Working in pairs to complete a project or to plan an activity provides the positive interaction of working together. We then move into sharing experiences in small groups which begins orally and gradually develops into sharing written material. The natural outcome of student sharing is one of being recognized as an individual with something important to say.

Paired students can be assigned the task of analyzing a piece of literature and sharing their responses to the author's style, the theme, the characters, and the conclusion. A panel can be created to critique books and present recommendations to the class. Responding to literature through creative dramatics, readers' theater, and choral reading requires group planning and provides a sense of achievement.

In responding to literature, students can work successfully in small groups on the following projects:

Developing timelines for events that happen by chapter or year

Mapping character development

Charting emotions or reactions to chapters

Creating still-lifes for events

Drawing cartoons or murals of characters

Sequencing events on jumbled cards

Organizing a chart to demonstrate character interactions

As students become more capable, require them to share poems, current events, or stories in small group responses to the subject matter. Initially, groups are instructed simply to respond in a positive manner to the selection. Later, response groups are directed to compile a list of questions, or they can be detectives who find clues (details) about the literature they are reading.

From the beginning, use answer keys, computer responses, or any form of self-evaluation that allows students to assess themselves. By utilizing answer keys, students experience the positive feedback of correction in a nonthreatening manner. In making corrections, they also are implementing the beginning stages of revising and editing.

Response groups don't just happen; they must be taught. The process must be *modeled*. It is important to be patient and consistent in developing group effort. The chatter of learning outweighs the disruption of quiet. Acquiring knowledge from peers is meaningful and beneficial. Even weaker students, who are grouped with stronger students, can provide positive feedback.

In forming response groups, we recommend that you:

1. Develop groups that normally don't work together, blending weak students with stronger students.
2. Use groups of three to five students.
3. Be positive and be constructive.
4. Build up expectations for response groups gradually.
5. Give concrete instructions for tasks to be completed in groups.
6. Develop a point system for group work.

Using Response Groups for Editing Writing

After students have begun to write, response groups serve an important role in active learning. First experiences in small group editing need to be very specific and nonthreatening. The first time students share, they simply share their stories. Students are directed to listen for something positive to say about each story while the writer reads aloud. Reading aloud gives the author a chance to *hear* the story and it often helps her or him find errors or awkward constructions. Students can make immediate revisions or note changes needed. Members of the response group talk about things they liked about the student's writing—the kind of language, the subject matter, the use of "showing" sentences, or the plot development. This positive and nonthreatening experience helps young authors build self-esteem and confidence.

Add to the responsibilities of the response group gradually but consistently. For example, the next responsibility of the group might be to develop questions about the story as it is read to them a second time. The first reading should always be done for enjoyment of content, whereas the second reading allows students to concentrate on fluency, grammar, and style. Later, the group could be directed to identify "telling" sentences rather than "showing" sentences as one specific way to improve writing.

After the groups are trained to make positive, supportive comments, they write responses that include not only good points but recommendations for improvement. Start simply by having students score a paper on the basis of one to ten, with the higher number being the better score. The score given reflects the listener's general reaction to the story on the basis of quality of language, development of the piece, clarity, and enjoyment. Provide half sheets of paper on which to write the evaluation, as shown here:

RESPONSE GROUP ASSIGNMENT

Paper Number _____
Score _____

Write a brief comment explaining why you gave the paper the score you did. For example: Did the author use colorful, vivid language? Was the paper exciting?

Did the paper follow a logical sequence? Were there good examples of showing sentences?

Scorer's Name _____

After groups feel comfortable with writing a simple comment, direct them to look for more specific details and to give more concrete suggestions. Hand out sample papers from anonymous authors. After listing some of the following on the board, discuss the papers:

What is the best sentence or word?

What is strong about this piece?

What do you like about it?

What don't you understand?

Are there good descriptions, effective use of words?

Are there words inappropriately used, ones that could be stronger?

Does the story have a clear beginning, middle, and end?

Does the story make sense?

What needs to be clarified?

Which part of the paper needs more specific descriptions?

What questions are left unanswered?

Find a good or weak example of a recently studied aspect of writing.

Hand out evaluation sheets for members of the response group to fill out for each paper. Encourage a workshop attitude so that all students share in a supportive manner. These three Response Sheets represent editing that progresses from positive support to the inclusion of constructive criticism and suggestions for improvement.

LEVEL 1

Author's Name _____   Your Name _____

What I liked best about the paper.

What I thought was a good sentence or word.

Some questions I have about the paper.

LEVEL 2

Author's Name _____   Your Name _____

Areas that were good in the story (be specific).

Does the paper flow (transition, beginning, middle, end)

Does the paper remain consistent in tense and point of view?

Where would you like more detail?

LEVEL 3

Author's Name _____   Your Name _____

What is good about the paper? (be specific).

What is your overall impression of the paper?

Where could the author improve the paper by adding more detail? dialogue?

Are there any irrelevant, repetitious, or uninteresting sentences?

How could this paper be improved? (be specific.)

Have the groups share their responses with the authors, stressing that they are not to take comments personally or be hurt by suggestions, but rather they are to ask questions and learn how to improve their papers. Students then use that information, incorporating it into their rewritten version of the paper. Students and teacher can decide on number values to assign for response group scores, original papers, and revised copies, which will all be considered part of the final grade. See the discussion of Holistic Scoring on pages 330–337.

Developing More Advanced Editing Skills

Study the author's style in the literature you present to your students. Conduct a class discussion about the characteristics of good writing. Students might suggest that authors not only apply the proper writing conventions but they also have the following:

A pattern or design

A hook for the reader

Cause and effect

A flow from one event to the next

Vivid details and actions

Relationships that are connected

Good choice of words

Point out that authors revise their stories several times in order to discover the proper shape of their stories. Each time they revise, authors may stress a different activity—sometimes they search for word order and grammatical errors, and sometimes they check the unity and flow. Stress that response groups can do the same. Elicit from students the "primary traits" that they can look for in papers. Their list may include some of the items below that you have placed on cards:

run-ons and fragments use of commas indentation of paragraphs capitalization

good imagery dialogue active verbs use of details

first or third person throughout consistency of tense use of transitions redundancies

spelling word endings repetitious words grammar

Hand out cards to the students, noting that each editing group can have different responsibilities. Have response groups convene a second time and a third time, if needed. Each time, the paper is read silently by all members of the group. Each member focuses on the primary traits assigned, commenting on weak or strong examples of the trait being examined. Students learn by discovering these examples.

Taking the information provided by their peers, students revise and rewrite their papers to improve them as they prepare for publication. All response papers from the editing meetings are attached to the final copy. Stress that authors need to be the final editors of their own papers, reading critically for style, grammar, capitalization, punctuation, and organization. Students need repeated experience with the full editing process, going through two or more drafts to polish their writing. Create a set of guidelines for proofreading, the final editing step before publication, thus:

GUIDELINES FOR PROOFREADING

I. Proofread for spelling. Read your paper backwards, asking
   A. Does the word look right?
   B. Is the word legible?
   C. Are you positive about the spelling? If not, circle it.
   Go through the entire paper in this fashion.

II. When you have finished reading, check the circled words.
   A. Ask a classmate to spell those words.
   B. Ask the teacher to spell them.
   C. Look them up in the dictionary.

III. Look for fragments and run-ons:
   A. Find the last sentence. Read it carefully.
   B. Does it make sense all by itself? Is it too long or does it combine too many ideas?
   C. Check each sentence in this manner.

IV. Check for capitalization errors. Apply all the rules.

V. Check your punctuation.
   A. Have you provided periods, question marks, or exclamation marks?
   B. Have you placed quotation marks appropriately?
   C. Have you used commas correctly?

VI. Did you give your writing a title?

Benefits of Response Groups

The response groups serve as a learning experience for every member of the group. Individuals stimulate the thinking of others. Small groups not only serve as a creative outlet in reading projects but encourage members to work cooperatively and constructively. Students learn more about written expression through the revision process than through grammar exercises, often being motivated to study usage and grammar. Members work with a common goal of helping peers improve their papers until they create finished products, free of errors.

Students also develop a sense of pride in their group effort and their own writing. From the beginning, they see that they are not producing something just for a teacher—they are working for another audience. This sense of audience enriches their abilities and provides stimulus for improvement. When individuals contribute thoughts that ignite the thinking of others or that foster a project, their self-esteem rises. Also, students working together in response groups learn about the writing process and develop a pride of ownership in the papers. The finished product has meaning to the student and the group; thus, it is usually of much higher quality.

HOLISTIC SCORING OF STUDENT WRITING

Holistic scoring is used widely as an efficient means of evaluating large samples of student writing. It differs from analytical scoring in that each paper is read as a whole and no attempt is made to count specific errors in the uses of conventions or grammatical constructions.

Holistic scoring provides a means of comparing student writing across a whole school district. Taking writing samples in the fall and in the spring enables districts (or schools or individual teachers) to assess the growth of students over the year. The holistic assessment involves the following procedures:

1. Decide on consistent methods of administering the test that all teachers will follow.
2. Select a prompt (a topic on which all students will write.)
3. Administer the test, taking a writing sample on a given day. Collect the papers.
4. Agree on a rubric (set of criteria) against which all papers will be scored.
5. Score the set of papers by all teachers involved.

The process of working with holistic scoring is especially valuable for both students and teachers because it involves determining the characteristics of good writing.

Selecting a Prompt

As you plan to take the writing sample, select a topic on which your students will write. Such concerns as the following should be considered:

General knowledge about the topic

Level of ability and sophistication of the students

Student interest in the topic

Whether students will write narrative or expository prose

Many varied topics have been used with writing assessment across the country, for example:

> Who is a special person in your life? Tell why this person is special and describe the kinds of things you do with this person.

> Pretend that you are invisible. Imagine what you might do and something that might happen. Tell a story about a day when you were invisible.

It is important that all teachers administering the writing test present it to the students in much the same way. Therefore, you should agree on a set of guidelines that all will follow. Here is one sample set of guidelines:

1. Directions, common to all students, should be in writing.
2. Set a time limit, possibly 45 minutes.
3. When presenting a prompt, do not provide extra information.
4. Do not assist students. Writing must be their own.
5. Keep the testing center quiet and free from distractions.

Preparing a Scoring Rubric

Before presenting the appropriate prompt, you need to consider the kind of writing you can expect from your students. What are quality indicators that will distinguish excellent writing from average writing? How will average (acceptable for grade level) writing differ from weak or unacceptable writing?

Creating the traits that will be characteristic of each level or score creates a rubric for use with holistic scoring. A rubric is simply a list or chart that describes the expected performance for each level. Varied performance indicators may be emphasized. For example:

1. The student follows directions and addresses the topic.
2. The student uses appropriate capitalization and punctuation.
3. A paragraph is developed with a topic sentence and supporting sentences.
4. The student uses interesting vocabulary and detail.
5. The student demonstrates some organization of work.

Before scoring the sample, train readers to score. During the training session, teach scorers to read stories or essays rapidly, absorbing the total impact before evaluating. They are to remain impartial as to the content and opinions, scoring only the quality of the paper. To further maintain impartiality, letter grades are not used, but rather scores of 1–9, 1–5, or mastery–nonmastery, which may seem less threatening to the students. When scoring, readers should not look at the previous reader's score, nor do they write on the paper itself. Usually two readers score each paper. If there is disagreement, then a third reader is necessary. If the stories or essays are written as competencies or if teachers, students, or parents have a need to know why a student failed, the last reader completes a rating sheet (a copy of the rubric), indicating deficiencies on nonmastery papers.

Introducing Holistic Evaluation to Your Class

Usually, holistic scoring is used to test writing competency, but it can be used in the classroom as a method of involving students in the grading/evaluation process. Teach students in response groups how to score papers with a simple two-point, pass-fail, system. Have the following prompt on the board.

> Describe your classroom. Write at least six complete sentences, including correct punctuation and capitalization. All sentences should relate to the topic and should be as interesting as possible.

Then pass out copies of two anonymous papers from another class that were written following this prompt:

Sample Paper 1

1. We have a t.v. it is back and whitte we have it for a year
2. their are for windos in this room they are always dirty.
3. I don't like my tabel it is all carved and writ on.
4. the room looks like a dump
5. the teacher nice but I steel don't like the room.

Sample Paper 2

Our classroom is in a portable and not very interesting. Our room is separeted by a moveable wall. We have lots of pictures on the walls and a green chalkboard. We have lots of windows and two doors. The teacher's desk is in the front and are desks are in rows. My desk is close to one of the two doors so I can look out at the playground. I wish I didn't have to work so hard in here, but the teacher is nice. That's what makes it fun to be in the classroom.

After reading the stories aloud, discuss both papers and decide why one paper is considered passing while the other is not. Point out the inappropriate use of numbering; the prompt did not ask them to list. Discuss the effect of misspelling and the poor use of punctuation and capitalization.

With your class, create a list of skills (a rubric) that identifies the quality indicators for nonmastery or mastery of the writing task.

Nonmastery	Mastery
Did not follow directions.	Followed all directions.
Listed or did not write in complete sentences.	Wrote in complete sentences.
Did not capitalize correctly.	Capitalized appropriately.
Has poor or no punctuation.	Uses appropriate punctuation, or makes few errors.
Uses run-ons or fragments.	Has few run-ons or fragments.
Strays from subject or does not develop ideas.	Sticks to topic or returns to topic after straying.
Shows limited vocabulary.	Uses good vocabulary, details, and descriptors.
Demonstrates poor spelling.	Spells most words correctly; few homonym errors.
Has no topic sentence and support is weak.	Has topic sentence and support, with a sense of beginning, middle, and end.
Does not show paragraphs.	Uses proper paragraphing.

Add any other criteria that are important for the type of writing or to your course of study. Hand out other anonymous examples of good writing and poor writing. The prompts can be your own—just make sure that both examples answer the same question. Again, have the students determine mastery or nonmastery. There should be a general agreement within the classroom as to mastery and nonmastery levels.

Display the rubric created by the class so that students observe it while writing their own stories. The chart acts as a writing guide and a reminder of quality indicators in writing so students are aware of how to write to get a passing score.

Have students apply the rubric to score some of their own papers. Provide a rating sheet and a copy of the rubric with a space for indicating nonmastery or mastery. Each paper is graded by two students; the first simply reads and scores mastery or nonmastery on the cover sheet; the second not only scores the paper but also circles the appropriate performance indicators on the cover sheet.

Developing Holistic Scoring Further

Have students develop a rubric for scoring papers on the basis of a 1–9 scoring system. The range of scores is defined thus:

9   outstanding
7   good
5   average
3   fair
1   weak

Papers with one sentence or less are marked 0. A score of 3 or 5 may be accepted as minimum competency according to the expectations appropriate for your students. Note that this process focuses student attention on identifying what good writing is. Their knowledge will expand over the years.

Develop a 1–7 rubric scoring system with the students. The following rubric offers criteria for quality indicators.

Score of 1—Weak	Score of 3—Fair
Writer does all or most of the following:	Writer does all or most of the following:
1. Minimal description.	1. Some details, but writing is colorless, flat.
2. Poor spelling.	2. Some common words and homonyms misspelled.
3. Confusing use of mechanics.	3. Frequent mechanical errors.
4. Poor use of capitalization.	4. Generally correct use of capitalization and periods.
5. Vocabulary limited with errors in agreement.	5. Limited vocabulary with some errors in agreement. Some use of slang.
6. Little or no organization.	6. Some organization, but tends to be mechanical.
7. Not legible.	7. Legible, possibly messy.
8. No paragraphing.	8. Little or some paragraphing.
Score of 5—Good	**Score of 7—Excellent**
Writer does all or more of the following:	Writer does all or most of the following:
1. General details, adjectives and adverbs in use.	1. Vivid details and images.

Score of 5—Good	Score of 7—Excellent
2. Adequate mechanics. Some errors that do not interfere with meaning.	2. Few mechanical errors. Internal punctuation correct.
3. Adequate vocabulary with few errors in agreement, person, or number.	3. Excellent vocabulary with good use of agreement and tenses.
4. Clear sense of organization with beginning, middle and end. May deviate from topic but returns.	4. Clear control of structure. Natural flow and unity. Moves towards completion and conclusion.
5. Spelling adequate, possible misspelled homonyms or difficult words.	5. Few spelling errors.
6. Proper paragraphing.	6. Proper paragraphing.
7. Varied sentence structure.	7. Obvious use of style.

After defining the characteristics of writing at each level, make a chart of the rubric to display so students use it as a guideline for papers written in class. Before scoring peer papers in response groups, practice the procedure on anonymous papers. Write the following prompt on the board.

> Describe an event in your earlier childhood that you remember and that has influenced your thinking. The event need not be an important one to anyone but yourself. Sentences should relate to the story and should explain what happened, what you thought, and what effect it had on you. Make sure that you write in complete sentences, using proper mechanics, correct punctuation, and capitalization. Don't forget to use paragraphing appropriately.

The prompt can be one of yours and the practice examples from another class. Note that a good prompt clearly states what is expected of the students. Make sure students understand what is required before they practice scoring. Hand out copies of the stories to each child. The following stories respond to the above prompt.

Holistic Score: 7

The Fair at Five Years Old

I'll always remember my first day at the County Fair when I was only 5 years old. My mother had to drag me through the amusement park because I wanted to stop at each and every ride. I was attracted to all of the wonderful sights, intersting sounds and delicious smells of the park and never wanted to leave.

Everywhere I saw rides that intrigued me. Roller coasters zoomed past me at about fifty miles an hour. The ferrywheel dangled with laughing and screaming people. Bright lights flashed everywhere, inviting me to stay.

Beside the sounds of the people on the rides, excited cheers came from the booths as someone won a prize. Popcorn salesmen called out and so did the people from the booths. Most of the people were talking happily that walked past me while others screamed with joy on the rides. I also heard little kids like me crying because they were scared to ride the roller coaster, but that didn't bother me.

The smells of all kinds of food like popcorn, hotdogs and hamburgers greeted my nose. Every time I got off a ride I started getting hungry because I wanted to eat all those smells. I really wanted some popcorn after I smelled it from the candy stand. At the end of the day I was eating the food instead of smelling it.

In conclusion, I will always think that amusement parks and fairs are a lot of fun, even now that I'm growing up. I can hardly wait for the next one.

Holistic Score: 3

The Day I Got Lost

I remember one day when I was about five year old, being dragged by my mother in a flea market. Becuase I went off and got lost. I left becuase of the nasty food.

I seen a man and I asked him could he help me. He look for my mom for a long time. But he gave up too. And then He left me.

Later I had heard my mom calling me. I could tell that she was mad by the way she hollored my name.

When we got home I got a spaking from my father. Because I had ran off, didn't stay with my mother. But I toold her why I ran off, she said, that is a real stupid reson.

Holistic Score: 5

Today my mother took me to an amusement park. I couldn't go anywhere by myself since I was only five years old.

It wasn't very fun because it was so crowed there I couldn't go on any ride or see any of the attractions. Being in crowds always reminds me of being small. All I could see was peoples feet and legs, nothing else. I could hear people talking about the rides and shows, but I was to small to see anything. The only thing that appealed to me was the smell of the food. I hate the feeling of being stepped on, pushed arond, knocked down. That's all I can think of when I think of an amusement park.

Holistic Score: 1

The Baseball Game

I member my first baseball game it was fun. Lots of bright lights in the stadium. I seen lots of peple wearing caps and carring penants. You could see noting but peple. Horns beeped. You could hear cheers. When peple cheered beer smelled terible. The night was cold you could feel the wind in my bones. Yes it was a cold night.

The students may not agree with all the scores indicated but they should be close. Come to some agreement on the scores assigned. Have students use the rubric in response groups to assign number scores to fellow members' papers. The process requires several class periods and should be repeated several times. You compile the scores assigned in the gradebook as one method of evaluation.

Benefits of Holistic Scoring

Holistic scoring is used to assess large group compositions. Schools use this means of evaluation for judging mastery or nonmastery on writing competencies. It can also be used for pre- and post-testing of projects. This method reduces the time spent on grading huge quantities of papers.

Holistic scoring also decreases the teacher's paperload while serving as a learning tool for students. Response groups work on the mechanics and details in the beginning stages as well as serve as holistic scorers for final copies. Students learn to differentiate between good papers and weak ones and tend to imitate the better examples.

EVALUATING PROGRESS

An important aspect of curriculum is evaluating and communicating progress of or to students. Evaluation should be an ongoing aspect of learning, with the students involved in the process. The process can begin with self-correction, move to teacher-student conferencing and self-evaluation, and evolve into peer evaluation.

The learning process of evaluation takes many forms. The use of answer keys and computer feedback allows students to assess themselves instantly. When students have a chance to sit down with a teacher who individually counsels them about their reading or writing, they absorb the lesson more clearly. By focusing each student's progress, the teacher-student conference becomes an effective learning tool.

   Another method of assessment reduces the number of letter grades assigned to students' papers by encouraging students to evaluate themselves. Implement self-appraisal as a natural part of your program. Develop a variety of tasks that allow students to self-evaluate and allow them to consider individual growth resulting from lessons. One such task might be to map out what they learned from a literature lesson in the following manner:

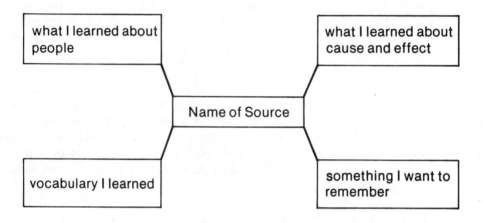

Another idea would involve students in clustering what they want to learn about a given subject as a prereading activity.

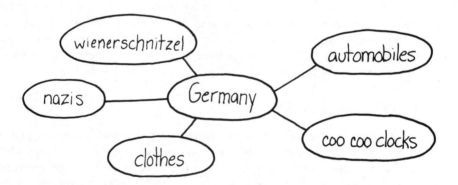

   After the reading/thinking/writing lesson, have students inventory which of the clustered items they learned. For example:

I now know this about Germany

Its people—

Its land—

Hitler—

Manufacturing—

Besides self-evaluation, students should learn to evaluate other students. Panels can critique the work of other small groups. Students can score (similar to Olympic score cards) small group presentations. Utilize response groups as revision and editing groups, having them maintain score sheets for each session. Resist overcorrecting and being the final assessor for the students. Students will learn to be honest in their evaluation of themselves and of others.

Reading Records

Individual records of reading assignments enable the students to see the results of their efforts. Present a lesson to show students how to record what they read. Some students need this as a motivation or goal. Tell students that they will receive effort points for reading and that all reading will count—even the books that they do not finish.

Give the students a sheet similar to the one below on which they can keep track. Set a minimum goal with the students. Check periodically to see that the students are filling in their form.

Date	Selection	Author	Pages Read
Monday			
Tuesday			
Wednesday			
Thursday			

(continued)

Friday
Weekends
Total for week
Comments about books
Name _____

Class Displays

Classroom displays of book reports, book charts, or bookworms remind children of the importance of reading for pleasure as well as recording their successful endeavors. Younger students will enjoy creating a bookworm that winds around the room above the chalkboard. Each student who completes a book adds a segment to the worm's body, as shown in this illustration.

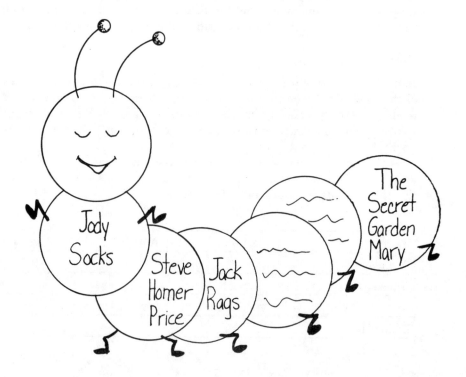

The Writing Portfolio

When students maintain a writing portfolio, they can see for themselves their own improvement. Have each student decorate a file folder in which to save all writing that is done during a grading period. Short writings that are shared, but not evaluated, will be stored here along with revised writings. A beginning writing sample may be stapled on the inside cover to use as a standard for evaluating progress; students will be pleased to note how they have progressed.

Use this portfolio as a basis for grading. This collection of student writing can be compiled into a magazine to be shared with parents in conferences or "Back to School."

Learning Logs

Keeping a reading or writing log also provides a means of evaluation. The following example is a log students can maintain to record progress. Students can record thinking notes on books they read, research notes, or use logs to gather thoughts about projects. Two examples are included here:

Assignment	Title	What I learned	What I need to know

Title	Pages	Thinking Notes

Transaction Logs

Students should enter into a transaction with the author. They should ask questions, predict what happens next, note their ideas and feelings about what they are reading, and relate the content to their own experience. Other activities that expand their thinking include drawing comparisons between events in one story and another, charting cause and effect, tracing the development of a thought or the plot, distinguishing between fact and opinion, and speculating about character development. Students should evaluate these learning logs based on their effort and knowledge they gained in the process.

When you read the students' transaction logs, you gain insight into each individual. The logs also provide topics to discuss during a student-teacher conference. Any grade assigned to these logs should also reflect the students' own assessment.

Completed Projects

The use of finished products for evaluation is an effective form of reporting student progress. Parents have a clear demonstration of their child's success, and students have something to keep of which they can be proud.

PUBLISHING STUDENT WORK

Lessons described in this book intend to help students to learn and succeed in reading/thinking/writing. Student success will depend on individual effort and ability, but the achievement can be enhanced by providing purposes for learning endeavors. Displaying student work should be an integral part of your program, as this kind of publication provides purpose and motivation. Any method you use—bulletin boards, class magazines, or picture books—encourages students to do their best. Publishing class anthologies, formally and informally, gives the students a purpose for genuine effort and produces a finished product that they can keep longer.

Displaying Work in the Classroom

Besides creating a positive learning atmosphere, displaying student products in the classroom enhances their self-esteem. Develop unique methods of exhibiting their work. Have students provide you with a picture of themselves to be posted on a bulletin board. Throughout the year, rotate products (reading projects, learning logs, written compositions) that each child has produced. Those projects completed by small groups could have their pictures clustered together. The pride students exhibit in this display will be genuine.

Another idea for display is to create a cardboard movable screen on which students can exhibit their work. Place the timelines, charts, and graphs that students have created on this screen, which could be placed in the reading circle. Use those items to stimulate further discussion when working with the reading groups.

Publishing a Class Anthology

About three weeks prior to the end of each semester, have students select one to three of their favorite stories, essays, or poems from their writing portfolios. These selections should be work that has been revised and rewritten previously. Have them reread their selections, looking for ways to revise them further. Review ways of revising—using more meaningful vocabulary, reworking paragraphs, developing weak descriptions, and making the work come together better. Remind students that authors may revise five to nine times before publication.

Allow enough class time for students to revise and edit these chosen stories. Encourage students to use a thesaurus to improve vocabulary. Post the rubric used to score papers. Confer with those students desiring your assistance about improving their work, or let students work together to discover where revision is recommended.

After students have revised their compositions and rewritten them, collect them but don't grade them. Find a resource (yourself, a parent, or a student in a typing class) to type the writing exactly as it is written. Preferably use a word processor so that the work can be saved in memory. Then return the papers to the students and ask them to proofread the stories for surface errors. Working in pairs increases the discovery rate. Students often are more successful in finding other people's mistakes, so allow them to work together.

Make the changes that the students find. Do this as many times as you feel necessary to find most of the errors. Do not be the final editor for the students—the end product should be a result of their efforts, not yours. Warn students that any errors not corrected will be in the published product.

Collect the last revision and make enough copies for each student. After the copies have been distributed, have students make covers and a Table of Contents. Bind the book with contact paper, or have students tie string through holes punched in the stories and cover. Students may present these books to their parents or you can use them in parent conferences. The feedback from student and parents will reward your efforts.

Exploring Further

Anderson, Richard (Chair), and the Commission on Reading. *Becoming a Nation of Readers*. National Academy of Education, National Institute of Education, Center for the Study of Reading, 1985.

Goodman, Kenneth (ed.). *Miscue Analysis: Applications to Reading Instruction*. ERIC/RCS and NCTE, 1973.

Myers, Miles. *A Procedure for Writing Assessment and Holistic Scoring*. NCTE and ERIC, 1980.

Myers, Miles, and Gray, James (eds.). *Theory and Practice in the Teaching of Composition*. NCTE, 1983.

Tiedt, Iris M. *Writing: From Topic to Evaluation*. Allyn and Bacon, 1989.

10

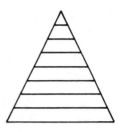

Resources for Students and Teachers

We recommend a well-stocked library in every school. Students and teachers need books that are readily accessible for pleasure and information. Books should also circulate to small classroom libraries that are changed to fit special studies or varied student interests.

The books and other materials listed in this chapter are selected for specific purposes. Books for the teacher are those that will update your professional growth and present new ideas in developing fields. Books for the students represent special groupings on topics that we recommend emphasizing in contemporary classrooms. No list is exhaustive, so you will need to read journals that review books and other instructional materials.

Enjoy exploring!

Especially for the Primary Grades

CALDECOTT AWARD BOOKS

The Caldecott Medal is awarded annually to the illustrator of an outstanding American picture book for children. The award honors Randolph Caldecott, an early American illustrator of children's books.

Because these awards are given to "picture books," the books have special appeal for primary grade children. Because they represent beautiful art and often present "big ideas," however, we recommend that all K–12 teachers take advantage of these exciting books. For example, they can be used as models for the writing of children's books by older students.

Note that the year listed is the year the award was given; books were published in the preceding year. The first name listed is that of the award winner—the illustrator. At times, the illustrator is also the author.

1938. Dorothy P. Lathrop. *Animals of the Bible* by Helen Dean Fish. Lippincott.

1939. Thomas Handforth. *Mei Lei*. Doubleday.

Honor books: Laura Adams Armer. *The Forest Pool*. Longman.
Robert Lawson. *Wee Gillis* by Munro Leaf. Viking.
Wanda Gag. *Snow White and the Seven Dwarfs*. Coward-McCann.
Clare Newberry. *Barkis*. Harper & Row.
James Daugherty. *Andy and the Lion*. Viking.

1940. Ingri and Edgar d'Aulaire. *Abraham Lincoln*. Doubleday.

Honor Books: Berta and Elmer Hader. *Cock-A-Doodle Doo*. Macmillan.
Ludwig Bemelmans. *Madeline*. Viking.
Lauren Ford. *The Ageless Story*. Dodd, Mead.

1941. Robert Lawson. *They Were Strong and Good*. Viking.

Honor Book: Clare Newberry. *April's Kittens*. Harper & Row.

1942. Robert McCloskey. *Make Way for Ducklings*. Viking.

Honor Books: Maud and Miska Petersham. *An American ABC*. Macmillan.
Velino Herrera. *In My Mother's House* by Ann Nolan Clark. Viking.
Holling C. Holling. *Paddle-to-the-Sea*. Houghton Mifflin.
Wanda Gag. *Nothing at All*. Coward-McCann.

1943. Virginia Lee Burton. *The Little House*. Houghton Mifflin.

Honor Books: Mary and Conrad Buff. *Dash and Dart*. Viking.
Clare Newberry. *Marshmallow*. Harper & Row.

1944. Louis Slobodkin. *Many Moons* by James Thurber. Harcourt.

Honor Books: Elizabeth Orton Jones. *Small Rain: Verses from the Bible* selected by Jessie Orton Jones. Viking.
Arnold E. Bare. *Pierre Pigeon* by Lee Kingman. Houghton Mifflin.
Berta and Elmer Hader. *The Mighty Hunter*. Macmillan.
Jean Charlot. *A Child's Good Night Book* by Margaret Wise Brown. Scott.
Plao Chan. *Good Luck Horse* by Chin-Yi Chan. Whittlesey.

1945. Elizabeth Orton Jones. *Prayer for a Child* by Rachel Field. Macmillan.

Honor Books: Tasha Tudor. *Mother Goose*. Walck.
Marie Hall Ets. *In the Forest*. Viking.
Marguerite de Angeli. *Yonie Wondernose*. Doubleday.
Kate Seredy. *The Christmas Anna Angel* by Ruth Sawyer. Viking.

1946. Maud and Miska Petersham. *The Rooster Crows*. Macmillan.

Honor Books: Leonard Weisgard. *Little Lost Lamb* by Golden MacDonald. Doubleday.
Marjorie Torrey. *Sing Mother Goose* by Opal Wheeler. Dutton.
Ruth Gannett. *My Mother Is the Most Beautiful Woman in the World* by Becky Reyher. Lothrop.
Kurt Wiese. *You Can Write Chinese*. Viking.

1947. Leonard Weigard. *The Little Island* by Golden MacDonald. Doubleday.

Honor Books: Leonard Weisgard. *Rain Drop Splash* by Alvin Tresselt. Lothrop.

Jay Hyde Barnum. *Boats on the River* by Marjorie Flack. Viking.

Tony Palazzo. *Timothy Turtle* by Al Graham. Welch.

Leo Politi. *Pedro, The Angel of Olvera Street*. Scribner.

Marjorie Torrey. *Sing in Praise: A Collection of the Best Loved Hymns* by Opal Wheeler. Dutton.

1948. Roger Duboisin. *White Snow, Bright Snow* by Alvin Tresselt. Lothrop.

Honor Books: Maria Brown. *Stone Soup*. Scribner.

Dr. Seuss. *McElligott's Pool*. Random.

George Schreiber. *Bambino the Clown*. Viking.

Hildegard Woodward. *Roger and the Fox* by Lavinia Davis. Doubleday.

Virginia Lee Burton. *Song of Robin Hood* edited by Anne Malcolmson. Houghton Mifflin.

1949. Berta and Elmer Hader. *The Big Snow*. Macmillan.

Honor Books: Robert McCloskey. *Blueberries for Sal*. Viking.

Helen Stone. *All Around the Town* by Phyllis McGinley. Lippincott.

Leo Politi. *Juanita*. Scribner.

Kurt Wiese. *Fish in the Air*. Viking.

1950. Leo Politi. *Song of the Swallows*. Scribner.

Honor Books: Lynd Ward. *America's Ethan Allen* by Stewart Holbrook. Houghton Mifflin.

Hildegard Woodward. *The Wild Birthday Cake* by Lavinia Davis. Doubleday.

Marc Simont. *The Happy Day* by Ruth Krauss. Harper & Row.

Dr. Seuss. *Bartholomew and the Oobleck*. Random.

Marcia Brown. *Henry Fisherman*. Scribner.

1951. Katherine Milhous. *The Egg Tree*. Scribner.

Honor Books: Marcia Brown. *Dick Whittington and His Cat*. Scribner.

Nicolas. *The Two Reds* by William Lipkind. Harcourt.

Dr. Seuss. *If I Ran the Zoo*. Random.

Helen Stone. *The Most Wonderful Doll in the World* by Phyllis McGinley. Lippincott.

Clare Newberry. *T-Bone, The Baby Sitter*. Harper & Row.

1952. Nicolas. *Finders Keepers* by William Lipkind. Harcourt.

Honor Books: Marie Hall Ets. *Mr. T. W. Anthony Woo*. Viking.

Marcia Brown. *Skipper John's Cook*. Scribner.

Margaret Bloy. *All Falling Down* by Gene Zion. Harper.

William Pene du Bois. *Bear Party*. Viking.

Elizabeth Olds. *Feather Mountain*. Houghton Mifflin.

1953. Lynd Ward. *The Biggest Bear*. Houghton Mifflin.

Honor Books: Marcia Brown. *Puss in Boots* by Charles Perrault. Scribner.

Robert McCloskey. *One Morning in Maine*. Viking.

Fritz Eichenberg. *Ape in a Cape*. Harcourt.

Margaret Bloy Graham. *The Storm Book* by Charlotte Zolotow. Harper.

Juliet Kepes. *Five Little Monkey*. Houghton Mifflin.

1954. Ludwig Bemelmans. *Madeline's Rescue*. Viking.

Honor Books: Robert McCloskey. *Journey Cake, Ho!* by Ruth Sawyer. Viking.
Jean Charlot. *When Will the World Be Mine?* by Miriam Schlein. Scott.
Marcia Brown. *The Steadfast Tin Soldier* by Hans Christian Andersen. Scribner.
Maurice Sendak. *A Very Special House* by Ruth Krauss. Harper.
A. Birnbaum. *Green Eyes*. Capitol.

1955. Marcia Brown. *Cinderella, Or the Little Glass Slipper* by Charles Perrault. Scribner.

Honor Books: Marguerite de Angeli. *Book of Nursery and Mother Goose Rhymes*. Doubleday.
Tibor Gergely. *Wheel on the Chimney* by Margarget Wise Brown. Lippincott.
Helen Sewell. *The Thanksgiving Story* by Alice Dagliesh. Scribner.
1956. Feodor Rojankovsky. *Frog Went A-Courtin'* edited by John Langstaff. Harcourt.
Honor Books: Marie Hall Ets. *Play with Me*. Viking.
Taro Yashima. *Crow Boy*. Viking.

1957. Marc Simont. *A Tree Is Nice* by Janice May Udry. Harper.

Honor Books: Marie Hall Ets. *Mr. Penny's Race Horse*. Viking.
Tasha Tudor. *1 Is One*. Walck.
Paul Galdone. *Anatole* by Eve Titus. McGraw.
James Gaugherty. *Gillespie and the Guards* by Benjamin Elkin. Viking.
William Pene duBois. *Lion*. Viking.

1958. Robert McCloskey. *Time of Wonder*. Viking.

Honor Books: Don Freeman. *Fly High, Fly Low*. Viking.
Paul Galdone. *Anatole and the Cat* by Eve Titus. McGraw.

1959. Barbara Cooney. *Chanticleer and the Fox* adapted from Chaucer. Crowell.

Honor Books: Antonio Fasconi. *The House That Jack Built*. Harcourt.
Maurice Sendak. *What Do You Say, Dear?* by Sesyle Joslin.
Taro Yashima. *Umbrella*. Viking.

1960. Marie Hall Ets. *Nine Days to Christmas* by Marie Hall Ets and Aurora Labastida. Viking.

Honor Books: Adrienne Adams. *Houses from the Sea* by Alice E. Goudey. Scribner.
Maurice Sendak. *The Moon Jumpers* by Janice May Udry. Harper.

1961. Nicholas Sidjakov. *Baboushka and the Three Kings* by Ruth Robbins. Parnassus.

Honor Book: Leo Lionni. *Inch by Inch*. Astor-Honor.

1962. Marcia Brown. *Once a mouse. . . .* Scribner.

Honor Books: Peter Spier. *The Fox Went Out on a Chilly Night*. Doubleday.
Maurice Sendak. *Little Bear's Visit* by Else Holmelund Minarik. Harper.
Adrienne Adams. *The Day We Saw the Sun Come Up* by Alice E. Goudey. Scribner.

1963. Ezra Jack Keats. *The Snowy Day*. Viking.

Honor Books: Bernarda Bryson. *The Sun Is a Golden Earring* by Natalia Belting. Holt.
Maurice Sendak. *Mr. Rabbit and the Lovely Present* by Charlotte Zolotow. Harper.

1964. Maurice Sendak. *Where the Wild Things Are*. Harper.

Honor Books: Leo Lionni. *Swimmy*. Pantheon.
Evaline Ness. *All in the Morning Early* by Sorche Nic Leodhas. Holt.
Philip Reed. *Mother Goose and Nursery Rhymes*. Atheneum.

1965. Beni Montresor. *May I Bring a Friend?* by Beatrice Schenk de Regniers. Atheneum.

Honor Books: Marvin Bileck. *Rain Makes Applesauce* by Julian Scheer. Holiday. Blair Lent. *The Wave* by Margaret Hodges. Houghton Mifflin. Evaline Ness. *A Pocketful of Cricket* by Rebecca Caudill. Holt.

1966. Nonny Hogrogian. *Always Room for One More* by Sorche Nic Leodhas. Holt.

Honor Books: Roger Duvoisin. *Hide and Seek Fog* by Alvin Tresselt. Lothrop. Marie Hall Ets. *Just Me*. Viking. Evaline Ness. *Tom Tit Tot*. Scribner.

1967. Evaline Ness. *Sam, Bangs & Moonshine*. Holt.

Honor Book: Ed Emberley. *One Wide River to Cross* by Barbara Emberley. Prentice-Hall.

1968. Ed Emberley. *Drummer Hoff* by Barbara Emberley. Prentice-Hall.

1969. Uri Shulevita. *The Fool of the World and the Flying Ship* by Arthur Ransome. Farrar.

Honor Book: Blair Lent. *Why the Sun and the Moon Live in the Sky* by Elphinstone Dayrell. Houghton Mifflin.

1970. William Steig. *Sylvester and the Magic Pebble*. Windmill.

Honor Books: Ezra Jack Keats. *Goggles*. Macmillan. Leo Lionni. *Alexander and the Wind-up Mouse*. Pantheon. Robert Andrew Parker. *Pop Corn & Ma Goodness* by Edna Mitchell Preston. Viking. Brinton Turkle. *Thy Friend, Obadiah*. Viking. Margot Zemach. *The Judge* by Harve Zemach. Farrar.

1971. Gail Haley. *A Story, A Story*. Atheneum.

Honor Books: Blair Lent. *The Angry Moon* by William Aleator. Little. Arnold Lobel. *Frog and Toad Are Friends*. Harper. Maurice Sendak. *In the Night Kitchen*. Harper.

1972. Nonny Hogrogian. *One Fine Day*. Macmillan.

Honor Books: Arnold Lobel. *Hildilid's Night* by Cheli Duran Ryan. Macmillan. Janina Domanska. *If All the Seas Were One Sea*. Macmillan. Tom Feelings. *Moja Means One* by Muriel Feelings. Dial.

1973. Blair Lent. *The Funny Little Woman* retold by Arlene Mosel. Dutton.

Honor Books: Gerald McDermott. *Anansi the Spider*. Holt. Leonard Baskin. *Hosie's Alphabet* by Hosea, Tobias and Lisa Baskin. Viking. Nancy Ekholm Burkert. *Snow White and the Seven Dwarfs*, translated by Randall Jarrell. Farrar. Tom Bahti. *When Clay Sings* by Byrd Baylor. Scribner.

1974. Margot Zemach. *Duffy and the Devil* retold by Harve Zemach. Farrar.

Honor Books: Susan Jeffers. *Three Jovial Huntsmen: A Mother Goose Rhyme*. Bradbury. David Macaulay. *Cathedral: The Story of Its Construction*. Houghton Mifflin.

1975. Gerald McDermott. *Arrow to the Sun*. Viking.

Honor Book: Tom Feelings. *Jambo Means Hello: A Swahili Alphabet Book* by Muriel Feelings. Dial.

1976. Leo and Diane Dillon. *Why Mosquitoes Buzz in People's Ears* retold by Verna Ardema. Dial.

Honor Books: Peter Parnall. *The Desert Is Theirs* by Byrd Balor. Scribner.
Tomie de Paola. *Strega Nona*. Prentice-Hall.

1977. Leo and Diane Dillon. *Ashanti to Zulu: African Traditions* by Margaret Musgrove. Dial.

Honor Books: William Steig. *The Amazing Bone*. Farrar.
Nonny Hogrogian. *The Contest*. Greenwillow.
M. J. Goffstein. *Fish for Supper*. Dial.
Beverly B. McDermott. *The Golem*. Lippincott.
Peter Parnell. *Hawk, I'm Your Brother* by Byrd Baylor. Scribner.

1978. Peter Spier. *Noah's Ark*. Translated by the illustrator. Doubleday.

Honor Book: Margot Zemach. *It Could Always Be Worse: A Yiddish Folktale*. Farrar.

1979. Paul Goble. *The Girl Who Loved Wild Horses*. Bradbury.

Honor Books: Donald Crews. *Freight Train*. Greenwillow.
Peter Parnall. *The Way to Start a Day* by Byrd Baylor.

1980. Barbara Cooney. *Ox-Cart Man* by Donald Hall. Viking.

Honor Books: Rachel Isadora. *Ben's Trumpet*. Greenwillow.
Uri Shulevitz. *Treasure*. Farrar.
Chris Van Allsberg. *Garden of Abdul Gaszai*. Houghton Mifflin.

1981. Arnold Lobel. *Fables*. Harper.

Honor Books: Molly Bang. *Grey Lady and the Strawberry Snatcher*. Scholastic.
Donald Crews. *Truck*. Greenwillow.
Joseph Low. *Mice Twice*. Atheneum.
Ilse Plume. *Bremen Town Musicians*. Doubleday.

1982. Chris Van Allsburg. *Jumanji*. Houghton Mifflin.

Honor Books: Maurice Sendak. *Outside, Over There*. Harper.
Arnold Lobel. *On Market Street*. Greenwillow.
Nancy Willard. *Visit to William Blake's Inn: Poems for Innocent and Experienced Travellers*. Harcourt.

1983. Marcia Brown. *Shadow* by Blaise Cendrars. Scribner.

Honor Books: Vera Williams. *Chair for My Mother*. Greenwillow.
Cynthia Rylands. *When I Was Young in the Mountains*.

1984. Alice and Martin Provensen. *The Glorious Flight* by Margaret Hodges. Viking.
Honor Books: Molly Bang. *1098*. Greenwillow.
Trina Schart Hyman. *Little Red Riding Hood*. Holiday House.

1985. Trina Schart Hyman. *Saint George and the Dragon*. Little.

Honor Books: Paul Zelinsky. *Have You Seen My Duckling?* by Nancy Tafuri. Greenwillow.
John Steptoe. *Story of Jumping Mouse*. Lothrop.

1986. Chris Van Allsburg. *The Polar Express*. Houghton Mifflin.

Honor Books: Stephen Gammell. *The Relatives Came* by Cynthia Rylant. Bradbury.
Don Wood. *King Bidgood's in the Bathtub* by Audrey Wood. Harcourt.

1987. Richard Egielski. *Hey, Al!* by Arthur Yorinks. Farrar, Straus.

Honor Books: Ann Grifalconi. *The Village of Round and Square Houses*. Little.
Suse MacDonald. *Alphabetics*. Bradbury.

Paul O. Zelinsky. *Rumpelstiltskin*. Dutton.

1988. John Schoenherr. *Owl Moon* by Jane Yoblen. Putnam.

READ BOOKS ALOUD TO STIMULATE THINKING

Reading books aloud to students introduces ideas and language patterns that facilitate the young students' oral or written response. Beginning writers find it easy to build on the pattern presented by a skilled author. First, read the story aloud, showing the illustrations that accompany the words. Afterwards, encourage the class to talk about the ideas presented and to suggest "variations on the theme" in the story. Students are excited, warmed up, and ready to collaborate on a class book that includes a contribution from each one—a book that everyone in the room will want to read!

Allard, Harry. *Bumps in the Night*. Doubleday, 1979. Children are well aware of mysterious noises of the night.

Allard, Harry. *I Will Not Go to the Market Today*. Dial, 1979. Imaginative excuses stimulates student ideas.

Allard, Harry. *It's So Nice to Have a Wolf Around the House*. Doubleday, 1977. Breaks down stereotyped ideas; students can compare other pictures of the wolf.

Allard, Harry. *Miss Nelson Is Missing*. Houghton Mifflin, 1977. Funny story for teachers; students write a new adventure.

Anglund, Joan W. *A Friend Is Someone Who Likes You*. Harcourt, 1958. Encourages students' ideas; suggests same format with other topics—love, winter, fun.

Barchas, Sara E. *I Was Walking Down the Road*.

Barker, Cicely M. *Flower Fairies*. Philomel. Enchanting book that young students enjoy.

Barrett, Judi. *Animals Should Definitely Not Wear Clothes*. Atheneum, 1970. Funny ideas that students can add to.

Brown, Margaret W. *The Important Book*. Harper. Wonderful pattern that students can replicate easily.

Brown, Margaret W. *Good Night Moon*. Harper, 1947. Sets up a pattern of good-nights.

Brown, Margaret W. *The Runaway Bunny*. Harper, 1972. (reissue)

Cameron, Polly. *I Can't, Said the Ant*. Coward, 1961. Nonsense rhymes to imitate.

Carle, Eric. *The Very Hungry Caterpillar*. Collins, 1970. Presents interesting information in story format.

Carle, Eric. *The Grouchy Ladybug*. Crowell, 1977.

Charlip, Remy. *What good Luck, What Bad Luck*. Scholastic. Fortunately–unfortunately pattern students can imitate.

Domanska, Janine. *If All the Seas Were One Sea*. Macmillan. Presents old rhyme students can rewrite with other ideas.

Einsel, Walter. *Did You Ever See?*

Einsel, Walter. *What Do You See?* Macmillan, 1974.

Grahm, John. *I Love You, Mouse*.

Hoberman, Mary Ann. *A House Is a House for Me*. Puffin.

Holl, Adelaide. *Have You Seen My Puppy?*

Hutchins, Pat. *Rosie's Walk*. Macmillan, 1968.

Hutchins, Pat. *The Wind Blew*. Bodley Head, 1974. A cumulative tale that shows the wind blowing an assortment of things up into the sky.

Jacobs, Leland. *Goodnight, Mr. Beetle*. Holt.

Kalan, Robert. *Rain*. Greenwillow, 1978. Exploration of a familiar topic; more ideas, then try new topics.

Kalan, Robert. *Blue Sea*. Greenwillow, 1979. Ideas about the ocean environment and inhabitants; suggests exploration of similar topic.

Keats, Ezra Jack. *Over in the Meadow*. Four Winds. An old song that children will enjoy adding ideas to.

Kent, Jack. *The Fat Cat*.

Kraus, Robert. *Leo the Late Bloomer*. Leo has a problem with which students can identify.

Kraus, Robert. *Whose Mouse Are You?* Macmillan, 1970.

Krauss, Ruth. *A Hole Is to Dig*. Harper, 1952. Share ideas orally; then add drawings and more definitions.

Krauss, Ruth. *Bears*.

Krauss, Ruth. *A Very Special House*. Harper, 1953.

Langstaff, John. *Oh, A Hunting We Will Go!*

Langstaff, John. *Over in the Meadow*. Harcourt, 1957. Songs that children can sing and add verses to.

Leman, Martin. *Comic and Curious Cats*. An alphabet book that students can use as a model.

Martin, Bill. *Brown Bear, Brown Bear, What Do You See?* Holt. Sets up pattern children can continue.

Martin, Bill. *Fire, Fire, Said Mrs. McGuire*. Holt. Old verse that children can chant and add verses to.

Martin Bill. *I Paint the Joy of a Flower*. Holt.

Martin, Bill. *My Days Are Made of Butterflies*. Holt. (adapted)

Martin, Bill. *When It Rains, It Rains*. Holt.

Martin, Bill. *The Wizard*. Holt.

Mayer, Mercer. *If I Had . . . .* Dial, 1968.

Mayer, Mercer. *What Do You Do with a Kangaroo?* Four Winds, 1974.

Mizumura, Kazue. *If I Were a Cricket*. Crowell, 1972. Stimulates imagination.

Mizumura, Kazue. *If I Were a Mother*. Crowell, 1968. Children write how they would behave as a mother.

Mosel, Arlene. *Tikki Tikki Tembo*. Holt, 1968. Pourquoi tale that students can imitate (explains why something is true); see other books by Mosel.

O'Neill, Mary. *Hailstones and Halibut Bones*. Doubleday, 1961. Poetry about color that children can imitate without rhyme. Also available on 2 short color films (Sterling).

Parish, Peggy. *Amelia Bedelia*. Harper, 1963. Wonderful humor based on language that children can imitate; other books about Amelia Bedelia will be enjoyed, too.

Piers, Helen. *The Mouse Book*. Watts, 1968.

Sendak, Maurice. *Chicken Soup with Rice*. Harper, 1962.

Sendak, Maurice. *Pierre*. Harper, 1962. Funny rhymed story that children can add to or imitate.

Sendak, Maurice. *Where the Wild Things Are*. Harper, 1963. Use with story theater; have students add new adventures for Max.

Shaw, Charles. *It Looked Like Spilt Milk*. Harper, 1947.

Showers, Paul. *The Listening Walk*. Crowell, 1961. Children take a walk and observe all the sounds they hear.

Spier, Peter. *Rain*. Doubleday, 1982. Talk about what happens when it rains; use with film "Rainshower."

Sullivan, Joan. *Round Is a Pancake*. Holt. Exploration of shapes can be continued orally and in writing.

Sutton, Eve. *My Cat Likes to Hide in Boxes*. Suggests pattern for cat activities and those of other pets.

Udry, Janice. *A Tree Is Nice*. Harper, 1956. Sets up pattern that children can extend, then use with other objects.

Viorst, Judith. *Alexander's Terrible, Horrible, No-good, Very Bad Day*. Atheneum, 1981. A natural listing that students of all ages enjoy imitating.

Viorst, Judith. *If I Were in Charge of the World and Other Worries*. Atheneum, 1981. Humorous poems suggest patterns for student poetry.

Waber, Bernard. *Dear Hildegarde*.

Waber, Bernard. *How to Go about Laying an Egg*. Houghton Mifflin. Funny model for a how-to book.

Waber, Bernard. *Lyle, Lyle, Crocodile*. Houghton Mifflin. Imaginative adventures that can be extended.

Waber, Bernard. *Nobody is perfick*. Houghton Mifflin, 1971. Humorous ideas about imperfection with which students identify.

Wright, H. R. *A Maker of Boxes*. Holt. Explores one topic; model for exploring other objects.

Zemach, Harve. *The Judge*. Farrar, 1969. Story to evaluate; older students can imitate form.

Zolotow, Charlotte. *Big Sister and Little Sister*. Harper, 1966. How it feels to have sisters and brothers.

Zolotow, Charlotte. *Do You Know What I'll Do?* Harper, 1958. A delightful pattern that all can join in.

Zolotow, Charlotte. *The Hating Book*. Harper, 1969.

Zolotow, Charlotte. *My Friend John*. Harper, 1968.

Zolotow, Charlotte. *One Step, Two. . . .* Harper, 1955. A counting book that can be imitated by young children.

Zolotow, Charlotte. *The Quarreling Book*. Harper, 1963.

Zolotow, Charlotte. *Someday*. Harper. Imaginative ideas about things to do.

Zolotow, Charlotte. *Some Things Go Together*. Harper. Language awareness that children can extend.

WORDLESS BOOKS

The wordless book has a special place in the language arts curriculum. Children can tell the story an illustrator-storyteller has presented, and it is amazing how the story content varies from child to child! Holding the book gives the storyteller confidence as he or she "reads" the words the author might have included. The pictures provide scaffolding for the speaker, and they also lead naturally to the writing of the story that has been told first orally. Wordless books provide a natural bridge between oral composition and composition in writing—a useful strategy for students of all ages.

Wordless books also promote thinking. Some author-illustrators present wonderful pictures that students of all ages can pore over as they discover concepts and ideas, as well as things to talk and think about.

Alexander, Martha. *Bobo's Dream*. Dial, 1970. When Bobo, a dachshund, loses his bone to a big dog, his owner retrieves the bone. Then Bobo dreams he returns his master's football when bigger boys take it.

Alexander, Martha. *Out! Out! Out!* Dial, 1968. A bird flies into the house through an open kitchen window. Neither mother, grocery man, nor custodian can chase it out. A little boy leads it back to the window with a trail of cereal.

Aruego, Jose. *Look What I Can Do*. Scribner, 1971. Two silly carabaos (water buffalo) play the "Anything you can do I can do better" game, getting themselves into some funny predicaments. Suggested from an old Philippine proverb.

Anno, Mitsumasa. *Anno's Flea Market*. Philomel, 1984. Wonderful paintings are rich with detail. Look for others by same illustrator: Anno's USA, etc.

Barton, Byron. *Elephant*. Seabury, 1971. A little girl sees a toy elephant, a poster elephant, an elephant in a book and on TV. She then has a wild dream about elephants. When she awakens, her parents take her to the zoo where she sees the most wonderful elephant of all—a real one.

Baum, Willi. *Birds of a Feather*. Addison-Wesley, 1969. An inventive bird decides to leave the flock and improve his plumage with the feathers from a passing lady's hat. He's trapped by a bird catcher, caged, then released when his ruse is discovered.

Bollinger-Savelli, Antonella. *The Knitted Cat*. Macmillan, 1971. A little girl knits a cat, leaving its tail unfinished. That night a mouse unravels the tail. The cat walks around outside, and an owl ties up the unraveling tail. The next morning the girl finishes the tail.

Carl, Eric. *Do You Want to Be My Friend?* Crowell, 1971. Little mouse is looking for a friend. On each page he finds a tail, and as the page is turned, the owner of the tail is revealed.

Carroll, Ruth. *The Christmas Kitten*. Walck, 1970. A little kitten, persistent in looking for a home, is finally allowed to stay with a family.

Carroll, Ruth. *What Whiskers Did*. Walck, 1932; 1965. The first of the wordless books, the story of a dog's adventures.

Goodall. *The Adventures of Paddy Pork*. Harcourt, 1968. Paddy, a pig, leaves home to join the circus. After some frightening and unsuccessful experiences, he returns home. See also, *The Ballooning Adventures of Paddy Pork*.

Goodhall. *Shrewbettina's Birthday*. Harcourt, 1971. Full-color drawings show the eventful day—Shrewbettina is robbed, does her shopping, cleans her house, and has a party. The ingenious use of half pages gives more visual detail in the Goodall books.

Goshorn. *Shoestrings*. Carolrhoda, 1975. A humorous portrayal of a child's trying to tie her shoestrings and the strange things that happen.

Hoban, Tana. *Is It Rough? Is It Smooth? Is It Shiny?* Greenwillow, 1984. Wonderful photography to stimulate thinking, talking, and writing. Numerous other titles by same author-illustrator.

Hoban, Tana. *Look Again*. Macmillan, 1971. No story is told, but this is one of the most fascinating of the textless picture books. A two-inch square peephole allows the viewer to see only a portion of a black and white photograph. After guessing, turning the page usually unveils a surprise close-up photograph. A third page puts the object in perspective or proportion. The book points to the beauty of simple things and our usual disregard for detail.

Hutchins, Pat. *Changes, Changes*. Macmillan, 1971. Children's play blocks are used to tell a fast-moving story. The figures build a house that catches fire. They build a fire engine that puts out the fire but causes a flood. So they move by boat, truck, and train to a new location and build another house.

Krahn, Fernando. *A Flying Saucer Full of Spaghetti*. Dutton, 1970. Small elf-like creatures entertain a rich little girl and fly her unwanted spaghetti across town to feed a hungry girl.

Mayer, Mercer. *A Boy, A Dog and A Frog*. Dial, 1967. Wonderful humorous stories of a little boy's rascality. See also *Frog, Where Are You? A Boy, A Dog, A Frog and a Friend, Frog on His Own,* and *Frog Goes to Dinner.*

Meyer, Renate. *Hide-and-Seek*. Bradbury, 1969. Two children play a game of hide and seek. Through the yard, into the barn, into the house, out to the garden the girl in pink chases the boy in blue. He is barely seen in the branches, behind the clothesline, under a chair, but he is finally caught.

Meyer, Renate. *Vicki*. Atheneum, 1969. Pictures not a sequence of events as much as a mood of friendlessness and loneliness.

Mordillo, Guillermo. *The Damp and Daffy Doings of a Daring Pirate Ship*. Quist, 1971. Daffy little characters build a sailing ship, launch it, and become pirates. Their ship sinks from the weight of their booty, so they bravely try again. Fascinating, light-hearted pictures.

Schick. *Making Friends*. Macmillan, 1969. Tells of a shopping trip with Mother and all the things a young child can notice along the way, many of which Mother did not see because she didn't look.

Wezel, Peter. *The Good Bird*. Harper, 1964. A bird sees an unhappy goldfish, catches a worm to share with the fish, and both are contented. Large, vivid pictures make it possible to use this book with large groups of children.

Sources

Bissett, Donald. "Literature in the Classroom," *Elementary English, 49* (November 1972): 1016–1019.

Tiedt, Iris M. *Exploring Books with Children*. Houghton Mifflin, 1979.

Reading in the Middle Grades

Once students have been introduced to the encoding-decoding processes, their chief need is to read quantity for enjoyment and information. The following books form a nucleus that offers something for every interest.

Avi. *The Fighting Ground*. Lippincott, 1984. Historical novel; war with the British seen by 13-year-old Jonathan.

Brown, Marc. *Arthur's April Fool*. Little, 1983. Getting the best of a bully.

Bulla, Clyde. *Charlie's House*. Crowell, 1983. A 12-year-old indentured servant.

Byars, Betsy. *The Computer Nut*. Viking Kestrel, 1984. Humorous story of Kate's mystery-romance via computer.

Cleary, Beverly. *Dear Mr. Henshaw*. Morrow, 1983. Letters to an author written by a sixth grade boy.

Cleary, Beverly. *Ramona Forever*. Morrow, 1984. Part of series about Henry and Ramona and her little sister, Beezus.

Conford, Ellen. *If This Is Love, I'll Take Spaghetti*. Four Winds, 1983. Short stories explore the problems of young girls.

Creswell, Helen. *The Secret World of Polly Flint*. Macmillan, 1984. Fantasy involving time travel.

Dahl, Roald. *James and the Giant Peach*. Knopf, 1961. High fantasy by noted adult author.

Duncan, Lois. *The Third Eye*. Little, 1984. Karen discovers she has unusual powers.

Gilson, Jamie. *4B Goes Wild*. Lothrop, 1983. Funny school story. See also: *Thirteen Ways to Sink a Sub* and *Harvey, the Beer Can King*.

Hurwitz, Johanna. *Aldo Ice Cream*. Morrow, 1981. Boy helps deliver Meals-on-Wheels.

Lindbergh, Anne. *Bailey's Window*. Harcourt, 1984. An unwelcome summer visitor discovers a magic window.

Lord, Bette Bao. *In the Year of the Boar and Jackie Robinson*. New York: Harper, 1984. Chinese-American Shirley Wong learns new ways.

Luen, Nancy. *The Ugly Princess*. Little, 1981. A princess learns new values.

Mark, Michael. *Toba*. Bradbury, 1984. Family story set in Poland in 1910.

Miles, Betty. *The Secret Life of the Underwear Champ*. Knopf, 1981. The fun of producing television commercials.

Peck, Robert. *Trig*. Little, 1984. An independent young girl chooses a new name.

Pfeffer, Beth. *What Do You Do When Your Mouth Won't Open?* Delacorte, 1981. Overcoming a phobia.

Roy, Ron. *Frankie Is Staying Back*. Clarion, 1981. Ups and downs of friendship.

Ruckman, Ivy. *Night of the Twisters*. Crowell, 1984. Children lose their home during a tornado in Nebraska.

Sachar, Louis. *Someday Angeline*. Avon, 1983. Fifth-grader keeps house for her dad, a garbage collector.

Salassi, Otto. *And Nobody Knew They Were There*. Greenwillow, 1984. Mystery of disappearing Marines solved by Jakey and Hogan.

San Souci, Robert. *Song of Sedna*. Doubleday, 1981. An Eskimo legend.

Shannon, George. *The Piney Woods Peddler*. Greenwillow, 1981. A father tries to bring his daughter a silver dollar.

Sharmat, Marjorie. *Chasing after Annie*. Harper, 1981. A dog disappears.

Snyder, Carol. *Memo: To Myself When I Have a Teenage Daughter*. Coward, 1983. Thirteen-year-old understands her mother better after reading the diary her mother kept at 13.

Springstubb, Tricia. *Which Way to the Nearest Wilderness?* Little, 1984. Realistic story of family problems.

Sutton, Jane. *Me and the Weirdos*. Houghton Mifflin, 1981. An eccentric, but lovable, family.

Terris, Susan. *Octopus Pie*. Farrar, 1984. Mystery of the missing octopus.

Van Allsburg, Chris. *Jumanji*. Houghton Mifflin, 1981. Provocative ideas; Caldecott winner.

Vogel, Ilse-Margaret. *Tikhon*. Harper, 1984. German Inge mourns the loss of her twin sister.

Yolen, Jane. *Children of the Wolf*. Viking, 1984. Based on fact, story of two wolf girls brought back to "civilization."

CHILDREN'S CLASSICS

Although student interests do vary, some books have almost universal appeal and are so good that we would hate to have any student miss knowing them. Such classics as *Charlotte's Web* are part of a child's literary heritage. Choose these titles for reading aloud, even to older students who may have missed them along the way. Students of different levels will see different things and can respond in varied ways.

Reading difficulty is indicated: P = Primary, I = Intermediate, and A = Advanced. Such a list can only be subjective and is far from exhaustive. Challenge your students to compile their own list of books they might share with younger children.

Aesop. *Fables*. Various editions. I-A

Alcott, Louisa May. *Little Women*. Various editions. 1868. Still a good family story about four sisters; strong image of young woman, Jo, and mother. I-A

Andersen, Hans Christian. *Andersen's Fairy Tales*. Several editions. I-A

The Arabian Nights. Folktales. Several editions. I-A

Barrie, James. *Peter Pan*. Several editions. I

Baum, Frank. *The Wizard of Oz*. Various editions. 1900. Story made famous by Judy Garland. I

Bemelmans, Ludwig. *Madeline*. Viking, 1939. Funny story in verse about audacious young girl. P

Burnett, Frances Hodgson. *The Secret Garden*. Several editions. A sour little girl and a crippled boy find love in a garden. I-A

Carroll, Lewis. *Alice's Adventures in Wonderland*. Several editions. I-A

Cervantes, Miguel de. *The Adventures of Don Quixote*. Trans. by J. Cohen. Methuen, 1980. I-A

Cleary, Beverly. *Henry Huggins*. Morrow, 1950. Adventures of young boy and his friends. I

Clemens, Samuel. (Mark Twain). *The Adventures of Huckleberry Finn*. Several editions. I-A

Clemens, Samuel. *The Adventures of Tom Sawyer*. Several editions. I-A

Craik, Dinah. *The Little Lame Prince*. Several editions. Fantasy of a prince imprisoned in a tower. I

Defoe. *Robinson Crusoe*. Several editions. A

Dickens, Charles. *A Christmas Carol*. Several editions. I-A

Dodge, Mary Mapes. *Hans Brinker* or *The Silver Skates*. Various editions. I-A

Forbes, Esther. *Johnny Tremain*. Houghton Mifflin, 1943. I-A

Geisel, Theodor (Dr. Seuss). *And to Think that I Saw It on Mulberry Street*. Vanguard, 1937. (First of many imaginative books) P-I

Grahame, Kenneth. *The Wind in the Willows*. Various editions. 1908. Story of Toad, Badger, Rat, and Mole who are friends. I-A

Grimm, Jakob and Wilhelm. *Grimm's Fairy Tales*. Several editions. I-A

Hale, Lucretia. *The Complete Peterkin Papers*. Houghton Mifflin, 1960. Funny story about a mixed-up family. I

Homer. *The Iliad* and *The Oddyssey*. Several editions. A

Irving, Washington. *Rip Van Winkle and The Legend of Sleepy Hollow*. Various editions. I-A

Kipling, Rudyard. *The Jungle Book*. Various editions. 1894. Story of boy raised by the wolves. I-A

Kipling, Rudyard. *Just So Stories*. Several editions. Pourquoi tales about animals. I

Lewis, C. S. *The Lion, the Witch, and the Wardrobe*. Four English children enter a fantasy world; part of the Narnia series. I

Lorenzini, Carlo (C. Collodi). *Pinocchio*. Various editions. 1892. Mischievous wooden puppet gives father a bad time. I

McCloskey, Robert. *Make Way for Ducklings*. Viking, 1941. Charming story of ducks in Boston. P

Milne, A. A. *Winnie-the-Pooh*. Various editions. 1926. Fantasy about Christopher Robin and his bear. P-I

Nesbitt, E. *Five Children and It*. Several editions. Children meet a Psammead, a sand fairy who makes dreams come true. I

Norton, Mary. *The Borrowers*. Harcourt, 1953. A fantasy of little people who "borrow" things. I

Perrault, Charles. *Perrault's Fairy Tales*. Various editions. I

Poe, Edgar Allan. *Tales*. Various editions. A

Potter, Beatrix. *The Tale of Peter Rabbit*. Various editions. 1901. One of series about small animals. P

Pyle, Howard. *Some Merry Adventures of Robin Hood*. Various editions. I-A

Pyle, Howard. *The Story of King Arthur and His Knights*. Various editions. I-A

Ruskin, John. *The King of the Golden River*. Various editions. I-A

Saint-Exupery, Antoine de. *The Little Prince*. Harcourt, 1943. (Trans. from French) I-A

Sewell, Anna. *Black Beauty*. Various editions. Story of a handsome stallion. I

Spyri, Johanna. *Heidi*. Various editions. 1884. Little girl brought up by her grandfather in Swiss Alps. I

Stevenson, Robert Louis. *Kidnapped* and *Treasure Island*. Various editions. A

Swift, Jonathan. *Gulliver's Travels*. Various editions. A

Tolkien, J. R. R. *The Hobbit*. Houghton Mifflin, 1938. Book that introduces trilogy, *Lord of the Rings*, popularized by films. I

Travers, Pamela. *Mary Poppins*. Harcourt, 1934. Humorous story of marvelous nanny. I

Verne, Jules. *Twenty Thousand Leagues under the Sea*. Various editions. A

White, E. B. *Charlotte's Web*. Harper, 1952. Wilbur the pig makes friends with Charlotte, a spider, who spins her web above his pen. I

Wilde, Oscar. *The Happy Prince and Other Stories*. Various editions. Modern fairytales. I

Wilder, Laura Ingalls. *Little House in the Big Woods*. Harper, 1953. First of Little House series; family story set in Wisconsin. I

Wyss, Johann. *The Swiss Family Robinson*. Various editions. A

Especially for Upper Elementary and Junior High

NEWBERY AWARD BOOKS

This medal is awarded annually in memory of John Newbery, a London bookseller of the eighteenth century and a first publisher of books for children. Selected by a committee of the American Library Association's Division of Libraries for Children and Young People, the award is given for excellence in writing literature for young people. The books, therefore, tend to be for middle school levels.

The year listed is the year of the award given for books published in the United States during the previous year.

1922. Hendrik Willem van Loon. *The Story of Mankind*. Liveright.

Honor Books: Charles Hawes. *The Great Quest*. Little.

Bernard Marshall. *Cedric the Forester*. Appleton.

William Bowen. *The Old Tobacco Shop*. Macmillan.

Cornelia Meigs. *Windy Hill*. Macmillan.

1923. Hugh Lofting. *The Voyages of Doctor Dolittle*. Lippincott.

1924. Charles Hawes. *The Dark Frigate*. Little.

1925. Charles Finger. *Tales from Silver Lands*. Doubleday.

Honor Books: Anne Carroll Moore. *Nicholas*. Putnam.

Anne Parrish. *Dream Coach*. New York: Macmillan.

1926. Arthur Bowie Chrisman. *Shen of the Sea*. Dutton.

Honor Book: Padraic Colum. *Voyages*. Macmillan.

1927. Will James. *Smoky, The Cowhorse*. Scribner.

1928. Dhan Gopal Mukerji. *Gayneck, The Story of a Pigeon*. Dutton.

Honor Books: Ella Young. *The Wonder Smith and His Son*. Longman.
Caroline Snedeker. *Downright Dencey*. Doubleday.

1929. Eric P. Kelly. *The Trumpeter of Krakow*. Macmillan.

Honor Books: John Bennett. *Pigtail of Ah Lee Ben Loo*. Longman.
Wanda Gag. *Millions of Cats*. Coward.
Grace Hallock. *The Boy Who Was*. Dutton.
Cornelia Meigs. *Clearing Weather*. Little.
Grace Moon. *Runaway Papoose*. Doubleday.
Elinor Whitney. *Tod of the Fens*. Macmillan.

1930. Rachel Field. *Hitty, Her First Hundred Years*. Macmillan.

Honor Books: Jeanette Eaton. *Daughter of the Seine*. Harper.
Elizabeth Miller. *Pran of Albania*. Doubleday.
Marian Hurd McNeely. *Jumping-Off Place*. Longman.
Ella Young. *Tangle-Coated Horse and Other Tales*. Longman.
Julia Davis Adams. *Vaino*. Dutton.

1931. Elizabeth Coatsworth. *The Cat Who Went to Heaven*. Macmillan.

Honor Books: Anne Parrish. *Floating Island*. Harper.
Alida Malkus. *The Dark Star of Itza*. Harcourt.
Ralph Hubbard. *Queer Person*. Doubleday.
Julia Davis Adams. *Mountains Are Free*. Dutton.
Agnes Hewes. *Spice and the Devil's Cave*. Knopf.
Elizabeth Janet Gray. *Meggy MacIntosh*. Doubleday.
Herbert Best. *Garram the Hunter*. Doubleday.
Alice Lide and Margaret Johansen. *Odd-Le-Uk the Wanderer*. Little.

1932. Laura Adams Armer. *Waterless Mountain*. Longman.

Honor Books: Dorothy P. Lathrop. *The Fairy Circus*. Macmillan.
Rachel Field. *Calico Bush*. Macmillan.
Eunice Tietjens. *Boy of the South Seas*. Coward.
Eloise Lownsbery. *Out of the Flame*. Longman.
Marjorie Alee. *Jane's Island*. Mifflin.
Mary Gould Davis. *Truce of the Wolf and Other Tales of Old Italy*. Harcourt.

1933. Elizabeth Lewis. *Young Fu of the Upper Yangtze*. Winston.

Honor Books: Cornelia Meigs. *Swift Rivers*. Little.
Hildegarde Swift. *The Railroad to Freedom*. Harcourt.
Nora Burglon. *Children of the Soil*. Doubleday.

1934. Cornelia Meigs. *Invincible Louisa*. Little.

Honor Books: Caroline Snedeker. *The Forgotten Daughter*. Doubleday.
Elsie Singmaster. *Swords of Steel*. Houghton.

Wanda Gag. *ABC Bunny*. Coward.
Erick Berry. *Winged Girl of Knossos*. Appleton.
Sarah Schmidt. *New Land*. McBridge.
Padraic Colum. *Big Tree of Bunlahy*. Macmillan.
Agnes Hewes. *Glory of the Seas*. Knopf.
Anne Kyle. *Apprentice of Florence*. Houghton.

1935. Monica Shannon. *Dobry*. Viking.

Honor Books: Elizabeth Seeger. *Pageant of Chinese History*. Longman.
Constance Rourke. *Davy Crockett*. Harcourt.
Hilda Van Stockum. *Day on Skates*. Harper.
1936. Carol Bring. *Caddie Woodlawn*. Macmillan.
Honor Books: Phil Stong. *Honk, The Moose*. Dodd.
Kate Seredy. *The Good Master*. Viking.
Elizabeth Janet Gray. *Young Walter Scott*. Viking.
Armstrong Sperry. *All Sail Set*. Winston.

1937. Ruth Sawyer. *Roller Skates*. Viking.

Honor Books: Lois Lenski. *Phebe Fairchild: Her Book*. Stokes.
Idwal Jones. *Whistler's Van*. Viking.
Ludwig Bemelmans. *Golden Basket*. Viking.
Margery Bianco. *Winterbound*. Viking.
Constance Rourke. *Audubon*. Harcourt.
Agnes Hewes. *The Codfish Musket*. Doubleday.

1938. Kate Seredy. *The White Stag*. Viking.

Honor Books: James Cloyd Bowman. *Pecos Bill*. Little.
Mabel Robinson. *Bright Island*. Random.
Laura Ingalls. *On the Banks of Plum Creek*. Harper.

1939. Elizabeth Enright. *Thimble Summer*. Rinehart.

Honor Books: Valenti Angelo. *Nino*. Viking.
Richard and Florence Atwater. *Mr. Popper's Penguins*. Little.
Phyllis Crawford. *Hello the Boat!* Holt.
Jeanette Eaton. *Leader by Destiny: George Washington, Man and Patriot*. Harcourt.

1940. James Daugherty. *Daniel Boone*. Viking.

Honor Books: Kate Seredy. *The Singing Tree*. Viking.
Mabel Robinson. *Runner of the Mountain Tops*. Random.
Laura Ingalls Wilder. *By the Shores of Silver Lake*. Harper.
Stephen Meader. *Boy with a Pack*. Harcourt.

1941. Armstrong Sperry. *Call It Courage*. Macmillan.

Honor Books: Doris Gates. *Blue Willow*. Viking.
Mary Jane Carr. *Young Mac of Fort Vancouver*. Crowell.
Laura Ingalls Wilder. *The Long Winter*. Harper.
Anna Gertrude Hall. *Nansen*. Viking.

1942. Walter D. Edmonds. *The Matchlock Gun*. Dodd.

Honor Books: Laura Ingalls Wilder. *Little Town on the Prairie*. Harper.
Genevieve Foster. *George Washington's World*. Scribner.
Lois Lenski. *Indian Captive: The Story of Mary Jemison*. Lippincott.
Eva Roe Gaggin. *Down Ryton Water*. Viking.

1943. Elizabeth Janet Gray. *Adam of the Road*. Viking.

Honor Books: Eleanor Estes. *The Middle Moffat*. Harcourt.
Mabel Leigh. *Have You Seen Tom Thumb?* Lippincott.

1944. Esther Forbes. *Johnny Tremain*. Houghton.

Honor Books: Laura Ingalls Wilder. *These Happy Golden Years*. Harper.
Julia Sauer. *Fog Magic*. Viking.
Eleanor Estes. *Rufus M*. Harcourt.
Elizabeth Yates. *Mountain Born*. Coward.

1945. Robert Lawson. *Rabbit Hill*. Viking.

Honor Books: Eleanor Estes. *The Hundred Dresses*. Harcourt.
Alice Dalgliesh. *The Silver Pencil*. Scribner.
Genevieve Foster. *Abraham Lincoln's World*. Scribner.
Jeanette Eaton. *Lone Journey: The Life of Roger Williams*. Harcourt.

1946. Lois Lenski. *Strawberry Girl*. Lippincott.

Honor Books: Marguerite Henry. *Justin Morgan Had a Horse*. Rand.
Florence Crannell Means. *The Moved-Outers*. Houghton.
Christine Weston. *Bhimsa, The Dancing Bear*. Scribner.
Katherine Shippen. *New Found World*. Viking.

1947. Carolyn Sherwin Bailey. *Miss Hickory*. Viking.

Honor Books: Nancy Barnes. *Wonderful Year*. Messner.
Mary and Conrad Buff. *Big Tree*. Viking.
William Maxwell. *The Heavenly Tenants*. Harper.
Cyrus Fisher. *The Avion My Uncle Flew*. Appleton.
Eleanore Jewett. *The Hidden Treasure of Glaston*. Viking.

1948. Wiliam Pene du Bois. *The Twenty-One Balloons*. Viking.

Honor Books: Claire Huchet Bishop. *Pancakes-Paris*. Viking.
Carolyn Treffinger. *Li Lun, Lad of Courage*. Abingdon.
Catherine Besterman. *The Quaint and Curious Quest of Johnny Longfoot*. Bobbs.
Harold Courlander. *The Cow-Tail Switch, and Other West African Stories*. Holt.
Marguerite Henry. *Misty of Chincoteague*. Rand.

1949. Marguerite Henry. *King of the Wind*. Rand.

Honor Books: Holling C. Holling. *Seabird*. Houghton.
Lousie Rankin. *Daughter of the Mountains*. Viking.
Ruth S. Gannett. *My Father's Dragon*. Random.
Arna Bontemps. *Story of the Negro*. Knopf.

1950. Marguerite de Angeli. *The Door in the Wall*. Doubleday.

Honor Books: Rebecca Caudill. *Tree of Freedom*. Viking.
Catherine Coblentz. *The Blue Cat of Castle Town*. Longman.
Rutherford Montgomery. *Kildee House*. Doubleday.
Genevieve Foster. *George Washington*. Scribner.
Walter and Marion Havighurst. *Song of the Pines*. Winston.

1951. Elizabeth Yates. *Amos Fortune, Free Man*. Aladdin.

Honor Books: Mabel Leigh Hunt. *Better Known as Johnny Appleseed*. Lippincott.
Jeanette Eaton. *Gandhi, Fighter without a Sword*. Morrow.
Clara Ingram Judson. *Abraham Lincoln, Friend of the People*. Follett.

Anne Parrish. *The Story of Appleby Capple*. Harper.

1952. Eleanor Estes. *Ginger Pye*. Harcourt.

Honor Books: Elizabeth Baity. *Americans before Columbus*. Viking.
Holling C. Holling. *Minn of the Mississippi*. Houghton.
Nicholas Kalashnikoff. *The Defender*. Scribner.
Julia Sauer. *The Light at Tern Rocks*. Viking.

1953. Ann Nolan Clark. *Secret of the Andes*. Viking.

Honor Books: E. B. White. *Charlotte's Web*. Harper.
Eloise McGraw. *Moccasin Trail*. Coward.
Ann Weil. *Red Sails to Capri*. Viking.
Alice Dalgliesh. *The Bears on Hemlock Mountain*. Scribner.
Genevieve Foster. *Birthdays of Freedom*. Scribner.

1954. Joseph Krumgold. *. . . And Now Miguel*. Crowell.

Honor Books: Claire H. Bishop. *All Alone*. Viking.
Meindert DeJong. *Shadrach*. Harper.
Meindert DeJong. *Hurry Home, Candy*. Harper.
Clara I. Judson. *Theodore Roosevelt, Fighting Patriot*. Follett.
Mary and Conrad Buff. *Magic Maize*. Houghton.

1955. Meindert DeJong. *The Wheel on the School*. Harper.

Honor Books: Alice Dalgliesh. *Courage of Sarah Noble*. Scribner.
James Ullman. *Banner in the Sky*. Lippincott.

1956. Jean Lee Latham. *Carry On, Mr. Bowditch*. Houghton.

Honor Books: Marjorie K. Rawlings. *The Secret River*. Scribner.
Jennie Lindquist. *The Golden Name Day*. Harper.
Katherine Shippen. *Men, Microscopes, and Living Things*. Viking.

1957. Virginia Sorensen. *Miracles on Maple Hill*. Harcourt.

Honor Books: Fred Gipson. *Old Yeller*. Harper.
Meindert DeJong. *The House of Sixty Fathers*. Harper.
Clara I. Judson. *Justice Holmes*. Follett.
Dorothy Rhoads. *The Corn Grows Ripe*. Viking.
Marguerite de Angeli. *Black Fox of Lorne*. Doubleday.

1958. Harold Keith. *Rifles for Watie*. Crowell.

Honor Books: Mari Sandoz. *The Horsecatcher*. Westminster.
Elizabeth Enright. *Gone-Away Lake*. Harcourt.
Robert Lawson. *The Great Wheel*. Viking.
Leo Gurko. *Tom Paine, Freedom's Apostle*. Crowell.

1959. Elizabeth G. Speare. *The Witch of Blackbird Pond*. Houghton.

Honor Books: Natalie Carlson. *The Family under the Bridge*. Harper.
Meindert DeJong. *Along Came a Dog*. Harper.
Francis Kalney. *Chucaro: Wild Pony of the Pampa*. Harcourt.
William Steele. *The Perilous Road*. Harcourt.

1960. Joseph Krumgold. *Onion John*. Crowell.

Honor Books: Jean C. George. *My Side of the Mountain*. Dutton.
Gerald Johnson. *America Is Born*. Morrow.
Carol Kendall. *The Gammage Cup*. Harcourt.

1961. Scott O'Dell. *Island of the Blue Dolphins*. Houghton.

Honor Books: Gerald Johnson. *America Moves Forward*. Morrow.
Jack Schaefer. *Old Ramon*. Houghton.
George Selden. *The Cricket in Times Square*. Farrar.

1962. Elizabeth G. Speare. *The Bronze Bow*. Houghton.

Honor Books: Edwin Tunis. *Frontier Living*. World.
Eloise McGraw. *The Golden Goblet*. Coward.
Mary Stolz. *Belling the Tiger*. Harper.

1963. Madeleine L'Engle. *A Wrinkle in Time*. Farrar.

Honor Books: Sorche Nic Leodhas. *Thistle and Thyme*. Holt.
Olivia Coolidge. *Men of Athens*. Houghton.

1964. Emily C. Neville. *It's Like This, Cat*. Harper.

Honor Books: Sterling North. *Rascal*. Dutton.
Ester Wier. *The Loner*. McKay.

1965. Maia Wojciechowska. *Shadow of a Bull*. Atheneum.

Honor Book: Irene Hunt. *Across Five Aprils*. Follett.

1966. Elizabeth B. de Trevino. *I, Juan de Pareja*. Farrar.

Honor Books: Lloyd Alexander. *The Black Cauldron*. Holt.
Randall Jarrell. *The Animal Family*. Pantheon.
Mary Stolz. *The Noonday Friends*. Harper.

1967. Irene Hunt. *Up a Road Slowly*. Follett.

Honor Books: Scott O'Dell. *The King's Fifth*. Houghton.
Isaac B. Singer. *Zlateh, the Goat, and Other Stories*. Harper.
Mary K. Weik. *The Jazz Man*. Atheneum.

1968. Elaine Konigsburg. *From the Mixed-Up Files of Mrs. Basil E. Frankweiler*. Atheneum.

Honor Books: Elaine Konigsburg. *Jennifer, Hecate, MacBeth, William McKinley, and Me, Elizabeth*. Atheneum.
Scott O'Dell. *The Black Pearl*. Houghton.
Isaac B. Singer. *The Fearsome Inn*. Scribner.
Zilpha K. Snyder. *The Egypt Game*. Atheneum.

1969. Lloyd Alexander. *The High King*. Holt.

Honor Books: Julius Lester. *To Be a Slave*. Dial.
Isaac B. Singer. *When Shlemiel Went to Warsaw & Other Stories*. Farrar.

1970. William Armstrong. *Sounder*. Harper.

Honor Books: Sulamith Ish-Kishor. *Our Eddie*. Pantheon.
Janet G. Moore. *The Many Ways of Seeing: An Introduction to the Pleasures of Art*. World.
Mary Steele. *Journey Outside*. Viking.

1971. Betsy Byars. *Summer of the Swans*. Viking.

Honor Books: Natalie Babbitt. *Knee-Knock Rise*. Farrar.
Sylvia L. Engdahl. *Enchantress from the Stars*. Atheneum.
Scott O'Dell. *Sing Down the Moon*. Houghton.

1972. Robert O'Brien. *Mrs. Frisby and the Rats of NIMH*. Atheneum.

Honor Books: Miska Miles. *Annie and the Old One*. Little.
Zilpha K. Snyder. *The Headless Cupid*. Atheneum.
Allan W. Eckert. *Incident at Hawk's Hill*. Little.
Virginia Hamilton. *The Planet of Junior Brown*. Macmillan.
Ursula K. LeGuin. *The Tombs of Atuan*. Atheneum.

1973. Jean C. George. *Julie of the Wolves*. Harper.

Honor Books: Arnold Lobel. *Frog and Toad Together*. Harper.
Johanna Reiss. *The Upstairs Room*. T. Y. Crowell.
Zilpha K. Snyder. *The Witches of Worm*. Atheneum.

1974. Paula Fox. *The Slave Dancer*. Bradbury.

Honor Book: Susan Cooper. *The Dark Is Rising*. Atheneum.

1975. Virginia Hamilton. *M. C. Higgins the Great*. Macmillan.

Honor Books: Ellen Raskin. *Figgs & Phantoms*. Dutton.
James and Christopher Collier. *My Brother Sam Is Dead*. Four Winds.
Elizabeth Pope. *The Perilous Gard*. Houghton.
Bette Green. *Phillip Hall Likes Me, I Reckon Maybe*. Dial.

1976. Susan Cooper. *The Grey King*. Atheneum.

Honor Books: Sharon Bell Mathis. *The Hundred Penny Box*. Viking.
Laurence Yep. *Dragonwings*. Harper.

1977. Mildren Taylor. *Roll of Thunder, Hear My Cry*. Dial.

Honor Books: William Steig. *Abel's Island*. Farrar.
Nancy Bond. *A String in the Harp*. Atheneum.

1978. Katherine Paterson. *Bridge to Terabithia*. Harper.

Honor Books: Beverly Cleary. *Ramona and Her Father*. Morrow.
Jamake Highwater. *Anpao: An American Indian Odyssey*. Lippincott.

1979. Ellen Raskin. *Westing Game*. Dutton.

Honor Book: Katherine Paterson. *Great Gilly Hopkins*. Harper.

1980. Joan Blos. *A Gathering of Days: A New England Girl's Journal*. Scribner.

Honor Book: David Kherdian. *Road from Home: The Story of an Armenian Childhood*. Greenwillow.

1981. Katherine Paterson. *Jacob Have I Loved*. Harper.

Honor Books: Jane Langton. *Fledgling*. Harper.
Madeleine L'Engle. *Ring of Endless Light*. Farrar.

1982. Nancy Willard. *A Visit to William Blake's Inn: Poems for Innocent and Experienced Travellers*. Harcourt.

Honor Books: Aranka Siegal. *Upon the Head of a Goat: A Childhood in Hungary 1939-1944*. Farrar.
Beverly Cleary. *Ramona Quimby, Age Eight*. Morrow.

1983. Cynthia Voight. *Dicey's Song*. Atheneum.

Honor Books: Paul Fleishman. *Graven Images*. Harper.
Jean Fritz. *Homesick: My Own Story*. Putnam.
Robin McKinley. *Blue Sword*. Greenwillow.

William Steig. *Doctor DeSoto*. Farrar.

Virginia Hamilton. *Sweet Whispers, Brother Rush*. Philomel.

1984. Beverly Cleary. *Dear Mr. Henshaw*. Morrow.

Honor Books: Elizabeth G. Speare. *Sign of the Beaver*. Harcourt.

Cynthia Voight. *Solitary Blue*. Atheneum.

Kathryn Lasky. *Sugaring Time*. Macmillan.

Bill Brittain. *The Wishgiver*. Harper.

1985. Robin McKinley. *The Hero and the Crown*. Greenwillow.

Honor Books: Mavis Jukes. *Like Jake and Me*. Knopf.

Bruce Brooks. *The Moves Make the Man*. Harper.

Paula Fox. *One-eyed Cat*. Bradbury.

1986. Patricia McLachlan. *Sarah, Plain and Tall*. Harper.

Honor Books: Rhoda Blumberg. *Commodore Perry in the Land of the Shogun*. Lothrop.

Gary Paulsen. *Dogsong*. Bradbury.

1987. Sid Fleischman. *The Whipping Boy*. Greenwillow.

Honor Books: Marion Dane Bauer. *On My Honor*. Clarion.

Patricia Lauber. *The Eruption and Healing of Mount St. Helens*. Bradbury.

Cynthia Rylant. *A Fine White Dust*. Bradbury.

1988. Russell Freedman. *Lincoln: A Photo-biography*. Tichnor-Fields.

LITERATURE WITH HIGH APPEAL FOR YOUNG ADULT READERS

Motivate adolescent readers by encouraging free reading and talking about books in your classroom. You read, too.

Ask students to add to this list of favorite authors and the books they have written. Reading level is fifth grade and up.

Adler, C. S.
   Get Lost, Little Brother. Clarion Brothers.

Aiken, Joan
   Bridle the Wind. Delacorte.
      Friendship; adventure; France; Spain
   A Whisper in the Night. Delacorte.
      Stories; suspense

Alcock, Vivien
   The Stonewalker. Delacorte.
      Fantasy; Great Britain
   The Sylvia Game. Delacorte.
      International conspiracy; supernatural

Alexander, Lloyd
   The Beggar Queen, Westmark, The Festrel—Triology. Dutton.
      Fantasy of Queen Augusta; futility of war

Allan, Mabel
   A Dream of Hunger Moss. Dodd.
      Great Britain; mystery

Almedingen, E. M.
  The Crimson Oak. Coward.
    Soviet Union; historical novel, Empress of Russia
Arrick, Fran
  Nice Girl from Good Home. Bradbury.
    Father-daughter relationship; family
Asimov, Isaac et al., eds.
  Sherlock Holmes through Time and Space. Bluejay Books.
    Mystery stories.
  Young Extraterrestrials. Bluejay Books.
    Stories; alien children
Avi
  Shadrach's Crossing. Pantheon.
    Smuggling; Depression period
  S.O.R. Losers. Bradbury.
    Soccer; friendship
Bauer, Marion
  Rain of Fire. Clarion.
    World War II; veterans; brothers
Bawden, Nina
  Squib. Lothrop.
    Child abuse
Beatty, Patricia
  Jonathan Down Under. Morrow.
    Australia; gold mines
  Melinda Takes a Hand. Morrow.
    Colorado; sisters
  Turn Homeward, Hannalee. Morrow.
    Civil War setting; prisoners of North
Bellairs, John
  The Curse of the Blue Figurine. Dial.
    Ghosts; mystery
Bethancourt, T. Ernesto
  Doris Fein: Legacy of Terror. Holiday.
    Mystery; Chicago in 20s
Blume, Judy
  Are You There, God? It's Me, Margaret. Bradbury.
    Growing up; religion
Brooks, Jerome
  Uncle Mike's Boy. Harper.
    Divorce; man-boy relationship
Bunting, Eve
  Someone Is Hiding on Alcatraz Island. Houghton.
    Bullies; self-reliance
Byars, Betsy
  Summer of the Swans. Viking.
    Mentally retarded boy; brother-sister relationship

The Glory Girl. Viking.
  Family life; singers

Carlson, Natalie
Ann, Aurelia and Dorothy. Harper.
  Black-white friends; foster home

Cassedy, Sylvia
Behind the Attic Wall. Crowell.
  Ghosts; orphans; uncles

Cleaver, Vera and Bill
Hazel Rye. Lippincott.
  Citrus farm; strong female character
Where the Lilies Bloom. Lippincott.
  Family ties; Appalachia

Clymer, Eleanor
Luke Was There. Holt.
  Running away; foster home
The Horse in the Attic. Bradbury.
  Horses; mystery

Cohen, Barbara
Thank You, Jackie Robinson. Lothrop.
  Adult-child relationship; lack of father

Conford, Ellen
The Luck of Pokey Bloom. Little.
  Growing up; parent-child relationship
Lenny Kandell, Smart Aleck. Little.
  Comedians

Cooper, Susan
Seaward. Atheneum.
  Fantasy

Corbett, W. J.
The Song of Pentecost. Dutton.
  Mice; allegory

Corcoran, Barbara
A Dance to Still Music. Atheneum.
  Deafness
The Woman in Your Life. Atheneum.
  Mexico; prison; drugs; self-confidence

Danziger, Paula
The Divorce Express. Delacorte.
  Parent-child relations; divorce; personal growth
There's a Bat in Bunk Five. Delacorte.
  Camp; sequel to *The Cat Ate My Gymsuit*; humor

Delton, Judy
Near Occasion of Sin. Harcourt.
  Catholicism; marriage; baby

Derman, Martha
And Philippa Makes Four. Four Winds.
    Stepparents; family life

Dygard, Thomas
Rebound Caper. Morrow.
    Basketball; school

Ellis, Ella
Hugo and the Princess Nena. Atheneum.
    Grandfathers; aging; California

Farley, Carol
The Garden Is Doing Fine. Atheneum.
    Death

Fenton, Edward
Duffy's Rocks. Dutton.
    Depression in American history

Fitzhugh, Louise
Harriet, the Spy. Harper.
    Parent-child relationships

Fleischman, Paul
Path of the Pale Horse. Harper.
    Physicians; yellow fever; Philadelphia

Fox, Paula
How Many Miles to Babylon? White.
    Gangs
The Slave Dancer. Harper.
    Historical fiction; slavery

George, Jean Craighead
Julie of the Wolves. Harper.
    Strong female character; Newbery award
The Talking Earth. Harper.
    Seminole Indians; Everglades; wilderness survival

Gordon, John
The Edge of the World. Atheneum.
    Fantasy; rural England

Greene, Bette
Philip Hall Likes Me, I Reckon, Maybe. Dial.
    Girl growing up

Greene, Constance
A Girl Called Al.
    Death; weight
Ask Anybody. Viking.
    Friendship; divorce

Greenwald, Sheila
Will the Real Gertrude Hollings Please Stand Up? Little.
    Dyslexia; cousins

Greer, Gery
Max and Me and the Time Machine. Harcourt.
Middle Ages; space and time; knighthood

Hahn, Mary
Daphne's Book. Clarion.
Friendship; writing; school

Hamilton, Virginia
The Magical Adventures of Pretty Pearl. Harper.
Blacks; fantasy
Willie Bea and the Time the Martians Landed. Greenwillow.
Blacks; Halloween; family life
The Planet of Junior Brown. Macmillan.
Loner; friendship

Haugaard, Erik.
The Samurai's Tale. Houghton.
Growing up in 16th Century Japan

Hentoff, Nat
This School Is Driving Me Crazy. Delacorte.
Father-son relationship

Hinton, Susan
The Outsiders. Delacorte.
Gang; brothers' relationship
Rumble Fish. Delacorte.
Brothers

Hermes, Patricia
Who Will Take Care of Me? Harcourt.
Mentally handicapped; orphans; brothers
You Shouldn't Have to Say Good-bye. Harcourt.
Mothers; death; parent-child

Holland, Isabelle
The Empty House. Lippincott.
Fathers; mystery

Holman, Felice
Slake's Limbo. Scribner.
Urban life

Hopper, Nancy
Hang On, Harvey! Dutton.
Musicians; school

Hughey, Roberta
The Question Box. Delacorte.
Conflict between parental authority and self-control

Hurmence, Belinda
Tancy. Houghton.
16-year-old slave in North Carolina

Ish-Kishor, Sulamith
Our Eddie. Scribner.
Family relationships

Jones, Diana
  Fire and Hemlock. Greenwillow.
    Fantasy; college

Klein, Norma
  Mom, the Wolfman and Me. Pantheon.
    Unmarried mother; stepfather

Konigsburg, Elaine
  About the B'Nai Bagels. Atheneum.
    Prejudice; growing up

Lampman, Evelyn
  The Year of Small Shadow. Harcourt.
    Prejudice

L'Engle, Madeleine
  A House Like a Lotus. Farrar.
    Sequel to *Arm of the Starfish, Dragons in the Waters*.
    Older-younger generations; Athens.
  Meet the Austins. Farrar.
  The Moon by Night. Farrar.
  The Young Unicorns. Farrar.
  A Ring of Endless Light. Farrar.
    Books about the Austin family; fantasy
  A Wrinkle in Time. Farrar.
  A Wind in the Door. Farrar.
  A Swiftly Tilting Planet. Farrar.
    The time trilogy; science fiction

Little, Jean
  Look through My Window. Harper.
    Family relationships

Lowry, Lois
  The One Hundredth Thing about Caroline. Houghton.
    Single parent; brothers and sisters
  Taking Care of Terrific. Houghton.
    Babysitters; Boston

Lunn, Janet
  The Root Cellar. Scribner.
    Orphans; farm life; history; space and time

McNamara, John
  Revenge of the Nerd. Delacorte.
    Crush; humorous results

Miles, Betty
  The Real Me. Knopf.
    Strong female character; family relationships

Murray, Michele
  Nellie Cameron. Seabury.
    Rejection; reading problem.

Myers, Walter
  Motown and Didi: A Love Story. Viking.
    Harlem; drugs; hero
  The Outside Shot. Delacorte.
    Sequel to *Hoops;* basketball; education; ethics

Naylor, Phyllis
  The Solomon System. Atheneum.
    Brothers; divorce

Newman, Robert
  The Case of the Etruscan Treasure.
    New York City; mystery

Newton, Suzanne
  An End to Perfect. Viking.
    Family problems; friendship
  I Will Call It Georgie's Blues. Viking.
    Growing up; characterization

Nixon, Joan
  The Ghosts of Now. Delacorte.
    Suspense; courage

O'Connor, Jane
  Just Good Friends. Harper.
    Growing up; parents

Okimoto, Jean
  Norman Schnurman, Average Person. Putnam.
    Fathers; football

Park, Barbara
  Beanpole. Knopf.
    Growing up

Paterson, Katherine
  Bridge to Terabithia. Crowell.
    Death
  The Great Gilly Hopkins. Crowell.
    Foster home
  Jacob Have I Loved. Crowell.
    Newbery award; competition between twins

Paulsen, Gary
  Dancing Carl. Bradbury.
    Iceskating

Peck, Richard
  The Dreadful Future of Blossom Culp. Delacorte.
    Space and time

Phipson, Joan
  The Watcher in the Garden.
    ESP

Rardin, Susan
  Captives in a Foreign Land. Houghton.
    Rome; courage; peace

Sachs, Marilyn
The Bear's House. Doubleday.
Divorce; mother image
Fourteen. Dutton.
Friendship; mothers

Sharmat, Marjorie
He Noticed I'm Alive . . . and Other Hopeful Signs. Delacorte.
Complicated family relationships
How to Meet a Gorgeous Girl. Delacorte.
Mark reads a helpful book

Shyer, Marlene
Adorable Sunday. Scribner.
Modeling; television commercials

Skurzynski, Gloria
Trapped in Slickrock Canyon. Lothrop.
Flash flood survival

Smith, Doris
A Taste of Blackberries. Crowell.
Death
The First Hard Times. Viking.
Stepfather

Sorensen, Virginia
Around the Corner. Harcourt.
Prejudice

Southall, Ivan
Let the Balloon Go. St. Martin.
Cerebral palsy

Speare, Elizabeth
The Sign of the Beaver. Houghton.
American Indians; history; friendship

Spinelli, Jerry
Space Station Seventh Grade. Dell.
Problems of being twelve

Stolz, Mary
The Noonday Friends. Harper.
Race; family relationships
Cat Walk. Harper.
Cat's adventures

Strasser, Todd
The Complete Computer Popularity Program. Delacorte.
Nuclear power plant; friendship; humor

Sweeney, Joyce
Center Line. Delacorte.
Five teenage brothers break free

Ter Haar, Jaar
Boris. Delacorte.
World War II

Uchida, Yoshiko
  The Best Bad Thing. Atheneum.
    Prejudice; Japanese-Americans; California history
Voigt, Cynthia
  The Callender Papers. Atheneum.
    Orphans; mystery; Massachusetts history
Weik, Mary
  The Jazz Man. Atheneum.
    Child abuse
White, Ellen
  The President's Daughter. Avon.
    Mother is President; understanding between mother and daughter
Wolitzer, Hilma
  Wish You Were Here. Farrar.
    Stepparent; boy-girl relationship
Wrightson, Patricia
  A Race Course for Andy.
    Mental retardation
  A Little Fear. Atheneum.
    Australia; fantasy
Yolen, Jane
  Dragon's Blood. Delacorte.
    Fantasy; galaxy
  Children of the Wolf. Viking.
    Feral children; based on fact

Language Books for K–8 Students

Turn students on to language study by introducing them to books about words and how the English language works. This annotated list includes an indication of the level of difficulty: Primary, Intermediate, or Advanced.

Adams, J. Donald. *The Magic and Mystery of Words*. Holt, 1963. Interesting essays for advanced students; good teacher resource. A

Adler, David A. *The Carsick Zebra and Other Animal Riddles*. Holiday, 1983. Fun with words. P

Adler, David A. *Finger Spelling Fun*. Watts, 1980. Good practice for spelling; aids understanding of deaf persons. P-I

Adler, Irving, and Adler, Joyce. *Language and Man*. Day, 1970. Importance of speech and communication. I

Alexander, Arthur. *The Magic of Words*. Prentice-Hall, 1962. Language development. I

Allard, Harry, and Marshall, James. *The Stupids Have a Ball*. Houghton, 1979. Fun with language. P

Applegate Mauree. *The First Book of Language*. Watts, 1962. Use of parts of speech in writing. I

Ashley, Leonard. *The Wonderful World of Superstition, Prophecy, and Luck*. Dembner, 1984. Discussion of superstition and predicting the future.

Asimov, Isaac. *Words from the Bible*. Houghton Mifflin. Also: *Words of Mathematics, Words of Science, Words on the Map, Words from the Myths*. Excellent books on the origins and meanings of words. I-A

Basil, Cynthia. *Nailheads and Potato Eyes*. Morrow, 1976. Body parts in language. P

Basil, Cynthia. *Breakfast in the Afternoon*. Morrow, 1979. Compound words. P

Batchelor, Julie. *Communication: From Cave to Television*. Harcourt, 1953. Explains the ways of communicating. I

Bayer, Jane. *A, My Name Is Alice*. Dial, 1984. Fun with language; great illustrations!

Bernstein, Joanne. *Fiddle with a Riddle*. Dutton, 1980. Riddles about famous names; treasure hunt with clues. I

Bishop, Ann. *Annie O'Kay's Riddle Round-up*. Dutton, 1982. Fun with language. I

Bishop, Ann. *Cleo Catra's Riddle Book*. Dutton, 1982. More fun with language. I

Borgmann, Dmitri A. *Language on Vacation: An Olio of Orthographical Oddities*. Scribner, 1965. For advanced students and teachers. A

Bossom, Naomi. *A Scale Full of Fish and Other Turnabouts*. Greenwillow, 1979. Multiple meanings. P

Bourke, Linda. *Handmade ABC: A Manual Alphabet*. Addison, 1981. Introduction to Sign. I-A

Briggs, A. Allen. *The Play of Words*. Harcourt, 1972. An excellent resource for the teacher. A

Brown, Marc. *Spooky Riddles*. Random, 1983. Fun with language. P-I

Burgess, Anthony. *The Land Where the Ice Cream Grows*. Doubleday, 1980. Manipulation of sounds and words. I

Caldwell, John. *Excuses, Excuses: How to Get Out of Practically Anything*. Crowell, 1982. Absurd excuses and illustrations. I

Cataldo, John W. *Words and Calligraphy for Children*. Van Nostrand, 1969. Brings words and art together in exciting ways. I-A

Charlip, Remy, et al. *Handtalk: An ABC of Finger Spelling & Sign Language*. Parents, 1974. Wonderfully illustrated introduction to Sign and Finger Spelling; good for understanding deaf persons. P-I-A

Chase, Stuart. *Danger—Men Talking!* Parents, 1969. An introduction to semantics. I

Cole, William, and Thaler, Mike. *Monster Knock Knocks*. Archway, 1983. Wordplay. I

Corbett, Scott. *Jokes to Read in the Dark*. Dutton, 1980. Fun with language. I-A

Davidson, Jessica. *How to Improve Your Grammar*. Watts, 1980. An overview of prescriptive grammar including usage. I

Davidson, Jessica. *How to Improve Your Spelling and Vocabulary*. Watts, 1980. Provides information about spelling and language. I

Davidson, Jessica. *Is That Mother in the Bottle? Where Language Came From and Where It Is Going*. Watts, 1972. Short chapters on various aspects of language. I-A

Davidson, Jessica. *The Square Root of Tuesday*. McCall, 1969. Logic. I

Davidson, Jessica. *What I Tell You Three Times Is True*. McCall, 1970. Information about language including ideas about semantics. I

Denison, Carol. *Passwords to Peoples*. Dodd, 1956. Entertaining introduction to history of language. I

DeVane, Lenchen. *The Adventures of Tony, David, and Marc*. Exposition, 1976. ABC vocabulary book with information about word origins. I

Dohan, Mary Helen. *Our Own Words*. Knopf, 1974. Interesting information for the teacher. A

Dugan, William. *How Our Alphabet Grew*. Golden, 1972. Information about the letters of the alphabet. I

Epstein, Samuel and Beryl. *The First Book of Words*. Watts, 1954. Beginning study of language. I

Epstein, Samuel and Beryl. *The First Book of Printing*. Watts, 1955. I

Ernst, Margaret. *Words*. Knopf, 1936. Development of the English language. I

Ernst, Margaret. *Words: English Roots and How They Grow*. Knopf, 1954. Origins of English words. I

Ernst, Margaret. *More about Words*. Knopf, 1951. An assortment of stories about words origins. I

Espy, Willard R. *A Children's Almanac of Words at Play*. Potter, 1982. Fun with language; good ideas for teachers. I-A
Look for adult books by Espy; for example: *An Almanac of Words at Play* and *Have a Word on Me*.

Esterer, Arnulf K., and Esterer, Louise A. *Saying It Without Words*. Messner, 1980. Using signs and symbols to communicate. I

Fadiman, Clifton. *Wally the Wordworm*. Macmillan, 1964. Wally's adventures as he eats his way through the dictionary. P-I

Farb, Peter. *Word Play: What Happens When People Talk*. Knopf, 1974. Good resource for teachers. A

Ferguson, Charles. *The Abecedarian Book*. Little, 1964. Clever observations about words. I-A

Ferguson, Charles. *Say It With Words*. University of Nebraska, 1959. Background for teachers. A

Fisher, Leonard E. *Alphabet Art: 13 ABCs from Around the World*. Four Winds, 1978. Comparative study. I

Folsom, Franklin. *The Language Book*. Grosset, 1963. Explores all aspects of language development. I

Foster, G. Allen. *Communication: From Primitive Tom-toms to Telstar*. Criterion, 1965. Presents various ways of communicating. I

Frasconi, Antonio. *See and Say: Guarda E Parla; Mira Y Hable; Regarde et Parle: A Picture Book in Four Languages*. Harcourt, 1955. Crosscultural study. I

Friend, M. Newton. *Words: Tricks and Traditions*. Scribner 1957. Introduction to word play. I

Funk, Charles. *Heavens to Betsy*. Harper, 1955. Humorous explanations of curious expressions. I

Funk, Charles. *Hog on Ice and Other Curious Expressions*. Harper, 1948. More about words in our language. I

Funk, Charles. *Thereby Hangs a Tale*. Harper, 1950. Exploration of cliches and idioms of English. I

Funk, Charles E., and Funk, Charles E. Jr. *Horsefeathers and Other Curious Expressions*. Harper, 1958. Word origins. I

Funk, Wilfred. *Word Origins and Their Romantic Stories*. Grosset, 1950. An excellent resource; includes affixes derived from both Greek and Latin. I-A

Garrison, Webb. *What's in a Word?* Abingdon, 1965. Origins of words. A

Gasiorowicz, Nina and Cathy. *The Mime Alphabet Book*. Lerner, 1974. Acting out words. P-I

Gomez, Victoria. *Wags to Witches: More Jokes, Riddles and Puns*. Lothrop, 1982. Fun with language. I

Gounaud, Karen Jo. *A Very Mice Joke Book*. Houghton, 1982. Funny mouse names. I

Greenfeld, Howard. *Sumer Is Icumen In*. Crown, 1978. Information about how language changes. I

Hanlon, Emily. *How a Horse Grew Hoarse on the Site Where He Sighted a Bare Bear*. Delacorte, 1976. Fun with homonyms. P-I

Hansen, Carl F., et al. *A Handbook for Young Writers*. Prentice-Hall, 1965. Handbook covering grammar and usage. I

Hanson, Joan. *Antonyms*. Lerner, 1972. P

Hanson, Joan. *Homographs*. Lerner, 1972. P

Hanson, Joan. *Homonyms*. Lerner, 1972. P

Hanson, Joan. *Synonyms*. Lerner, 1972. P

Hautzig, Esther. *At Home: A Visit in Four Languages*. Macmillan, 1968. Introduces children to French, Spanish, and Russian; good for multicultural teaching. Also: *In School* and *In the Park*. P-I

Helfman, Elizabeth. *Signs and Symbols Around the World*. Lothrop, 1967. Use of written language to communicate. I

Hill, Donna. *Ms. Glee Was Waiting*. Atheneum, 1979. All kinds of excuses. P

Hofsinde, Robert. *Indian Sign Languages*. Morrow, 1956. Presents Indian "vocabulary." I

Hogben, Lancelot. *Wonderful World of Communication*. Garden City, 1959. History of communication. I-A

Holt, Alfred H. *Phrase and Word Origins*. Dover, 1961. Interesting information about history of language. A

Holzer, Hans. *Word Play*. Strawberry Hill Press (616 44th Avenue, San Francisco CA 94121), 1978. Humorous definitions add interest to the study of words. A

Hook, J. N. *The Story of American English*. Harcourt, 1972. Good background for the teacher. A

Hudson, Peggy, comp. *Words to the Wise*. Scholastic, 1971. Paperback about words. I

Hunt, Bernice. *The Whatchmacallit Book*. Putnam, 1976. Vocabulary development. I

Hymes, Lucia, and Hymes, James M. *Oodles of Noodles*. Scott, Foresman, 1964. Introduction to word play. P

Irwin, Keith G. *The Romance of Writing*. Viking, 1957. Early developments of writing. A

Jacobs, Frank. *Alvin Steadfast on Vernacular Island*. Dial, 1965. Fun with words in a fictional context. I

Janeczko, Paul B. *Loads of Codes and Secret Ciphers*. Macmillan, 1984. Ideas for using and breaking codes. I

Johnson, Wendell S. *Words, Things, and Celebrations*. Harcourt, 1972. Useful information for the teacher. A

Juster, Norton. *The Phantom Tolbooth*. Epstein/Random, 1961. Fiction that presents many concepts about words and the dictionary. I

Katan, Norma Jean, and Mintz, Barbara. *Hieroglyphs: The Writing of Ancient Egypt*. Atheneum, 1981. Combines language study with history. I-A

Kaufman, Joel. *The Golden Happy Book of Words*. Golden, 1963. Introduces many words. P

Keller, Charles. *Norma Lee, I Don't Knock on Doors: Knock, Knock Jokes*. Prentice, 1983. Wordplay. I

Keller, Charles. *Smokey the Shark*. Prentice, 1982. A very funny collection of jokes, riddles, and puns. I

Kohn, Bernice. *What a Funny Thing to Say!* Dial, 1974. Discusses modern usage, for example, slang and jargon. I-A

Kraske, Robert. *The Story of the Dictionary*. Harcourt, 1975. Dictionary-making and the great lexicographers. I-A

Laird, Charlton. *Thinking about Language*. Holt, 1964. Discussion of words, grammar, and man's use of language in society. A

Laird, Charlton, and Laird, Helene. *Tree of Language*. World, 1957. Development of the English language. I

Lamb, Geoffrey. *Secret Writing Tricks*. Nelson, 1975. Fun with codes and other language activities. I

Lambert, Eloise. *Our Language*. Lothrop, 1955. History of English. I

Lambert, Eloise, and Pei, Mario. *Our Names: Where They Came from and What They Mean*. Lothrop, 1960. Exploration of names. I

Lipton, James. *An Exaltation of Larks or The Venereal Game*. Grossman, 1968. Focuses on collective nouns. A

Maestro, Betsy and Guilio. *Traffic: A Book of Opposites*. Crown, 1981. Opposites used in sentences. P

Mathews, Mitford M. *American Words*. World, 1959. Origins of words. I-A

Merriam, Eve. *AB to ZOGG: A Lexicon for Science-Fiction and Fantasy Readers*. Atheneum, 1977. A spoof for fantasy lovers. I-A

Merriam, Eve. *A Gaggle of Geese*. Knopf, 1960. Explores unusual words for groups of things. P-I

Merriam, Eve. *Ab to Zogg: A Lexicon for Science Fiction and Fantasy Readers*. Atheneum, 1978.

Merriam, Eve. *What's in the Middle of a Riddle?* Knopf, 1964.

Merriam, Eve. *What Can You Do with a Pocket?* Knopf, 1963.

Michel, Anna. *The Story of Nim: The Chimp Who Learned Language*. Knopf, 1980. Interesting nonfiction; photographs. I-A

Moorhouse, Alfred C. *The Triumph of the Alphabet; A History of Writing*. Abelard, 1953. The story of writing. I-A

Morris, William and Morris, Mary. *Dictionary of American Word Origins*. Harper, 1963. Up-to-date words and their origins. I-A

Nilsen, Don L., and Nilsen, Alleen P. *Language Play: An Introduction to Linguistics*. Newbury, 1978. A good resource for teachers.

Ober, J. Hambleton. *Writing: Man's Great Invention*. Peabody Institute, 1965. History of writing. I-A

Ogg, Oscar. *The Twenty-Six Letters*. Crowell, 1948. History of writing. I

O'Neill, Mary. *Words Words Words*. Doubleday, 1966. Rhymes about sounds and words. I

O'Neill, Mary. *Hailstones and Halibut Bones*. Doubleday, 1961. Wonderful poems about colors that provides models for children's writing. Available on 2 short films (Sterling).

Opie, Iona, and Opie, Peter. *The Lore and Language of Schoolchildren*. Oxford, 1967. Good resource for teacher. A

Osmond, Edward. *From Drumbeat to Tickertape*. Criterion, 1960. Development of writing and printing techniques. I

Palmer, Robin. *A Dictionary of Mythical Places*. Walck, 1975. A useful book for a unit on myths. I-A

Parish, Peggy. *Amelia Bedelia*. Harper, 1963. One of series; fiction about humorous maid who interprets language literally. P-I

Parish, Peggy. *Amelia Bedelia and the Baby*. Greenwillow, 1982.

Partridge, Eric. *A Charm of Words*. Hamilton, 1960. Stories about words. I

Pei, Mario, *All about Language*. Lippincott, 1954, I-A

Pei, Mario. *Our National Heritage*. Houghton, 1965. Cultural and linguistic heritage of Americans. I-A

Perl, Lila. *Candles, Cakes, and Donkey Tails*. Houghton, 1984. Birthday traditions, symbols, and celebrations. I

Provensen, Alice, and Provensen, Martin. *Karen's Opposites*. Golden, 1963. Introduction to antonyms. P

Radlauer, Ruth S. *Good Times with Words*. Melmont, 1963. Using varied words in creative writing. I

Rand, Ann, and Rand, Paul. *Sparkle and Spin*. Harcourt, 1957. Enjoying words together; excellent illustrations. P

Raskin, Ellen. *The Mysterious Disappearance of Leon (I Mean Noel)*. Dutton, 1971. Fiction with a word puzzle. I

Reid, Alastair. *Ounce, Dice, Trice*. Little, 1958. Introduction to wordplay by an imaginative collector of words. I

Rogers, Frances. *Painted Rock to Printed Page*. Lippincott, 1960. How writing developed from primitive efforts. I

Roget, Peter M. *New Roget's Thesaurus of the English Language*. Rev. by Norman Lewis. Putnam, 1961. An excellent edition of the famous thesaurus. I-A

Rossner, Judith. *What Kind of Feet Does a Bear Have?* Bobbs, 1963. Introduction to wordplay. P

Russell, Solveig P. *A Is for Apple and Why*. Abingdon, 1959. How our alphabet developed. I

Sage, Michael. *Words Inside Words*. Lippincott, 1961. Stresses enjoyment of words. I

Sarnoff, Jane, and Ruffins, Reynold. *Words: A Book about the Origins of Everyday Words and Phrases*. Scribner, 1981. Introduction to etymology. I

Scarry, Richard. *Early Words*. Random, 1976. A book for preschool and early reading. P

Scheier, Michael, and Frankel, Julie. *The Whole Mirth Catalog*. Watts, 1979. Humorous ways of working with language. A

Schultz, Sam. *101 Monster Jokes*. Lerner, 1983. Funny jokes and riddles. I

Schwartz, Alvin. *The Cat's Elbow and Other Secret Languages*. Farrar, 1982. Describes 13 different secret codes or languages beginning with Pig Latin. I

Schwartz, Alvin. *Scary Stories to Tell in the Dark*. Lippincott, 1982. Also: *More Scary Stories to Tell in the Dark*. Lippincott, 1983. Stories often told as part of our folklore. I

Schwartz, Alvin. *Ten Copycats in a Boat and Other Riddles*. Harper, 1980. Riddles from folklore. I

Schwartz, Alvin. *A Twister of Twists, A Tangler of Tongues*. Lippincott, 1972. A fascinating collection of twisters from different language. I

Schwartz, Alvin. *Witcracks: Jokes and Jests from American Folklore*. Lippincott, 1973. A humorous approach to language study. I

Schwartz, Alvin. *Tomfoolery: Trickery and Foolery with Words*. Lippincott, 1973. New and old tricks that students enjoy.

Scott, Joseph and Lenore. *Hieroglyphs: Your Own Secret Code Language*. Van Nostrand, 1974. Encoding-decoding. I

Segal, Joyce. *It's Time to Go to Bed*. Doubleday, 1980. Creative excuses. P-I

Severn, Bill. *People Words*. Washburn, 1966. Word origins. I-A

Severn, Bill. *Place Words*. Washburn, 1969. Word origins. I-A

Shipley, Joseph T. *Playing with Words*. Prentice-Hall, 1960. Written for adults; provocative for advanced students. I-A

Shipley, Joseph T. *Word Games for Play and Power*. Prentice-Hall, 1962. A second book about wordplay and the fascination of words. I-A

Sparke, William. *Story of the English Language*. Abelard, 1965. The development of the English language. I

Steig, William, *CDC?* Farrar, 1984. Fun with letters that make words. I-A

Supraner, Robyn. *Giggly-Wiggly, Snickety-Snick*. Parents, 1978. Textures. P

Vasilu. *The Most Beautiful Word*. Day, 1970. Search ends with discovery; stimulates discussion. P

Waller, Leslie. *Our American Language*. Holt, 1960. Introduction to the story of English. P

Williams, Kit. *Masquerade*. Schocken, 1980. Verbal and visual riddles. I

Wiseman, Bernard. *Morris Has a Cold*. Dodd, 1979. Fun with language. P

White, Mary S. *Word Twins*. Abingdon, 1961. Fun with homonyms. P

Yates, Elizabeth. *Someday You'll Write*. Dutton, 1962. Specific information for the young writer on plot development, and so on. I

Zim, Herbert S. *Codes and Secret Writing*. Morrow, 1948. Fascinating language activities. I

Books for the Teacher:
Reading/Thinking/Writing

TEACHING READING

The books in this section provide the latest information about reading instruction. Included here are books that focus on the use of literature in the reading program.

Allen, P. David, and Watson, Dorothy. *Findings of Research in Miscue Analysis: Classroom Implications*. NCTE, 1976.

Applebee, Arthur N. *The Child's Concept of Story: Ages Two to Seventeen*. University of Chicago Press, 1980.

Bailey, Richard W., and Fosheim, Robin M. (Eds.). *Literacy for Life: The Demand for Reading and Writing*. Modern Language Association, 1983.

Bingham, Jane, and Scholft, Grayce. *Fifteen Centuries of Children's Literature*. Greenwood Press, 1980.

Cameron, Eleanor. *The Green and Burning Tree: On the Writing and Enjoyment of Children's Books*. Atlantic Monthly, 1969.

Cianciolo, Patricia (Ed.) and NCTE Committee on the Elementary School Booklist. *Adventuring with Books: A Booklist for Pre-K–Grade 8*. NCTE, 1977.

Cullinan, Bernice, and Weiss, M. Jerry. *Books I Read When I Was Young*. Commission on Literature. NCTE, 1981.

Daniels, Steven. *How 2 Gerbils, 20 Goldfish, 200 Games, 2,000 Books and I Taught Them How to Read*. Westminster Press, 1971.

Guthrie, John T. (Ed.). *Comprehension and Teaching: Research Reviews*. International Reading Association, 1981.

Hains, Maryellen (Ed.). *A Two-Way Street: Reading to Write/Writing to Read*. Michigan Council of Teachers of English and the Michigan Department of Education, 1982.

Hearne, Betsy. *Choosing Books for Children*. Dell, 1981.

Heilman, Arthur W., and Holmes, Elizabeth Ann. *Smuggling Language into the Teaching Reading*. Merrill, 1972.

Huck, Charlotte S. *Children's Literature in the Elementary School*. Holt, 1983.

International Reading Association/Children's Books Council Joint Committee. "Children's Books for _____ ." Annual publication in October *Reading Teacher*.

Johnson, Edna, et al. *Anthology of Children's Literature*. Houghton Mifflin, 1977.

Judy, Stephen N. *The ABC's of Literacy: A Guide for Parents and Educators*. Oxford, 1980.

Lamme, Linda L. (Ed.). *Literature: Making It the Foundation of Your Curriculum*. NCTE, 1981.

McCracken, Robert, and McCracken, Marlene. *Reading, Writing, and Language*. Penguin, 1979.

Nilsen, Alleen Pace, and Donelson, Kenneth L. *Literature for Today's Young Adults*, 2nd ed. Scott Foresman, 1985.

Page, William D. and Pinnell, Gay Su. *Teaching Reading Comprehension*. NCTE, 1979.

Smith, Frank. *Comprehension and Learning: A Conceptual Framework for Teachers*. Holt, 1975.

Smith, Frank. *Reading without Nonsense*. Teachers College Press, 1978.

Spache, Evelyn B. *Reading Activities for Child Involvement*. Allyn and Bacon, 1981.

Sutherland, Zena, et al. *Children & Books* Scott, Foresman, 1985.

Tiedt, Iris M. *Exploring Books with Children*. Houghton Mifflin, 1979.

Tiedt, Pamela L., and Tiedt, Iris M. *Multicultural Teaching: Activities, Information and Resources*, 2nd ed. Allyn and Bacon, 1986.

Tway, Eileen (Ed.). *Reading Ladders for Human Relations*, 6th ed. American Council on Education, 1981.

Weaver, Constance. *Psycholinguistics and Reading: From Process to Practice*. Winthrop, 1980.

White, Mary Lou. *Children's Books: The Best of the Past Decade*. NCTE, 1981.

THINKING: INFORMATION AND STIMULUS

This bibliography includes books about thinking that provide information about the brain and thinking processes for teachers and students. Most of these resources provide information about working with students in the classroom.

Almy, Millie, et al. *Young Children's Thinking: Studies of Some Aspects of Piaget's Theory*. Teachers College Press, 1966.

Berthoff, Ann E. *The Making of Meaning*. Boynton/Cook, 1981.

Bloom, Benjamin. *All Our Children Learning: A Primer for Parents, Teachers and Other Educators*. McGraw-Hill, 1981.

Bogen, Joseph E. "The Other Side of the Brain VII: Some Educational Aspects of Hemispheric Specialization." *UCLA Educator*, 17 (1975): 24–32.

PAR Thinking Skills Resource Panel. "Thinking about the Teaching of Thinking." *Phi Delta Kappa* (September 1980). *Practical Applications of Research: Newsletter of Phi Delta Kappa's Center on Evaluation, Development, and Research*.

Lewis, David, and Greene, James. *Thinking Better: A Revolutionary New Program to Achieve Peak Mental Performance*. Rawson, Wade, 1982. A five-step method for problem solving.

Moore, Linda P. *You're Smarter Than You Think: At Least 500 Fun Ways to Increase Your Intelligence*. Holt, 1985. Dealing realistically with IQ and intelligence.

Parnes, Sidney J., et al. *Guide to Creative Action*. Scribner, 1977.

Rico, Gabriele L. "Metaphor and Knowing: Analysis, Synthesis, Rationale." Dissertation, Stanford University, 1976.

Samples, Bob. "Holonomic Knowing: A Challenge for Education in the 80s," in R. Baird Shuman (Ed.), *Education in the 80s*. National Education Association, 1981.

Smith, Frank. *Comprehension and Learning*. Holt, 1975.

Tarnopol, Lester, and Tarnopol, Muriel (Eds.). *Brain Function and Reading Disabilities*. University Park Press, 1976.

Tiedt, Iris M. *Teaching Thinking in K–12 Classrooms*. Allyn and Bacon, 1989.

Zepezauer, Frank. "Consciousness Shifting: Intellectual Training in the Schools." *California English* (March-April 1981).

BOOKS ABOUT WRITING AND TEACHING STUDENTS TO WRITE

These titles are directed toward K–12 teachers who are working with young writers in the classroom. They suggest many ideas and techniques for encouraging students to write more effectively. They also provide a theoretical background for accepted approaches to teaching composition today.

Applebee, Arthur. *The Child's Concept of Story: Ages Two to Seventeen*. University of Chicago, 1978.

Applebee, Arthur. *Writing in the Secondary School: English and the Content Areas*. National Council of Teachers of English, 1981.

Berthoff, Anne E. *Forming-Thinking-Writing: The Composing Imagination*. Hayden, 1978.

Berthoff, Anne E. *The Making of Meaning: Metaphors, Models, and Maxims for Writing Teachers*. Boynton/Cook, 1981.

Camp, Gerald (Ed.). *Teaching Writing: Essays from the Bay Area Writing Project*. Boynton/Cook, 1983.

Cooper, Charles, and Odell, Lee (Eds.). *Evaluating Writing: Describing, Measuring, Judging*. National Council of Teachers of English, 1977.

Elbow, Peter. *Writing without Teachers*. Oxford, 1973.

Flower, Linda. *Problem-Solving Strategies for Writing*, 2nd ed. Harcourt, 1985.

Garrison, Roger. *How a Writer Works: Through the Composing Process*. Harper, 1981.

Graves, Donald H. *Writing: Teachers & Children at Work*. Heinemann, 1983.

Grossman, Florence. *Getting from Here to There: Writing and Reading Poetry*. Boynton/Cook, 1982.

Grubb, Mel. *Using Holistic Evaluation*. Glencoe, 1981.

Jensen, Julie (Ed.). *Composing and Comprehending*. NCRE and NCTE, 1984.

Johnson, Ferne. *Start Early for an Early Start: You and the Young Child*. American Library Association, 1976.

Judy, Stephen N., and Judy, Susan J. *An Introduction to the Teaching of Writing*. Wiley, 1981.

Krashen, Stephen. *Second Language Acquisition and Second Language Learning*. Pergamon, 1981.

Kroll, Barry, and Vann, Roberta. *Exploring Speaking-Writing Relationships: Connections and Contrasts*. NCTE, 1981.

Lawlor, Joseph (Ed.). *Computers in Composition Instruction*. SWRL Educational Research and Development, 1962.

Loban, Walter. *Language Development: Kindergarten through Grade Twelve*. National Council of Teachers of English, 1976.

Macrorie, Ken. *Searching Writing*. Boynton/Cook, 1984.

McWilliams, Peter A. *The Word Processing Book: A Short Course in Computer Literacy*. Prelude Press, 1982.

Moffett, James, and Wagner, Betty Jane. *Student-Centered Language Arts and Reading, K-13: A Handbook for Teachers,* 3rd ed. Houghton Mifflin, 1983.

Myers, Miles. *A Procedure for Writing Assessment and Holistic Scoring*. National Council of Teachers of English, 1980.

Myers, Miles, and Gray, James. (Eds.). *Theory and Practice in the Teaching of Composition: Processing, Distancing, and Modeling*. NCTE, 1983.

Rico, Gabriele. *Writing the Natural Way*. Tarcher/Houghton Mifflin, 1983.

Schultz, John. *Writing from Start to Finish*. Boynton/Cook, 1982.

Shaughnessy, Mina P. *Errors and Expectations: A Guide for the Teacher of Basic Writing*. Oxford, 1977.

Smith, Frank. *Writing and the Writer*. Holt, 1982.

Stillman, Peter. *Writing Your Way*. Boynton/Cook, 1984.

Strong, William. *Sentence Combining and Paragraph Building*. Random, 1981.

Thaiss, Christopher J., and Suhor, Charles. (Eds.). *Speaking and Writing K-12*. NCTE, 1984.

Tiedt, Iris M. *Editing and Evaluating Student Writing: A Workshop Approach*. Allyn and Bacon, 1986.

Tiedt, Iris M. *The Language Arts Handbook*. Prentice-Hall, 1983.

Tiedt, Iris M., et al. *Reading, Thinking, Writing: Ideas, Resources, and Information*. Allyn and Bacon, 1986.

Tiedt, Iris M., et al. *Writing from Topic to Evaluation*. Allyn and Bacon, 1989.

Tiedt, Pamela, and Tiedt, Iris. *Multicultural Teaching,* 2nd ed. Allyn and Bacon, 1986.

Tollefson, Stephen K. *Shaping Sentences: Grammar in Context*. Harcourt, 1985.

Turbill, Jan. *No Better Way to Teach Writing*. Primary English Teaching Assn., 1983.

Weaver, Constance. *Grammar for Teachers: Perspectives and Definitions*. National Council of Teachers of English, 1979.

Wresch, William. (Ed.) *The Computer in Composition Instruction, A Writer's Tool*. NCTE, 1984.

Zinsser, William. *Writing with a Word Processor*. Harper, 1983

Index

A Friend Is, 296
"Abe's Longest Walk," 313
Active verbs, 276
Activity, 20
Adjectives, 171
Aesop, 131–132
Affixes, 208
Alcott, Louisa May, 296
Allard, Harry, 91
Alphabet, 77–79
Alphabet Song, 78
Anglund, Joan, 296
Anthology, 343–344
Applebee, Arthur, 58
Appleseed, Johnny, 228–229
Art, 258–262
Assumptions, 15–16
Audience, 172, 330
Authors, 10, 14, 18
Awareness, 27

Babar, 83
Back to School Night, 322
Bartoli, Jennifer, 19
Basal reader, 284
Benet, Rosemary and Stephen, 308
Bias, 214–215, 246–247
Big Book of Stories, 279
Bilingual, 19
"Bill of Rights," 309–312
Biography, 210–211, 262
Body language, 307–308
Book reviews, 124–126
Bookbinding, 137, 183–191
Bookfinder, 142
Booklists, 18, 23, 39, 61, 99–100, 106–107, 112, 145–146, 345–384
Books:
    language, 374–381

middle grades, 356–366
primary, 345–351
teaching reading, 381–382
thinking instruction, 382–383
writing instruction, 383–384
young adults, 366–374
Bookworms, 340
Brainstorming, 119, 126, 139, 163, 173, 201, 203, 207, 211, 236, 241, 247
Britton, James, 5
Brown Bear, Brown Bear, 90
Brunhoff, Laurent de, 83
Bulletin board, 45, 92, 99, 220, 284, 343

Calculators, 257
Caldecott Award books, 345–351
California State Department of Education, 318
Cameron, Polly, 165
Careers, 162
Carroll, Lewis, 308
Cat in the Hat, The, 129–133
Categorizing, 165–168, 171, 200–202, 207
Cause and effect, 221, 225–226
Chanting, 140
Character traits, 226–227
Characteristics of a strong Reading/Thinking/Writing program, 319–320
Characterization, 128, 207, 217–218, 228–229, 231–232, 265–266, 302
Characters, 88–90, 140–141
Charlotte's Web, 11
Checklists for programs, 319
Child's Concept of Story, The, 58
Children and Books, 272
Children's Catalog, 24, 142
Children's Literature in the Elementary School, 271
Chomsky, Noam, 2

Choral reading, 59, 276
Choric speaking, 294–295
Class books, 90–91, 191, 260, 357–359
Classification, 32–38
Classroom climate, 142
Clichés, 285
"Cloud, The," 291
Close reading, 284
Cloze technique, 94–95, 208, 296
Clustering, 150, 156, 162, 166–167, 203, 212, 262–263, 277, 292
Collage, 237
Commas, 163–165, 274–277
Commercials, 246
Communication, 323
Comparing, 88–94, 159–161
Composers, 266–267
Composing and Comprehending, 5, 6, 58, 149, 239
Composition, 13
Compound sentences, 164–165
Comprehension, 11, 13, 17, 27, 28, 38, 194, 263–264, 286, 289–290, 317–318
Computers, 137, 141, 257
Conferences, 341–342
Conflict, 246
Context, 122, 277
Convergences: Transactions in Reading and Writing, 6, 149
Cooperative learning, 329–337
Crane, Ichabod, 169
Creative drama, 140, 297–309
Creative thinking, 272
Creativity, 13, 285, 351–353
Critical thinking, 286, 297
Cross-level tutoring, 168
Crossword puzzle, 252
Crow Boy, 236
Cullinan, Bernice, 271
Culture, 237, 247
Cunningham, Julia, 18
Curriculum, 15, 316–344

Data collection, 195–202
De La Mare, Walter, 230
Death, 19
Decoding, 58
Découpage, 139
Dialogue, 284
Diamond, Neil, 310
Diary, 125
Dictation, 19, 64–65, 272–278
Dictionary, 126
Diphthongs, 75–76

Directions, 29
Divergent thinking, 233
Diversity, 233–237
Donelson, Kenneth, 272
Dr. Seuss, 129–131
Dragonwings, 236
Dramatization, 38–39, 127–129, 140, 271, 285, 296–309 (*see also* Puppetry)
Drawing, 260–261
Dynamics of Language Learning: Research in Reading & English, 239
Dyson, Anne Haas, 58

Echo reading, 45–46
Economics, 246
Editing writing, 136, 172–191, 325–337
Egoff, Sheila, 271
"Elf and the Doormouse, The," 308
Emotions, 276, 299
Encoding, 58
English, teaching, 26
Environment, 9, 113
ESL students, 19, 279, 297
Essay, 159–161, 236, 246
Evaluating writing, 337–344
Evaluation, 15, 20, 318
Evaluation forms, 325–327
Exposition, 285
Expressions, 122–123

Fables, 131–133
Fact, 13, 218–219
Fairytale, 301–302
Family tree, 235
Farewell to Manzanar, 236, 247, 276–277
Father's Day, 136, 171
Field trip, 250–251
Figurative language, 122–123, 204–205, 306–307
Film, 45, 219
Flannelboard, 280–281, 303–304
"Fog," 220
Folksongs, 267
Folktale, 199–200
Follow-up, 20
Fools Rush In, 245
Form, 17, 163
Forum: Reflections on Theory and Practice in the Teaching of Foundations of Literacy, The, 58
"Fox and the Crow, The," 131, 132
Freedom, 309–313
Fulwiler, Toby, 239

Games, 233
Geography, 247
Gifts, 136–140
Giving Tree, The, 144
Goal setting, 250
Good teacher, 321–322
Goodman, Kenneth, 5, 58
Goodman, Yetta, 5
Graham, Loren, 247
Grahame, Kenneth, 208
Grammar, 2, 10, 17, 27, 175–177, 208, 275–277
Graphemes, 9, 68–82
Graphing, 236
Graves, Donald, 5
Greeting cards, 171
Groups, 130, 156, 219, 323–342
Gwynne, Fred, 122

Haiku, 285
Handbook for Planning an Effective Reading Program, 318
Handbook for Planning an Effective Writing Program, 318
Handbook for Teachers, A, 5
Handwriting, 68, 139
Happiness Is, 296
"Hare and the Tortoise, The," 132
Heide, Florence, 217, 226
Henry, O., 225, 232
Herford, Oliver, 308
"Highwayman, The," 282–284
Historical accuracy, 247
History, 160–161, 247
Holdaway, Donald, 58
Holidays, 235
Holistic evaluation, 67, 177–179, 317
Holistic model, 6–7
Holliday, J. S., 245
Homonyms, 122–123
Houston, James D., 247, 276–277
Houston, Jeanne Watsuki, 247, 276–277
Huck, Charlotte, 271
Huckleberry Finn, 202–204
Humor, 91–93, 122–123

I Can't Said the Ant, 165
I Search, 236, 240–245
I-Statements, 288
Idioms, 122–123, 126, 204–205, 305–306
Imagery, 282–284, 285
Immigrants, 236
Indentation, 285
Index, 160

Individualization, 10, 15, 23, 323–344
Inference, 13, 215–216, 220–221, 284
Inner City Mother Goose, 233
Integrative thinking, 221–234
International Reading Association, 23
Interviews, 191, 235, 257
Intonation, 17, 128–129
Involving students, 322–323
Ira Sleeps Over, 64
Irving, Washington, 169
Issues, 207, 232

Jack and the Beanstalk, 279
"Jack and Jill," 60–61
Japanese Americans, 276–277
Jaques, Florence P., 293–294
Jensen, Julie, 5, 6, 58, 149, 239
Jeopardy, 126
Johnny Appleseed, 207
"Johnny Cake," 309
Journals, 221–226, 261–262
Judgment, 13
Jumping rope, 61–63
Just For You, 164

Keats, Ezra Jack, 44
Key words, 253–254
King, Martin Luther, 310, 312
King Who Reigned, The, 122
Knowledge level, 195–202

La Dictée, 272–278
La Dictée: A Dictation Method for Learning to Write, 272
Language, 22
  books, 374–381
Language acquisition, 2, 8, 27, 194
Language Arts Handbook, The, 6, 239, 272
Language Connections: Writing & Reading Across the Curriculum, 239
Language Development: Kindergarten Through Grade Twelve, 58, 149
Language experience, 82–88
Language and Learning, 5
Lazarus, Emma, 309–310
Leaf, The, 225, 232
Lear, Edward, 308
Learning, 114–116
Learning Log, 200–202, 248–249, 255–256, 341–342
"Legend of Sleepy Hollow, The," 222
Lesson, 20

Letters, 66–67, 139–140, 145, 245–256, 262, 322–323
"Lewis and Clark," 308
Library, 22, 24, 242–243, 270, 345
Light in the Forest, 210, 217
Listening, 27, 38, 44, 64, 81, 274–278
Literal meaning, 122–123, 204–205
Literature, 14, 16, 18, 44, 45, 58, 59–63, 127–136, 168–171, 198–200, 269–315
Literature and the Child, 271
Literature as Exploration, 5
Literature for Today's Young Adults, 272
Little Red Riding Hood, 13, 232
Little Women, 296
Loban, Walter, 58, 149
Logs, 114, 341–342 (*see also* Learning Logs)
London, Jack, 219, 231
Longfellow, Henry Wadsworth, 246
Love, 141
Lyrics, 266–267

Macaroon, 18
Make New Friends, 268
Manuscript printing, 69–70
Mapping, 67, 195–202, 220–226, 252, 263, 301–302, 338
Maps, 30–32
Marshall, James, 91
Martin, Bill, 90
"Mary Had a Little Lamb," 268
Mathematics, 252–257
Mayer, Mercer, 164
Mechanics, 163–165
Memory, 111
Merriam, Eve, 233
Metacognition, 10, 27, 45, 150, 193
Metaphor, 168–170, 220
Miller, George, 58
Model, writing, 274, 276
Modeling, 324
Models, 19, 168–171
Moffett, James, 3, 5
Mood, 263–264, 267
Moore, Clement, 308
Morals, 131–133
Mother Goose, 59–61
Mother's Day, 136, 171
Mothers, 145
"Mouse Princess, The" 301–302
Multicultural education, 233–237
Multicultural Teaching: A Handbook of Activities, Information and Resources, 107, 239, 272

Music, 41–43, 78, 79, 263–268
"My Bonnie Lies Over the Ocean," 42

National Council of Teachers of English, 22
National Geographic, 220
National Wildlife, 220
"New Colossus, The," 309–310
Newbery Award books, 359–366
Newspapers, 171, 196–198, 205–206, 246, 251, 285
Nilsen, Aileen, 272
Nonna, 19
North American Indian, 236
Note taking, 248–249
Noyes, Alfred, 282–284
Nursery rhymes, 59–61, 233

Objectives, 320–321
Observations, 20, 250–251
"Old MacDonald," 268
"One, Two, Buckle My Shoe," 62, 257
Open House, 45, 322
Opinion, 218–219
Oral interpretation, 130
Oral language, 8, 57, 59, 164, 354
"Owl and the Pussycat, The," 308
Ownership, 330

Pantomime, 297, 305
Paragraphing, 285
Paragraphs, 274–277, 289–290
Parallel structure, 274–275
Paraphrasing, 284
Parents, 15, 55, 65, 79, 99, 113, 205, 258, 322–323, 344
Pattern books, 351–353
Pattern, puppet, 48
Patterning, 163, 268
Patterns, 90–91, 293–296
"Paul Revere's Ride," 246
Pearson, P. David, 58
Peer-editing, 172, 209
Personification, 22, 229–230, 251–252, 291–293
Petersen, Bruce T., 6, 149
Phonemes, 9, 68–82
Phonics, 4, 9, 16, 68–82, 295
Photographs, 140
Picture books, 127–131
Pioneers, 245–246
"Pirate Captain Jim," 281
Play, 125
Plays, 127–129

Plays, The Drama Magazine for Young People, 309
Poetry, 21, 22, 53, 54, 59–61, 63, 113, 140, 252, 262, 267, 280–285, 291–296, 299–300
Point of view, 277, 286–290
Portfolios, 65, 323
Positive attitude, 17
Prairie Winter, 216
Prediction, 40–41, 126, 210–211, 232
Prewriting, 22, 150–156, 162, 163
Pride, 330
Primary traits, 328
Prior knowledge, 8, 9, 16, 27, 59
Problem solving, 207
Prompt, 330–331
Proofreading, 329
Propaganda, 247
Prose, 285
Publishing, 191, 258–263, 342–344
Punctuation, 140, 273–275, 284
Puppetry, 47–51, 125, 205–206

Quality indicators, 331–333
Questioning, 209–214, 220–222, 224, 235–236, 342
Quotation marks, 220, 281–282, 284

Readers' theater, 129–133, 317
Reading, 3, 10, 17, 27, 44, 56–100, 116–119
Reading aloud, 17
Reading center, 105
Reading Log, 222–224, 339–340
Reading Teacher, 23
Reading without Nonsense, 3, 5
Reading/writing connections, 82
Red Badge of Courage, 246
Repetition, 293–296
Research, 26–27
Response groups, 323–342
Response Guides for Teaching Children's Books, 272
Responses, 209
Retelling, 46, 278–279
Revere, Paul, 285
Revision, 172–191, 343
Revolutions, 241–242
Rhyming, 165, 295
Rhythm, 45, 46, 63, 266–267
"Richard Cory," 265
Richter, Conrad, 210, 217
Right-brain thinking, 194
Risk, 143

Robinson, E. A., 266
Rockwell, Norman, 310
Role playing, 113, 120, 121, 142, 247, 288–290
Rosenblatt, Louise, 5
Rubric, 173, 330–337
"Runaway Pancake, The," 309

SAFE Model, 20 (see examples in each chapter)
Sandburg, Carl, 220
Scaffolding, 354
Schlein, Miriam, 145
Science, 20, 248–252
Self-esteem, 66–67, 95–100, 119, 325, 330, 343
Self-evaluation, 209, 323–329, 338–339
Sendak, Maurice, 39, 89
Senior citizens, 140
Senses, 20
Sentence patterns, 275–277
Sentences, 19
Sequence, 29, 44
Setting, 247, 267
"Sh," 280
Shelley, Percy Bysshe, 291
Short story, 198–200
Shultz, Charles, 296
"Silver," 230
Silverstein, Shel, 144, 281–282
Simile, 168–170, 219, 285
Simon and Garfunkel, 265
Singing, 42, 43, 77–79
"Sleepy Hollow," 169
Smith, Frank, 3, 5
Snow White, 127
Snowflakes, 45
Snowy Day, The, 44
Social studies, 159–161, 239–247
Software, 137, 141
Somers, Albert B., 272
Songs, 126, 144, 162, 171, 256–257
Sound effects, 162
Sound of Sunshine, Sound of Rain, 217, 226
Sound-symbol relationships, 64
South Town, 247
Speaking, 27, 47–56
Speeches, 51–54
Spelling, 9, 68–82, 175–177
Spontaneous Apprentices: Children and Language, 58
Springsteen, Bruce, 310
Squire, James, 8, 26, 58, 239

Stationery, 139–141, 145
Statue of Liberty, 309
Stevenson, Robert Louis, 273–275
Stimulus, 20
Stock, P., 149
Story, 206
  sense of, 64–65
Story theater, 28, 306–308
Storytelling, 133–136
Stotsky, Sandra, 149
Student-centered curriculum, 316–344
Student-centered Language Arts and Reading Curriculum, K–13, A, 5
Students, 15
Stupids Step Out, The, 91
Style, 17, 163, 168–170, 328
Superstitions, 203
Sutherland, Zena, 272
Syllables, 81
Symbolism, 219, 252

Taylor, Mildred D., 289
Teacher, 24, 145
Teachers & Children at Work, 5
Teaching Thinking in K–12 Classrooms, 6, 318
Teaching the Universe of Discourse, 5
Teaching Writing in K–8 Classrooms, 6
Telephone, 47
Television, 47, 57, 68, 95, 121, 125, 142
"Ten Little Indians," 256
Tests, 207
Theme, 233, 264, 266, 141–146, 309–313
"There Once Was a Puffin," 293–294
"There's a Place for Us," 266
Thesaurus, 343
Thinking, 3, 8, 12, 13, 14, 17, 27, 47, 82, 94, 113, 150–162, 193–237, 270, 351–353
"Three Little Pigs, The," 40, 127, 307
Thursday's Child: Trends & Patterns in Contemporary Children's Literature, 271
Tiedt, Iris M., 6, 107, 239, 272, 318
Tiedt, Pamela L., 107, 239, 272
Tierney, Robert, 58
Time-on-task, 10
Tippett, James S., 280
To Build a Fire, 219, 231
Tom Sawyer, 17
Trade books, 270
Transaction, 12, 13, 16, 114–119
Transaction logs, 342

Transparencies, 174, 281–284, 293–296
Treasure Island, 273–275
"Tree Stands Very Straight and Still, The," 300
Tremain, Johnny, 285

Uninterrupted Sustained Silent Reading, 103–105
Unit, 141–146, 233–237, 309–313
United States Constitution, 311

Values, 141–146, 267
Velveteen Rabbit, The, 143
Venn Diagram, 156–162, 217, 226, 266
Verbs, 169–170, 291–293
Videotape, 52–53, 110–111, 128–129, 134, 145
"Visit from St. Nicholas, A," 308
Visualization, 28–32, 133–136, 140, 247–272
Vocabulary, 59, 67, 126, 181, 182, 208, 211–214, 253, 254, 256, 276, 282–284, 303–304
Vulnerability, 143

Waber, Bernard, 64
Wagner, Betty Jane, 3, 5
"Walrus and the Carpenter, The," 308
Way Mothers Are, The, 145
"West Side Story," 266
What's Whole About Whole Language?, 5, 58
"Where Have All the Flowers Gone?", 312
Where the Sidewalk Ends, 281–282
Where the Wild Things Are, 39, 8
White, E. B., 11
Whole language, 271
Wilder, Rose, 216
Williams, Margaret, 143
Wind in the Willows, 208
Word problems, 253–256
Wordless books, 354–356
Worthington, Janet E., 272
Writing 10, 14, 17, 27, 56–100
Writing: From Topic to Evaluation, 318
Writing portfolio, 341
Writing skills, 42–43
Wynne, Annette, 300

YA books, 366–374
"You Are Old, Father William," 308
Young, Art, 239